Erk Volkmar Heyen
Kultur und Identität
in der europäischen Verwaltungsrechtsvergleichung
– mit Blick auf Frankreich und Schweden

Schriftenreihe
der
Juristischen Gesellschaft zu Berlin

Heft 168

W
DE
G

2000

Walter de Gruyter · Berlin · New York

Kultur und Identität
in der europäischen
Verwaltungsrechtsvergleichung –
mit Blick auf Frankreich
und Schweden

Von
Erk Volkmar Heyen

Vortrag
gehalten vor der
Juristischen Gesellschaft zu Berlin
am 26. Januar 2000

W
DE
G

2000

Walter de Gruyter · Berlin · New York

Dr. *Erk Volkmar Heyen,*
o. Universitätsprofessor
an der Ernst-Moritz-Arndt-Universität Greifswald

♾ Gedruckt auf säurefreiem Papier,
das die US-ANSI-Norm über Haltbarkeit erfüllt.

Die Deutsche Bibliothek – CIP-Einheitsaufnahme

Heyen, Erk Volkmar:
Kultur und Identität in der europäischen Verwaltungsrechtsvergleichung – mit Blick auf Frankreich und Schweden : Vortrag gehalten vor der Juristischen Gesellschaft zu Berlin am 26. Januar 2000 /
von Erk Volkmar Heyen. - Berlin ; New York : de Gruyter, 2000
(Schriftenreihe der Juristischen Gesellschaft zu Berlin ; H. 168)
ISBN 3-11-016982-7

Satz: OLD-Satz digital, Neckarsteinach
Druck: Druckerei Gerike GmbH, Berlin
Buchbinderische Verarbeitung: Industriebuchbinderei Fuhrmann GmbH & Co. KG, Berlin

Inhaltsübersicht

I. Einleitung

Mit der in den 90er Jahren zunehmend beachteten und kommentierten Europäisierung des Verwaltungsrechts – d. h. der durch die Rechtssetzung und Rechtsprechung der Organe der Europäischen Union bewirkten Harmonisierung der mitgliedstaatlichen Verwaltungsrechtsordnungen[1] – hat auch die europäische Verwaltungsrechtsvergleichung eine deutliche Verlebendigung erfahren. Gab es zuvor kaum allgemeine Berichte über Stand und Probleme der Rechtsvergleichung im öffentlichen Recht, so wurde in den letzten drei Jahren allein in Deutschland bald ein halbes Dutzend davon veröffentlicht[2].

Auch von Kultur und Identität ist im Zusammenhang mit Recht oder Verwaltung neuerdings des öfteren die Rede. 1998 hatte der „32.

---

[1] Vgl. dazu aus der reichen Literatur *J. Schwarze* (Hrsg.), Das Verwaltungsrecht unter europäischem Einfluß. Zur Konvergenz der mitgliedstaatlichen Verwaltungrechtsordnungen in der Europäischen Union, 1996, und zwei Habilitationsschriften: *Th. v. Danwitz*, Verwaltungsrechtliches System und Europäische Integration, 1996; *S. Kadelbach*, Allgemeines Verwaltungsrecht unter europäischem Einfluß, 1999; einen Überblick gibt *F. Schoch*, Die Europäisierung des Allgemeinen Verwaltungsrechts und der Verwaltungsrechtswissenschaft, in: Die Verwaltung, Beiheft 2: Die Wissenschaft vom Verwaltungsrecht. Werkstattgespräch aus Anlaß des 60. Geburtstages von Prof. Dr. Eberhard Schmidt-Aßmann, 1999, S. 135-154.

[2] Vgl. *Ch. Starck*, Rechtsvergleichung im öffentlichen Recht, in: Juristenzeitung, 52 (1997), S. 1021-1030; *H. Krüger*, Eigenart, Methode und Funktion der Rechtsvergleichung im öffentlichen Recht, in: Festschrift Martin Kriele, 1997, S. 1393-1405; *G. Trantas*, Die Anwendung der Rechtsvergleichung bei der Untersuchung des öffentlichen Rechts, 1998; *K.-P. Sommermann*, Die Bedeutung der Rechtsvergleichung für die Fortentwicklung des Staats- und Verwaltungsrechts in Europa, in: Die Öffentliche Verwaltung (DÖV), 52 (1999), S. 1017-1029; *I. Lipowicz*, Rechtsvergleichende Perspektiven der Verwaltungsrechtswissenschaft, in: Die Verwaltung, Beiheft 2 (Fn. 1), S. 155-164. Aus der älteren Literatur ist vor allem zu nennen: Zeitschrift für ausländisches öffentliches Recht und Völkerrecht (ZaöRV), 24 (1964), H. 3, insbes. *H. Strebel*, Vergleichung und vergleichende Methode im öffentlichen Recht, S. 405-430, und *R. Bernhardt*, Eigenheiten und Ziele der Rechtsvergleichung im öffentlichen Recht, S. 431-452. In historischer Sicht: *E. V. Heyen*, Französisches und englisches Verwaltungsrecht in der deutschen Rechtsvergleichung des 19. Jahrhunderts: Mohl, Stein, Gneist, Mayer, Hatschek, in: *ders.* (Hrsg.), Verwaltung und Verwaltungsrecht in Frankreich und England (18./19. Jh.), 1996 (= Jahrbuch für europäische Verwaltungsgeschichte, Bd. 8), S. 163-189; *M. Stolleis*, Nationalität und Internationalität: Rechtsvergleichung im öffentlichen Recht des 19. Jahrhunderts, 1998.

Deutsche Rechtshistorikertag" in Regensburg mehrere Beiträge zum
Verhältnis von Rechtsgeschichte, Rechtsvergleichung und Rechtskultur vorgesehen[3]. Im selben Jahr wurde in der Zeitschrift „Rechtstheorie" – aus Anlaß des auch einem breiteren Publikum bekannt geworde-
nen Buches von Samuel Huntington über den nach Ende des Ost-
West-Konflikts von ihm erwarteten „Clash of Civilizations" – ein Son-
derheft herausgebracht mit dem Titel „Konvergenz oder Konfronta-
tion? Transformationen kultureller Identität in den Rechtssystemen an
der Schwelle zum 21. Jahrhundert"[4]. 1999 befaßte sich die „Gesellschaft für Rechtsvergleichung" auf ihrer Tagung in Freiburg i. Br.
gleich zweifach mit dem Thema Rechtskultur. In der Fachgruppe für
Grundlagenforschung diskutierte man über die Internationalisierung
und die Europäisierung des Rechts als Grund und Folge konvergieren-
den Rechtsdenkens in unterschiedlichen Rechtskulturen, in der Fachgruppe für Rechtsgeschichte und Rechtsethnologie über Rechtskreis
und Rechtskultur[5]. Die „Vereinigung der Deutschen Staatsrechtsleh-
rer" nahm sich wenige Wochen später auf ihrer Heidelberger Tagung in
der Arbeitsgruppe für Verwaltungslehre des Themas der Verwaltungskultur an; es wurden u. a. die Auswirkungen der nationalen Verwaltungskulturen auf die Umsetzung des Verwaltungsrechts der Europäi-

---

[3] Ein Teil der Vorträge ist erschienen in: Zeitschrift für Europäisches Privat-
recht (ZEuP), 7 (1999), H. 3; vgl. dort insbes. *M. Graziadei*, Comparative Law,
Legal History, and the Holistic Approach to Legal Cultures, S. 531-543. Der
Mitherausgeber dieser Zeitschrift und Rechtshistoriker Reiner Schulze hat
schon vorher einschlägig betitelte Sammelbände herausgebracht: *R. Schulze*
(Hrsg.), Deutsche Rechtswissenschaft und Staatslehre im Spiegel der italieni-
schen Rechtskultur während der zweiten Hälfte des 19. Jahrhunderts, 1990; *A.
Mazzacane / R. Schulze* (Hrsg.), Die deutsche und die italienische Rechtskultur
im „Zeitalter der Vergleichung", 1995.
[4] Bd. 29, H. 3/4; vgl. dort insbes. *K. Veddeler*, Rechtstheorie versus Kulturtheorie? Plädoyer für eine aufgeklärte Kulturtheorie des Rechts, S. 453-473.
Schon vorher sind einschlägig betitelte rechtstheoretische Tagungsbände erschienen: *S. Jørgensen u. a.* (Hrsg.), Tradition and Progress in Modern Legal
Cultures, 1985 (= ARSP, Beiheft 23); *E. Mock / C. Varga* (Hrsg.), Rechtskultur
– Denkkultur, 1989 (= Archiv für Rechts- und Sozialphilosophie [ARSP], Beiheft 35); *P. Sack u. a.* (Hrsg.), Monismus oder Pluralismus der Rechtskulturen?
Anthropologische und ethnologische Grundlagen traditioneller und moderner
Rechtssysteme, 1992 (= Rechtstheorie, Beiheft 12). Schließlich gibt es auch einschlägig betitelte Reader für Jurastudenten: *C. Varga* (Hrsg.), Comparative Legal Cultures, Aldershot u. a. 1992; *V. Gessner u. a.* (Hrsg.), European Legal
Cultures, Aldershot u. a. 1996.
[5] Mit ihrem Interesse für Rechtskultur steht die deutsche Rechtsvergleichung nicht allein; vgl. etwa *M. van Hoecke / M. Warrington*, Legal Cultures
and Legal Paradigms: Towards a New Model for Comparative Law, in: International and Comparative Law Quarterly, 47 (1998), S. 495-536.

schen Union in ihren Mitgliedstaaten behandelt. Schließlich wurde –
ebenfalls im Herbst 1999 – vom Verfassungsrechtler Peter Häberle, der
wie kein anderer ausdauernd und variantenreich für eine sog. kultur-
wissenschaftliche Betrachtung vor allem des Verfassungsrechts eintritt[6],
ein „Bayreuther Institut für Europäisches Recht und Rechtskultur" ins
Leben gerufen.

Möglicherweise liegt es an der gängigen Assoziation von Kultur und
Kultiviertheit, wenigstens fällt auf, daß das Thema Rechtskultur gern zu
feierlichen Anlässen – also bei einem Blick über den juristischen Alltag
hinaus – aufgegriffen wird[7]. Da begriffliche Klarstellungen dabei nicht
gerade im Vordergrund stehen, drängt sich zuweilen der Verdacht auf,
das Thema sei vielleicht doch von einem eher feuilletonistischen Reiz.

Darin mag man sich angesichts mancher anzutreffender Stilisierun-
gen bestätigt fühlen. So meint Konrad Zweigert, einer der großen Re-
präsentanten der bundesdeutschen Zivilrechtsvergleichung[8], in einem
Festschriftbeitrag aus den 60er Jahren: „In Frankreich ist die Jurisprudenz ein Zweig der allgemeinen Kultur, in Deutschland ist sie ein
Fach"[9], dort die „hohe Schule des klaren Denkens, des deutlichen Aus-
drucks und der Kunst der Rhetorik", hier die „Tür zu bestimmten Berufen"[10]. Den französischen Juristentyp sieht er im „plädierenden An-
walt" verwirklicht, den deutschen im „gelehrten Doctor iuris"[11] (wohl
im Widerspruch zur gerade festgestellten besonderen Berufsbezogen-
heit der deutschen Jurisprudenz). Diese Etikettierung wird noch politisch eingefärbt, wenn es mit Bezug auf das 19. Jahrhundert – einge-

---

[6] Vgl. vor allem *P. Häberle*, Verfassungslehre als Kulturwissenschaft, 2.
Aufl. 1998 (1. Aufl. 1982); *ders.*, Europäische Rechtskultur. Versuch einer An-
näherung in zwölf Schritten, 1994 (Taschenbuchausgabe 1997).
[7] Vgl. etwa *H. Coing*, Das Recht als Element der europäischen Kultur. Text
eines am 31. Mai 1983 in der öffentlichen Sitzung des Ordens Pour le Mérite ge-
haltenen Vortrags, in: Historische Zeitschrift, 238 (1984), S. 1-15; *I. von Münch*,
Rechtskultur. Vortrag anläßlich der Entgegennahme des Emile-v.-Sauer-Preises
des Hamburgischen Anwaltsvereins, in: Neue Juristische Wochenschaft, 46
(1993), S. 1673-1678. Die 1997 erschienene Festschrift für den Rechtshistoriker
Karl Kroeschell trägt den Titel „Wirkungen europäischer Rechtskultur".
[8] Zu ihrer Entwicklung vgl. *M. Martinek*, Wissenschaftsgeschichte der
Rechtsvergleichung und des Internationalen Privatrechts in der Bundesrepublik
Deutschland, in: *D. Simon* (Hrsg.), Rechtswissenschaft in der Bonner Republik.
Studien zur Wissenschaftsgeschichte der Jurisprudenz, 1994, S. 529-619; *E. Wad-
le*, Einhundert Jahre Rechtsvergleichende Gesellschaften in Deutschland, 1994.
[9] *K. Zweigert*, Der Jurist in Frankreich und Deutschland. Versuch einer ver-
gleichenden Typologie, in: Festschrift Hans G. Ficker, 1967, S. 498-507 (498).
[10] Ebd., S. 499.
[11] Ebd.

standenermaßen „zugespitzt" – heißt: „[...] der Typus des französischen Advokaten ist das Produkt erfolgreicher Revolutionen, der Typus des gelehrten deutschen Juristen ist das Ergebnis der Anpassung"[12]. Schließlich wird der „europäische Jurist" beschworen: „Was könnten wir uns mehr wünschen, als daß der Sachernst und die Gründlichkeit des Deutschen auf der einen Seite, die französische Lebenskunst, Klarheit, Eleganz und Wortkraft auf der anderen sich zu einer neuen Einheit verbinden, zu der auch noch die gelassene Weisheit des englischen Richters, wenn das Glück es so fügt, sich gesellen könnte"[13].

Nach diesem Strauß von Stichworten, der einen ersten Eindruck von der Aktualität der Thematik und ihrer bisherigen Präsentation vermitteln sollte, sei der Sache etwas auf den Grund gegangen. Zunächst möchte ich zur Relativierung des Rechts durch Kultur eine kleine historisch-systematische Reflexion anstellen, dabei einige Punkte fixieren, die mir für die europäische Verwaltungsrechtsvergleichung relevant erscheinen, und sodann diese Relevanz anhand zweier Beispiele veranschaulichen, von denen das erste Frankreich, das zweite Schweden betrifft.

II. Zur theoretischen Fassung der kulturellen Relativierung des Rechts im allgemeinen

1. Ein Stück Geschichte: Anfänge kulturwissenschaftlicher Rechtsbetrachtung

Recht und Kultur auch terminologisch miteinander zu verbinden, kommt vor rund hundert Jahren auf und hat zu tun mit einer epistemologischen Krise der Rechtswissenschaft. Wie die Wende zum 21. Jahrhundert war schon die Wende zum 20. Jahrhundert eine Zeit vorher nie gekannter Dynamisierung in allen Bereichen des wirtschaftlichen und gesellschaftlichen Lebens und eine Zeit der Globalisierung, allerdings weniger in der Perspektive freier unternehmerischer Konkurrenz, als vielmehr in der Perspektive einer der Tendenz nach expansiven natio-

---

[12] Ebd., S. 505.
[13] Ebd., S. 507. Vgl. dazu aus heutiger und nichtdeutscher Sicht *L. Moccia*, Les bases culturelles du juriste européen: un point de vue continental, in: Revue internationale de droit comparé, 49 (1997), S. 799-811. Neuerdings zeigen sich Ansätze einer Amerikanisierung des europäischen Juristen.

nalen Selbstbehauptung, was der ganzen Epoche das Etikett des Imperialismus eingebracht hat. Dynamisierung und Globalisierung machten auch die Rechtsordnung zu einem Aspekt des Wettbewerbs, zugleich aber zu einem Ausdruck nationaler Identität. Diese doppelte Funktionalisierung der Rechtsordnung relativierte ihren Geltungsanspruch, oder anders ausgedrückt: eine gesetzespositivistische Begründung des Geltungsanspruchs wurde auch in rechtswissenschaftlicher Sicht zunehmend als unzureichend empfunden.

Auf diese Herausforderung konnte man im wesentlichen auf zwei Weisen reagieren: empirisch-erklärend oder normativ-rechtfertigend. Der eine Ansatz förderte eine über die bisher schon betriebene Auslandsrechtskunde hinausgehende Rechtsvergleichung (unter Einschluß der Universalrechtsgeschichte und Rechtsethnologie), der andere die Rechts- und Wirtschaftsphilosophie.

In Person und Werk Josef Kohlers (1849-1919) – vor allem Wirtschaftsrechtler und ein weithin anerkannter, wenngleich nicht unumstrittener Repräsentant der Rechtswissenschaft im wilhelminischen Deutschland[14] – verbanden sich beide Ansätze beispielhaft[15]. Kohler war Mitbegründer einschlägiger Periodika, namentlich der „Zeitschrift für vergleichende Rechtswissenschaft" und des „Archivs für Rechts- und Wirtschaftsphilosophie", das sich heute „Archiv für Rechts- und Sozialphilosophie" nennt. Die Herstellung des Zusammenhangs von Rechtsphilosophie und Rechtsvergleichung – der sich freilich alsbald wieder verlieren sollte[16] und erst heute vielleicht erneut aufgenommen

---

[14] Vgl. des näheren G. *Spendel*, Josef Kohler. Bild eines Universaljuristen, 1983; W. *Gast*, Historischer Optimismus. Die juristische Weltsicht Josef Kohlers, in: Zeitschrift für vergleichende Rechtswissenschaft (ZVglRWiss), 85 (1986), S. 1-10; A. *Gängel* / M. *Schaumburg*, Josef Kohler – Rechtsgelehrter und Rechtslehrer an der Berliner Alma mater um die Jahrhundertwende, in: ARSP, 75 (1989), S. 289-312.

[15] Programmatisch J. *Kohler*, Rechtsphilosophie und Rechtsvergleichung, in: ARSP, 1 (1907/1908), S. 192-199; vgl. auch die Würdigung aus Anlaß seines 70. Geburtstages von L. *Adam*, Josef Kohler und die vergleichende Rechtswissenschaft, in: ZVglRWiss, 37 (1919), 1-31.

[16] Die Literatur dazu wird nach den 20er Jahren äußerst spärlich; vgl. A. *Blomeyer*, Zur Frage der Abgrenzung von vergleichender Rechtswissenschaft und Rechtsphilosophie, in: RabelsZ, 8 (1934), S. 1-16; W. *Wengler*, Gedanken zur Soziologie und zur Philosophie der Rechtsvergleichung, in: M. *Rotondi* (Hrsg.), Inchiesti di diritto comparato, Bd. II, Padova / New York 1973, S. 723-733; H.A. *Schwarz-Liebermann von Wahlendorf*, Méthode comparée et philosophie du droit, in: ebd., S. 611-621. In den 70er/80er Jahren rückt die Beschäftigung mit dem Verhältnis zwischen Rechtsvergleichung und Rechtssoziologie in den Vordergrund; vgl. den Sammelband von U. *Drobnig* / M. *Rehbinder* (Hrsg.), Rechtssoziologie und Rechtsvergleichung, 1977; ferner D. *Martiny*,

wird – geschah unter Verwendung des für die damalige Zeit insgesamt wissenschaftsprägenden und geradezu populären Kulturbegriffs. In seinem Leitaufsatz für das „Archiv für Rechts- und Wirtschaftsphilosophie" von 1907 bezeichnet Kohler das Recht zugleich als „Kulturerscheinung und Kulturbedingung"[17].

„Kultur" war, wie auch heute, ein Sammelbegriff für alles, was dem menschlichen Verhalten innerlich und äußerlich Sinn gibt und insofern zum Handeln macht, desgleichen was von dieser Sinnstiftung zeugt: Sprache, Religion, Wissenschaft, Technik, Kunst und eben auch Recht[18]. Die Anbindung des Rechtsbegriffs an den Kulturbegriff verhieß der Rechtswissenschaft Selbständigkeit gegenüber Gesetzgebung und Rechtsprechung und damit eigene Dignität[19]. Folgerichtig wurde Rechtswissenschaft auch von manchen als Kulturwissenschaft begriffen, freilich nicht ohne Widerspruch zu erfahren[20].

Als Erkennungsmerkmal einer Kulturwissenschaft wurde die Untersuchung der Wertbezogenheit kultureller Phänomene genannt. Gustav

---

Rechtsvergleichung und vergleichende Rechtssoziologie, in: Zeitschrift für Rechtssoziologie (ZfRSoz), 1 (1980), S. 65-84, und *K.A. Zweigert*, Juristische und soziologische Empirie des Rechts. Genese und Zukunft der Rechtsvergleichung als wissenschaftliches Problem des europäischen Rechts, in: Zeitschrift für ausländisches und internationales Privatrecht (RabelsZ), 45 (1981), S. 51-72.

[17] *J. Kohler*, Wesen und Ziele der Rechtsphilosophie, in: ARSP, 1 (1907/08), S. 3-15 (6); so auch schon – aber nur illustrierend – *ders.*, Das Recht als Kulturerscheinung. Einleitung in die vergleichende Rechtswissenschaft, 1885. Über die Einbettung solcher Verknüpfung in die zeitgenössische Diskussion unterrichtet *G. Sprenger*, Recht als Kulturerscheinung, in: *ders.* (Hrsg.), Deutsche Rechts- und Sozialphilosophie um 1900. Zugleich ein Beitrag zur Gründungsgeschichte der Internationalen Vereinigung für Rechts- und Sozialphilosophie (IVR), 1991 (= ARSP, Beiheft 43), S. 134-153.

[18] Zum heutigen Kulturbegriff und dem Zusammenhang der Kulturerscheinungen vgl. *F.H. Tenbruck*, Die Aufgaben der Kultursoziologie [1985], in: *ders.*, Perspektiven der Kultursoziologie. Gesammelte Aufsätze, hrsg. von *C. Albrecht u. a.*, 1996, S. 48-74 (52 ff.).

[19] Vgl. *F. Münch*, Kultur und Recht. Nebst einem Anhang: Rechtsreformbewegung und Kulturphilosophie, 1918; *M. Angerthal*, Untersuchungen zur Kulturidee in der neueren Rechtsphilosophie, Diss. jur. Königsberg 1929; *A. Gysin*, Recht und Kultur auf dem Grunde der Ethik, 1929.

[20] Bekannt wurde vor allem die Auseinandersetzung zwischen *H. Rickert*, Rechtswissenschaft als Norm- und Kulturwissenschaft, 1916, und *H. Kelsen*, Rechtswissenschaft als Norm- und Kulturwisssenschaft, in: Schmollers Jahrbuch für Gesetzgebung, Verwaltung und Volkswirtschaft im Deutschen Reich, 40 (1916), S. 1181-1239. Zum Verständnis solcher Kulturwissenschaft vgl. *R. vom Bruch u. a.* (Hrsg.), Kultur und Kulturwissenschaften um 1900. Krise der Moderne und Glaube an die Wissenschaft, 1989, insbes. den Einleitungsaufsatz der Herausgeber.

Radbruch (1878-1949) hat seine Rechtsphilosophie in dieser Richtung entwickelt[21]. Als Rechtsvergleicher, der er auch war, versuchte Radbruch dem Dualismus von Sein und Sollen, den er seinen neukantianischen Grundüberzeugungen entsprechend für unentrinnbar hielt, durch eine entsprechende Differenzierung der Rechtsvergleichung gerecht zu werden. Referenzpunkt der Rechtsvergleichung kann danach sein: zum einen der deskriptiv begriffene „Rechtstypus, d. h. das System der durchschnittlichen Eigenschaften der Rechtssysteme eines bestimmten Kulturkreises und einer bestimmten Entwicklungsstufe", zum anderen das normativ begriffene „Rechtsideal, d. h. das System der vom Standpunkte eines bestimmten Individuums an das Recht eines bestimmten Kulturkreises und einer bestimmten Entwicklungsstufe zu stellenden Anforderungen"[22]. Beim „Rechtsideal" wird demnach zwar die Sollenssubjektivität als Ausgangspunkt genommen, aber durch ihre Verknüpfung mit „Kulturkreis" und „Entwicklungsstufe" gewissermaßen gedämpft und insofern dann doch wieder ein Stück verobjektiviert. Die Richtigkeitsfrage wird nicht aufgegeben, aber sie wird relativiert durch Bezugnahme auf Raum und Zeit, auf Gesellschaft und Individuum[23].

---

[21] G. *Radbruch*, Grundzüge der Rechtsphilosophie, 1914, S. 2: „Recht ist die Wirklichkeit, die den Sinn hat, dem Rechtswerte, der Rechtsidee zu dienen". Schon vor Rickert und Radbruch hatte Emil Lask Rechtswissenschaft kulturwissenschaftlich verstanden und den Sinn von Normen aus ihrer Beziehung auf sozial anerkannte Werte und Zwecke gewonnen; vgl. *E. Lask*, Rechtsphilosophie, in: Festschrift Kuno Fischer, 2. Aufl., 1907, S. 269-320 (298 ff.).

[22] G. *Radbruch*, Über die Methode der Rechtsvergleichung, in: Monatsschrift für Kriminalpsychologie und Strafrechtsreform, 2 (1905/06), S. 422-425 (423). Vgl. dazu *H. Scholler*, Rechtsvergleichung als Vergleichung von Rechtskulturen. Ein Beitrag zu Gustav Radbruchs Rechtsvergleichung, in: Festschrift Arthur Kaufmann, 1993, S. 743-759.

[23] Der Neukantianismus wirkt sich auch in der Methodologie der Rechtsvergleichung aus: Für *M. Salomon*, Grundlegung der Rechtsphilosophie, 1919, S. 41, besteht das *tertium comparationis* rechtsvergleichender Arbeit im „Rechtsproblem"; in ihm wird „den Rechtsnormen der verschiedenen Rechtskreise, die zur Vergleichung stehen, ihre Rolle zuerkannt. Sie erscheinen als die voneinander abweichenden Lösungsversuche eines identischen Rechtsproblems. Die Einheit des Problems ist es, die ihre Vergleichbarkeit gewährleistet." *Blomeyer* (Fn. 16), S. 12 f., kritisiert daran, die das Rechtsproblem konstituierenden Elemente seien apriorischer Natur und Salomon daher ein Vertreter einer „Topik apriorischer Begriffe", die zu einer empirischen Rechtsvergleichung nichts beitragen könne. *E.A. Kramer*, Topik und Rechtsvergleichung, in: RabelsZ, 33 (1969), 1-15 (4 f.) sieht in Salomon einen Vorläufer Theodor Viehwegs in der Entwicklung der topischen Methode des Problemdenkens: Rechtsvergleichung sei „nicht anderes als angewandte Topik".

14

Solche neukantianischen Skrupel kennt der Neuhegelianer Kohler nicht. Radbruchs Sollenssubjektivität wird geschichtsphilosophisch überspielt: Das Recht, so schreibt er, „bedarf der tieferen Begründung der Bedeutung der menschlichen Kultur und des menschlichen Daseins im Laufe der Zeiten, es bedarf des Begriffes der Entwicklung und des Verständnisses unseres Völkerdaseins als einer zeitlichen Ausgestaltung des göttlichen Wesens mit der Aufgabe, unter Anwendung aller Hilfsmittel unseres geistigen Lebens viele und reiche Kulturbildungen [zu] schaffen und sich dadurch zur Göttlichkeit aufzuschwingen"[24]. Dementsprechend wäre es aus Kohlers Sicht auch irrig, die Gesetzesauslegung an den Vorstellungen des historischen Gesetzgebers auszurichten; Maßstab sei vielmehr der „Kulturfortschritt"[25].

Aber dieser geschichtsphilosophische Impetus bedarf der empirischen Abstützung, namentlich seitens der Rechtsvergleichung. „Das Wort Kultur ist ein blosser Schall, wenn man nicht die einzelnen Arten der Kultur kennt", heißt es; andernfalls gliche die Rechtsphilosophie einem „Kartenhaus"[26]. Daher wendet sich Kohler, auch wenn er in hegelscher Manier ein „Walten des Weltgeistes"[27] unterstellt, nicht nur gegen den Dualismus von Sein und Sollen, sondern auch gegen Hegels „Begriffsdialektik"[28]: „Nicht Begriffsdialektik, sondern Realdialektik ist die Eigenart der Welt, und erst aus der tausendfältigen Erfahrung, nicht aus den Hegelschen Triaden, lässt sich die Welt verstehen. Aber darin halten wir fest an der ungeheuren Tat Hegels, dass die Kultur uns eine Entwicklung darstellt, d. h. eine zeitliche Entfaltung von Mächten, welche in der Potenz bereits ausserzeitlich vorhanden waren. Denn die Kultur als bewegende Geisteskraft ist eine Emanation des ewigen Gottes."

Wem das alles sehr fremd erscheint, der möge bedenken, daß auch Otto Mayer (1846-1924) zu seiner grundlegenden Konstruktion eines allgemeinen deutschen Verwaltungsrechts durch ein nicht zuletzt von Hegel inspiriertes Theorem der Rechtsentwicklung ermutigt worden ist[29].

---

[24] *Kohler* (Fn. 15), S. 193; ähnlich schon *Kohler*, Recht als Kulturerscheinung (Fn. 17), S. 3 (Vorrede).
[25] *Kohler*, Wesen und Ziele (Fn. 17), S. 6.
[26] *Kohler* (Fn. 15), S. 195.
[27] Ebd., S. 198.
[28] Ebd., S. 199. Vgl. dazu *W. Schild*, Die Ambivalenz einer Neo-Philosophie. Zu Josef Kohlers Neuhegelianismus, in: *Sprenger* (Fn. 17), S. 46-65.
[29] Vgl. *E.V. Heyen*, Otto Mayer. Studien zu den geistigen Grundlagen seiner Verwaltungsrechtswissenschaft, 1981, S. 111 ff., 162 ff.; zur Art seiner Beiziehung ausländischen Verwaltungsrechts vgl. *ders.* (Fn. 2), S. 181 ff.

Was immer wir heute von Kohlers oder Radbruchs rechtsphiloso-
phischen Ansätzen halten mögen, sie bringen im Zusammenhang mit
der Rechtsvergleichung eine starke Relativierung des Rechts durch
Kultur zum Ausdruck, gleichzeitig aber auch die identitätsstiftende
Wirkung dieser kulturellen Einbettung[30]. Zu fragen ist, ob und inwie-
weit solche Kulturbedingtheit von Recht innerhalb der Rechtsvergleichung auch einen Begriff der Rechtskultur rechtfertigt.

2. Ein Stück Systematik:
Rechtskulturbegriffe für die Rechtsvergleichung

Es geht mir hier nicht um eine auf Vollständigkeit bedachte Aufli-
stung der in der rechtswissenschaftlichen Literatur auffindbaren Be-
griffsbestimmungen und deren Bewertung. Das Verständnis variiert
beträchtlich[31]. Eine erste und bereits recht wirksame Einschränkung
der Variationsbreite ließe sich erreichen, wenn man den Begriff der
Rechtskultur für Dinge reservierte, die unsere Rechtssprache nicht
schon durch andere, etablierte Termini, wie z. B. „Rechtsordnung"
oder „Rechtssystem", erfaßt. Mir erscheint es wenig sinnvoll, Differenzen zwischen Rechtsordnungen ohne weiteres als Differenzen von
Rechtskulturen anzusehen; ein Bundesstaat wie der deutsche wäre andernfalls von vornherein zum rechtskulturell fragmentierten Raum er-

---

[30] Auf solche Wirkung hinzuweisen, ist auch eine Funktion der Rechtsgeschichte gegenüber der Rechtsvergleichung; vgl. *E. Genzmer*, Zum Verhältnis
von Rechtsgeschichte und Rechtsvergleichung. Eine Vortragsskizze, in: ARSP,
41 (1954/55), S. 326-347; *ders.*, Über historische Rechtsvergleichung, in: *Rotondi* (Fn. 16), S. 233-254; *J. Gilissen*, Histoire comparée du droit. L'expérience de la
Société Jean Bodin, in: ebd., S. 255-297; *H. Coing*, Die Bedeutung der europäischen Rechtsgeschichte für die Rechtsvergleichung, in: RabelsZ, 32 (1968), S. 1-
23; *H. Hübner*, Sinn und Möglichkeiten retrospektiver Rechtsvergleichung, in:
Festschrift Gerhard Kegel, 1987, S. 235-252; *M. Reimann*, Rechtsvergleichung
und Rechtsgeschichte im Dialog, in: ZEuP, 7 (1999), S. 496-512.
[31] Eine Vorstellung von der anzutreffenden Vielfalt vermitteln *A. Erh-Soon
Tay*, Law and „Legal Culture", in: *Jørgensen* (Fn. 4), S. 165-171; *G. Rebuffa*,
Culture juridique, in: *A.-J. Arnaud u. a.* (Hrsg.), Dictionnaire encyclopédique
de théorie et de sociologie du droit, Paris / Bruxelles 1988, S. 89-91; *W. Gephart*,
Kulturelle Aspekte des Rechts. Vom Klassen- zum Kulturparadigma, in:
ZfRSoz, 11 (1990), S. 177-187; *R. Cotterell*, The Concept of Legal Culture, in:
D. Nelken (Hrsg.), Comparing Legal Cultures, Aldershot u. a. 1997, S. 13-31; *P.
Gabel*, Critical Legal Studies et la pratique juridique: la conception de la culture
juridique et de la pratique du droit comme interventions culturelles, in: Droit et
Société, 36/37 (1997), S. 369-400; *G. Mohr*, Zum Begriff der Rechtskultur, in:
Dialektik, 1998, H. 3: Kulturen des Rechts, hrsg. von *W. Goldschmidt*, S. 9-29.

klärt. Im übrigen sollte die Fruchtbarkeit der durch die Begriffsbildung
eröffneten Untersuchungsperspektive maßgeblich sein.

Ich möchte hier im wesentlichen nur zwei Rechtskulturbegriffe vor-
schlagen, einen für die Makrovergleichung und einen für die Mikrovergleichung, diese aber unter bestimmten, auch für die europäische Verwaltungsrechtsvergleichung wichtigen Aspekten in sich differenzieren.
Beide Begriffe verstehen sich rein deskriptiv, intendieren also keine Bewertung.

Ein Rechtskulturbegriff für die Makrovergleichung: „Rechtskultur"
bezeichnet hier eine Gesamtheit von 1. Rechtsnormen, 2. Institutionen
der Rechtsnormerzeugung und -anwendung, 3. Kenntnissen, Einstellungen (Werthaltungen) und Verhaltensweisen mit Bezug zu diesen
Rechtsnormen und Rechtsinstitutionen, jeweils einschließlich ihrer
physischen, stilistischen und symbolischen Repräsentation (z. B. Geset-
zestexte, Vertragsurkunden, Gerichtsgebäude, Amtsroben u. ä.). Diese
Gesamtheit konstituiert sich durch ihren Bezug auf eine bestimmte gesellschaftliche Einheit. Das muß nicht notwendigerweise ein Staat sein;
es sind auch überstaatliche und unterstaatliche Einheiten denkbar[32].

Ein Rechtskulturbegriff für die Mikrovergleichung: Dieser Begriff
beschränkt sich auf das dritte Element des eben genannten Rechtskulturbegriffs für die Makrovergleichung[33], d. h. „Rechtskultur" bezeichnet hier eine Gesamtheit von Kenntnissen, Einstellungen (Werthaltungen) und Verhaltensweisen mit Bezug auf Rechtsnormen und Rechtsinstitutionen, jeweils einschließlich ihrer physischen, stilistischen und
symbolischen Repräsentation. Auch diese Gesamtheit konstituiert sich
durch ihren Bezug auf eine bestimmte gesellschaftliche Einheit (von
der Rechtskultur eines Individuums zu sprechen ist zwar semantisch
denkbar, für die Rechtsvergleichung aber – also pragmatisch – uninter-
essant). Je nachdem, ob es um Kenntnisse, Einstellungen usw. von Per-
sonen innerhalb oder außerhalb der Rechtsinstitutionen geht, kann
man – einem vor allem in der Rechtssoziologie verbreiteten Sprachge-
brauch folgend[34] – interne und externe Rechtskulturen unterscheiden.

---

[32] Insofern kann man z. B. auch von europäischer Rechtskultur sprechen;
vgl. etwa *Häberle*, Europäische Rechtskultur (Fn. 6); *P. Stein*, Römisches Recht
und Europa. Die Geschichte einer Rechtskultur, 1996.
[33] Hinsichtlich der ersten beiden Elemente allein will mir die Bildung eines
Rechtskulturbegriffs entbehrlich scheinen. Man könnte sie unter den Begriff
der Rechtsordnung oder des Rechtssystems fassen.
[34] Vgl. *Rebuffa* (Fn. 31); *Cotterell* (Fn. 31); ferner die Beiträge zur Rechtskultur in: ZfRSoz, 6 (1985), H. 2, und 7 (1986), H. 1.

Zur internen Rechtskultur gehört dann die des sog. Rechtsstabes, differenzierbar u. a. nach Richtern, Anwälten und Rechtsprofessoren, zur externen Rechtskultur die der Rechtslaien, d. h. des Publikums der Rechtsinstitutionen, ebenfalls in sich vielfältig differenzierbar. Externe wie interne Rechtskulturen entscheiden darüber, ob und wie von Rechtsnormen Gebrauch gemacht und Rechtsinstitutionen in Anspruch genommen bzw. eingesetzt werden.

Bei beiden Rechtskulturbegriffen, dem der Makrovergleichung und dem der Mikrovergleichung[35], kann man einen engeren Gebrauch unterscheiden. Angesichts der – auch historisch begründeten – Bedeutung der Identitätsproblematik für den Begriff der Rechtskultur, soll hier von Rechtskultur im engeren Sinne dann gesprochen werden, wenn es in der Selbstwahrnehmung der Angehörigen dieser Rechtskultur um identitätsstiftende Merkmale geht. In solchen Fällen entwickelt die Berufung auf die Rechtskultur in rechtsrelevanten Entscheidungsprozessen ein eigenes Gewicht, sozusagen einen Mehrwert.

Beide Rechtskulturbegriffe, einschließlich ihrer hier vorgestellten Binnendifferenzierungen, sind auch relevant für die Erfassung von „Verwaltungskultur"[36]. Die Begriffe der Rechtskultur und der Verwaltungskultur sind nicht deckungsgleich, sondern überschneiden sich. So könnte man als interne Verwaltungrechtskultur die Rechtskultur des auf die öffentliche Verwaltung bezogenen Rechtsstabes bezeichnen (vor allem Verwaltungsbeamte, Verwaltungsrichter, Professoren des Verwaltungsrechts[37]).

Was leistet nun diese Begriffsbildung? Sie schafft vor allem Aufmerksamkeit dafür, daß Rechtsnormen und Rechtsinstitutionen in einen größeren Kommunikationskontext eingebettet sind, der nicht nur ihre Wirklichkeit bestimmt – deren Erforschung man besonderen, empirisch ausgerichteten Disziplinen, wie der Rechtssoziologie und

---

[35] Es lassen sich natürlich auch Begriffsmischungen denken. So könnte man zur Rechtskultur beispielsweise der Anwälte auch die einschlägigen Berufsgesetze und Standesordnungen zählen.

[36] Der Ausdruck tritt vermehrt in den frühen 80er Jahren auf, und zwar im Zusammenhang mit politikwissenschaftlichen Untersuchungen zur „politischen Kultur"; zur bisherigen Literatur vgl. die Nachweise bei *S. Römer-Hillebrecht*, Verwaltungskultur. Ein holistischer Modellentwurf administrativer Lebensstile, 1998.

[37] Über die Auswirkungen des jeweiligen professionellen Milieus auf die Handhabung von Verwaltungsrechtswissenschaft vgl. *E. V. Heyen*, Profile der deutschen und französischen Verwaltungsrechtswissenschaft 1880-1914, 1989.

Rechtspolitologie, überlassen könnte –, sondern auch ihren normativen Gehalt und Geltungsanspruch, womit sich die Kerndisziplin der Rechtswissenschaft: die Rechtsdogmatik und auch die Rechtsvergleichung zu befassen haben.

Teilweise ist dies ein durchaus vertrauter Gedanke: Das aus ständiger Rechtsprechung erwachsende Richterrecht z. B. ist ein sichtbarer Ausdruck eines Segments interner Rechtskultur, nämlich richterlicher Rechtskultur. Solche Rechtskultur ermöglicht es denen, die an ihr teilhaben und sie im Urteil autoritativ auszudrücken berufen sind, passenden und weniger passenden Umgang mit dem geltenden Recht zu unterscheiden. Und dies, ohne sich darüber immer Rechenschaft zu geben, so wie ja der Fisch das Wasser, in dem er schwimmt, auch kaum jemals wahrnimmt. Die Rechtsordnung hat etliche Stellen, an denen man die Rechtsnormen aus der richterlichen Rechtskultur – einem Magma gleich – aufsteigen und sich ausformen sieht: z. B. das Prinzip von Treu und Glauben im Zivilrecht und im öffentlichen Recht das Verhältnismäßigkeitsprinzip, aus dem heraus das Preußische Oberverwaltungsgericht entscheidende Teile des allgemeinen Polizeirechts entwickelt hat und das Bundesverfassungsgericht Möglichkeiten und Grenzen der Grundrechtseinschränkung. Die allgemeine gesellschaftliche und die besondere juridische Akkulturation (das „Judiz") der professionellen Rechtsanwender entscheiden über das jeweils rechtlich Denkbare und das rechtlich Naheliegende.

Zur internen Rechtskultur gehört auch die sog. juristische Methodenlehre: die Anleitung zur Normauslegung und Normfortbildung, wie sie in der Rechtsprechung und einer der Rechtsprechung vorarbeitenden Rechtsdogmatik praktiziert werden. Die Rechtsdogmatik hat, wenigstens bei uns in Deutschland, bezüglich des geltenden Rechts nicht nur Beschreibungs- und Dokumentationsfunktionen, Strukturierungs- und Klarstellungsfunktionen, die manche vielleicht noch einer kulturindifferenten Wissenschaftsebene zuzuordnen geneigt sein könnten. Sie hat vielmehr auch die Funktion, innerhalb des geltenden Rechts auftretende Regelungswidersprüche und -lücken zu beheben, und zwar in der Perspektive der Gewinnung bzw. Erhaltung eines identitätsstiftenden, dabei entwicklungsfähigen, also Stabilität ohne Stagnation gewährleistenden Systems (Pflegefunktion). Schließlich hat Rechtsdogmatik die Funktion, auf die Dynamik gesellschaftlich-politisch relevanter Interessen- und Werteartikulationen zu reagieren und Vorschläge zur Modifizierung von Gesetzgebung, Verwaltung und Rechtsprechung zu erarbeiten (Änderungsfunktion). Es sind vor allem die Pflege- und Änderungsaspekte, die dazu geführt haben, die „politischen Funktion" der Methode bzw. ihren Charakter als „Machtfaktor"[38] zu untersuchen und damit ihre rechtskulturelle, durch kaum eine Rechtsnorm erfaßte und gesteuerte Bedeutung an den Tag zu bringen. In Krisenzeiten ist der rechtskulturelle Gehalt des Streites um die richtige Methode geradezu mit Händen zu greifen[39]. Aber Richterrecht und juristische Methodenlehre betreffen nur die interne Rechtskultur und hier auch nur Teilaspekte. Die kulturelle Relativierung des Rechts geht weit darüber hinaus, wie man sich insbesondere anhand des Begriffs der externen Rechtskultur vergegenwärtigen kann. Beide, die internen und die externen Rechtskulturen, bestimmen, ob und in welchem Umfang Legalität und Legitimität einer Rechtsordnung zusammen- oder auseinanderfallen und damit ob und in welchem Umfang die Rechtsordnung akzeptiert, modifiziert oder revolutioniert wird. Sie sind gewissermaßen entweder das Öl, das die Rechtsmaschine am Laufen hält, oder der Sand in dessen Getriebe, mit anderen Worten – um es nicht technisch, sondern ökologisch zu sagen – sie bilden das Biotop, das das Rechtsleben entweder begünstigt oder beeinträchtigt, in jedem Fall aber prägt.

Ich komme damit zu meinen zwei Beispielen, die nunmehr mit Bezug auf die europäische Verwaltungsrechtsvergleichung die praktische

---

[38] Vgl. G. *Haverkate*, Gewißheitsverluste im juristischen Denken. Zur politischen Funktion der juristischen Methode, 1977; D. *Grimm*, Methode als Machtfaktor, in: Festschrift Helmut Coing, Bd. I, 1982, S. 469-492.

[39] So z.B. anschaulich im sog. Methoden- und Richtungsstreit der deutschen Staatsrechtswissenschaft zur Zeit der Weimarer Republik, der vor allem mit den Namen Carl Schmitt, Erich Kaufmann, Hermann Heller, Rudolf Smend und Hans Kelsen verbunden ist. Vgl. dazu B. *Schlink*, Weimar – von der Krise der Theorie zur Theorie der Krise, in: Gedächtnisschrift Bernd Jeand'Heur, 1999, S. 43-55 (55): „In ihrer Grundsätzlichkeit schöpfen diese Antworten theoretisch aus, wie Krisen begegnet werden kann. Es kann versucht werden, der Kampf, der mit der Krise einhergeht, in den Rahmen und unter die Regeln der vorgegebenen Verfassungs- und Rechtsordnung zu zwingen. Es kann auch versucht werden, die brüchig gewordene oder gar zerbrechende Einheit kulturell-geistig oder organisatorisch-institutionell zusammenzuhalten, den Staat als Smendschen Integrations- oder Hellerschen Organisations- und Entscheidungszusammenhang zu stärken und gegen den Kampf zu setzen. Ob das unter Beibehaltung, Veränderung oder auch Verletzung der vorgegebenen Verfassungs- und Rechtsordnung geschieht, ist dabei lageabhängig und sekundär. Schließlich kann versucht werden, den Kampf anzunehmen, eine klare Freund-Feind-Unterscheidung zu treffen und sich auf die eine oder andere Seite zu schlagen, wieder je nach Lage unter Wahrung oder Preisgabe des Rahmens und der Regeln der vorgegebenen Verfassungs- und Rechtsordnung." Zu den Auswirkungen dieses Methodenstreits in der Bundesrepublik vgl. H. *Schulze-Fielitz*, Grundsatzkontroversen in der deutschen Staatsrechtslehre nach 50 Jahren Grundgesetz – in der Beleuchtung des Handbuchs des Staatsrechts, in: Die Verwaltung, 32 (1999), S. 241-282 (270 ff.).

Relevanz der kulturellen Relativierung des Rechts veranschaulichen sollen. Sie handeln beide von Rechtskultur im engeren Sinne, also von identitätsstiftenden Merkmalen, und zwar sowohl auf der Makro- als auch auf der Mikroebene.

III. Zur praktischen Relevanz der kulturellen Relativierung des Verwaltungsrechts

1. Erstes Beispiel: Frankreich – Stärkung francophoner Identität?

Im Dezember 1998 veröffentlichte das Pariser „Internationale Institut für Öffentliche Verwaltung" (IIAP: *Institut international d'administration publique*) ein knapp 200 Seiten starkes Heft, dessen Titel in deutscher Übersetzung etwa lauten würde: „Die öffentliche Verwaltung der francophonen Länder bei Anbruch des 21. Jahrhunderts"[40]. Es dokumentiert eine zwei Jahre zuvor mit großem äußeren Aufwand, viel Selbstbewußtsein und beachtlicher Aufmerksamkeit in der Tages- und Wochenpresse inszenierte wissenschaftliche und zugleich höchst politische Tagung. Die Teilnehmer kamen aus über 40 Ländern: Minister, hohe Beamte, Direktoren von Verwaltungsschulen, Universitätsprofessoren. Formeller Anlaß war das 30jährige Bestehen des von Charles de Gaulle gegründeten Instituts, das seit den 60er Jahren Tausende von Verwaltungsbeamten ausgebildet hatte, vor allem aus den ehemaligen französischen Kolonialgebieten in Afrika und Indochina, aber auch aus den mittel- und osteuropäischen Transformationsländern. Die Veranstaltung stand unter der Schirmherrschaft des Staatspräsidenten Jacques Chirac, die Eröffnungsansprache hielt der damalige Ministerpräsident Alain Juppé.

Vergleicht man die Schlußerklärung der Tagung mit dieser Eröffnungsansprache, so sieht man, daß eine konzertierte Aktion von Wissenschaft und Politik vorlag. Die besondere Zielsetzung der Tagung trat bereits in den Worten Juppés zutage. Dem wissenschaftlichen Programm war zwar entnehmbar, daß es um Verwaltungsmodernisierung

---

[40] *Institut international d'administration publique* (Hrsg.), L'administration publique des pays francophones à l'aube des années 2000. Assises francophones de l'administration publique organisées par l'Institut international d'administration publique, Paris 12-14 décembre 1996, Paris 1998.

und ihre Folgen für Verwaltungsausbildung und Entwicklungsverwaltung sowie um die Kennzeichen des französischen und francophonen Verwaltungsverständnisses gehen sollte. Aber die pragmatische Stoßrichtung, die der Ministerpräsident vorgab – inbesondere die mit entschlossenem Tone vorgetragene Verteidigung eines historisch gewachsenen Staatskonzepts – war in dieser Form nicht selbstverständlich.

Die Versammlung möge darüber nachdenken, so sagt Juppé[41], was die francophone Gemeinschaft auf der Grundlage ihrer institutionellen Traditionen in einer Welt des stetigen Wandels dazu beitragen könne, daß der Staat in allen Ländern stark sei und zugleich geachtet werde. Der Staat sei der Garant der Freiheiten, der Garant des gesellschaftlichen Zusammenhalts, der Garant der Prinzipien des gleichen Zugangs zu den öffentlichen Leistungen (*service public*), deren Fortbestand er sichere. Gerade durch seine Einheit stiftende und Schutz gewährende Rolle gewinne er die Zuneigung der Nation. Nur er könne den Vorrang des Gemeinwohls (*intérêt général*) gewährleisten und die Gleichheit aller in den Bereichen der Gesundheit, der Sicherheit, der Justiz, der Erziehung oder des Umweltschutzes. Die allgemeinen Prinzipien guter Verwaltung – Durchsichtigkeit, Verantwortung, Solidität des Finanzgebarens, Aufstieg der Führungskräfte nach Leistung – müßten aufrechterhalten und gestärkt werden.

Es sei die Aufgabe aller Francophonen, fährt Juppé fort[42], auf der Bühne der Welt gemeinsam ihre Konzeption des Staates im Dienste der Menschen zu verteidigen. Denn sie seien mehr als eine Sprachgemeinschaft, nämlich eine Gemeinschaft von Menschen, die danach trachteten, ein Gleichgewicht zu finden zwischen einer aktiven Teilnahme an der Entwicklung der Welt, der Achtung der Kultur eines jeden, der Wurzeln seiner Gesellschaft, und den Grundwerten der Freiheit, der Gleichheit und der Brüderlichkeit, die nicht irgendeiner Marktideologie oder irgendeinem Marktmechanismus geopfert werden dürften.

In dem anschließenden Einleitungsreferat durch den ehemaligen Sektionsvorsitzenden im *Conseil d'Etat* Guy Braibant wird beides – Staatsverständnis und Francophonieverständnis – aufgegriffen und auf die öffentliche Verwaltung bezogen. Die Einheit in der Vielfalt eines francophonen Verwaltungsverständnisses wird im gemeinsamen Gegensatz zu den angelsächsischen Konzepten gesehen[43].

---

[41] A. *Juppé*, Allocution d'ouverture, in: *Institut* (Fn. 40), S. 11-14 (12).

[42] Ebd., S. 13 f.

[43] G. *Braibant*, La place de la francophonie dans la coopération administrative internationale, in: *Institut* (Fn. 40), S. 15-20 (15).

Braibant konstruiert dabei eine unauflösbare Einheit von Werten und Wörtern. Illustriert wird dies am Beispiel von Etat, volonté géné-rale, service public, fonction publique – Termini, für die es im Englischen keine angemessene Übersetzung gebe. Inhaltlich sei die französische wie die francophone Konzeption der Verwaltung dadurch gekennzeichnet, daß sie als Konsequenz des Rechtsstaats (Etat de droit) eine Rechtsverwaltung (administration de droit) zu sein beanspruche; demgemäß werde der gerichtlichen Verwaltungskontrolle ein beträchtliches, den angelsächsischen Konzepten fremdes Gewicht eingeräumt[44].

. In dieser entschlossenen Zuspitzung – die vielleicht für ein Mitglied des Conseil d'Etat, des obersten Verwaltungsgerichts in Frankreich, nur allzu natürlich ist – gewinnt die Francophonie mit ihrer verwaltungskulturellen Ausformung also zugleich einen wesentlich rechtskulturellen Gehalt mit etatistischer Leuchtkraft. Darin liegt nun keine bloß deskriptive Selbstanalyse des französischen Mutterlandes, sondern ein programmatischer Anspruch auf Besserung des bisher als zu gering eingeschätzten Stellenwerts solcher Rechts- und Verwaltungskultur in der internationalen Gemeinschaft: Zwar spiele das Pariser IIAP mit seinen Ausbildungsangeboten, Büchern und Dokumentationen sowie seiner Zeitschrift (*Revue française d'administration publique*) eine herausragende Rolle und sei eine Trumpfkarte im internationalen Wettbewerb; auch gelte gleiches für das Brüsseler „Internationale Institut für Verwaltungswissenschaften" (IISA: *Institut international des Sciences administratives*), welches das Französische neben dem Englischen als offizielle Sprache anerkannt habe (wenngleich aus finanziellen Gründen diese Gleichberechtigung immer wieder in Frage gestellt werde). Aber ansonsten – in der UNO, in der Weltbank, ja selbst innerhalb der EU – könne von einem angemessenen Platz für die Francophonie nicht die Rede sein[45]. Auch sprachlich sei das Französische unter Druck geraten. Beklagt wird die Übernahme einer Vielzahl nicht nur überflüssiger, sondern irreführender Ausdrücke aus dem Englischen, wie management, guidance, governance (anstelle von *gestion, directive* oder *incitation administrative, gouvernement*). Zur Abhilfe wird u. a. eine stärkere Präsenz francophoner Länder auf internationalen Veranstaltungen, eine noch stärkere Nutzung von IIAP und IISA (!) vorgeschlagen, ferner die Förderung der bisher kaum entwickelten Verwaltungsrechtsvergleichung unter den francophonen Ländern selbst, da sie es gestatten würde, die gemeinsamen Elemente besser her-

---

44 Ebd., S. 16 f.
45 Ebd., S. 18 f.

auszuarbeiten und über die wichtigen Fragen der Terminologie nachzudenken[46].

Auch im Schlußbericht der Tagung – erstattet vom Vorsitzenden der internationalen Konferenz der Dekane der francophonen Rechtsfakultäten, dem Belgier Francis Delpérée – wird die französische Rechtskultur als Bestandteil der Francophonie herausgestellt. Sie reiche deutlich über den französischen Sprachraum hinaus (z. B. nach Syrien, Brasilien, Argentinien, Italien, Griechenland u. a.), denn nicht die Apartheid, sondern der Universalismus sei ihre Berufung[47]. Auch Delpérée beschwört als wesentliches Merkmal der Francophonie die Ideen- und Wertegemeinschaft. Hinsichtlich der Verwaltung heißt das für ihn, wie schon für Braibant, daß die Verwaltung eine rechtsstaatliche zu sein habe, eine Verwaltung, die durch ein besonderes Verwaltungsrecht und die gerichtliche Kontrolle seiner Einhaltung geprägt sei. Als weitere Kennzeichen der francophonen Verwaltung werden herausgestellt: ihre Ausrichtung auf das demokratische Ideal; die – freilich inzwischen vielfältig modifizierte, nämlich benutzer- und mitarbeiterfreundlicher sowie transparenter gewordene – Tradition des napoleonischen Modells, d. h. eines Verwaltungssystems, das auf der Hierarchisierung der Grade und Funktionen aufbaue; schließlich der Staatssinn (*sens de l'Etat*), der Sinn für eine Verwaltung, die nicht mit einem Privatunternehmen verwechselt werden dürfe, der Sinn für den *service public*, wo der Staat sich nicht damit begnüge, die Spielregeln festzulegen, sondern Ziele definiere und selbst für deren Verwirklichung sorge[48]. Differenzen zwischen den Verwaltungssystemen der francophonen Länder werden im Schlußbericht, entsprechend den Landesberichten, zwar ohne weiteres zugestanden[49], gleichwohl aber ruft Delpérée auf – wie schon Juppé und Braibant – zur Verbesserung des francophonen Zusammenhalts im Bereich der öffentlichen Verwaltung.

---

[46] Ebd., S. 20.
[47] F. *Delpérée*, Rapport de synthèse, in: *Institut* (Fn. 40), S. 181-188 (183 f.).
[48] Ebd., S. 186.
[49] Ebd., S. 187. Durchaus unterschiedlich waren dann auch die Motivationen für eine Teilnahme an der Tagung: Die kanadische Provinz Québec beteiligte sich nicht zuletzt deswegen, weil sie in ihrer Verwaltung ein Bollwerk in der Verteidigung der französischen Sprache sah, und dies, obwohl die Verwaltung selbst auf britischer Tradition beruht, also keinerlei Bezug zur Französischen Revolution oder zu den napoleonischen Verwaltungsreformen aufweist. Kamerun dagegen suchte wohl einfach verzweifelt Halt in den schweren wirtschaftlichen und gesellschaftlichen Turbulenzen seiner Staatlichkeit, mag die eigene Verwaltung faktisch auch nur noch ein Zerrbild der aus den Kolonialzeiten überkommenen französischen Vorlage liefern.

Folgerichtig dann die schon erwähnte Schlußerklärung aller Teilnehmer[50]: Unter Hinweis darauf, daß das francophone Band einen wesentlichen Faktor der Verwaltungsentwicklung ihrer Herkunftsländer dar-
stelle, daß der Verwaltung die zentrale Rolle in der Förderung der ökonomischen und sozialen Entwicklung zukomme, daß die Globalisierung die Staaten zwinge, über ihre Aufgaben und Handlungsweisen gegenüber der Gesellschaft grundsätzlich nachzudenken, wird u. a. be-
schlossen, im Sinne der Förderung des Zusammenhalts regelmäßige
Treffen von Verwaltungsspezialisten aus Theorie und Praxis der francophonen Länder zu organisieren und ein Netzwerk zum Austausch ver-
waltungsrelevanter Informationen und Dokumentationen aufzubauen.

Soweit die Pariser Tagung des IIAP. Sie fügt sich ein in eine sehr französische Tradition außenpolitischer Dimensionierung innenpolitischer
Strukturen. Genannt sei insofern eine für das Vortragsthema ebenfalls
aufschlußreiche Tagung der französischen „Vereinigung für eine Na-
tionalstiftung zum Rechtsstudium" über die internationale Rechtskooperation im November 1992[51]. Diese Gesellschaft, wesentlich getra-
gen von Rechtsprofessoren, hat zum Ziel, wie es in ihrem Programm
heißt, die Entwicklung anspruchsvoller, den Anforderungen der wirtschaftlichen und gesellschaftlichen Entwicklung angepaßter Rechtsaus-
bildung zu fördern und dabei zur Ausstrahlung (*rayonnement*) des
französischen Rechts beizutragen. Dementsprechend betonte man auf
der Tagung von 1992 allenthalben die Bedeutung der Rechtshilfe für
den ökonomischen und kulturellen Einfluß Frankreichs in der Welt. In
der Eröffnungsansprache von Marceau Long, dem damaligen Vizeprä-
sidenten des *Conseil d'Etat* und Präsidenten der Vereinigung, wurde
die Wahl Braibants zum Präsidenten des Brüsseler IISA als Erfolg und
Anerkennung solcher Einflußbemühungen angesehen[52].

Wie ernst diese Aufgabe genommen wird, zeigt am besten wiederum
Braibant selbst mit einem Vortrag über die Verbreitung des Rechts-
staatsmodells nach dem Zusammenbruch der Sowjetunion. Als Leitprinzip solcher Verbreitungstätigkeit nennt er das Prinzip des französischen Vorzugs (*principe de préférence française*)[53]. „Man hat wiederholt

---

[50] Ebd., S. 190.
[51] *Association pour une fondation nationale des études de droit* (Hrsg.), La
coopération juridique internationale. Actes de la Sixième journée nationale du
Droit, organisée par la A.F.N.E.D. et l'Institut français des Sciences administratives avec le concours du Conseil d'Etat, Paris 1994.
[52] Ebd., S. 6.
[53] G. *Braibant*, La diffusion de l'Etat de droit, in: *Association* (Fn. 51),
S. 79-86 (81).

gesagt", heißt es sodann, wörtlich übersetzt, „daß das Interesse an der Rechtskooperation auch ein nationales sei, ein Mittel politischer Einflußnahme, ein Mittel wirtschaftlichen Eindringens, und all dies ist wahr; wir müssen es im Kopf behalten. Daraus folgt, daß wir vor allem, meiner Meinung nach, bei unserem Bemühen um die Verbreitung des Rechtsstaats diesen *à la française* entwickeln müssen, d. h. eine französische Form der Verfassungskontrolle, eine französische Form der Dualität der Gerichtsbarkeit, die französischen Prinzipien des Strafrechts usw. Das ist zunächst, was wir am besten kennen; sodann ist das wahrscheinlich, was wir für das beste halten; drittens ist es das, was man von uns erwartet."

Aber Braibant sieht auch, daß dieses Leitprinzip des französischen Vorzugs eine Abmilderung verdient, nämlich im Hinblick auf eine Anpassung an die Verhältnisse vor Ort, denn – so meint er unter Berufung auf den Oxforder Politologen und Verwaltungswissenschaftler Vincent Wright – in Verwaltungsdingen entscheide letztlich die Geschichte des jeweiligen Landes[54].

Daß Braibants Thesen in der francophonen Welt weithin als berechtigt angesehen werden, zeigt nicht zuletzt das Grußwort des damaligen Generalsekretärs der UNO, Boutros Boutros-Ghali, zu einem 1993 stattfindenden Kolloquium über den Einfluß französischer Rechtsfakultäten außerhalb Frankreichs. Selbst promoviert an einer französischen Universität und Professor des Rechts in Ägypten bekennt er sich in angesichts seines hohen Amtes verblüffender Offenheit zur französischen Sprache und zum französischen Recht, die ihm beide am besten geeignet erscheinen, um – wie er sagt – den hohen Wert der Gerechtigkeit zu vermitteln[55].

---

[54] Ebd., S. 82. Noch bescheidener gibt sich *G. Vedel* – 1992 Vorsitzender des Verwaltungsrats der Vereinigung, außerdem *doyen honoraire* der Rechtswissenschaftlichen Fakultät der Universität Paris und ehemaliges Mitglied des *Conseil constitutionnel* – in seinem Schlußwort ebd., S. 212 f.: Er wünscht sich auch Anerkennung eigener Fehler und eigener Reformbedürftigkeit sowie Ehrlichkeit und Vorsicht im Umgang mit anderen Ländern.
[55] *B. Boutros-Ghali*, in: Revue d'histoire des facultés de droit et de la science juridique, 15 (1994), S. 15-17 (15).

2. Zweites Beispiel:
Schweden – Schwächung nordischer Identität?

In den nordischen Ländern im allgemeinen und in Schweden im besonderen erleben wir, wenn ich es recht sehe, etwas anderes als in Frankreich und dem francophonen Raum[56]. Ein ähnlich zielstrebig organisiertes Zusammenrücken angesichts von Globalisierung und Europäisierung ist – wohl mangels einer anerkannten Führungsmacht – nicht zu erkennen, wenngleich die Identitätsfrage auch in rechtskultureller Hinsicht durchaus gestellt wird[57]. Die traditionelle Rechtszusammenarbeit[58], die sich allerdings kaum auf das öffentliche Recht bezogen hat[59], verliert an Bedeutung gegenüber der EU-Rechtssetzung. Die Funktion einer nicht zuletzt außenpolitischen Stabilisierung des nordischen Raums, namentlich im Verhältnis zu Rußland und Deutschland, scheint sich erübrigt zu haben. Es wird auch offener und betonter über den Einfluß des kontinentalen *ius commune* auf den sog. nordischen Rechtskreis und seine Rechtskultur gesprochen[60]. Die größte Gemein-

---

[56] Während man sich über Struktur und Entwicklung des französischen Verwaltungsrechts auch in deutscher Sprache leicht informieren kann – vgl. jetzt vor allem *H.J. Sonnenberger / Ch. Autexier*, Einführung in das französische Recht, 3. Aufl. 2000 –, ist das für das schwedische Verwaltungsrecht nicht der Fall. *G. Ring / L. Olsen-Ring*, Einführung in das skandinavische Recht, 1999, konzentrieren sich vor allem auf das Privatrecht; eine erste Orientierung in englischer Sprache bietet *S. Jägerskiöld*, Administrative Law, in: *S. Strömholm* (Hrsg.), An Introduction to Swedish Law, 2. Aufl., Stockholm 1988, S. 79-102. Im Gegensatz zur deutsch-französischen Rechtsvergleichung – vgl. insoweit *O. Beaud / E.V. Heyen* (Hrsg.), Eine deutsch-französische Rechtswissenschaft? Kritische Bilanz und Perspektiven eines kulturellen Dialogs, 1999 – ist die deutsch-schwedische Rechtsvergleichung im Bereich des öffentlichen Rechts wenig entwickelt. Zusammenfassende Berichte gibt es nicht; das Interesse scheint von Zufälligkeiten abhängig zu sein.
[57] Vgl. insbes. *P. Letto-Vanamo* (Hrsg.), Nordisk Identitet. Nordisk rätt i europeisk gemenskap, Helsinki 1998, mit einem kleinen Beitrag auch zum Verwaltungsrecht: *O. Mäenpää*, Nordisk förvaltningsrätt söker europeisk identitet, S. 129-137; ferner *P. Letto-Vanamo*, Det Nordiska rättsområdet i Unionens Europa, in: Nordisk Administrativt Tidskrift, 80 (1999), S. 233-241.
[58] Vgl. *Ring / Olsen-Ring* (Fn. 56), S. 4 ff.; *G. Carsten*, Hundert Jahre Nordischer Juristentag 1872-1972, in: RabelsZ, 37 (1973), S. 80-100.
[59] Vgl. *N. Herlitz*, Elements of Nordic Public Law, Stockholm 1969; *D.C. Rowat* (Hrsg.), Public Administration in Developed Democracies. A Comparative Study, New York / Basel 1988, Abschnitt II, mit Landesberichten zu den Verwaltungssystemen der nordischen Länder und einem Vergleichsbericht.
[60] Vgl. etwa *D. Tamm*, The Nordic legal tradition in European context – Roman law and the Nordic countries, in: *Letto-Vanamo*, Nordisk Identitet (Fn. 57), S. 15-31.

samkeit im öffentlichrechtlichen Bereich, der Wohlfahrtsstaat, wurde bereits vor dem Beitritt Schwedens und Finnlands zur EU abgebaut, und zwar im Gefolge der allgemeinen Entbürokratisierungs- und Globalisierungsdebatte.

Die schwedische Verwaltungsrechtskultur weist mehrere Besonderheiten auf. Am bekanntesten in Deutschland dürfte die Institution des Ombudsmans als Instrument parlamentarischer Verwaltungskontrolle sein; erst recht spät wurde eine Verwaltungsgerichtsbarkeit eingerichtet, die aber nach wie vor als Bestandteil der Verwaltung gilt, mit der Folge, daß zwischen Rechtmäßigkeits- und Zweckmäßigkeitskontrolle nicht klar unterschieden wird und eine dogmatisch ausgebaute Ermessensfehlerlehre nicht besteht[61]. Ich möchte hier jedoch auf ein Element zu sprechen kommen, das weniger bekannt ist und durch den Beitritt Schwedens zur EU ohne formalen Änderungszwang eine Herausforderung erfahren hat[62]. Es geht um einen Aspekt der juristischen Methodenlehre, nämlich das Gewicht der Gesetzesmotive (Materialien) bei der Normauslegung[63]. Dieses Gewicht ergibt sich aus keiner Rechts-

---

[61] Vgl. *H. Ragnemalm*, Administrative Justice in Sweden, Stockholm 1991; aus der deutschsprachigen Literatur: *W. Haller*, Der schwedische Justitieombudsman. Eine Einrichtung zur Verstärkung des Rechtsschutzes und der parlamentarischen Kontrolle im Hinblick auf das Verhalten von Organen der Verwaltung und der Rechtspflege, Zürich 1964; *M.-D. Forstmann*, Der Rechtsschutz im schwedischen Verwaltungsverfahren, in: Verwaltungsarchiv, 62 (1971), S. 313-390, und 63 (1972), S. 10-54; *K.-M. Ortloff*, Die Bedeutung des Begriffes „Zweckmässigkeit (Lämplighet)" für die Kontrolle behördlicher Entscheidungen. Eine rechtshistorische Untersuchung des Schwedischen Rechts, Diss. jur. München 1972; *G. Hahn*, Das neue schwedische Verwaltungsgesetz, in: Verwaltungsarchiv, 64 (1973), S. 260-282; *ders.*, Die Reform der Verwaltungsgerichtsbarkeit in Schweden, in: Verwaltungsarchiv, 64 (1973), S. 335-398; *R. Hofmann*, Landesbericht Schweden, in: *J.A. Frowein* (Hrsg.), Die Kontrolldichte bei der gerichtlichen Überprüfung von Handlungen der Verwaltung, 1993, S. 105-120.

[62] Zu den Veränderungen schwedischer Rechtskultur im allgemeinen vgl. *K.Å. Modéer*, European Legal Cultures. Traditions and Cultures in Contemporary Europe, in: *T. Forsgren* (Hrsg.), Cultural Crossroads in Europe, Uppsala 1997 (Forskningsradsnämnden, Report 97:3), S. 70-77; *ders.*, Den svenska domarkulturen – europeiska och nationella förebilder, Lund 1994. Zu den Veränderungen schwedischer Verwaltungskultur vgl. *W. Jann*, Verwaltungskulturen im internationalen Vergleich. Ein Überblick über den Stand der empirischen Forschung, in: Die Verwaltung, 33 (2000), im Druck.

[63] Vgl. vor allem *T. Bjerkén*, Le droit et l'administration de la Suède face à l'intégration européenne, in: *G. Marcou* (Hrsg.), Les mutations du droit de l'administration en Europe. Pluralisme et convergences, Paris 1995, S. 263-293 (284 ff.); ferner *Ring / Olsen-Ring* (Fn. 56), S. 8 ff.; *Letto-Vanamo*, Det Nordiska rättsområdet (Fn. 57), S. 238 f.; *A. Peczenik*, Grundlagen der juristischen Argumentation, Wien 1983, S. 75 ff.

norm; es ist ein Element der internen Rechtskultur im engeren Sinne, also von identitätsstiftender Bedeutung, und betrifft nicht nur die Richter, sondern auch die Rechtsprofessoren.

Die starke Stellung der Gesetzesmotive hat verschiedene Gründe. Zu nennen ist zum einen ein ausgeprägter, metaphysikkritischer Skeptizismus gegenüber Ansprüchen normativer Erkenntnis, der unter dem Stichwort „skandinavischer Rechtsrealismus" auch international bekannt geworden ist und eine Jahrzehnte dauernde Hinwendung zu einem im Kern gesetzespositivistischen Verständnis von Rechtswissenschaft bewirkt hat, auf dessen Grundlage Generationen schwedischer Juristen ausgebildet worden sind[64]. Zum anderen kann das demokratietheoretische Argument angeführt werden, für eine über das Gesetz hinausgehende Rechtsschöpfung fehle die nötige Legitimation. Beide Begründungselemente konnten bislang in Schweden weithin überzeugen, weil sich – von 1932 bis 1976, als die Sozialdemokratie die Regierungsverantwortung innehatte, – eine Tradition der Konsens-Demokratie oder doch zumindest die Ideologie einer solchen etabliert hatte, die sich u. a. in einem auf breite Konsultationen ausgerichteten, besonders sorgfältigen und transparenten Gesetzgebungsverfahren[65] niederschlug und darum den Gesetzesmotiven eine besondere Überzeugungskraft verschaffte. Folgerichtig werden die Gesetzesmotive in Schweden von der höchstrichterlichen Rechtsprechung traditionell intensiv zitiert. Das färbt auf Art und Weise der Rechtswissenschaft ab und macht die Gesetzeskommentare, meist geschrieben von den Gesetzgebungsreferenten in den Ministerien, zu einer zentralen Literaturgattung.

Dieser gesetzespositivistische Umgang mit den Motiven, der Verwaltungsbeamte, Richter und Rechtsprofessoren zu besonderem Respekt gegenüber dem Willen des Gesetzgebers erzog, schien auch des-

---

[64] Vgl. *S. Jørgensen*, Grundzüge der Entwicklung der skandinavischen Rechtswissenschaft, in: Juristenzeitung, 25 (1970), S. 529-535; *S. Strömholm*, Hauptströmungen der schwedischen Rechtsphilosophie und Rechtstheorie in der Nachkriegszeit, in: Rechtstheorie, 2 (1971), S. 35-61; *H.-H. Vogel*, Der skandinavische Rechtsrealismus, 1972; *E. Kamenka u. a.* (Hrsg.), Soziologische Jurisprudenz und realistische Theorien des Rechts, 1986 (= Rechtstheorie, Beiheft 9), Abschnitt III, auch mit kritischen Beiträgen skandinavischer Autoren zu diesem Verständnis von Rechtswissenschaft.

[65] Vgl. *W. Jann*, Die Vorbereitung von Gesetzen in Schweden, in: Zeitschrift für Parlamentsfragen, 12 (1981), S. 377-398; *E. Haslauer*, Das schwedische Modell des Gesetzgebungsverfahrens, in: Österreichische Zeitschrift für öffentliches Recht und Völkerrecht, 33 (1982), S. 101-124; *W. Maihofer* (Hrsg.), Theorie und Methode der Gesetzgebung. Kolloquium der deutschen und schwedischen Gesellschaft für Rechtsvergleichung in Freiburg i. Br. vom 28.-31. März 1982, 1983.

wegen angebracht, weil er wesentlich mit dafür sorgte, daß die legisla-
tiven Entscheidungen des Parlaments auch administrativ umgesetzt
wurden. Dies ist nach schwedischem Verwaltungsaufbau nicht ganz so
selbstverständlich, wie es die deutschen Verwaltungsjuristen anmuten
mag. Nicht nur die Lokalverwaltungen genießen große Autonomie[66],
sogar die entsprechend ihren unterschiedlichen Aufgaben reich geglie-
derten Zentralverwaltungen sind den Ministerien nicht nachgeordnet
und untereinander unabhängig[67]. Die Ministerien dienen der Politik
und der Gesetzesvorbereitung und sind entsprechend klein; nur das
Außenministerium ist Ministerium und Zentralbehörde in einem. Die
Zentralbehörden unterliegen nur der Rechtsaufsicht der Regierung,
nicht eines Ministeriums, und dies auch nicht in Einzelfällen der
Rechtsanwendung.

Mit dem Beitritt Schwedens zur EU ist sowohl dieser besondere Verwaltungsaufbau, der ebenfalls zur schwedischen Verwaltungsrechtskultur im engeren Sinne gehört, als auch die Stellung der Gesetzesmotive in der Normauslegung unter Druck geraten. Ich möchte hier nur
auf den zweiten Aspekt eingehen[68].

Schweden wird, wie alle anderen Mitgliedsstaaten auch, mit der Ver-
pflichtung konfrontiert, EU-Recht in nationales Recht umzusetzen[69].

---

[66] Vgl. *C. Krage*, Einführung in das schwedische Kommunalrecht. Ein Vergleich zur Bundesrepublik Deutschland, 1990. Zur weiteren Entwicklung vgl.
die Beiträge in: Stadt und Gemeinde, 1997, H. 10, insbes. *C. Riberdahl*, Stand
und Entwicklung der kommunalen Gesetzgebung in Schweden, S. 280-286.

[67] Einen knappen Überblick zur schwedischen Verwaltungsorganisation
bietet *L. Sjöbert*, Aufbau der öffentlichen Verwaltung in Schweden, in: Stadt und
Gemeinde, 1997, S. 276-278. Zur schwedischen Verwaltungsgeschichte vgl. des näheren den Literaturbericht von *T. Bjerkén*, Administrative History in Sweden,
in: Jahrbuch für europäische Verwaltungsgeschichte, 10 (1998), S. 333-347.

[68] Zum ersten Aspekt vgl. *Bjerkén* (Fn. 63), S. 274 ff.

[69] Schweden empfängt natürlich nicht nur Rechtssetzungsimpulse seitens der
EU, sondern sendet auch welche dorthin aus. Sie können dann auch auf das deutsche Verwaltungsrecht wirken. Davon zeugt die aktuelle Diskussion um das allgemeine Akteneinsichtsrecht, das in Schweden eine lange Tradition hat und ebenfalls
ein identitätsstiftendes Moment seiner Verwaltungsrechtskultur darstellt. Das
schwedische Akteneinsichtsrecht hat schon immer das Interesse der deutschen
Verwaltungsrechtswissenschaft geweckt. Bei den Dissertationen bildet das Thema
einen frühen Schwerpunkt deutsch-schwedischer Verwaltungsrechtsvergleichung: *I. Voigt*, Das Recht auf Einsicht in die Akten der Verwaltungsbehörden
unter vergleichender Darstellung des Rechts auf Einsicht nach der schwedischen Pressefreiheitsverordnung, Diss. jur. Hamburg 1957; *J. Conradi*, Das Öf-
fentlichkeitsprinzip in der schwedischen Verwaltung, Diss. jur. Berlin 1968; *H.
Bergner*, Das schwedische Grundrecht auf Einsicht in öffentliche Akten, Diss.
jur. Heidelberg 1969. Zur jüngsten Diskussion vgl. *G. Nolte*, Die Herausforderung für das deutsche Recht der Akteneinsicht durch europäisches Verwal-

Dafür erweist sich das landeseigene Gesetzgebungsverfahren nunmehr als zu umständlich und langwierig, die Beibehaltung von pluralistisch zusammengesetzten Studienkommissionen und vielseitigen Anhörungen als zweifelhaft. Bei einem anderen, weniger gesellschaftlich abgestimmten Typus der Gesetzgebung wird aber die bisherige starke Orientierung der Normauslegung an den Gesetzesmotiven fragwürdig.

Diese Bedeutungsabnahme der Gesetzesmotive wird noch unterstützt durch die ganz andere juristische Methodik des EuGH, dessen offen in Anspruch genommene, ja betonte Rechtsschöpfungsfunktion der schwedischen Gerichtsbarkeit, nicht zuletzt der Verwaltungsgerichtsbarkeit, fremd ist[70]. In der Rechtsprechung des EuGH tritt das Gewicht des Wortlauts einer Norm angesichts so vieler unterschiedlicher Amtssprachen in seiner Bedeutung ebenso zurück wie die Verwendung von historisch-systematischen Argumenten angesichts des oft kompromißhaften, sprunghaften Charakters europäischer Rechtssetzung, die weder Vollständigkeits- noch Systemabsichten verfolgt[71]. In den Vordergrund rückt statt dessen die teleologische Auslegung, die in ihrer Berufung auf die sog. objektive Zweckrichtung des Gemeinschaftsrechts rechtspolitische Züge trägt. Die besondere richterliche Rechtskultur des EuGH, in welcher verschiedene nationale Komponenten sich mischen, tritt deutlich hervor[72]. Sie könnte daher die Auslegungspraxis schwedischer Gerichte, was die Berücksichtigung der Gesetzesmotive betrifft, nachhaltig verändern, ohne daß dazu eine formelle Änderung des Rechts erforderlich wäre. Es würde sich um eine Änderung der internen Rechtskultur handeln, welcher allerdings die Bedeutung einer stillschweigenden Verfassungsänderung zukommen könnte[73].

---

tungsrecht, in: DÖV, 52 (1999), S. 363-374; *Bjerkén* (Fn. 63), S. 289 ff., meint, daß es auch in Schweden zu Anpassungen kommen dürfte.

[70] Vgl. *Modéer*, Den svenska domarkulturen (Fn. 62).

[71] Vgl. etwa *H. Schulte-Nölke*, Elf Amtssprachen, ein Recht? Folgen der Mehrsprachigkeit für die Auslegung von Verbraucherschutzrichtlinien, in: *R. Schulze* (Hrsg.), Auslegung europäischen Privatrechts und angeglichenen Rechts, 1999, S. 143-160.

[72] Vgl. *P. Demaret*, Le juge et le jugement dans l'Europe d'aujourd'hui: la Cour de Justice des Communautés européennes, in: *R. Jacob* (Hrsg.), Le juge et le jugement dans les traditions juridiques européennes. Etudes d'histoire comparée, Paris 1996 (= Droit et Société, vol. 17), S. 303-377.

[73] So *Bjerkén* (Fn. 63), S. 288 f.

IV. Zusammenfassung und Ausblick

Nach diesen beiden Beispielen für die praktische Relevanz der kulturellen Relativierung des Rechts aus dem Bereich europäischer Verwaltungsrechtsvergleichung möchte ich abschließend eine kleine Summe ziehen, und zwar zu den Stichworten Kultur und Identität.

Erstens zur Kultur: Zum Verständnis der in Europa vorgehenden Rechtsentwicklung ist es wichtig, diese Entwicklung auch in Hinblick auf ihre kulturelle Bedingtheit und Ausformung im Blick zu haben. Andernfalls lassen sich Angleichungsbereitschaft und Angleichungswiderstand nicht zutreffend einschätzen, vor allem dann nicht, wenn es nicht nur um Rechtsnormen und Rechtsinstitutionen in ihrer Textgestalt, sondern um die dazugehörige Rechtswirklichkeit, sozusagen die Kontextgestalt des Rechts geht. Die internen und externen Rechtskulturen modifizieren erheblich die normative wie die faktische Tragweite des positiven Rechts. Das gilt nicht zuletzt für das EU-Recht[74].

Hinsichtlich der Verwaltungsrechtsentwicklung in Europa kommt der internen Rechtskultur besondere Bedeutung zu. Der Denkstil der auf die öffentliche Verwaltung und ihr Recht bezogenen Wissenschaften und Professionen wirkt selektiv in Hinblick auf Problemwahrnehmung, Problemdefinition und Problemlösung. Im Rahmen der internationalen Rechts- und Verwaltungskommunikation erfüllt insbesondere die Rechts- und Verwaltungsvergleichung eine bedeutsame Schleusen- oder Membranfunktion. Solche Kommunikation – mag sie nun manifest und absichtsvoll oder latent und unabsichtlich erfolgen – kann zu normativ-institutioneller Infiltration führen, ohne daß es dazu besonderer Ermächtigungen bedürfte. Wissenschaftstransfer kann auf diese Weise auch zu Institutionentransfer führen; nicht immer folgt also die Wissenschaft dem Gegenstand, es geht auch umgekehrt. Dies liegt an der eigentümlichen Funktionenvielfalt der hier angesprochenen Rechts- und Verwaltungswissenschaften, vor allem an ihren Pflege- und Änderungsfunktionen.

Zweitens zur Identität: Individuell wie kollektiv ist Identitätsgewinnung unvermeidlich, und sie muß auch rechtskulturell ernstgenommen werden. Aber nicht zuletzt die historische Perspektive zeigt, daß es wenig angemessen ist, Identitäten zu verdinglichen. Sie bilden sich im Zusammenhang mit bestimmten pragmatischen – ökonomisch, politisch,

---

[74] Insofern ist es nicht unbedenklich, hinsichtlich einer Erweiterung der EU nur die Übernahme des rechtsnormativ-textlichen, nicht aber die Erreichung des rechtskulturellen *Acquis communautaire* zum Maßstab der Beitrittsmöglichkeit zu machen.

rechtlich usw. konturierten – Anforderungen. Insofern erscheinen sie bei näherer Betrachtung als ein Arrangement aspekt- und fallbezogener Identifizierungen. Sie bleiben offen für Veränderungen und bilden insofern keine Substanzen, sondern gewissermaßen „Fluktuanzen"[75].

Das bedeutet aber, daß der Hinweis auf Kultur und damit Geschichte noch nichts darüber sagt, wie es weitergehen soll und schließlich wird. Das gilt auch für den Einigungsprozeß der EU und das Verhältnis der in ihr wirksamen Rechtskulturen untereinander. Sicher ist Geschichte ein Strukturaspekt der Gegenwart, die ohne ihn nicht zutreffend erfaßt wäre. Allerdings ist damit die Zukunft nicht determiniert; es gilt nicht die Formel „Zukunft ist Herkunft", es gilt nur, daß die Herkunft über die Zukunft mitentscheidet. Nicht alles ist möglich, aber doch vieles.

Rechtskulturelle Forschung, zumal wenn vergleichend und historisch betrieben, kann sensibilisieren für die Implementationsprobleme voluntaristisch inszenierter Reformprozesse, aber auch die Augen öffnen für die Mythisierung des Überkommenen und Eigenen. Am besten ist es, wenn solche Forschung sich möglichst ungeschminkt aufklärend verhält, auch wenn damit das Prekäre des scheinbar Selbstverständlichen in beunruhigender Weise zutage tritt.

Was aus francophoner bzw. nordischer Identität letztlich wird, was aus europäischer Identität, das weiß man nicht, auch nicht im Bereich der Rechts- und Verwaltungskultur. Was die einen bedauern, begrüßen die anderen. Es spricht derzeit vieles dafür, daß sich ein mittlerer Weg durchsetzen wird, d. h. eine Öffnung bisher vor allem national definierter Identitäten zum Sub- bzw. Supranationalen hin; aber mehr als eine Öffnung dürfte es auf absehbare Zeit nicht werden. Allein, dies ist Spekulation. Es scheint mir nicht zu den vorrangigen Aufgaben der Verwaltungsrechtsvergleichung zu gehören, Rechts- und Verwaltungspolitik zu betreiben, und wenn dies geschieht, dann sollte es offen gesagt und auch als Politikum debattiert werden. Die in Unterstützung des EuGH vielfach praktizierte Harmonisierungfunktion der europäischen Rechtsvergleichung ist nicht deren einzig denkbare Funktion. Rechtsvergleichung läßt sich auch empirisch-erklärend und ideologiekritisch einsetzen; hier gäbe es noch viel zu tun.

---

[75] Vgl. dazu *W. Stegmaier*, Die fließende Einheit des Flusses. Zur nachmetaphysischen Ontologie, in: *K. Gloy / E. Rudolph* (Hrsg.), Einheit als Grundfrage der Philosophie, 1985, S. 355-379, insbes. 363 ff.

Schriftenreihe der Juristischen Gesellschaft zu Berlin

Frühere Hefte auf Anfrage
Mitglieder der Gesellschaft erhalten eine Ermäßigung von 40 %

ISBN 3 11 016982 7

Preface

The pandemic, first seen in patients with respiratory symptoms in Wuhan Province, China at the end of December 2019 and defined as COVID-19 on January 13, 2020, affected almost all countries and millions of people worldwide. With the COVID-19 pandemic, state administrations required efforts to develop politics in an uncertain conjuncture, adapting process of health, economy, social life, education, and all other social institutions with difficult and sometimes challenging results.

The world has experienced different types of closures with strong containment regulations prior to the pandemic. However, COVID-19 situation affected a disparate group of areas, bringing along unprecedented crises. In the short term, we will continue to observe the effects of the economic and health crises that the world has fallen into, as well as the long term impacts on key areas such as education, family, law, technology, digitalization, industry and commerce, productivity, and social–individual behavior. In this sense, this crisis brings the winds of change and has affected our tendencies, needs, and behaviors within different paradigms.

The editors are all from different fields from education to statistics to international relations. As three women academicians, as we have worked on the effects that COVID-19 has had on our fields, we noticed that it is not possible to grasp the essence of the effects of COVID-19 without a holistic perspective. More interestingly, we noticed that scholars across the disciplines have been afraid to see COVID-19 and its implications through multidisciplinary and transdisciplinary perspectives, an unfortunate and old-fashioned attitude.

COVID-19 pandemic is just one of the cornerstones in the course of our history, however its effects will be undeniably influential for our future. In this respect, we see this book as a unique opportunity to discuss effects of COVID-19 upon specialist areas and efforts of strong coordination and foresight to overcome the crises we are in.

In this context, **Chapter 1** addressed by two of our editors Şuay Nilhan Açıkalın and Şefika Şule Erçetin titled "Understanding COVID-19 with Chaos Theory", initiates studies and discussions on other fields in this book by revealing the dynamics and implications of pandemic for societies for upcoming chapters.

In **Chapter 2**, André Olbrich explores the relationship of COVID-19 and the Infodemic with a typology through government measures to condemn false information, also discussing social reaction under the shadow of misinformation. **Chapter 3**, by Mehmet Cem Şahin, touches upon social change after COVID-19 using Ulrich Beck and his risk society approach. In **Chapter 4**, Luis Tomé opens new discussion on how COVID-19 will influence international politics. Mariam Kavakci analyses the implications of COVID-19 on healthcare service delivery in a case study in **Chapter 5**.

In **Chapter 6**, Onur Uraz discusses whether a structural change is necessary to achieve international cooperation in the context of international law. **Chapter 7** is written by Çağatay Özdemir and questions liberal international order *vis-à-vis* US leadership during the COVID-19 period. Helena Belchior-Rocha and Rosário Mauritti in **Chapter 8** bring a different perspective to the COVID-19 pandemic, "Can We Stop and Listen Now?" Emphasizing that we need to rethink the new normal. In **Chapter 9**, Dilek İlhan-Beyaztaş and Nuray Senemoğlu examine differences created by the COVID-19 pandemic in our learning approaches and processes — vital to understanding the future of education.

In **Chapter 10**, Nail Alkan and Berkan Alkan specifically focus on the future of the European Union, which has been shaken with health and social crises. In addition to this, **Chapter 11** by Selim Kanat draws attention to how terrorism will be impacted by COVID-19. In Chapter 12, Esra Akyol argues that people with mental health disorders can be considered as the most vulnerable group during COVID-19 and explores their treatment during the pandemic.

Chapter 13 by Kanupriya asks an old question with a new perspective, citing the current situation of India as an example: Is globalization a dead or timeless notion? In **Chapter 14**, Shan Qiyue argues that the role of high technologies in China's fight against COVID-19 has been advantageous in preventing the transmission of viruses. Lastly, **Chapter 15** by Özlenen Özdiyar and Abdul Samet Demirkaya unfolds the transformation of distance education in higher education with the COVID-19.

The content of this book provides an abundance of unique topics with which to discuss the impact of COVID-19 on different aspects of our lives. All these chapters have encouraged academics to work harder, produce information, and analyze the information produced in different fields. We hope that this book will help the reader explore the functioning of different disciplines in order to understand how the COVID-19 pandemic will shape our future, contributing to the work of all practitioners, policymakers, and the scientific community.

Şefika Şule ERÇETİN
Nihan POTAS
Şuay Nilhan AÇIKALIN

About the Editors

Şefika Şule ERÇETİN is currently Dean of Education Faculty of Hacettepe University. In 1991, she completed her Ph.D. from Division of Educational Administration, Supervision, Planning, and Economics in Hacettepe University. Since 2003, she has been working as a professor. She has been a visiting scholar in various national and international universities. She has worked in many national and international projects as a member of the project team or as the project coordinator. She is the president, board member, and founder member of the International Science Association (ISCASS). She is the editor-in-chief of several national and international journals. She has written a number of national books. She has also edited and authored chapters in international books published by well-known international publishers. She is one of the rare academicians in Turkey who works in "chaos, complexity, quantum leadership" and has so since 1990. She has directed many theses, and she gives seminars regularly on these topics. Her other main research fields are comparative education policies, research methods organizational intelligence and stupidity and wisdom, leadership, migration, fuzzy logic, children at risk, women and peace studies, social media, plasma leadership, quantum leadership, and women leadership model.

Nihan POTAS, Ph.D., is an Assistant Professor of the Faculty of Economics and Administrative Sciences, Department of Healthcare Management at the Ankara Hacı Bayram Veli University. She graduated from Başkent University, Department of Statistics and Computer Sciences. She had completed her master's education at Gazi University Department of Statistics, Faculty of Science. She got her Ph.D. degree from Ankara University Department of Statistics, Faculty of Science. She has been the project manager, Principal Investigator, and co-Principal Investigator on several national and international projects which are funded grants. Her research interests are in the areas of non-parametric statistics, categorical data analysis, survival analysis, and applied statistics.

Şuay Nilhan AÇIKALIN is currently working as an Assistant Professor and vice director of Graduate School at Ankara Hacı Bayram Veli University, Department of International Relations. Dr. Açıkalın received her doctorate degree from Middle East Technical University with "Political Leadership and Foreign Policy: Recep Tayyip Erdoğan and Angela Merkel". She has been a visiting researcher at Lancaster University in UK and Humboldt Universitat zu Berlin with the Jean Monnet Scholarship Program. Throughout her education life, she has been working as coordinator of national and international projects on integration and education of refugees based on field research. Dr. Açıkalın has authored various international book chapters and articles from reputable publishing house. She is the founding member and vice president of the International Science Association, which carries out studies on disadvantaged groups such as refugees, youth, women, and girls.

She was participant of the world's largest organization of Bali Democracy Forum and Asian Civilizations Dialogue. Dr. Açıkalın has interests in leadership, migration and refugee, Turkey-EU relations, chaos and complexity studies, Europeanization and diplomacy in theory and practice, as well as other study subjects.

Contents

Chapter 1

Understanding COVID-19 with Chaos Theory: Dynamics and Implications for Societies

Şuay Nilhan AÇIKALIN[*,‡] **and Şefika Şule ERÇETİN**[†,§]

*Department of International Relations,
Ankara Hacı Bayram Veli University, Ankara, Turkey*

†*Department of Educational Sciences, Hacettepe University,
Ankara, Turkey*

‡*suay.acikalin@hbv.edu.tr*
§*sefikasule@gmail.com*

Abstract

Humanity has experienced different pandemics throughout history which have altered social, political, and economical life in each era. The 21st century has its own catastrophe, COVID-19 is not an exception but with differences. Today, the world is more interdependent and globalized than ever before, bringing diverse, multidimensional, and complex dynamics and implications. In this respect, the COVID-19 pandemic is not only a health crisis but also a multifaceted social crisis which cannot be solved with a linear approach. This chapter, as the first chapter of the book, is going to analyze COVID-19 with properties of chaos theory. In addition, this chapter functions as an open discussion of the diverse dynamics and implications of COVID-19, introducing upcoming chapters by different authors.

1. Introduction

The word pandemic refers to the state of an outbreak of a new virus spreading worldwide and causing an epidemic disease through transmission from one person to another. The word has now become one of the most extensively used in daily life since the final days of 2019. Similar pandemics have occurred many times throughout the history of humanity, with millions of people affected by the outcomes of such incidents (Drezner, 2020). Following the declaration of COVID-19 as a pandemic, extensive studies on the disease, from medical to social perspectives, have been carried out (Fauci *et al.*, 2020; Velavan *et al.*, 2020; Pfefferbaum *et al.*, 2020). The extent and speed of the spread of COVID-19 pandemic in the last one year has shown that its effects on human life varies across different dimensions, which has made it very important to research these dimensions and the levels of the pandemic's effectiveness on human life.

Chaos theory is derived from mathematics and has various applications in physics, meteorology, engineering, economics, as well as different branches of social sciences. Chaotic systems have unique features compared to conventional (linear) systems. Sensitivity to initial conditions, having multi-actors, nonlinearity, and interdependence are determinants of a chaotic system. Chaos theory has been applied to different phenomena, from economic to social crises, in order to understand the essence of dynamics and implications with holistic and realistic perspectives. Although there is already extensive literature on the application of chaos theory to COVID-19, the cynosure has been mostly treatment algorithms and predictions for future measurements (Piotrowski, 2020; Speakman & Sharpley, 2012; Tabor, 2021). However, analyzing social effects of COVID-19 has been limited to traditional approaches and theories, which created a gap in the literature. Hence, COVID-19 and its multidimensional nature, including changing dynamics and implications for societies, ought to be dissected using chaos theory. As the first chapter of the book, we will analyze COVID-19 using chaos theory in terms of its dynamics and implications for societies.

In this chapter, we first briefly revisit the history of pandemics. Second, we make the case for why we should see pandemics as multidimensional crises. Third, we expand on the definition of chaos theory and its characteristics, including **sensitivity to initial conditions, bifurcation points, nonlinearity, and self-organization**. Fourth, we discuss why

COVID-19 should be deemed as different and unique considering the medical and social effects of COVID-19. Last, we propose a redefinition of social and political effects of COVID-19 using chaos theory *vis-á-vis* public policymaking.

2. Pandemics in History

There have been only few catastrophes that have shaped our societies and lives, and pandemics are among the incontestable cornerstones in history. In order to understand why we aimed to analyze COVID-19 using chaos theory, an overview of pandemics and their impact on history is definitely vital. In view of this reality, this section discusses previous pandemics in history (since the common era) and their major consequences briefly.

1. **The Black Death:** *Yersinia pestis* (in its various bubonic, pneumonic, and septicemic manifestations) was a global outbreak that originated in China in 1334, arriving in Europe in 1347 thanks to the Silk Road. Within a short period of time, it led to a huge number of causalities in the global population, falling from 450 million to below 350 million, possibly even below 300 million (Britannica, 2020). Some estimates claim that the Black Death claimed up to 60% of lives in Europe at that time, which was the most destructive after WW2 in the continent (Oldstone, 1998). As expected, the spread of the disease created fear and anxiety, which in turn led to societal and psychological trauma within the affected population. Along with this, the epidemic caused demographical changes in all continents: mass movement from urban to safer rural areas resulting in depopulation and famine (Borsch & Sabraa, 2017; Jedwab *et al.*, 2019). In other words, the Black Death was the reason for detrimental effects on regional economies as well as population, economic activity, and governance ability of states, especially in the continent of Europe. In the long term, because of the lack of population in urban cities, workers' wages had increased and technological development regarding production was paved (Voigtländer & Voth, 2013). Naturally, new medical knowledge, tools, and the notion of quarantine were discovered during this era (Mackowiak & Sehdev, 2002).
2. **Spanish Flu:** The Spanish flu pandemic, which happened between 1918 and 1920 in the early decades of the 20th century, can be deemed

the first true global pandemic since the adoption of modern medicine. Although the country of origin of the virus was not clear, (possibly USA, China, Spain, France, or Austria) it is called Spanish because the country's press was the first to report it (Trilla *et al.*, 2008; Maas, 2020). The pandemic in the United States occurred in three waves between 1918 and 1919. The first wave began in March 1918 and lasted throughout the summer of 1918. The second and third waves were more devastating and occurred in the fall of 1918 and the spring of 1919, respectively (Garrett, 2007). It should be noted that the Spanish flu emerged in the midst of WWI, which accelerated mobilization of the virus across the world through military movement and the high number of refugees, leading to the deaths of more than 50 million people in a year (Humphries, 2014; Whiting, 2020). Measures implemented against the Spanish flu, including closing public places, forcing people to wear masks, and closing borders, were similar in all affected countries (McQueen, 1976). When it comes to social, economic, and political consequences of the Spanish Flu, though they were not easy to identify because of the then war, slowdown of economic activity and lack of social trust were to be expected. Interestingly, the Spanish Flu faded quickly in the eyes of the public, which is why it is not easy to comment on political consequences (Crosby, 2013).

3. **SARS:** It was the first outbreak in the 21st century sourced from the SARS coronavirus (SARS-CoV), which started in China and affected fewer than 10,000 individuals, with high fatality rate mainly in China, Hong Kong, Singapore, but also in other countries, including Canada (Harwyluck, 2004). Contrary to previous pandemics, the SARS epidemic of 2002–2003 was more of an epidemic of fear, generated by great levels of uncertainty about the pathogen, although it was contained in the middle of 2003 (Person *et al.*, 2004). Especially, the psychological sequelae of SARS has been quite invincible. SARS created fear and anxiety; an entire population of people was at risk of becoming stigmatized in society and health workers suffered psychological distortion (Person *et al.*, 2004; Huremović, 2019). In addition to this, Stephan Roach, an economist from Morgan Stanley, estimated the global economic cost of SARS to be around US$30 billion (Cooper, 2016). Notwithstanding the economic and psychological consequences, SARS did increase the power and visibility of the WHO: the shift of power from sovereign states to the international organization exercised to contain the pandemic and take measures

globally (Price-Smith, 2009). Also, influence of the SARS outbreak on politics have been quite interesting and have divided scholars on whether the outbreak diminished the increasing global role of China or not; however, it seemed that China was late to inform the world, but they managed to keep their economic and political rise in international system (Drezner, 2020).

4. **Swine Flu, Ebola, and MERS:** The 2009 H1N1 pandemic was a reprise of the "Spanish flu" pandemic from 1918 with estimated death toll varying from 20,000 to over 500,000 (Wilson, 2012). Although it ended in 2010, it is a type of flu that continues to circulate seasonally around the globe (Türk *et al.*, 2020). As seen in previous pandemics, economic activities declined not due to deaths or dismissals but because of changing consumer behavior (McKibbin and Sidorenko, 2006).

   Ebola virus was first seen in 1976 near the Ebola river but the disease was defined as an epidemic in 2013 December in Guinea. Since then, the virus has emerged periodically infecting people in various African countries. The Ebola epidemic in 2014 led to a reduction in household incomes and poverty in the countries affected (Gatiso *et al.*, 2018).

   In June 2012, a new type of coronavirus was reported in a case of viral pneumonia in Saudi Arabia. This mysterious and deadly viral pneumonia had mobilized in the Arabian Peninsula and the Republic of Korea in a short time which was announced as MERS-CoV. It mostly had an economic impact on tourism sectors of Saudi Arabia and Republic of Korea corresponding to about US\$2.6 billion in lost tourism revenue (Delivorias & Scholz, 2020).

3. Pandemics as Multidimensional Crises

The previous section gave a quick glance on previous pandemics in modern history and their social, political, economic, and also psychological impacts. The Black Death can be deemed as the most destructive pandemic, regarding its major impact such as changing geopolitical balances and political systems in the affected country, that also triggered discovery of new medical methods. However, the Black Death is also the least known pandemic in terms of its psychological, social, and economic consequences due to lack of scientific works and cumulative perspective for evaluating dynamics. As clearly divulged in the above, humanity has been more aware of roots and consequences of pandemics with globalization and increasing role of technological and scientific developments that exposed a holistic picture of pandemics and their impact in history: pandemics are not solely health crises but are multidimensional crises at national and international levels. In other words, they have the potential to weaken many societies, political systems, and economies simultaneously (Davies, 2018). From this point of view, the nature of pandemics and their impact should be addressed using a multidimensional approach.

First of all, pandemics can emerge anytime and anywhere, so the unpredictability is the main characteristic of pandemics, whereas being prepared is stressed upon by governments and international organizations. Second, the capacity of crisis management is a remarkable determinant when fighting against pandemics, which requires multidisciplinary crisis management teams and approaches within different administrative levels. This realistic perspective to crisis management brings more actors and complex decision-making processes for policymakers at all levels. Third, efficient and effective policymaking serve as pillars for combating pandemics. Policymakers are charged with taking actions to protect their population from the disease while lacking reliable information about the virus, possible measures, and their direct or indirect health and socioeconomic consequences (Berger *et al.*, 2021). Furthermore, as underlined, it is not enough to hinder transmission at the national level, which is why policymakers at the national level should be also consistent with those at the international level.

Thus, the uncertainties of its emergence and course make pandemics multidimensional crises that cannot be understood and tackled with classical approaches. Chaos theory is a resilient alternative to understand the nature of pandemics and generate efficient and effective policies.

4. Chaos Theory: An Alternative Novelty to Old Stories

For centuries, human beings have been looking for concrete predictions, including predictability of human behavior. However, social behavior and social systems are inherently unpredictable. As Krasner suggests, chaos theory emerged as a means to understand and examine unpredictability and nonlinearities of social life (1990). In other words, the social realm is determined with a nonlinear structure. Chaos behavior is not a newly discovered phenomenon in the world of science. Edward Lorenz, from the Massachusetts Institute of Technology (MIT), is the discoverer of chaos who first observed the phenomenon as early as in 1961, and by chance what would later be called chaos theory in 1963, while making calculations with uncontrolled approximations aimed at predicting the weather (Oestriechter, 2007). If we look over the general characteristics of chaos and chaotic systems, they include **sensitivity to initial conditions, bifurcation points, nonlinearity, and self-organization**.

First, sensitivity to initial conditions is one of the distinguishing properties of chaotic systems. Basically, small disturbances are going to have explosive and nonlinear effects in chaotic systems — also named the "butterfly effect". Lorenz determined that that there would be completely different variations of output when he entered 0.561 and 0.5617 as inputs during weather predictions. In other words, the butterfly effect can highlight small differences between numbers that are very close to each other in the continuum of real numbers — differences that may evade the experimental interpretation of data but may increasingly amplify in the system's dynamics (Bertuglia & Vaio, 2005). As expected, such characteristics can be deemed a source of unpredictability within the system hindering long term predictions and identification of overall behavior (Kauffman, 1996).

Second, critical moments or junctures, scientifically called as a bifurcation points, are vital in chaotic systems to see the trajectory of the system. Having bifurcation points is also directly linked with sensitivity to initial conditions because until bifurcation points in the system the trajectory of the system might be considered as predictable, but once the system reaches a bifurcation point, the system is led by patterns of behavior less predictable than before (i Font & Regis, 2006). In this respect, bifurcations points are extremely important regarding their nature and historical consequences for the system and actors within.

Third, nonlinearity is an inherent property of chaotic systems that naturally includes multi-actors. As aforementioned, considering the sensitivity to initial conditions and bifurcation points, chaotic systems are not as same as linear systems that have causality principle. Strogatz (2003) emphasized this property of chaotic system along with realities of the universe where most things in nature are nonlinear, whereas linear equations tend to describe idealized situations. Naturally occurred disproportion between a change in one part of a complex system and its subsequent effect in another part of the system (Bright & Pryor, 2005). As a result, predicting final outcomes beyond the very short term becomes impossible. In addition to this, multi-actors in the chaotic system also have nonlinear relationships (Tomé & Açıkalın, 2017). However, it does not mean that the nonlinearity lacks structure, which is a set of motions, known as attractors, to which a complex system is attracted. "According to Newton's laws of motion, each attraction or repulsion is accompanied by an equal and opposite reaction. If you are attracted by a force, you will also attract the source of that force with an equal force in the opposite direction" (Erçetin *et al.*, 2012). These reactions comprise "strange attractions" in the chaotic system. It is a kind of an equilibrium point in the system but definitely a dynamic equilibrium. The interesting point with strange attractors is that they are embedded within their composition. Due to sensitivity to initial conditions, while the orbits are moving further away from each other, they also gather together in a limited space without intersecting or retracing the same path. This contradictory behavior is the most critical property of strange attractors, and they have limits in the system; as the limits are getting clearer in the system, order seems closer. Thus, strange attractors are the only way to understand the structure of a chaotic systems as Wheatley concluded that we need to look at the whole picture in order to understand how order emerges in a system, and defined strange attractors as the form of the whole (1999).

Fourth and last, is self-organization, which can be defined as spontaneous emergence of major structure from local interactions (Heylighen, 2015). Behavior of systems can be seen as an abstract mathematical space that is known as phase space. Phase space shows how the system being studied changes with respect to time and various other variables (Erçetin *et al.*, 2012, p. 95). In other words, phase space shows evolution of a system and how the system transforms into a new system. In this sense, chaos is deterministic where chaos itself can generate order. Based on this, Wheatley points out that in order to understand the generation of new order, there is a need to look at the whole picture, which emphasizes an amazing feature of chaotic systems where individual motions looks like a chaos but the whole system has order. Thus, generating a new order in chaotic systems takes a long time because the whole system is composed of chaotic behavior of its elements. "... dynamical systems are historical systems they can reveal many types of behavior over time" (Kiel & Elliott, 1996, p. 2). Thus, chaotic systems will generate their own new forms from inner guidelines rather than the imposition of form from outside. The ability to reorganize is inherent in the chaotic system itself and does not require external intervention. In other words, the capacity for self-organization enables complex systems to develop or change their internal structure spontaneously and in order to cope with their external environment.

5. COVID-19: Turmoil in Post Globalization Era

In late December 2019, a new type of pneumonia characterized by fever, dry cough, fatigue, and various other symptoms was reported in the Huanan Seafood Wholesale Market in Wuhan, Hubei, China (Wu *et al.*, 2020). On January 13, the first case of COVID-19 was reported outside China when a female patient was diagnosed with COVID-19 in Thailand. In the following two weeks, first cases emerged in Europe (Aytekin, 2020). The World Health Organization (WHO) declared the COVID-19 outbreak a global emergency on January 30, 2020. In a response to the mysterious virus, governments followed similar measures as follows: enforced border shutdowns, travel restrictions, and quarantine (Nicola *et al.*, 2020). Only after two months, WHO declared the coronavirus a global pandemic on March 11.

Since first emerging in China, COVID-19 transformed into a global crisis after spreading to 191 countries and regions so far. Based on the numbers till mid of April 2021, the official global total of COVID-19 cases has topped 236 million and around 5 million people lost their lives (COVID Live Update, 2021). The genetic sequence of COVID-19 was published on January 11, 2020, which led to global research activities to develop a vaccine against the disease. The scale of the high tech and economic impact of the COVID-19 pandemic has been a driving force to have fastest vaccine technology platforms in the history. The first COVID-19 vaccine candidate was ready for human clinical testing with unexpected rapidity on March 16, 2020 (Le, 2020).

Although the story of the emergence of COVID-19 is almost similar to previous pandemics, its biological sequence and course have been quite distinct, especially in its effects on the world. Humanity and the world have witnessed lots of "firsts" in history. Economically, central banks even decided to come up with "whatever it takes" approach (Nicola *et al.*, 2020). Furthermore, people resorted to "panic buying" and stockpiling even in the most developed countries, leading to short-term shortages and possibly, increased prices in the long term, which is an undeniable damage to agriculture. More interestingly, the world has witnessed unrest over wearing of masks and also vaccines in the last few weeks. In other words, COVID-19 has been not only challenging but also caused turmoil for humanity showing how individuals and societies are interconnected with each other.

6. Application of Chaos Theory to COVID-19

Application of chaos theory to pandemics has been used as a mathematical model to track behavior of viruses regarding transmission that shows a nonlinear trend (Piotrowski, 2020; Postavaru *et al.*, 2021; Tabor, 2021). On the other hand, we are going to apply chaos theory to its characteristics to comprehend holistic picture of its dynamics and implications for societies.

First, sensitivity to initial conditions is characteristic of chaotic systems. Similar to previous pandemics, COVID-19 has more than one initial condition determining how it spreads in a spatial and temporal setting. The initial point was the emergence of virus at the Wuhan seafood market. Depending on the analysis perspective, following initial points can be differentiated. For example, if an infected person had not caught a plane to Italy, the disease might have appeared weeks later and its effects would be less severe in Italy and across Europe. Figure 1 shows a timeline for different countries as local initial conditions. From this figure, the various turning points for countries and the world can be seen. Initial conditions may not necessarily always be the emergence of virus. Decisions of policymakers and their policies can be deemed as initial conditions. If Brazil had a different president, the progress of the epidemic in Latin America might have been different.

Second, bifurcation points are vital in chaotic systems to see the trajectory of the system. For pandemics, especially for COVID-19, it can be said that mutations and its variations are the bifurcation points within the pandemic course. Through these mutations, viruses basically change their genome structure from time to time, originating in emergent infections composed of a new RNA genome (Eskier *et al.*, 2021). This understanding of these mutations and the consequences for the entire RNA genome of these viruses requires also a new algorithm for containment. In other words, each mutation of COVID-19 has been a bifurcation point in the course of the pandemic. Similar to this perspective,

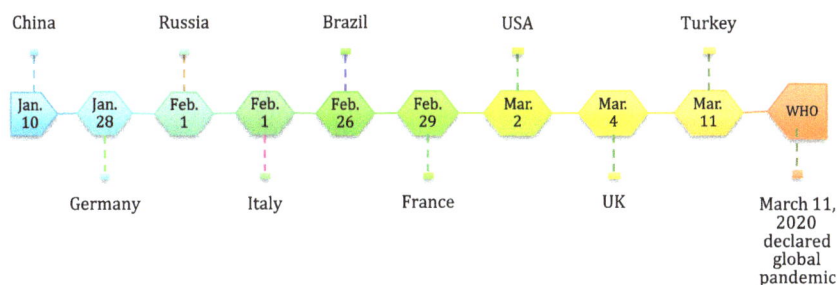

Figure 1:   Timeline of first cases in various countries.

e Fernandes *et al*. (2020) applied the methods based on nonlinear dynamics for understanding the pattern of coronaviruses in order to obtain its fractal signature for better understanding of its origin, mutations, and for faster identification of its genome in the diagnostic of COVID-19.

Third, nonlinearity of the pandemic is inherited in human behavior. Simply, human behavior is a nonlinear phenomenon that is difficult to catch in linear modeling. This explains why mathematical models developed to explore the evolution of the COVID-19 crisis could not predict the explosion of the number of infected people in the period following the state of emergency. External dynamics, such as regulations and restrictions, also affect the nonlinearity of people's behavior during the emergency state that created psychological pressure as well, which had a natural tendency of relaxation and ignoring the basic need of social distancing (Bratianu, 2020). In conjunction with this nonlinear understanding of people's behavior, nonlinear mathematical models have examined COVID-19 transmission and how to control transmission (Rohith & Devika, 2020; Tang *et al*., 2020).

Fourth and last is the self-organization property of chaotic systems. As we illustrated in the first and second properties of chaotic structure of COVID-19 pandemic, self-organization also has implications for COVID-19. In other words, the self-organization property will bring new order with new actors. From this perspective, every new system needs flexibility and the ability to adapt to internal and external environments. Self-organization especially plays a key role in determining the course of a pandemic that would bring new conditions- so go with the flow is the only principle! (Millierd, 2020).

Self-organization has both advantages and disadvantages in a pandemic. To exemplify, the worst scenario will be self-organization leading to the pandemic getting out of control, allowing the percentage of the infected population to go beyond a threshold — known as herd immunity — in the long term (Contoyiannis, 2020). On the contrary, understanding self-organization is the key for flexible and efficient policymaking considering the emerging structures, forms, and hierarchies. In the beginning of COVID-19, most of the governments followed similar measures; however, viruses affected each country in a unique way that triggered decisions at national and even district level in most of the countries (Han *et al.*, 2020). Beyond the measures for the pandemic, even legislative processes related to economic, social, and health have been influenced by COVID-19 through the self-organizational capacity of the system.

7. Conclusion: The Nature of Public Policymaking, COVID-19 and Chaos Theory

The public policy process is a dynamic, complex, and interactive process through which public problems are identified and countered by creating new approaches or reforming existing approaches, which are composed of governmental and non-governmental actors (Erkoçak & Açıkalın, 2015). In the last decade, new notions in public policymaking became a dominant discourse in discussions that are evidence based, innovation, metagovernance and experimental governance to simplify public policymaking (Erkoçak & Açıkalın, 2015; Laakso *et al.*, 2017). However, an unexpected phenomenon, like a pandemic, can create catastrophic effects in public policymaking.

As aforementioned, COVID-19 is understood with chaos theory through sensitivity to initial conditions, bifurcation points, nonlinearity, and self-organization. All these properties address how COVID-19 and its implications at the social level are chaotic, which has undeniably reflected on public policymaking. Although we touched upon this partially under the previous subsection, it should be underlined how public policy could be formulated during COVID-19 era. As Geyer and Rihani suggests, thinking in terms of complexity does not give the final answer to any policy area but rather gives a more realistic picture of social, economic, and political dimensions (2010).

First of all, policymakers should accept that COVID-19 is a multifaceted crisis, which has been sensitive to various initial conditions across the globe. This fact drives policymakers to overestimate actors and dynamics at local, national, and international level, where arresting the pandemic is one country is not solely enough to overcome it completely. Interestingly, policymakers during previous pandemics have suffered from technological limitations and lack of information (Colvin, 2020). Whereas, policymakers during COVID-19 have suffered from information overload that mostly included misinformation. Camargo and Camargo (2020) recall this situation as an "infodemic". With the number of users of social media increasing day by day, such platforms have become the prime source of information for increasingly more people. Misinformation has been transformed into a political tool for groups which are anti-lockdown and anti-vaccine to further promote their non-scientific agenda within the masses. Misinformation and the age of post-truth also influence international aspects of policymaking during COVID-19. The outstanding spread of deception drove WHO authorities of significant position to participate with an end goal to control its multiplication, collaborating with customary news sources and significant Internet organizations. Even the Director-General of WHO, Dr. Tedros Adhanom Ghebreyesus, underlined this reality in his words, "We're also battling the trolls and conspiracy theorists that push misinformation and undermine the outbreak response" (WHO, 2020).

Throughout history, humanity has faced different pandemics at different times and locations. All these pandemics changed the existing economic, social and political order in a peculiar way. Profound of changing after pandemic had been evolved to be more complicated and deep through centuries. When the Black Death emerged across Europe, no one could imagine the weakened perception of religion and later relations between church and politics. While the world was shaking with the fear of WWI, the Spanish flu infected around 100 million people, which led to the establishment of the first modern public healthcare system by Lenin. Similar examples can be given from different social and historical realities, which unveiled unique consequences of pandemics.

When COVID-19 was first identified in the beginning of 2020, the average number of total flights per day in March 2019 was 176,000, with discussion of globalization and glocalization overlapping (Thiessen, 2020; Açıkalın & Erçetin, 2020). Simply, humanity has never experienced such levels of interdependency, technological advancement, and mobilization before. So, the effects and implications of COVID-19 cannot be compared with those of any previous pandemics. Under this reality, COVID-19 and its implications should be dissected with more comprehensive and holistic, as well as a nonlinear, approach.

Consequently, chaos theory is an alternative way to analyze COVID-19 and its societal implications that has been already used to build more realistic models for predicting disease spread. Thus, chaos theory is not solely used for mathematical modeling but also a great tool to bring up a realistic picture of COVID-19 and how it would have implications on societies. Main properties of chaos theory can be summarized as follows: sensitivity to initial conditions, bifurcation points, nonlinearity, and self-organization. Within this framework, in this chapter, we discussed how COVID-19 can be analyzed to flaunt its multifaceted nature which challenged our lives and would be effective in the long term. In this respect, this chapter can be deemed as an introduction to upcoming chapters in the book that discusses how different fields would be affected by COVID-19.

References

Açıkalın, Ş. N. & Erçetin, Ş. Ş. (2020, December 20). *Understanding Global Reflexes to Covid-19 with Autopoiesis System Approach (Conference Presentation)*. 20th International Symposium on "Disordered Systems: Theory and Its Applications" (DSS-2020), İstanbul, Turkey.

Berger, L., Berger, N., Bosetti, V., Gilboa, I., Hansen, L. P., Jarvis, C., Marinacci, M., & Smith, R. D. (2021). Rational policymaking during a pandemic. *Proceedings of the National Academy of Sciences*, *118*(4), e2012704118, https://doi.org/10.1073/pnas.2012704118.

Bertuglia, C. S. & Vaio, F. (2005). *Nonlinearity, Chaos, and Complexity: The Dynamics of Natural and Social Systems*. Oxford: Oxford University Press on Demand.

Borsch, S. & Sabraa, T. (2017). Refugees of the Black Death: Quantifying rural migration for plague and other environmental disasters. *Annales de démographie historique*, *2*(2), 63–93, https://doi.org/10.3917/adh.134.0063.

Bratianu, C. (2020). Toward understanding the complexity of the COVID-19 crisis: A grounded theory approach. *Management & Marketing*, *15*(s1), 410–423.

Bright, J. E. & Pryor, R. G. (2005). The chaos theory of careers: A user's guide. *The Career Development Quarterly*, *53*(4), 291–305.

Britannica, T. Editors of Encyclopaedia (2020, November 9). *Black Death. Encyclopedia Britannica*, https://www.britannica.com/event/Black-Death.

Colvin, C. (2020). Does the Spanish flu offer lessons in how to tackle a pandemic? — Economics Observatory. Retrieved from: https://www.economicsobservatory.com/does-spanish-flu-offer-lessons-how-tackle-pandemic on April 25, 2021.

Contoyiannis, Y., Stavrinides, S. G., Hanias, M. P., Kampitakis, M., Papadopoulos, P., & Potirakis, S. (2020). On the effectiveness of imposing restrictive measures in a graded Self-Organized Criticality epidemic spread model the case of COVID-19. *arXiv e-prints*, arXiv-2004.

COVID Live Update. (2021). 142,563,976 Cases and 3,039,403 Deaths from the Coronavirus — Worldometer. (n.d.). Retrieved from: https://www.worldometers.info/coronavirus/ on April 19, 2021.

Delivorias, A. & Scholz, N. (2020). *BRIEFING EPRS | European Parliamentary Research Service*.

Drezner, D. W. (2020). The song remains the same: International relations after COVID-19. *International Organization*, 1–18.

e Fernandes, T. D. S., de Oliveira Filho, J. S., & da Silva Lopes, I. M. S. (2020). Fractal signature of coronaviruses related to severe acute respiratory syndrome. *Research on Biomedical Engineering*, 1–5.

Erkoçak, E. & Açıkalın, Ş. N. (2015). Complexity theory in public administration and metagovernance. In *Chaos, Complexity and Leadership 2013*, pp. 73–84. Springer: Cham.

Eskier, D., Akalp, E., Dalan, Ö., KarakÜlah, G., & Oktay, Y. (2021). Current mutatome of SARS-CoV-2 in Turkey reveals mutations of interest. *Turkish Journal of Biology*, *45*(1), 104–113.

Fauci, A. S., Lane, H. C., & Redfield, R. R. (2020). Covid-19 — Navigating the Uncharted. *New England Journal of Medicine*, *382*(13), 1268–1269, https://doi.org/10.1056/nejme2002387.

Garrett, T. A. (2007). Economic effects of the 1918 influenza pandemic. *Federal Reserve Bank of St. Louis*, 26.

Gatiso, T. T., Ordaz-Németh, I., Grimes, T., Lormie, M., Tweh, C., Kühl, H. S., & Junker, J. (2018). The impact of the Ebola virus disease (EVD) epidemic on agricultural production and livelihoods in Liberia. *PLoS neglected tropical diseases*, *12*(8), e0006580, https://doi.org/10.1371/journal.pntd.0006580.

Geyer, R. & Rihani, S. (2010). *Complexity and Public Policy: A New Approach to Twenty-First Century Politics, Policy and Society*. Routledge: Taylor and Francis.

Han, E., Tan, M. M. J., Turk, E., Sridhar, D., Leung, G. M., Shibuya, K., ... & Legido-Quigley, H. (2020). Lessons learnt from easing COVID-19 restrictions: An analysis of countries and regions in Asia Pacific and Europe. *The Lancet*.

Humphries, M. O. (2014). Paths of infection: The first world war and the origins of the 1918 influenza pandemic. *War in History*, 21(1), 55–81, https://doi.org/10.1177/0968344513504525.

Huremović, D. (2019). Brief history of pandemics (pandemics throughout history). In D. Huremović (Ed.), *Psychiatry of Pandemics: A Mental Health Response to Infection Outbreak,* pp. 7–35. Springer International Publishing, https://doi.org/10.1007/978-3-030-15346-5_2.

i Font, J. P. P., Pere, J., & Régis, D. (2006, July). Chaos theory and its application in political science. In IPSA-AISP World Congress, Session "Beyond Linearity: Research Methods and Complex Social Phenomena", Fukuoka, Japan (9–13 July 2006).

Jedwab, R., Johnson, N. D., & Koyama, M. (2019). Pandemics, places, and populations: Evidence from the Black Death.

Kauffman, S. (1996). *At Home in the Universe: The Search for the Laws of Self-Organization and Complexity.* Oxford University Press.

Kiel, L. D. & Elliott, E. (Eds.). (1996). *Chaos Theory in the Social Sciences: Foundations and Applications.* University of Michigan Press, https://doi.org/10.3998/mpub.14623.

Krasner, S. (1990). *The Ubiquity of Chaos.* Washington.

Laakso, S., Berg, A., & Annala, M. (2017). Dynamics of experimental governance: A meta-study of functions and uses of climate governance experiments. *Journal of Cleaner Production, 169,* 8–16.

Le, T. T., Andreadakis, Z., Kumar, A., Román, R. G., Tollefsen, S., Saville, M., & Mayhew, S. (2020). The COVID-19 vaccine development landscape. *Nature Reviews Drug Discovery, 19*(5), 305–306.

Maas, S. (2020). Social and Economic Impacts of the 1918 Influenza Epidemic. *NBER.* Retrieved from: https://www.nber.org/digest/may20/social-and-economic-impacts-1918-influenza-epidemic on April 17, 2021.

Mackowiak, P. A. & Sehdev, P. S. (2002). The origin of quarantine. *Clinical Infectious Diseases, 35*(9), 1071–1072.

McKibbin, W. J., & Sidorenko, A. (2006). *Global Macroeconomic Consequences of Pandemic Influenza (p. 79).* Sydney: Lowy Institute for International Policy.

McQueen, H. (1976). The 'Spanish' influenza pandemic in Australia, 1912–19. In J. Roe (Ed.), *Social Policy in Australia — Some Perspectives 1901–1975,* pp. 131–147. Cassell Australia: Stanmore NSW.

Millierd, P. (2020). Integrating chaos: Building resilient organizations with chaos theory. Retrieved from: https://think-boundless.com/chaos-theory/ on April 23, 2021.

Nicola, M., Alsafi, Z., Sohrabi, C., Kerwan, A., Al-Jabir, A., Iosifidis, C., Agha, M., & Agha, R. (2020). The socio-economic implications of the coronavirus pandemic (COVID-19): A review. *International Journal of Surgery, 78,* 185–193, https://doi.org/10.1016/J.IJSU.2020.04.018.

Oldstone, M. B. (1998). Introduction to the principles of virology. In *Viruses, Plagues, and History,* pp. 11–22. Oxford: Oxford University Press.

Person, B., Sy, F., Holton, K., Govert, B., Liang, A., & National Center for Inectious Diseases/SARS Community Outreach Team (2004). Fear and stigma: The epidemic within the SARS outbreak. *Emerging Infectious Diseases, 10*(2), 358–363, https://doi.org/10.3201/eid1002.030750.

Pfefferbaum, B. & North, C. S. (2020). Mental health and the Covid-19 pandemic. *New England Journal of Medicine, 383*(6), 510–512.

Piotrowski, C. (2020). Covid-19 pandemic and chaos theory: Applications based on a bibliometric analysis. *Journal of Projective Psychology & Mental Health, 27*(2), 1–5.

Postavaru, O., Anton, S. R., & Toma, A. (2021). COVID-19 pandemic and chaos theory. *Mathematics and Computers in Simulation, 181*, 138–149.

Rochel De Camargo, K. & Camargo, C. K. R. (2020). Trying to make sense out of chaos: Science, politics and the COVID-19 pandemic As tentativas de explicar o caos: A ciência, a política e a pandemia da COVID-19 Intentos de explicar el caos: Ciencia, política y la pandemia de COVID-19 (Explaining the Chaos: Science, Politics, and the COVID-19 Pandemic). *Cad. Saúde Pública (Cad. Saúde Publication), 36*(5), 88120, https://doi.org/10.1590/0102-311X00088120.

Rohith, G. & Devika, K. B. (2020). Dynamics and control of COVID-19 pandemic with nonlinear incidence rates. *Nonlinear Dynamics, 101*(3), 2013–2026.

Speakman, M. & Sharpley, R. (2012). A chaos theory perspective on destination crisis management: Evidence from Mexico. *Journal of Destination Marketing & Management, 1*(1–2), 67–77.

Strogatz, S. (2003). *Sync: The Emerging Science of Spontaneous Order*. New York: Hyperion Books.

Tabor, J. W. (2021). Chaos: Exploring an engaging online model for rapid application during the pandemic. *Educational Technology Research and Development, 69*(1), 97–100.

Tang, B., Bragazzi, N. L., Li, Q., Tang, S., Xiao, Y., & Wu, J. (2020). An updated estimation of the risk of transmission of the novel coronavirus (2019-nCov). *Infectious disease modelling, 5*, 248–255.

Thiessen, T. (2020). 40% less flights worldwide: This is what's happening with air travel. Retrieved from: https://www.forbes.com/sites/tamarathiessen/2020/04/01/40-percent-less-flights-worlwide-air-travel-restrictions/?sh=3b8f208c6079 on April 24, 2021.

Tomé, L., & Açıkalın, Ş. N. (2017, October). Complexity theory as a new Lens in IR: System and change. In *International Symposium on Chaos, Complexity and Leadership* (pp. 1–15). Springer: Cham.

Trilla, A., Trilla, G., & Daer, C. (2008). The 1918 "Spanish flu" in Spain. *Clinical Infectious Diseases, 47*(5), 668–673.

Velavan, T. P. & Meyer, C. G. (2020). The COVID-19 epidemic. *Tropical Medicine & International Health, 25*(3), 278.

Voigtländer, N. & Voth, H. J. (2013). The three horsemen of riches: Plague, war, and urbanization in early modern Europe. *Review of Economic Studies, 80*(2), 774–811.

Whiting, K. (2020). COVID-19: How did Spanish flu change the world? *World Economic Forum.* Retrieved from: https://www.weforum.org/agenda/2020/04/covid-19-how-spanish-flu-changed-world/ on April 17, 2021.

WHO. (2020). Immunizing the public against misinformation. Retrieved from: https://www.who.int/news-room/feature-stories/detail/immunizing-the-public-against-misinformation on April 26, 2021.

Wilson, K. (2012). Revisiting influenza deaths estimates — Learning from the H1N1 pandemic. *The European Journal of Public Health, 22*(1), 7–8.

Wu, Y. C., Chen, C. S., & Chan, Y. J. (2020). The outbreak of COVID-19: An overview. *Journal of the Chinese Medical Association, 83*(3), 217–220, https://doi.org/10.1097/JCMA.0000000000000270.

https://doi.org/10.1142/9781800611450_0002

Chapter 2

COVID-19 and the Infodemic — A Typology of Government Measures to Condemn False Information

André OLBRICH

Department of Political Science, University of Göttingen, Göttingen, Germany

dr.andre.olbrich@outlook.com

Abstract

The year 2020 was not only characterized by combat against a virus, but also by a struggle with various kinds of mis- and disinformation. During 2020, governments around the globe were highly active in enacting new policies, decrees and laws to alleviate the effects of false information. This paper shows and compares different government measures to overcome this information crisis. A typology of the different measures and escalation stages gives insight into how governments reacted to such a challenge and will show at the same time what kind of problems lawmakers and government officials face when they try to reduce the spread of false information.

1. Introduction

Little did we know in summer 2019 that in the following year, we would experience a worldwide pandemic that would change the world as we knew it. But at least some of us had an idea of how a worldwide pandemic could look in our technologized age. Security expert Bruce Schneider wrote in June 2019 for the *New York Times* that fighting a virus would not be the only challenge to overcome: "When the next pandemic strikes, we'll be fighting it on two fronts. The first is the one you immediately think about: understanding the disease, researching a cure, and inoculating the population. The second is new, and one you might not have thought much about: fighting the deluge of rumors, misinformation, and flat-out lies that will appear on the internet" (Schneider, 2019). In the same way responded Tedros Adhanom Ghebreyesus, Director-General of the World Health Organization (WHO), in February 2020 at the Munich Security Conference: "We're not just fighting an epidemic; we're fighting an infodemic. Fake news spreads faster and more easily than this virus, and is just as dangerous" (Ghebreyesus, 2020).

The reason why the fight against false information is equally weighted as the fight on the medical front seems obvious. To mitigate the impact of the virus and to ensure that the people act in a way which allows to control the disease are the main goals during a pandemic. But false news can undermine all kinds of efforts of health institutions and governments in their struggle to protect people from infection, not only when it comes to the condemnation of the virus itself, but also when it comes to introducing vaccines for prevention or medicine to help people who have already caught the deadly disease. False information might also lead to a significant mobilization of anti-restrictions, anti-mask, and anti-vaccination protests. People might hurt themselves or put others in danger based on their uninformed decisions. Clearly, the best health policies could be much less effective if they are not accompanied by consequent measures to cut or at least slow down the spread of false information.

In the past, the problem of misleading information was especially in the focus of interest during major political events, like the US presidential election and the Brexit vote in 2016, the same year when the word "post-truth" was announced as the Word of the Year by the Oxford Dictionary. A term which not so much contains a temporal dimension in the sense that we would live somehow past the truth but rather functions as an angle for a serious debate about the question if the truth is, in our time, of any practical relevance anymore (McIntyre, 2018, pp. 1–5). The outbreak of COVID-19 and the new wave of all kinds of false information shows that this problem not only concerns the conduct of fair political processes but also affects the health and lives of the people themselves. While reacting rather helplessly and without much ideas during the last years, governments found themselves under pressure to find solutions for this problem. During the whole year of 2020, we can observe high government activity regarding the topic of false information. In this paper, I will show how governments reacted during this crisis and classify the different kinds of measures and policies that were taken.

In order to give a typology, it is important to understand in what way false information has already influenced past pandemics. I will show that the scale of this problem has changed since COVID-19 was discovered and why governments suddenly saw a strong incentive to enact new policies, decrees, and laws to alleviate the effects of false information. We will see that different governments went through different escalation stages or chose different approaches from rather soft measures like the implementation of task forces to rather hard measures like the introduction of new laws with severe punishments. This typology and comparison can give us insight about the ways in which governments react to such a crisis. At last, it might also show us the dilemma governments find themselves when on the one hand they have to regulate the spread of misleading information while on the other hand want to protect the freedom of expression.

2. Fake News, Misinformation, and Disinformation

In accordance with Lazer *et al.* (2018), I regard the term fake news as "fabricated information that mimics news media content in form but not in organizational process or intent". Other terms which are overlapping with fake news, but not identical are "misinformation", which is regarded as "false or misleading information", and "disinformation", which is understood as "false information that is purposely spread to deceive people" (Lazer *et al.*, 2018, p. 1094). While misinformation could be simply inaccurate or erroneous without intention, disinformation is spread with the specific goal of manipulation and is partly used as a weapon by various actors like governments, intelligence services, extremists groups, etc. In the following, I will use the term "false information" in a general sense and specify, where necessary, with the terms misinformation and disinformation. I avoid the very popular term "fake news" since I agree with Freelon and Wells (2020, p. 146) that "its use by Trump and his followers to delegitimize unfavorable news coverage has stripped it of any analytical value it may have once held". Another important term is "info-demic". In a joint statement by the WHO and other UN organizations, infodemic is defined as "an overabundance of information, both online and offline. It includes deliberate attempts to disseminate wrong informa-tion to undermine the public health response and advance alternative agendas of groups or individuals. Mis- and disinformation can be harmful to people's physical and mental health; increase stigmatization; threaten precious health gains; and lead to poor observance of public health mea-sures, thus reducing their effectiveness and endangering countries' ability to stop the pandemic" (WHO 2020). While infodemic also can mean just the overabundance of true information, with all the different news around a prominent issue like COVID-19, the WHO sees first and foremost the danger that so much output could cloud the difference between true and false information.

3. The Role of False Information During Past Pandemics

Although the spread of false information during natural disasters is noth-ing new, there has clearly been a surge with the invention of social media. While in the past the media was a gatekeeper and it was not easy for an individual to reach out to thousands or even millions of others, social media has torn down this gate. Every comment, every post, and every tweet can now reach a worldwide audience much easier. Especially during natural disasters, this fact is a curse and a blessing at the same time. Where social media has, on the one hand, the potential to deliver valuable infor-mation quickly to the people who need them (and much more effectively than traditional media), it has, on the other hand, the potential to further destabilize an already critical situation, for example with the encourage-ment of wrong behavior or the spread of additional worries and panic within the population. Such problems could be observed, be it during earthquakes or hurricanes (Alexander, 2014, pp. 724–726).

Natural disasters are events of high activity on social media. A cross analysis of the behavior of Twitter users during a variety of catastrophes found that those users with only an average amount of followers are the ones with the highest activity during these events (Niles *et al.*, 2019, pp. 10–12). Major events draw the attention of the average user and the greater amount of activity sets the conditions for the fast spread of misleading information. There are at least three aspects which make pandemic times even more prone to false information than other natural disasters. Because of these factors, "infodemic" and "pandemic" can go hand in hand:

1. *Invisibility*: The pandemic disaster is not easily visible and brings with it a high level of uncertainty. Unlike the cases of hurricanes or earthquakes, people have a much harder time accepting even the bare existence of the event. Other natural disasters produce impressive footage and are immediately felt by the people who are exposed to them. Compared to that, a pandemic is a much more nebulous event, which invites speculation on a much greater scale.
2. *Long duration*: A pandemic is, in its time frame, an event with an open ending. Other natural disasters are more restricted in their appearance. Over its duration, there is enough time to go through different stages of rumors, conspiracies, and manipulation.
3. *Limited knowledge*: The knowledge about a new virus might be extremely limited. The less information is available, we might say, the more the empty information space will get filled up with all kinds of rumors and misinformation. When a virus appears, there usually needs to be a lot of research carried out: about its ways of transmission, about its fatality, or about how to combat it. It can be much more demanding to transmit knowledge about epidemiology and biology to ordinary people, who, without a basic understanding of the facts, might easily doubt the health benefits of a vaccine or certain preventive measures. And this transmitting process might be easily sabotaged by false information.

The history of pandemics offers a wide range of misbeliefs and conspiracy theories. One of the main precedences of a successful disinformation campaign was the so-called "Operation Infection", executed by the KGB of the Soviet Union in the 1980s, which was supposed to spread disinformation about HIV. It was propagated that the HIV epidemic was a failed or targeted US bioweapons operation. "Operation Infection" used the whole portfolio to support its claims, like vast conspiracy theories, faked academic papers, and statements from alleged health experts. And it was so successful that media outlets covered this story around the globe in dozens of languages (United States Department of State, 1987). It is assumed that the HIV disinformation campaign had an impact long after the KGB stopped its efforts. One survey in 1992 found out that 15% of a representational group of Americans in US believed that the virus was created by the US Government (Boghardt, 2009, p. 19). Groups who are especially suspicious about the government due to their experience with discrimination and racism in society seemed to be even more inclined to believe these theories. A survey from 2004 found out that 24.5% of questioned African Americans agreed somewhat or strongly with "AIDS was produced in a government laboratory" (Bogart & Thorburn, 2005, p. 215).

While this example shows that governments should have an interest in fighting false information to not endanger the trust of its citizens, it gets even worse when a government itself is convinced of some kind of misleading information. This happened with the presidency of Thabo Mbeki from 1999 on in South Africa. The government refused to act according to medical consensus and denied antiretroviral drugs for citizens infected with HIV. This fatal policy was driven by a mix of persistent false information and the belief in conspiracy theories. Later studies have estimated the loss of lives because of this policy at around 330,000 (Chigwedere et al., 2008, p. 412).

A study of the past Ebola outbreak between 2018 and 2019 in DR Congo has shown that people who are exposed to false information are less likely to follow government advice. Of a representative interview group of Congolese citizens, 45.9% believed in some kind of misinformation (that Ebola does not exist or that it was either fabricated for financial gains or in order to destabilize the country). Believing in this kind of misinformation lowered the willingness of the citizens living in DR Congo to accept a vaccine in the future or to adopt other preventive measures (Vinck et al., 2019, pp. 533–534). In general, studies have shown that people who believe in conspiracy theories are less likely to get vaccinated (Jolley & Douglas, 2014, p. 6).

Reports from Liberia during the Ebola outbreak of 2014 showed a significant amount of rumors which ranged from downplaying the severity of the virus to claiming that it was a hoax. Such conspiracy theories may have impeded the ability of healthcare workers to carry out their job and had a huge impact on the control and management of the crisis (Cheung, 2015, p. 72). Conspiracy theories have also developed around the Zika virus outbreak during 2015–2016, where it was mostly claimed that Zika is a biological weapon (Klofstad et al., 2019).

All these cases show that false information can undermine the trust in the government as well as in health institutions during pandemics. It can lead to a behavior that contributes to the further spread of a virus and the combat against the virus can be sabotaged, for example, by anti-vaccine conspiracies.

4. Why Governments Needed to Act During the COVID-19 Outbreak

Besides various experiences with false information during pandemics, the impact of COVID-19 might be only comparable with the Spanish Flu, which occurred at a time when our modern communication technology was not even in the slightest way imaginable. More than 70% of Britons and Americans use online media (including social media) as a source of news. In some countries like Argentina this value goes up to 90% (Newman *et al.*, 2020, p. 10). During the pandemic, with its lockdown measures and curfews, the importance of online media has increased even more. Online traffic to the BBC website in the UK has doubled in March 2020 as social distancing and lockdown measures were put in place (Newman *et al.*, 2020, p. 11). At the same time, rumors and false information were also spreading on a great scale (Cinelli *et al.*, 2020). A broad study of reports on social media platforms but also websites of television networks and online presences of newspapers in 87 countries from January to April 2020 found that 89% of the reports were based on unverified rumors, 7.8% of the content could be classified as conspiracy theory, and another 3.5% contained stigma, for example, against foreigners and healthcare workers (Islam *et al.*, 2020, p. 1622).

For a long time, social media companies were relatively unregulated regarding the content which they allow on their platforms. Earlier, Facebook, YouTube, or Twitter were regarded only as platforms which are not directly responsible for the content which various users produce. They could set their own policies regarding what they tolerate and what not. At least since the US presidential election in 2016, politicians have set their eyes on Big Tech and partly have already passed regulations which demand more responsibility from social media platforms. All of them have in some way updated their policies since the appearance of COVID-19. Twitter, for example, has further expanded their understanding of harm to combat misleading information that contradicts official health guidelines (Twitter, 2020). Social media platforms are also partnering with international organizations to deliver accurate information.

Facebook has partnered with the WHO and other health authorities to bring educational pop-ups on Facebook and Instagram, and on Facebook's messenger services, it was possible to get the latest update from the WHO health alert (Facebook Newsroom, 2020). But these are all measures which are taken on a voluntary basis. It remains a controversial discussion to which extent the state should actually get involved in what people write and say online.

But during the pandemic, the need for regulation seemed to be more urgent for governments than ever before. False information not only could cost lives, they also could lead to a destabilization of a country itself when people take to the streets and protest because of claims that a worldwide conspiracy is going on, that the vaccines are there to control the minds of the people, or because they believe that the whole virus is a hoax (Burki, 2020). Especially at the early stages of the pandemic when clear information and studies were lacking, it invited wild speculations. Among them were also harmful health claims. Recommendations which were shared online that highly concentrated alcohol could disinfect and kill the virus has led to at least 800 deaths, thousands of hospitalizations, and several more people ending up blind (Islam *et al.*, 2020, p. 1624). Stigma led to discrimination and fired racism against people of Asian descent (*Ibid.*, p. 1627). It led to breaking of restriction rules and to unhealthy practices (Tasnim *et al.*, 2020, p. 171). People died from an overdose of chloroquine, a medicine which some people hailed as a miracle drug, or were drinking bleach as an alleged cure for the virus (Reimann, 2020). Other effects are the undermining of the trust in the government authorities and sparking protests that led, for example in Germany, almost to a storming of the Parliament (Bennhold, 2020). Mass mobilization with violent outcomes happened in several countries during the whole year. Governments never had to deal with such consequences at such scales before because the influence of false information during elections and other events seemed to be much more subtly compared to what happened in 2020. Consequently, several states have passed laws and new regulations in that year alone.

Furthermore, pressure came also from international organizations. The WHO gave their recommendation to the member states to do what is in their power to spread scientific information and to take action against mis- and disinformation: "We call on Member States to develop and implement action plans to manage the infodemic by promoting the timely dissemination of accurate information, based on science and evidence, to all communities, and in particular high-risk groups; and preventing the spread, and combating, mis- and disinformation while respecting freedom of expression" (WHO, 2020). The expansion of online social media and the appearance of a worldwide pandemic have led to a completely new perspective on false information. It seems that the harm which can be done by that means is perceived as highly dangerous, so that many states saw it as a public interest to take measures against it.

While the condemnation of false information might be seen as beneficious in the matter of protecting the health of the people and to stabilize the internal affairs of states, another motivation, less oriented toward the well-being of citizens, was also present. The combat of false information gave governments a justification to strengthen their control over the media. Organizations like Freedom House saw a rise of internet restrictions, especially in states which rank low on their democracy index. The measures had led to a restriction of free online speech and increased arrests (Freedom House, 2020, p. 10).

5. A Typology of Government Measures to Condemn False Information

What were the policies which states implemented to combat the infodemic? We see in many different countries various measures and escalation stages. Lazer *et al.* (2018) divides "interventions", in the matter of false information, into two categories:

(A) Empowerment of individuals to recognize and evaluate false informations and
(B) Structural changes to prevent the exposure to false information.

While these interventions are not exclusively political since in the past, it was mostly the free press, NGOs, or the social media platforms themselves who were active in this matter, I will show which kind of specifically political interventions were made during the COVID-19 pandemic in 2020. The following types of government actions against false information could be observed:

(1) Issuing guidelines to strengthen information literacy,
(2) Implementing task forces,

(3) Centralization of news flow in the matter of COVID-19,
(4) Criminalization of spreading false information,
(5) Passing new laws or expanding the scope of existing legislation, and
(6) Internet shutdowns.

Only some of these measures try to function in a corrective way without intervening too much into the whole information economy. These are typically the types 1 and 2 (Category A). The types 3 to 6 (Category B) try to combat the spread of false information directly, either with stronger punishments, regulations which demand the removal or moderation of false information, or even shut down of the whole news flow to prevent possible spread of harmful dis- and misinformation.

5.1. *Issuing guidelines to strengthen information literacy*

Strengthening information literacy was the dominant strategy in pre-COVID times. With the goal to protect future elections for the European Parliament, the EU Commission formed an expert group of 39 members in 2018 with different backgrounds in journalism, fact checking organizations, academia, etc. The threat of false information was already known from the US Elections of 2016, but the advisors of this expert group made no fundamental recommendation for a law initiative; instead they suggested a soft approach to the European Commission, which should promote media and information literacy, develop tools for empowering journalists and users, and fund further research about the dangers of false information. A joint communication in 2020 about "Tackling COVID-19 disinformation" has not changed that soft policy. To combat false information the EU relies on strengthening awareness of its citizens, support of fact-checkers and researchers, and cooperation with social media platforms. Greater law initiatives were not planned, but the EU has presented, by the end of the year, the draft of the Digital Services Act (DSA), which is not a temporary solution for COVID-19 false information but for the problem as a whole, and the attention for this project and the necessity for a regulation of Big Tech has only grown even further since the infodemic.

Most governments have launched their own information campaigns and guidelines to make people aware of false information. In the UK, the government started the "Don't Feed The Beast" campaign, especially trying to improve people's sharing behavior on social media (UK Government, 2020). They provided a checklist on how to identify trustworthy information and demanded reflection before spreading certain information even further. In Spain, the National Police has published a guide which should help people not to be manipulated through false information during COVID-19 (Ministerio del Interior, 2020). And in Italy, which was the first country that has been hit badly by COVID-19, the Ministry of Health started a campaign to counter false information, which made up 7.1% of its overall newsflow. They marked posts as fake and linked to official statistics and data to prevent people from believing in unproofed statements (Lovari, 2020, p. 460). Many governments have used similar approaches or have at least supported the information campaign "#PledgetoPause", initiated by the WHO and linked to their official sites accompanied by fact checks of common false information like in Germany (Bundesregierung, 2020).

Sponsoring media literacy and guidelines are among the easiest political measures which can be taken to combat false information. But they might be too little considering the large amount of information that is circulating. Fact checking and in-depth analysis consumes time, while in the meantime, false information can spread without obstacles. Besides that, positive effects of strengthening awareness of manipulative news might turn out useful long-term, but during an acute crisis, it might be a less useful way of dealing with false information.

5.2. *Implementing task forces*

Several states have founded special task forces in response to the threat of false information. It is one of the easiest measures a government can take since it usually does not require immediate parliamentary approval. Besides that, task forces to combat false information are already widely used. In 2015, the EU implemented "EUvsDisinfo" as part of the European External Action Service's East StratCom Task Force. They tackle especially misleading information launched by russian disinformation campaigns. Prominently, Canada founded such a task force to protect their elections (CTV News, 2019).

One of the first governments who implemented a task force to combat specific false information about COVID-19 was the United Kingdom in March 2020. The simple goal of this unit was to ensure that the public will get correct news and to tackle dangerous misinformation and harmful narratives. After identifying such issues, a direct rebuttal over the appropriate social media channels of the government was delivered. At the same time, the unit worked together with social media platforms to remove the potential harmful content (UK Government, 2020).

If countries did not implement a specific task force during COVID-19, they could instead rely on their already existing press departments, either of the Health Ministry or other government organizations. A specific unit which is dealing only with this issue might be more effective, but this is highly dependent on how much a government is willing to pay for that. It is so far unknown how successful the British task force was, but it was handling around 70 incidents of false information per week, which seems to be a small fraction of all the untrustworthy information which was out there.

5.3. *Centralization of news*

Some governments took rather radical measures and responded to the infodemic with a centralization of all COVID-19 news. According to the government of Serbia, information spread by private individuals without authorization cannot be considered accurate or liable beyond doubt. It declared that information about COVID-19 from health institutions have to be sent to the national crisis staff which reports directly to Prime Minister Ana Brnabic. Health institutions could no longer give statements directly to the public or media outlets. Only through the crisis staff, information could be transmitted to the public. Some NGOs have criticized this centralization of COVID-19 news since it would be a restriction of the freedom of the press (Stojanovic, 2020). Something similar has also happened in Hungary, where an operational group of the government has centralized the information about COVID-19. Its press conferences are the only source of information, while other public institutions are much more unlikely to disclose information about the COVID-19 situation in Hungary (Hungarian Civil Liberties Union, 2020).

5.4. *Criminalization of spreading misinformation*

Criminalization of false information does not necessarily come from a law which specifically regulates false information. Some are part of emergency powers given to the government for limited time or in a temporary state of exception. We can see that some countries choose the way of criminalization over decrees or emergency states. In Peru, the Ministry of Justice announced in April 2020 that people who share false information could be sanctioned with a prison sentence up to six years. Peru was then the first country in South America which criminalized the creation and sharing of false information in the context of COVID-19 (Alvarez-Risco *et al.*, 2020, p. 584). A decree, issued by the Bolivian interim President Jeanine Añez, stated that individuals who spread false information or spread panic would have to face criminal charges and a punishment of up to ten years in prison (Committee to Protect Journalists, 2020). Hungary has passed a so-called "Enabling Act". With this law, the government can rule by decree with the purpose of combating COVID-19. A more specified duration was not given. The act also consists of regulations regarding the spread of untrue facts or misrepresentation of facts during the emergency period, which is regarded now as a felony and will be punished with up to five years imprisonment (Ministry of Justice Hungary, 2020, p. 3).

Criminalization is a strong intervention in the problem of false information. Individuals can be held responsible for their actions, and this might be an effective deterrence. The problem with criminalization is, on the one hand, the difficulty of enforcing this act due to the various ways in which users have means to stay anonymous on the internet and that strong cooperation with technology companies is necessary in addition to a legal basis for obtaining private data. On the other hand, the spectrum of what can be considered as mis- or disinformation is very wide, and to let a government interpret this matter equals a huge amount of power, which could be also used to suppress free media or the opposition within a country.

5.5. *New and updated legislation*

Legislation against false information already has precedence. Between 2016 and 2019, 13 countries worldwide have implemented regulations regarding this matter (De Gregorio & Radu, 2019, p. 7). In 2020 alone, 17 countries passed specific laws justifying it with the severe impact of false information around COVID-19. While it might, on the one hand, be desirable to take out wrong information and to do something against the manipulation with legal means, COVID-19 might be also a favorable opportunity to restrict the freedom of speech. As known, the term "fake news" can be also used as a term to denounce critical media outlets and to undermine the public trust in them (International Press Institute, 2020).

Some countries updated or interpreted existing laws in a new way to make them fit to regulate the spread of false information. Since new legislation is sometimes not possible in a timely manner, governments tend to be creative in using the already existing legal framework as a basis for their actions against misleading news. The Indian Ministry of Electronic and Information Technology has published an advisory in March 2020, in which it demands social media platforms to spread awareness of the problem of untrustworthy news, that misleading content has to be removed and that they should promote authentic information (Indian Ministry of Electronic & Information Technology, 2020). The base for India is the Disaster Management Act from 2005, with which it is not only possible to justify a lockdown but also to make it illegal to "spread panic", which according to the government, also includes the spread of false information (Rodrigues & Xu, 2020, p. 128). The strict manner in which the government was involved in this process led to massive criticism by the free press. The Indian Prime Minister, Narendra Modi, asked several owners of news media to focus on positive stories around the pandemic. Additionally, the Indian Government even requested a ruling from the Supreme Court that news outlets needed clearance from the government before they publish any news related to the new pandemic, which is another example for a news centralization attempt. Even if this was denied, the supreme court at least ruled that news outlets must use official information for their articles, which they have never been forced to do before (*Ibid.*).

China, on the other hand, had already implemented several modern mechanisms to combat false information before the COVID-19 crisis and was, in that way, well prepared. Since 2017, a cybersecurity law regulates, among other things, various kinds of misleading information. And since 2018, the Illegal and Unhealthy Information Reporting Centre is responsible for detecting and refuting false information (Rodrigues & Xu, 2020, p. 127). National and local rumor-refuting platforms were then especially used during the COVID-19 crisis. Major news sites have provided special fact checking sites. China has also used its Public Security Administration Punishment Law to detain people who spread misleading information (*Ibid.*, pp. 127–128).

Russia already had since March 2019 a law which regulated false information. People had to pay fines if it was proved that they spread false information, and websites could be blocked in case they contain untrue news. After the COVID-19 crisis started, the country rushed several changes to the Criminal Code. Not only would people have to face fines up to the equivalent of 23,000 Euro as individuals, also media outlets could be fined up to the equivalent of 117,000 Euro. The difference between the old and the new legislations is that spreading false information found its way into the Criminal Code and can now also be sanctioned with imprisonment.

5.6. *Internet shutdown*

The most radical measure (the nuclear option, we might say) is a shutdown of the Internet to prevent the further spread of false news. The Indian government made use of that means and ordered several regional shutdowns in the country, officially to condemn the spread of misleading information (Rodrigues & Xu, 2020, p. 128). India is not new to internet shutdowns. Even before the COVID-19 crisis, the government used shutdowns for various reasons. In 2019 alone, Internet was shut down at least 95 times in India (Nazmi, 2019).

6. Governments as a Driver of False Information

While governments do not only have means to combat false information, they can on the other hand also spread false information themselves. The political ideology of the ruling parties and individuals in a certain country has an effect on how the government deals with false information. If a government takes measures at all, they might be used to accuse the free press or the opposition of spreading "fake news" and therefore giving a justification to silence the press as we can assume in Hungary and Russia.

Some governments might take almost no measures at all because it finds itself actually on the side of the spectrum which spreads these false information. Calvillo *et al.* (2020, p. 1125) found a relation between presidential approval and knowledge about COVID-19 in the US. US citizens who supported Donald Trump usually had less knowledge about epidemiological facts. This seems to be connected to the statements of the former US president himself. A major study of 38 million news articles in

English found that Trump was mentioned in 37.9% of all articles which consists of false information. Therefore, the authors of the study conclude "that the President of the United States was likely the largest driver of the COVID-19 misinformation 'infodemic'" (Evanega *et al.*, 2020).

Another case in which false information was spread by the government itself is the denialism of the Brazilian government under Jair Bolsonaro. Parts of the Brazilian government and especially the president himself have "sustained their denialist stance by conveying misinformation, particularly regarding the symptoms, risks, and cures of the virus, and instigating risky behavior" (Ricard & Medeiros, 2020, p. 2). Bolsonaro defended certain medications as useful despite no evidence for their effectiveness, breached quarantine, or acted against the advice of the WHO to reduce contacts. Even some of his tweets on Twitter were deleted because they violated the platform's own implemented policy on COVID-19 disinformation (*Ibid.*, p. 4).

7. Conclusion

COVID-19 has changed the perception of the problem of false information in an eruptive way. While it is a constant problem in the age of social media, it got the attention of only the governments as a possible target of regulation during single events, especially elections. Now with COVID-19, the whole world experiences the same crisis and has to react to false information in some way.

In this chapter, I classified different government reactions to false information during the pandemic of 2020 with various examples of different escalation stages. Some countries adopted several of these measures, others only one or none. We gained insights into how the kind of measure a government is choosing might be related to the political ideology of the government which is in power and is also related to the political system itself. We also can build on the hypothesis that the combat against false information might come at the cost of the freedom of expression, which seems, at first glance, too high a price to pay. On the other hand, we have learned that false information has a serious impact on the health and life of citizens around the world. A government which would simply ignore the fact would not only threaten its people but also the stability of the country as a whole. Therefore, it is recommended that governments continue with soft measures against false information and ensure a legislation process which is open and transparent with the goal to regulate especially the spread of misleading news on social media platforms.

We can observe worldwide the emergence of stronger national approaches to the problem of false information. It seems that most of the states are not willing to let technology companies decide what should or should not appear on their platforms. COVID-19 could be the main driver in a new era in which the state acquires some competencies which private companies claim for themselves these days. In a post-COVID era, we might see more restrictive measures in various states appearing to regulate the publishing of information, especially on social media platforms. The challenge of false information is more and more perceived as a matter of public interest.

References

Alexander, D. E. (2014). Social media in disaster risk reduction and crisis management, *Science and Engineering Ethics*, *20*, 717–733.

Alvarez-Risco, A., Mejia, C. R., Delgado-Zegarra, J., Del-Aguila-Arcentales, S., Arce-Esquivel, A. A., Valladares-Garrido, M. J., Rosas del Portal, M., Villegas, L., Curioso, W. H., Sekar, M. C., & Yañez, J. A. (2020). The Peru Approach against the COVID-19 infodemic: Insights and strategies. *The American Society of Tropical Medicine and Hygiene*, *103*(2), 583–586.

Bennhold, K. (2020). Far right germans try to storm reichstag as virus protests escalate. *New York Times*. 31 August 2020, https://www.nytimes.com/2020/08/31/world/europe/reichstag-germany-neonazi-coronavirus.html (Accessed on 01.02.2021).

Bogart, L. M. & Thorburn, S. (2005). Are HIV/AIDS conspiracy beliefs a barrier to HIV prevention among African Americans? *Journal of Acquired Immune Deficiency Syndromes*, *38*(2), 213–218.

Boghardt, T. (2009). Operation INFEKTION — Soviet bloc intelligence and its AIDS disinformation campaign, *Studies in Intelligence*, *53*(4), 1–24.

Bundesregierung (2020). Kampagne #pledgetopause — Einen moment gegen desinformation. 10 November 2020, https://www.bundesregierung.de/breg-de/themen/coronavirus/einen-moment-gegen-desinformation-1809908 (Accessed on 28.01.2021).

Burki, T. (2020). The online anti-vaccine movement in the age of COVID-19. *The Lancet*. *2*(10), 504–505.

Casey, A., Klofstad, J. E., Uscinski, Connolly, J. M., & West, J. P. (2019). What drives people to believe in Zika conspiracy theories? *Palgrave Communications*, *5*(36), 1–8.

Calvillo, D. P., Ross, B. J., Garcia, R. J. B., Smelter, T. J., & Rutchick, A. M. (2020). Political ideology predicts perceptions of the threat of COVID-19 (and susceptibility to fake news about it). *Social Psychological and Personality Science*, *11*(8), 1119–1128.

Cheung, E. (2015). An outbreak of fear, rumours and stigma: Psychosocial support for the Ebola Virus Disease outbreak in West Africa. *Intervention*, *13*(1), 45–84.

Chigwedere, P., Seage, G. R., Gruskin, S., & Lee, T. (2008). Estimating the lost benefits of antiretroviral drug use in South Africa. *Journal of Acquired Immune Deficiency Syndromes*, *49*(4), 410–415.

Cinelli, M., Quattrociocchi, W., Galeazzi, A., Valensise, C. M., Brugnoli, E. Schmidt, A. L., Zola, P., Zollo, F., & Scala, A. (2020). The COVID-19 social media infodemic. *Scientific Reports, 10*, 16598.

Committee to Protect Journalists (2020). Bolivia enacts decree criminalizing "disinformation" on COVID-19 outbreak. 9 April 2020, https://cpj. org/2020/04/bolivia-enacts-decree-criminalizing-disinformation/ (Accessed on 25.01.2021).

CTV News (2019). Feds unveil plan to tackle fake news, interference in 2019 election, https://www.ctvnews.ca/politics/feds-unveil-plan-to-tackle-fake-news-interference-in-2019-election-1.4274273 (Accessed on 22.01.2021).

De Gregorio, G. & Roxana, R. (2019). Counter-disinformation around the world: Comparing state actions. 2019 Global Internet Governance Academic Network Annual Symposium, Berlin, Germany.

European Commission (2018). A multi-dimensional approach to disinformation — Report of the independent High level Group on fake news and online disinformation, Luxemburg: Publications Office of the European Union.

Evanega, S., Lynas, M., Adams, J., & Smolenyak, K. (2020). Coronavirus misinformation: Quantifying sources and themes in the COVID-19 "infodemic". *The Cornell Alliance for Science*, https://allianceforscience. cornell.edu/wp-content/uploads/2020/09/Evanega-et-al-Coronavirus-misinformationFINAL.pdf.

Facebook Newsroom (2020). Combating COVID-19 Misinformation Across Our Apps. 25 March 2020, https://about.fb.com/news/2020/03/combating-covid-19-misinformation/ (Accessed on 22.01.2021).

Freedom House (2020). Freedom on the Net 2020 — The Pandemic's Digital Shadow, https://freedomhouse.org/sites/default/files/2020-10/10122020_FOTN2020_Complete_Report_FINAL.pdf (Accessed on 21.01.2021).

Freelon, D. & Wells, C. (2020). Disinformation as political communication. *Political Communication*, *37*(2), 145–156.

Ghebreyesus, T. A. (2020). Speech at the Munich Security Conference, 15 February 2020, https://www.who.int/director-general/speeches/detail/munich-security-conference (Accessed on 01.12.2020).

Hungarian Civil Liberties Union (2020). Research on the obstruction of the work of journalists during the coronavirus pandemic in Hungary. 15 April 2020, https://tasz.hu/a/files/coronavirus_press_research.pdf (Accessed on 25.01.2021).

Indian Ministry of Electronic & Information Technology (2020). Advisory to curb false news/misinformation on Corona Virus, 20 March 2020, https://www.meity.gov.in/writereaddata/files/advisory_to_curb_false_news-misinformation_on_corona_virus.pdf (Accessed on 22.01.2021).

International Press Institute (2020). Rush to pass "fake news" laws during Covid-19 intensifying global media freedom challenges, 22 October 2020, https://ipi.media/rush-to-pass-fake-news-laws-during-covid-19-intensifying-global-media-freedom-challenges/ (Accessed on 28.01.2021).

Islam, S., Sarkar, T., Khan, S. H., Kamal, A. M., Hasan, S. M. M., Kabir A., Yeasmin, D., Islam, M. A., Chowdhury, K. I. A., Anwar, K. S., Chughtai, A. A., & Seale H. (2020). COVID-19–Related infodemic and its impact on public health: A global social media analysis. *The American Journal of Tropical Medicine and Hygiene*, *103*(4), 1621–1629.

Lazer, D. M., Baum, M. A., Benkler, Y., Berinsky, A. J., Greenhill, K. M., Menczer, F., Metzger, M. J., Nyhan, B., Pennycook, G., Rothschild, D., Schudson, M., Sloman, S. A., Sunstein, C. R., Thorson, E. A., Watts, D. J., & Zittrain, J. L. (2018). The science of fake news — Addressing fake news requires a multidisciplinary effort. *Science*, *359*(6380), 1094–1096.

Lovari, A. (2020). Spreading (dis)trust: Covid-19 misinformation and government intervention in Italy. *Media and Communication*, *8*(2), 458–461.

McIntyre, L. (2018). *Post-Truth*, London: The MIT Press.

Ministerio del Interior (2020). La Policía Nacional presenta la primera guía para evitar ser manipulados por las fake news, 27 March 2020, http://www.interior.gob.es/prensa/noticias/-/asset_publisher/GHU8Ap6ztgsg/content/id/11676535 (Accessed on 22.01.2021).

Ministry of Justice Hungary (2020). Act XII of 2020 on the containment of coronavirus. 31 March 2020, http://abouthungary.hu/media/DocumentsModell-file/1585661547-act-xii-of-2020-on-the-containment-of-coronavirus.pdf (Accessed on 25.01.2021).

Nazmi, S. (2019). Why India shuts down the internet more than any other democracy, *BBC News*, 19 December 2019, https://www.bbc.com/news/world-asia-india-50819905 (Accessed on 22.01.2021).

Newman, N., Fletcher, R., Schulz, A., Andı, S., & Nielsen, R. K. (2020). *Digital News Report 2020*. Retrieved from: https://reutersinstitute.politics.ox.ac.uk/sites/default/files/2020-06/DNR_2020_FINAL.pdf.

Niles, M. T., Emery, B. F., Reagan, A. J., Dodds, P. S., & Danforth, C. M. (2019). Social media usage patterns during natural hazards. *PLOS ONE*, *14*(2), e0210484.

Reimann, N. (2020). Some Americans Are Tragically Still Drinking Bleach As A Coronavirus "Cure". *Forbes*. Aug 24, 2020, https://www.forbes.com/sites/nicholasreimann/2020/08/24/some-americans-are-tragically-still-drinking-bleach-as-a-coronavirus-cure/?sh=2374e0d26748 (Accessed on 21.01.2021).

Ricard, J. & Medeiros, J. (2020). Using misinformation as a political weapon: COVID-19 and Bolsonaro in Brazil. *The Harvard Kennedy School Misinformation Review, 1*(2), 1–6.

Rodrigues, U. M. & Xu, J. (2020). Regulation of COVID-19 fake news infodemic in China and India, *Media International Australia, 177*(1), 125–131.

Schneider, B. (2019). We must prepare for the next pandemic — We'll have to battle both the disease and the fake news. *New York Times*, 17 June 2019, https://www.nytimes.com/2019/06/17/opinion/pandemicfake-news.html (Accessed on 27.11.2020).

Stojanovic, M. (2020). Serbian Govt takes control of information flow about pandemic, *Balkan Insights*, 1 April 2020, https://balkaninsight.com/2020/04/01/serbian-govt-takes-control-of-information-flow-about-pandemic/ (Accessed on 25.01.2021).

Tasnim, S., Hossain, M., & Mazumder, H. (2020). Impact of rumors and misinformation on COVID-19 in social media. *Journal of Preventive Medicine & Public Health. 53*, 171–174.

Twitter (2020). Coronavirus: Staying safe and informed on Twitter, 3 April 2020, https://blog.twitter.com/en_us/topics/company/2020/covid-19.html#misleadinginformation (Accessed on 22.01.2021).

UK Government (2020). Press releases, 30 March 2020, https://www.gov.uk/government/news/government-cracks-down-on-spread-of-false-coronavirus-information-online (Accessed on 21.01.2020).

UN News (2020). UN urges people to #PledgetoPause before sharing information online, 21 October 2020, https://news.un.org/en/story/2020/10/1075742 (Accessed on 28.01.2021).

United States Department of State (1987). *Soviet Influence Activities: A Report on Active Measures and Propaganda 1986–87*, Department of State Publication.

Vinck, P., Pham, P. N., Bindu, K. K., Bedford, J., & Nilles, E. J. (2019). Institutional trust and misinformation in the response to the 2018–19 Ebola outbreak in North Kivu, DR Congo: A population-based survey. *The Lancet, 19*(5), 529–536.

World Health Organization (2020). Managing the COVID-19 infodemic: Promoting healthy behaviours and mitigating the harm from misinformation and disinformation. 23 September 2020, https://www.who.int/news/item/23-09-2020-managing-the-covid-19-infodemic-promoting-healthybehaviours-and-mitigating-the-harm-from-misinformation-and-disinformation (Accessed on 13.12.2020).

Chapter 3

A Social Change Theorist Recalled by the COVID-19 Pandemic: Ulrich Beck and the Risk Society

Mehmet Cem ŞAHİN

*Department of Sociology of Religion,
Dokuz Eylül University, İzmir, Turkey*

mcemsahin@gmail.com

Abstract

Ulrich Beck is a well-known German sociologist and one of the most cited social scientists in the world. His theory of social change focuses on questions of uncontrollability, ignorance, and uncertainty in the modern age, and he created the terms "risk society" and "second modernity" or "reflexive modernization". He also defines three features that characterize global risks: de-localization, incalculableness, and non-compensability. Beck's risk society theory offers a functional perspective in which very accurate sociological theses are put forward in terms of containing the basic concepts that reside at the center of the phenomenon and the many discussions about the global epidemic that occupy the agenda of the countries and societies of the world. The COVID-19 pandemic justifies Beck's theory. From Beck's theoretical perspective, COVID-19 pandemic is characterized as a manufactured risk.

1. Introduction

Upon the emergence of a new respiratory disease, which started on December 1, 2019, with a case in Wuhan (the capital of the Hubei region of China) and progressed in a short period in various patients without a specific cause and did not respond to any known treatment or vaccines, a novel coronavirus strain designated as SARS-CoV-2 was identified by epidemiologists. The respiratory disease caused by SARS-CoV-2 was given the name COVID-19 referring to the new coronavirus disease that emerged first in the year 2019.

The transmission rate of the virus increased in mid-January 2020. Later, SARS-CoV-2 infection cases diagnosed in various countries in Europe, North America, and Asia Pacific began to be reported, and on March 11, 2020, the World Health Organization declared a global epidemic. On March 13, 2020, it was reported that Europe had become the epicenter of the coronavirus crisis. During the past year, as of the end of April 2021, there were 147,662,276 confirmed cases and 125,592,640 recovering patients worldwide, while 3,119,459 people died due to the virus.

In the face of the global epidemic threat, all countries of the world put into effect a series of emergency action plans. The most important of these protection methods are the measures to reduce human mobility. Therefore, depending on the speed of viral transmission, curfews, partial and full lockdown measures were implemented in various countries of the world except for isolated cases. It has become mandatory to wear masks in closed areas. Travel restrictions have been introduced, and maximum attention has been paid to sanitation rules in public and private areas.

As in previous epidemic periods, the COVID-19 pandemic undoubtedly had economic, social, and psychological consequences. In addition to millions of people who lost their lives, rising unemployment and the bottleneck that the health sector has fallen into, as a result of the exponential increase in the number of cases, have thrown everything off balance. For humanity, which tries to cope with all the negativities caused by the epidemic process and heal its wounds, a period has started where old normals lose their function and new normals dominate life.

Theories that are capable of explaining the causes and effects of the phenomenon are often the starting point for a sociologist in a very comprehensive, and at the same time, complicated issue, such as embarking on the sociological analysis of this new stage experienced by humanity in the process of social change. In this context, in explaining the sociological dimensions of socioeconomic, cultural, political, technological, ecological, and other transformations occurring with the COVID-19 pandemic, the perspective offered by the German sociologist Ulrich Beck's "Risk Society" theory deserves to be reconsidered in this process. Beck's theory was put forward at the end of the cold war and in the 20th century in general, and has the feature of a precaution and warning against the possible problems that the West faces and will face. It is a common point of Beck's work to stand "consciously" in the face of problems and, with new policies, to be proposed based on this consciousness. Beck first described the theory of Risk Society, which has earned him a reputation in social science circles, in the work *Risikogesellschaft? Auf dem Weg in eine andere Moderne* he authored in 1986. With the publication of the English translation of this book in 1992, the theory began to spread and be debated in wider circles, and many of the works that Beck wrote in the following years were translated into different languages.

2. Risk Society Theory

Risk is a word that has been used to describe dangerous situations that can be encountered for ages and people's concerns. Within the framework of this definition, humans have faced dangers and risks that have threatened them throughout the ages. Risks are not present-day threats and dangers that arise today. Risks are as old as human history, but there are differences between their use before the ages and their current use in terms of meaning and content. In addition to the meanings of threat and danger that have survived from the past centuries to the present, today it is used for dangers created by human beings who are personally responsible for their consequences that also concern other living creatures. In these risks, the effect of man, but not its coincidence, is more important. Beck explains this by referring to today's society, which he defines as a risk society from the industrial society process characterized by unconscious and unlimited use of science and technology. Beck's theory, which turned to this issue especially after the disintegration of the USSR, aims to explain the social structure of the 21st century and the cultural, political, economic, social, technological, and scientific uniqueness of this society. Risk society includes environmental, cultural, social, scientific side effects, including danger, threat, and risk factors of the industrial society.

Beck conceptualized the risk society as a continuation, a new version of the industrial society as a type of society prepared by the developing industrial society of the 19th century, and at the same time, as the new form taken by modernity — a new stage. While Beck describes the 19th century as a period dominated by the logic of reaching univocity, the 20th century is defined by concepts such as "pluralist", "indeterminate", "double-valued". He sees the period as neither an industrial society nor a service society nor a post-modern society. He defines this social process as "a society that contains doubt, self-doubt and by this way lays the foundations for a change, and can be liberated through doubts".

Beck says that modernity is experienced randomly and unconsciously. He claims that within this modernity, two types of societies are intertwined in the continuation of industrial society, even in the process that occurred while industrial society was ending. Naming it as the risk society, he took this social stage as the starting point of the risk society theory. Beck also saw this stage he mentioned as the last stage Western society has reached today. He argued that in the present risk society, the risks that have existed for a long time emerge in many different ways and encompass and threaten the whole society. It has revealed a certain development process as a solution for society and individuals against risks, dangers, and threats. This is the theory of "reflexive modernization" (*reflexiver modernisierung*), which is called "contemplative modernization".

Beck sees the decisions taken in the industrial society of the 19th century, the policies implemented, and the progress and developments of the industrial society constitute the process of preparing the risk society. Beck defines the stage that the industrial society has reached at the end as the "risk society" that also bears the traces of the industrial society.

Beck is of the view that society today consists of uncertain risks and that techno-industrial development also supports these risks (see Table 1). He states that the dimensions of these uncertainties and dangers seen in the risk society cannot be predicted, and in this case, the past loses its power to determine the future, and a fictional future expectation emerges. According to him, at this stage, forecasts are needed in the face of uncertainties and dangers for the future, and this leads to an increase in the need for experts. However, he states that specializing in risks will be possible through experience and that it seems quite difficult to generate ideas, make suggestions, or provide guidance in the face of dangers and risks that were not present and encountered for the first time. At this stage, Beck portrays a pessimistic and blurred future. According to him, the

Table 1:   Characteristic features of the risk society.

Traditional Society	Industrial Society	Risk Society
Incalculable threat: No knowledge of when the next catastrophe will come	Calculable risk	Incalculable risk: Uninsurable
Organizational logics: Local	Organizational logics: National	Organizational logics: Global
Limited specific threats	Temporally and spatially bound threats	Threats unbounded in time and space
Simple understanding of blame and causality	Complex understanding of blame and causality	Incomprehensible in standard terms of blame and causality
Prevailing beliefs anchored in tradition	First modernity: Faith in progress and reason	Reflexive modernity: All knowledge and practice called into question
Manufactured risks: Insignificant	Manufactured risks: Latent	Manufactured risks: Dominant
Paradigmatic risk: Natural catastrophe	Paradigmatic risk: Industrial accident	Paradigmatic risk: Radioactive leak
Subjectivity informed by hunger	Subjectivity informed by inequality	Subjectivity informed by fear

Source: Adapted from Beck, 1996 by Matthewman (2015, p. 74).

main purpose of those who say they are experts is to try to make the society accept risks (Beck, 1994, p. 9). Beck explains the greatest advantages of risks as "being easily legitimate since no one is an expert on this subject and cannot clearly give an idea of the consequences" (*Ibid.*, 1992, p. 34). According to Beck, risks that are in "acceptability" during the decision-making process are already accepted (*Ibid.*, 1999, p. 58). However, he states that it does not seem possible to predict whether the results will be positive or negative. According to Beck, risks do not tell what to do, but what not to do. (*Ibid.*, 1999, p. 141). Beck's particular emphasis is on the realization of risks based on preliminary decisions. Beck defines risks as packages that are opened by planning, knowing the consequences, and ignoring the dangers and side effects, and as formations that have all kinds of political, social, and institutional support (*Ibid.*, 1999, pp. 48–50).

The most distinctive difference between the risk society and the industrial society is seen as the emergence of risks in the risk society as a result of the decisions taken. It is accepted that external dangers and threats are not as effective as individual decisions in the formation of risks. This process is considered an incomplete learning process. According to Beck, in this process, in which old methods are invalid, new institutions are needed to be trusted in the face of risks, risks increased dependence on experts, and one of the most prominent features of the risk society is uncertainty and unpredictability (Beck, 1992, p. 34; 1994, p. 9).

According to Beck, the age we live in is not a nation-state modernity. According to him, globalization is also an ongoing and irreversible process just like modernization. Emphasizing that the impact area of risks is expanded in this process, Beck states that the risk society has transformed into a "world risk society". According to him, it does not seem possible to exclude risks at this stage. In the period from the beginning of the 17th and 18th century industrial modernity, which is regarded as the first stage of modernity, to the early 20th century, the risk was seen as a way of measuring unpredictable results. Beck stated that in the age we live in, nature is industrialized and new uncertainties emerge. According to him, efforts to control risks turn into uncertainties and dangers. It is acknowledged that it is difficult to find an institution that specializes in the effects of risks and makes decisions. Beck points out that denying risks in such a situation will cause them to grow in an immeasurable and uncontrollable way.

One of the most prominent features of the risk society is the distribution and sharing of risks. Western societies continue to see their own social processes as a common destiny for other world societies. Beck points out that while wealth distribution adheres to class patterns, risk distribution does not differentiate between rich and poor. This is also a sign that the distinction between the world's wealthy, prosperous countries and other societies has disappeared. Beck points out that the "invisible side effects", previously legitimized, are suddenly "visible". According to him, those who produce risks and try to benefit from them are somehow caught in this cycle of dangers even if they take risks away from them. Beck points out that risks will sooner or later return to those who produce them and benefit from them with a boomerang effect (Beck, 1992).

Another determination of Beck is that as the risk society develops, the hostile relationship between those affected by risk and those who benefit from it increases. He gave the example, in this regard, of those who first cause people to get sick for various reasons and then try to treat them with medication. According to him, atomic, chemical, and genetic technologies, which were sources of wealth, have become a concern today. Beck states that being affected by risks is different from being affected by class situations. According to him, unemployment due to job loss is an obvious phenomenon for everyone, there is no need for measurements, whereas the situation of people who encounter toxic additives in food cannot be predicted with consciousness and experience. According to him, risks are man-made mixtures, a combination of politics, morality, mathematics, technology, cultural definitions, assumptions, and risk society is also a mixed society (Beck, 1999, p. 146), and the world risk society will become a conscious society when it begins to understand itself. Believing that in a situation where everything is in danger, all decisions should be re-examined, rethought, and reconsidered, Beck argues that this will happen with the transformation of society into a self-critical form.

Stating that risk society emerges as a result of common decisions, Beck explains the conditions of the occurrence of risks with the concept of "produced uncertainties". He explains this in two ways: according to him, excess information can be the source of new risks, which depends on who has the information and how it is used. On the contrary, risks can also occur as a result of unconsciousness. Not knowing enough to participate in the decision process or making wrong decisions due to unconsciousness and ignorance leads to "produced uncertainties". Beck emphasizes that too much information, unconsciousness, and ignorance can lead to risk formation in various ways.

Beck criticizes the insistence of scientists that analyses are done innocently in the face of the visible landscape. According to him, behind this logic lies the desire of scientists to keep their careers and monetary success high by asserting that the risks are at an "acceptable" level. Beck calls this "being intoxicated to the tolerable extent" (Beck, 1992, p. 65). In Beck's opinion, while chemical products that are first tested on animals, they will now have to be tested on humans to see their real effects, and this circumstance will turn the society into a laboratory and the world into a test tube (*Ibid.*, 1995, p. 8).

Defending the need to review the relationship between nature and society in the century we live in, Beck believes that nature cannot be understood apart from society and society cannot be understood outside of nature. According to Beck, who thinks that risks are a threat not only to humans but also to nature and all other living creatures in nature, "environmental problems are not only problems that concern us and our environment, they are completely social problems. The person who continues to say that nature is out of society is speaking from another century that no longer concerns our reality" (Beck, 1992, p. 81). Questioning the definition of "nature" in the age we live in, Beck defines humans as the ruler, director, and in a harmful relationship with nature. He emphasizes that human beings are also a part of nature and asks "Where does nature begin?" (*Ibid.*, 1995, p. 37). He frequently emphasizes the view that people lead completely far from being natural in nature and that nature turns into an unnatural artificiality. According to Beck, in the relationship between society and nature, human beings started to dominate nature and the natural balance is disrupted; this dominance causes the socialization of nature. According to Beck, the source of the risks that threaten nature is the "inappropriate" policies that science and technology stated.

Beck emphasizes that if the choices made are not reviewed, the consequences are not considered, and if they are not analyzed with a conscious and logical view, the limits of great dangers will be encountered. In another definition, Beck says that self-reflecting modernization is confronting the consequences of risk society. With these definitions, Beck states that negativities can be prevented by reviewing, questioning, and making decisions in the face of threats and dangers seen in the risk society. According to Beck, the process he defines as the second modernity should be regarded as a second chance and a new option for people. Making judicious, rational, and logical decisions that prioritize reason, logic, questioning and criticism, and implementing these decisions constitute the basic skeleton of Beck's self-thinking modernization theory. Beck defines this formation as a "double modernization". According to him, the important thing is to learn the necessary lessons from the mistakes made in previous modernities and to carry the modernity process to a conscious stage (Beck, 1992, 1999).

According to him, with the concept of risk society, new and different formations and forms of production that were not seen in previous periods have emerged. He defines these formations as nuclear and chemical giant technology, genetic research, environmental threat, extreme militarization, and impoverished societies. Beck underlines the necessity for everyone to have a questioning, awareness, and control mechanism against these formations, which he sees as side effects of modernization. The dimensions of the risks, threats, and dangers, which he said to emerge with the risk society, are much larger than they are in the industrial society, and they are no longer innocent. Beck says that these dangers cannot be perceived by the senses and cannot be determined by science. Beck defines the world risk society as "a threatening future caused by the uncertainties produced by the lack of control, knowledge and unconsciousness, knowledge and its consequences, the dilemma between nature and culture, and a man-made mixture world" (Beck, 1999, p. 147). In the age we live in, risk includes more and more future-oriented dangers that will affect the future. In previous ages, risks were thought to be due to coincidence. There are differences between the concept of risk in traditional societies and the concept of risk in the modernization and industrialization process (*Ibid.*, 1992, p. 33). Risk is also a map that controls the future. Risk is also in a position to control the future by foreseeing the consequences of human movements and radicalized modernization (*Ibid.*, 1992, p. 3).

3. Conclusion

According to Beck, risks are unpredictable, so it is difficult to take action against them (Beck, 1992, p. 21). At the most advanced stage of modernization, uncertainty and uncontrollability problems arose. The emerging risks indicate the don'ts but what should be done remains unclear. This uncertainty and unpredictability affect all levels: national, local, class, individual, etc. The unpredictable and unrecognizable risks reveal the concept of "uninsurability". Medical precautions have become difficult. Atomic hazards and nuclear accidents cannot be covered by insurance as they were not included in the previous definition of "accident" (*Ibid.*, p. 21). Today, the distribution of risk and distribution of wealth is different. Risks go beyond the boundaries of all classes and countries, affecting both the rich and the poor. Just like a boomerang, risks return to those who created them, who profited from them (*Ibid.*, p. 22). There are many who lose because of the risks as well as those who win because of them. With the lack of authority and control, risks pose a potential danger (*Ibid.*, p. 23) Risks arise in a specific geographic area but become universal by spreading all over the world. Risks spread in complex ways that spread unpredictably (Pesticides, breast milk, baby, …) (*Ibid.*, p. 27). Risks arising in the risk society increase dependence on experts (*Ibid.*, p. 30). On the other hand, there is no expert on risks. Risks can only be learned through experimentation. Since there is no expert, risk can be easily justified and therefore becomes a danger (*Ibid.*, 1992, p. 28). Today, destroyed forest lands, polluted groundwater, and seas, toxic accidents are the visible side effects of the risks. Radiation, toxic waste, and nuclear activities are unseen side effects that Beck refers to as the "shadow kingdom" (*Ibid.*, p. 55).

Beck's risk society theory offers a functional perspective in which very accurate sociological theses are put forward in terms of containing the basic concepts that reside at the center of the phenomenon and many discussions that occupy the agenda of the countries and societies of the world, which as of today, are faced with the global epidemic threat.

References

Beck, U. (1992). *Risk Society: Towards a New Modernity*, London: Sage Publications.

Beck, U. (1994). *Reflexive Modernization*, Cambridge: Polity Press.

Beck, U. (1995). *Ecological Politics in an Age of Risk*, Cambridge: Polity Press.

Beck, U. (1996). Risk society and the provident state. In S. Lash, B. Szerszynski & B. Wynne (Eds.), *Risk, Environment, Modernity: Towards a New Ecology*, pp. 27–43. London: Sage.

Beck, U. (1999). *World Risk Society*, Cambridge: Polity Press.

Matthewman, S. (2015). Disasters, risks and revelation: Making sense of our times, Palgrave, Macmillan. DOI:10.1057/9781137294265.

Chapter 4

The Impacts of the Pandemic Crisis on International Politics

Luis TOMÉ*

*Director of the International Relations Department,
Autónoma University of Lisbon, Lisbon, Portugal*

ltome@autonoma.pt

Abstract

The purpose of this chapter is to examine the main impact of COVID-19 on international politics about a year after it was declared a pandemic. Our main argument is that this pandemic crisis underlined and accelerated trends that already existed while triggering dynamics that may redefine world geopolitics and international order. The essay follows a demonstrative analytical model, being also based on an "eclectic approach" and a multidisciplinary perspective that crisscrosses the areas of international relations, geopolitics, and security studies. In line with the central purpose and argument of this chapter, the text is structured into eight major topics. In the first, we analyse the performance of countries in managing the pandemic, trying to understand if there is an association with the level of wealth and the type of political regime. In the second, the impact of COVID-19 on the nationalism vs. internationalism

---

*Where he also coordinates the Ph.D. in International Relations: Geopolitics and Geoeconomics. Director of the research unit OBSERVARE-Observatory of Foreign Relations.

and multilateralism equation is examined, and in the third we reflect on its impact on *hyperglobalization*. In the three parts that follow, we look at the stance of China and the US in the context of the pandemic, then analyzing its effects on the whole of the "West". In the next topic, we try to explain the impact of the pandemic crisis on the world power structure and on the pattern of interactions between the main international actors. The eighth and final topic reflects on the effects of this pandemic on the international order.

1. Introduction

The world was already facing serious problems before the COVID-19 pandemic arose, as attested by the wide-ranging speech United Nations (UN) Secretary-General António Guterres made to the General Assembly on January 22, 2020 — the UN's 75th anniversary year — referring to what he called the *four horsemen* that "can jeopardize every aspect of our shared future: epic geopolitical tensions, climate crisis, global mistrust and the downsides of technology" (Guterres, 2020). No reference was made, then, to the new coronavirus that had emerged in China in late 2019. In early 2020, neither the UN SG (Secretary General) nor anyone else could predict the brutal impact COVID-19 would have. On January 30, 2020, the World Health Organization (WHO) declared the COVID-19 outbreak a Public Health Emergency of International Concern, the WHO's highest level of alarm. On March 11, 2020, the WHO's Director-General Tedros Adhanom Ghebreyesus declared, for the first time, a pandemic due to a coronavirus, the "severe acute respiratory syndrome coronavirus 2" (SARS-CoV-2) or COVID-19. It is true that the world had faced other pandemics before but none so widespread as this one. The virus spread rapidly by taking advantage of globalization and interconnectedness, virtually affecting all peoples, states, and regions of the world. In addition to the huge human tragedy, which in just over a year already accounts for around 2.5 million dead and 110 million infected (numbers continue to increase every day and certainly for many months to come), there is the devastating economic, social, and political effects. Governments and societies, almost without exception, face tremendous public health challenges, economic, and employment difficulties, security issues, and social and political instability. In other words, in a world that was already volatile and problematic, the COVID-19 pandemic added a crisis with dramatic impacts across the globe.

The concept of "crisis" has a wide variety of meanings and is used in most fields — from medicine (from where the term originates) to international relations, economics, and public administration. In social relations, "crisis" always means "disorder" or alteration of the existing order and therefore uncertainty: "a time of great danger, difficulty, or confusion" (Oxford Learner's Dictionaries); "a situation which is not normal or stable … an urgent situation that suddenly happens and breaks the routine processes of any system" (Işyar, 2008, p. 2); "crises are defined by threat, uncertainty, and time pressure" (Lipscy, 2020, p. E98). On the other hand, "crisis" has entered the theoretical–conceptual framework of international relations first as a situation where there is no war but there is no peace either (no war no peace) between states — the so-called "international crisis" — evolving and then expanding the concept regarding "crisis management" (in pre-conflict, conflict, or post-conflict situations between and within states) and also to refer to "global crisis" (such as the 2008–2010 financial crisis or the climate change crisis). This last notion of "global crisis" is the one that best characterizes the situation caused by COVID-19 as it describes something that happens in all parts of the world and affects all parts of the world. Inevitably, major crises have major consequences, usually unforeseen. As we are in the midst of a global pandemic crisis and much can still happen or be changed, it is premature to draw definitive conclusions about all its consequences. And it is very likely that, as John Allen (2020) put it, "The History of COVID-19 Will Be Written by the Victors". Still, about a year after the pandemic was declared, it is possible to identify multiple impacts of COVID-19.

As such, the objective of this chapter is to examine the main impacts of the pandemic crisis on international politics. Our main argument is that COVID-19 pandemic underlined and accelerated trends that already existed, while triggering dynamics that may redefine world geopolitics and international order. The essay follows a demonstrative analytical model, being also based on an "eclectic approach" and a multidisciplinary perspective that crisscrosses the areas of international relations, geopolitics, and security studies (see on this Tomé (2016)). At a theoretical level, we prefer the referential framework of chaos and complexity theories (see, e.g., Erçetin & Açıkalın, 2020) for two fundamental reasons. First, because "chaos" is one of the meanings closest to the concept of "crisis". In fact, pre-crisis, crisis, and post-crisis periods are generally considered chaotic processes once the situation expresses a nonlinear developing process. Second, at the core of the contribution of chaos and complexity theories lies the notion of "complex adaptive systems" (CAS), emphasizing the ideas of unpredictability and adaptation, thus also contradicting the sense of linearity. It is worth remembering the main characteristics of CAS: numerous independent and interdependent agents/actors, infinite interaction/feedback systems within units/actors, emergence, self-organization, and coevolution and coadaptation. As we have argued in other works (e.g., Tomé, 2016; Tomé & Açıkalın, 2019), these characteristics coincide with those of the international system, which in reality, is not only a complex system but an adaptive one. Moreover, change is something inherent to the international CAS, alongside a certain notion of order — change and order are indeed the two sides of the same coin. Thus, the complex adaptive international system should be understood with regard to these change and order approaches.

In line with the central purpose and argument of this chapter, the text is structured into eight major topics. In the first, we analyse the performance of countries in managing the pandemic, trying to understand if there is an association with the level of wealth and the type of political regime. In the second, the impact of COVID-19 on the nationalism vs. internationalism and multilateralism equation is examined, and in the third we reflect on its impact on *hyperglobalization*. In the three parts that follow, we look at the stance of China and the US in the context of the pandemic, then analyzing its effects on the whole of the "West". In the next topic, we try to explain the impact of the pandemic crisis on the world power structure and on the pattern of interactions between the main international actors. The eighth and final topic reflects on the effects of this pandemic on the international order. In the final remarks, we will present a summary of our conclusions and arguments about the visible impacts of COVID-19 on international politics about a year after it was declared a pandemic.

2. Better or Worse Performance Is Not the Result of the Development Level nor of the Political Regime

Over the past year, governments and societies have been turning inwards to fight COVID-19, exposing vulnerabilities and hard political choices. The pandemic crisis has also given rise to many distinct narratives and counter-narratives about what kind of states and political regimes are inherently better suited to fight COVID-19. Data on the number of infected and dead and testing capacity (see WHO, *COVID-19 situation report*) reveal substantial differences between countries and regions in terms of pandemic management. Although the coronavirus outbreak started in China, Asia-Pacific countries, in general, have been more successful in containing the pandemic. On the contrary, in Europe and North America, the results are truly tragic. Many countries in the Middle East and Africa have managed to halt the progress of the pandemic with robust preventive measures, unlike Central and South America, where the situation is generally bad. On the other hand, unsurprisingly, the "Corruption Perceptions Index" shows that corruption undermines the global health response to COVID-19; corruption and emergencies feed off each other, creating a vicious cycle of mismanaged deepening crisis; corruption undermines an equitable response to COVID-19, and corruption diverts funds from essential services, such as healthcare, leaving countries around the world vulnerable and under-prepared to deal with public health crises (Transparency International, 2021).

However, and much more relevant, the data show that the best or worst performance in facing the COVID-19 pandemic is not associated with either the level of development or the type of political regime. For example, in the *Worldometers.info* ranking of 220 countries and territories, the ten worst are, in that order, the US, India, Brazil, Russia, UK, France, Spain, Italy, Turkey, and Germany. Likewise, in a ranking of almost 100 countries, established based on six criteria — confirmed cases, confirmed deaths, confirmed cases per million people, confirmed deaths per million people, confirmed cases as a proportion of tests, and tests per thousand people — the Australian think tank Lowy Institute (2021) places in the top ten New Zealand (with the best performance), Vietnam, Taiwan, Thailand, Cyprus, Rwanda, Iceland, Australia, Latvia, and Sri Lanka; at the bottom of the table stand Brazil (the worst), Mexico, Colombia, Iran, US, Bolivia, Panama, Oman, Ukraine, Chile, and Guatemala (China was not included in this ranking due to a lack of publicly available data on testing). Although these rankings are always debatable and may change with the evolution of the situation, it is clear that, in general, the richest countries — which have, therefore, greater and better resources — have not been more effective in combating the pandemic than the poorest or developing countries: "Richer countries were quickly overwhelmed when the virus first emerged. International air travel accelerated virus transmission from abroad in these countries. By contrast, many governments in developing countries had more lead time — and often a greater sense of urgency — to put in place preventative measures after the scale and severity of the global crisis became known. The relatively "low-tech" nature of the health measures used to mitigate the spread of the virus to date, including large-scale lockdowns, may have created a more level playing field between developed and developing countries in the management of COVID-19" (Lowy Institute, 2021). Still, as we entered the vaccination phase against COVID-19 at the end of 2020, the difference in wealth and unequal access to the first vaccines gave a decisive advantage to the richest countries, suggesting that the poorest countries will be facing the pandemic longer. On the other hand, the data demonstrate that success/failure in responding to the pandemic is not a matter of political regime: some democracies perform well but others have truly catastrophic results; and the same is true regarding autocracies and hybrid regimes.

The COVID-19 pandemic has triggered a number of exceptional legal/constitutional responses from governments of all types as they seek extraordinary measures to manage the threat. And "despite initial differences, the performance of all regime types in managing the coronavirus converged over time … The tools to contain the spread of COVID-19 — stay-at-home orders, lockdowns, and border closures — have been common to most countries" (Lowy Institute, 2021). However, the way how governments convinced or compelled their citizens to adhere to these measures often reflected the nature of their political systems. Therefore, unsurprisingly, COVID-19 has served as a pretext for autocratic regimes to accentuate repression and oppression over populations: "repressive governments used the pandemic as an opportunity to introduce or implement additional restrictions on civic freedoms" (CIVICUS Monitor, 2020). According to this CIVICUS research tool, whose information was obtained through collaboration with more than 20 civil society research partners, the top global violations in 2020 include detainment, harassment, censorship, and intimidation of protestors, attack on journalists, protest disruption, restrictive laws, excessive force, and the imprisonment of human rights defenders (*Ibid.*).

However, while safeguarding the necessary differences, democratic societies also experienced restrictions and violations of civil liberties and rights in the context of a worldwide pandemic, as denounced by CIVICUS and many organizations and reports. For example, in its "Global State of Democracy Report", while recognizing and praising cases where it was possible to effectively fight the pandemic while preserving democratic rights and freedoms, the *International IDEA* (2020) reveals that almost half of democracies have implemented restrictions that were illegal, disproportionate, or unnecessary under the guise of the pandemic and that 43% of democracies have applied measures to combat the health crisis that have undermined essential political and civic values, such as freedom of expression, movement, and assembly. Along the same lines, "Almost 70% of countries covered by The Economist Intelligence Unit's Democracy Index recorded a decline in their overall score, as country after country locked down to protect lives from a novel coronavirus. The global average score fell to its lowest level since the index began in 2006" (EIU, 2021). This "Democracy Index 2020" also states that "Global Democracy has a very bad year. The pandemic caused an unprecedented rollback of democratic freedoms in 2020", adding that "No country in Western Europe recorded an increase in its overall civil liberties score, while Eastern Europe's regression means the region has deteriorated most since the report was first established" (*Ibid.*).

3. More Nationalism, Less Multilateralism and Internationalism ... But Also Some Positive Developments

The data shows that national populist leaders like Trump in the US, Modi in India, Bolsonaro in Brazil, Obrador in Mexico, Putin in Russia, Erdogan in Turkey, or Duterte in the Philippines have seriously failed to fight the COVID-19 pandemic. Despite this failure, nationalist, populist, and protectionist movements, as well as attacks on the liberal international order, seek to exploit the pandemic crisis to promote their agendas. Of course, the virus of populism and nationalism also tends to take advantage of the economic and social crisis associated with the pandemic. Nationalism, isolationism, xenophobia, and attacks on the liberal world order have been growing for years, and this trend has been accelerated by the pandemic. But more than that, most governments and political leaders, regardless of their democratic/autocratic/hybrid character and respective ideological orientation, faced the pandemic crisis by overstressing the rhetoric of "national interest" and adopting a stance of "national selfishness" of "us first". In the face of the greatest emergency since World War II, most countries returned to a very limited self-interest.

The problem is not that governments defend the national interest (it would be strange if they did not!), but how they define and promote that interest. As stated by J. Nye (2020), "Every country puts its national interest first; the important question is how broadly or narrowly this interest is defined. COVID-19 shows we are failing to adjust our strategy to this new world". In general, instead of cooperating constructively for the common benefit, promoting collective and coordinated efforts in the face of a global crisis, countries turned to themselves, sought essentially "national" responses, spoke against each other, fostered "protectionism", revalued "national borders" as a protection mechanism and often turned rival countries into scapegoats for their own mistakes. This stance has been noticeable at all times and levels, including in the initial race to ventilators and protective materials, followed by the creation of the first vaccine, and more recently, by the acquisition of vaccines — in many ways like the classic "arms race". If the rise of nationalism in the context of a pandemic is consolidated, this will favor the possibility of international and domestic conflicts: "Leaders may see fights with foreigners as useful domestic political distractions, or they may be tempted by the weakness or preoccupation of their opponents and take advantage of the pandemic to destabilize favourite targets or create new facts on the ground" (Fukuyama, 2020). Still, as acknowledged by Fukuyama, "given the continued stabilizing force of nuclear weapons and the common challenges facing all major players, international turbulence is less likely than domestic turbulence" (*Ibid.*).

The national egoisms highlighted in the context of a pandemic crisis also fuel another earlier trend: the weakening of multilateralism and internationalism. The coronavirus pandemic has thrown a harsh spotlight on the state of global governance. The attacks on the World Health Organization (WHO) are the best example of this — including the withdrawal of the United States from the organization by the Trump Administration, meanwhile corrected by the new White House tenant, Joe Biden — in a context that would precisely advise international cooperation and support to the main international institution with responsibilities for the coordination and global management of the pandemic. In addition, many other international institutions were, as it were, paralyzed by the "self-lockdown" of their member states, caught up in the "national" management of the pandemic, as if multilateral organizations had no relevance in terms of global health, regulation of the protection goods market, or any other of the many matters that link national, regional, and global interests.

Similarly, looking essentially at themselves, countries seemed to look at "others" only through the prism of statistical comparisons of the pandemic situation, "forgetting" the many other issues that require international attention and cooperation. Despite persistent calls from voices such as those of the UN's SG António Guterres or Pope Francis, the COVID-19 pandemic made countries "forget" practically everything else, ranging from the climate crisis to the countless violent conflicts that went on — in Eastern Ukraine, Afghanistan, Libya, Syria, Yemen, DR Congo, or South Sudan — the protection of refugees, alleviation of extreme poverty and hunger, or aid to the populations most in need of international emergency aid. Similarly, national selfishness and the absence of international solidarity persist in the distribution of vaccines against COVID-19, leaving the poorest countries and peoples behind. According to *The Economist Intelligence Unit*, "Rich countries will get access to coronavirus vaccines earlier than others … the rollout in middle-income and emerging countries will take much longer; we do not expect it to take place at a game-changing scale before 2022. The picture appears even bleaker for low-income countries; we do not expect most of these states to have wide access to a vaccine before 2022-23" (EIU, 2020). This situation led WHO's DG (Director General) Tedros Adhanom Ghebreyesus to say that the world faces a "catastrophic moral failure" because of unequal COVID vaccine policies (cit. in BBC, 2021).

Fortunately, in the context of a pandemic crisis, there are countless actions of solidarity and human generosity in all societies and all over the world. We fully subscribe to the words of Nicholas Burns (2020): "In every country, however, there are many examples of the power of the human spirit — of doctors, nurses, political leaders, and ordinary citizens demonstrating resilience, effectiveness, and leadership. That provides hope that men and women around the world can prevail in response to this extraordinary challenge". Still, there are other very positive developments to note. From the outset, unlike most governments, international cooperation between medical and scientific communities in different countries was extraordinary, namely regarding sharing data and knowledge about the new coronavirus, and in the search for anti-COVID-19 treatment and vaccines. It was this transnational scientific cooperation that made it possible to know the particular characteristics of this coronavirus and its successive mutations and variants, to share experiences and treatment techniques, to provide advisories backed by scientific evidence to policymakers, or to produce vaccines in record time — vaccines that used to take 10–20 years to create but which, in this case, took just 8–10 months in the case of the first ones. In addition, transnational scientific research is producing valuable advances in vaccine research, as multinational and multidisciplinary teams gain knowledge about the virus and achieve good results from different angles. Strangely, some political leaders disregarded science and scientists' recommendations for their own reasons. Were it not for this international cooperation, or if doctors and scientists had the same stance as some political leaders, COVID-19 would certainly cause many more deaths and infections for a much longer time, prolonging the climate of chaos and other crises directly related to the pandemic.

The COVAX initiative is another significant development. It results from an extraordinary and unique global collaboration, with more than two-thirds of the world engaged. COVAX is one of the three pillars of the "Access to COVID-19 Tools Accelerator", which was launched in April 2020 by the WHO and the European Commission in response to this pandemic — bringing together governments, global health organizations, manufacturers, scientists, private sector, civil society, and philanthropists. Its aim is to accelerate the development and manufacture of COVID-19 vaccines and to guarantee fair and equitable access to every country in the world. It is the only truly global solution to this pandemic because it is the only effort to ensure that people in all corners of the world will get access to COVID-19 vaccines once they are available, regardless of their wealth. Coordinated by GAVI, the Vaccine Alliance, the Coalition for Epidemic Preparedness Innovations (CEPI), and the WHO, COVAX is trying to achieve this by acting as a platform that supports the research, development, and manufacturing of a wide range of COVID-19 vaccine candidates and negotiating their pricing. All participating countries, regardless of income levels, are supposed to have equal access to the approved vaccines. COVAX has the world's largest and most diverse portfolio of COVID-19 vaccines, and as such, represents the world's best hope of bringing the acute phase of this pandemic to a swift end (see GAVI website and the WHO website: COVAX). It is a pity that national selfishness and "vaccine nationalism" have not yet allowed to take advantage of the full potential of partnerships such as the Vaccine Alliance or to achieve the objectives of initiatives such as COVAX. Anyway, let us hope that G. John Ikenberry (2020) is right when he said, at the beginning of the pandemic, "it is hard to see anything other than a reinforcement of the movement toward nationalism, great-power rivalry, strategic decoupling, and the like ... but over the longer term, the democracies will come out of their shells to find a new type of pragmatic and protective internationalism".

4. Questioning Hyperglobalization, Stressing Asia-Pacific's Economic Centrality, and a More China-Centric Globalization

The emergence of the pandemic made *hyperglobalization* questionable for two main reasons, favoring several instrumentalizations. First, the easy and intense movement of people contributed to the speed with which the pandemic spread from country to country and from region to region. Hence the impetus for many governments to ban international travel and close borders. Unfortunately, the same reason was used by many nationalist, populist, supremacist, racist, and xenophobic leaders and movements to promote their agendas and instigate "fear" or even "hatred" against "others", namely foreigners, immigrants, and refugees. The second reason is the vulnerability of the overwhelming majority of countries to the dependence on certain international production and supply chains — initially, those healthcare materials that are urgently needed, from masks to ventilators, and more recently, vaccines. COVID-19 also questioned the basic tenets of global manufacturing: factory closings in afflicted areas have left other manufacturers,as well as hospitals, pharmacies, supermarkets, and retail stores, bereft of inventories and products. Companies started rethinking and shrinking the multistep, multicountry supply chains that dominated production until now. And faced with difficulties in the supply of medical equipment and protective materials, many governments and countries claimed to have "strategic reserves" so as not to depend (at least, not so much) on external supply, seeking to have a certain level of national production and diversify their suppliers. This situation was also exploited by political leaders and movements with different motivations, from the traditional antagonists of globalization and economic liberalism to new protectionisms and nationalisms. But it was not just that because many "liberal" and "internationalist" observers also took COVID-19 as the death certificate of *hyperglobalization*. For example, in a special edition of the *Foreign Policy* journal, when asked about "How the World Will Look After the Coronavirus Pandemic", Stephen M. Walt predicted "A World Less Open, Prosperous, and Free" and that "We will see a further retreat from hyperglobalization"; also Robin Niblett anticipated "The End of Globalization as We Know It", adding that "The coronavirus pandemic could be the straw that breaks the camel's back of economic globalization"; and Laurie Garrett sees "a dramatic new stage in global capitalism, in which supply chains are brought closer to home" (Foreign Policy, 2020).

It is not possible to guess, at this point, the final result of the pandemic crisis on such *hyperglobalization*, nor what differences there will be between before and after COVID-19. However, after more than a year of living with this coronavirus, the trend is not to reverse globalization, much less its end. It is likely that there will be some adjustments: "more companies will demand to know more about where their supplies come from and will trade off efficiency for redundancy. Governments will intervene as well, forcing what they consider strategic industries to have domestic backup plan and reserves" (O'Neil, 2020). But adjustments in the production and distribution chains are normal and natural in a globalized market economy and have been happening for a long time due to several factors. And just as the financial crisis of 2008–2010 led to adjustments, but not to an end or to a reversal of globalization, there is no added reason to assume that the pandemic crisis will do so. In addition, criticism and attacks on globalization, economic liberalism, free trade, and global production and distribution chains existed long before the pandemic crisis and will certainly continue later.

On the other hand, the advantages of economic globalization far outweigh its disadvantages (as exemplified by the escape from poverty of hundreds of millions of Chinese and Indians and the economic development of these two Asian giants since they internationalized their economies), and most of the main international actors remain interested in maintaining and promoting their essential foundations. No free trade or investment agreements were cancelled or denounced during the pandemic crisis. On the contrary, some quite significant ones have been concluded after long years of negotiations, such as the "Regional Comprehensive Economic Partnership" (RCEP) between 15 countries in Asia Pacific and the "Comprehensive Agreement on Investment" (CAI) between China and the 27 EU member states. In the meantime, Trump's former US isolationist and protectionist policy has also been reversed by the new American administration: "we can build better global preparedness to counter COVID-19, as well as detect and prevent future pandemics…

When we invest in the economic development of countries, we create new markets for our products and reduce the likelihood of instability, violence, and mass migrations. When we strengthen health systems in far regions of the world, we reduce the risk of future pandemics that can threaten our people and our economy" (Biden, 2021b). In addition, there is the obvious finding that globalization is crucial to producing and distributing goods and medical equipment and vaccines essential to combat COVID-19, as well as for the necessary economic recovery.

In other words, everything points to *hyperglobalization* surviving the pandemic crisis, although with adjustments and some differentiating aspects compared to the previous configuration. Still, what the pandemic crisis has also revealed is that globalization needs more and better governance and regulation to be more just — a decisive aspect both to correct certain distortions and inequalities between the main economies of the world, and above all, to mitigate the terrible effects that the dual pandemic and economic crisis have, and will continue to have for a long time, on the poorest and most vulnerable.

The differentiating aspects — and also trends underlined by the pandemic crisis — include accentuating the Asia-Pacific economic centrality and a slightly more China-centric globalization. As we pointed out earlier, Asia Pacific as a whole is performing much better in managing the pandemic than Europe, the Americas, or any other macro-region in the world. Now, the same is true of the economic crisis associated with it. The shift of the global economic centrality from the North Atlantic to Asia Pacific is something that had occurred earlier. Take, for example, the evolution of GDP based on the purchase power parity (PPP) world share: In 1990, North America had a share of 26.6%, Western Europe of 26.2% (added together they represented a world share of 52.8%), and Asia Pacific had a share of 27.37%; in 2010, these shares were 20.41%, 17.23% (37.64% joint share) and 38.35%, respectively; and in 2021, the IMF estimates a share of 18.99% for North America, 15.36% for Western Europe (34.35% joint share) and 45.31% for Asia Pacific (IMF Datamapper). This systemic change seems to have been accentuated by the pandemic crisis: In 2020, Asia Pacific had a drop in the real GDP of "just" −2.3%, while Europe fell −7.2%, the EU −7.6%, the American continent −5.6%, and North America −4.9%. Economic recovery will also be faster in Asia Pacific which, according to IMF estimates, will have a real GDP growth of 6.7% in 2021, while Europe's will be 4.7%, the EU's 5%, and both all Americas and North America 3.3%. In 2022, the trend is the same, with

Asia Pacific having a real GDP growth of 5.4%, Europe 3.1%, the EU 3.3%, the Americas 2.9%, and North America also 2.9% (*Ibid.*).

Likewise, thanks to a very sharp and continuous growth, China's share in the world's GDP in purchase power parity (PPP) jumped from 2.27% in 1980 to 18.56% in 2020 — surpassing the US, whose share in the same period decreased from 21.41% to 15.41% (*Ibid.*). China may soon have the world's largest real/nominal GDP, which seems to be accelerated by the pandemic crisis: according to the IMF, China will be the only major economy to have a real GDP growth in 2020 (about 1.9%), while the US and the Eurozone will have very negative variations (−4.3% and −8.3%, respectively); and in 2021, the Chinese economy will recover more quickly with a real GDP growth of 8.2%, compared to only 3.1% in the US and 5.2% in the Eurozone (IMF Datamapper). Under these conditions, it will be very difficult for other major players to opt for "decoupling" strategies *vis-à-vis* China. Two examples, in particular, confirm this, in the context of a pandemic: on 15 November 2020, the ten ASEAN countries, Japan, South Korea, Australia, and New Zealand signed the *Regional Comprehensive Economic Partnership* (RCEP) with China, negotiated for a decade and establishing the largest free trade area in the world; and on 30 December 2020, the EU and China agreed to the terms of the "Comprehensive Agreement on Investment" (CAI) that had been negotiated for seven years. It is therefore very likely that Kishore Mahbubani's prediction (2020) will be confirmed: "The COVID-19 pandemic will not fundamentally alter global economic directions. It will only accelerate a change that had already begun: a move away from U.S.-centric globalization to a more China-centric globalization". Inevitably, this situation will reflect on all other dimensions of power and on global geopolitical balances.

The pandemic and economic "double crisis" could also have important repercussions in strategic terms, although the trends are ambivalent. More than ever, pandemics have come to be seen as a matter of "national security" by virtually all countries, which can favor the strengthening of budgets in the areas of security and defense. At the same time, however, the increase in health budgets and the necessary additional resources, both to mitigate the effects of the serious economic and social situation and to launch the recovery of economies, may compromise or compel to readjust certain programs, investments, and budgets previously foreseen in the fields of security and defense. Likewise, depending on the scale and duration of the economic crisis and the speed of recovery, some states will be in a better position than others, or will be able to do it sooner, to strengthen their military capabilities and/or invest in "dual-use" equipment and technologies. As it is, this type of readjustment may imply significant changes in the strategic balances between powers and in certain regions, as well as question certain previous commitments (as in NATO, in which by 2024 all member states should reach a minimum of 2% of GDP on total defense spending, and at least 20% of annual defense expenditure on major new equipment, which is very difficult to achieve by most European allies), with unpredictable consequences.

5. Confirming China's Growing Assertiveness

As we have just shown, no country has benefited more than China from the post-"double Cold War" (USSR–US and China–USSR) order. China's resurgence is one of the most impactful forces of global geopolitics, and its evolution and interactions are increasingly determining for the world order. Chinese leaders see value in a stable order and economic globalization (see Xi, 2021). Within the framework of the proclaimed "Chinese dream", Beijing continues to assert that it has no hegemonic intentions; its foreign policy is based on the traditional "five principles of peaceful coexistence"; its strategy is one of "peaceful rise" and "win win", taking advantage of a "period of opportunity"; and its defense policy is purely "defensive" (China, PR 2019). The ideal international order for Beijing is one that favors the self-legitimation of the leading role of the Chinese Communist Party (CCP), facilitates China's continued economic growth, and helps the CCP to maintain "harmful" foreign influences at a distance, such as the liberal ideas of democracy, rule of law, and human rights. At the same time, China thinks and acts like a traditional great power, and Chinese leaders declare a "New Era": "China moving closer to centre stage ... new era of great power diplomacy with Chinese characteristics... take an active part in leading the reform of the global governance system ... a leading position in terms of economic and technological strength, defence capabilities, and composite national strength... crossed the threshold into a New Era" (Xi, 2017). Xi and the CCP believe that China, as a great power and civilization, is entitled to play a leading role in the world, and the Chinese communist regime is showing itself to be increasingly assertive in its claims. In recent years, four game-changing events have accelerated this incrementalist calculus: the advent of Xi

Jinping as China's paramount leader in 2012, the growth of China's "comprehensive national power", a perception of continued US decline, and the COVID-19 pandemic.

China has the inglorious burden of being the "womb" that spawned the new coronavirus and of not having prevented a global pandemic or sharing information as soon as it emerged. The Chinese regime's initial attempts to hide data and silence doctors were latter followed — with the implementation of strict restrictive measures and lockdowns — by the difficulties of the country (factory of the world) in supplying ventilators and protective materials to dozens of countries that began to be swept away by the pandemic. As a result, the CPP's "leading role" and China's international image were severely damaged. Meanwhile, Beijing began to control the pandemic, at the same time COVID-19 decimated other countries and regions, with emphasis on Europe and the US. As if in a "boomerang effect", the global expansion of COVID-19 started to be quickly and skilfully used by Beijing to try to position China as a reference and leader in the management of the pandemic: by promoting its own system, "lessons learned" and measures taken; by providing aid to other countries; and by resuming large-scale production and worldwide export of ventilators and protective materials crucial in the face of COVID-19.

More relevantly, in the midst of a pandemic crisis, China showed an unusual assertiveness, seeming to abandon both the principle of "keeping a low profile" associated with the "24-character strategy" since Deng Xiaoping and the traditional line of essentially non-confrontational "peaceful coexistence". Beijing used the distraction of the COVID-19 emergency both to increase surveillance and repression mechanisms against the Chinese population, notably against the Uighurs in Xinjiang and Hong Kong's freedom, and to expand operations against Taiwan and to engage in territorial disputes against its neighbors, pursuing intense international propaganda. For example, China intensified militarization in the South China Sea and the East China Sea. imposed a "National Security Law" on Hong Kong, had the first military deadly clash with India in a disputed Himalayan border area in 45 years, and was involved in successive diplomatic frictions and threats of sanctions with several countries, from the US to Australia, Canada, and the United Kingdom.

In the context of the COVID-19 pandemic, China has taken a "great leap forward" in realizing its ambitions. However, Beijing may be going too far and too fast, risking a real anti-China "front". Indeed, for many countries and political leaders, the pandemic crisis has underlined or contributed to changing the perspective about China, from a "benign giant panda" whose growth everyone can benefit from to the "threatening dragon" that the resurgent China also represents. Basically, Chinese assertiveness in a pandemic crisis can help to affirm China as an emerging superpower but also bring the inherent costs.

6. American Failure in the Face of COVID-19, the End of Trump's Presidency, and Further Questioning of US Leadership

Despite its immense power and impressive resources, the United States is one of the countries most affected by COVID-19, a direct result of its highly polarized society and President Trump's incompetence. Considering that his personal purposes would be better served by playing down the pandemic and discrediting scientists and by confrontation rather than national cohesion, President Trump's stance has aggravated the social and political divides in the US, preventing it from effectively combating COVID-19. The tragic performance of the US has multiple causes, but perhaps the most significant is Trump's abject leadership, which resulted in the largest public health emergency since the 1918 flu pandemic. In parallel, coronavirus has plunged a hitherto buoyant US economy into the worst depression since the Great Crash of 1929. COVID-19 hit the US in the midst of a campaign toward the November 2020 Presidential elections. Most likely, the tragic management of the pandemic crisis was one of the main reasons for Trump's defeat in these elections, which, by the way, took place when the country registered new highs of people infected and killed by COVID-19. As if that were not enough, Trump tried to stop his defeat/victory by Joe Biden–Kamala Harris by inventing "frauds" that were proven not to exist, encouraging the popular attack on the Capitol, and finally, plunging the US, the "land of Democracy", into an "uncivil war", as President Biden described it in his inauguration speech (Biden, 2021a). Trump left the White House through the "back door" and was the object of an unprecedented second impeachment process in the US, tainting the image of American democracy like never before.

The same incompetence of President Trump in the context of the pandemic crisis was manifested on the external front: COVID-19 evidenced the superpower's lack of will and/or ability to lead the world in a global crisis as well as to articulate with allies and partners in finding common solutions. At the same time, Trump attacked international institutions instead of galvanizing them — targeting, in particular, the WHO from which he withdrew the US. This stance — supported by many Republican Congressmen and Senators and by a large part of the American public opinion — may be due, in part, to a certain "hegemonic fatigue" or a cyclical isolationism of the US, but the protectionist and "Trump brand" nationalist populism is unquestionable, subverting and limiting collective and more concerted efforts in the face of the global pandemic crisis.

Anyway, the important question is that "The United States Has Failed the Leadership Test" (Schake, 2020). The US position had been questioned for years, but the failure in the face of COVID-19, Trump's turbulent departure from the presidency, and the inept American leadership in a global crisis all contribute to questioning it further. It is quite symptomatic, moreover, that when looking at "The New US Foreign Policy" in the Biden administration, the influential American journal *Foreign Affairs* (March/April 2021) published in the same special issue titles such as "Gone But Not Forgotten. Trump's Long Shadow and the End of American Credibility" (by Jonathan Kirshner); "Rogue Superpower. Why This Could Be an Illiberal American Century" (by Michael Beckley); "How Hegemony Ends. The Unravelling of American Power" (by Alexander Cooley and Daniel H. Nexon); "The End of American Illusion. Trump and the World as It Is" (by Nadia Schadlow); and "The Self-Destruction of American Power. Washington Squandered the Unipolar Moment" (by Fareed Zakaria).

It was in the context of a very serious pandemic crisis that the Biden–Harris administration began the Herculean task of trying to recover the United States, internally and externally. As a White House candidate, Joe Biden said that "The next U.S. President will have to address the world as it is in January 2021, and picking up the pieces will be an enormous task. He or she will have to salvage our reputation, rebuild confidence in our leadership, and mobilize our country and our allies to rapidly meet new challenges. There will be no time to lose" (Biden, 2020). And as soon as he started the Presidency, Biden launched a vigorous US "National Strategy for the COVID-19 Response and Pandemic Preparedness" and an "American Rescue Plan" to support and stimulate the recovery of the economy (including a US$1.9 trillion fiscal stimulus package), also reversing the American departure from the WHO and rejoining the Paris Climate Agreement. At the same time, President Biden announced that "America is back. Diplomacy is back at the center of our foreign policy…

we will repair our alliances and engage with the world once again, not to meet yesterday's challenges, but today's and tomorrow's ... We must meet the new moment of accelerating global challenges — from the pandemic to the climate crisis to nuclear proliferation — challenging the will only to be solved by nations working together and in common ... we can build better global preparedness to counter COVID-19, as well as detect and prevent future pandemics" (Biden, 2021b). But despite this predisposition and the many expectations toward the Biden administration, neither the United States nor the world are what they were before Trump or even before COVID-19. And among many other differences, three stand out: the lesser relative power of the US (namely in the face of the resurgence of China), the loss of credibility of the US, and the fragmentation of the "West" or of the "concert of democracies".

7. The Polarization of the "West"

The divergences between the US and many of its allies and partners that have been growing for years have dramatically worsened in the four years of the Trump presidency. The trade protectionism of the Trump "America First" not only attacked China, but also targeted Canada and Mexico (dismantling NAFTA and creating the new UMSCA), the EU, and Asia-Pacific allies and partners (including withdrawing the US from the TTIP negotiations with the EU and TPP with 11 other Asia-Pacific partners). Factors such as the "China factor" or the blackmail of the Trump administration about "burden sharing" became divisive in Washington's relations with its allies and partners. And the dissonance was such that traditional US allies and partners were often on the opposite side of Washington (and often on the same side of China and Russia) in matters such as free trade, protection of refugees, and regulation of migratory movements, Israeli–Palestinian conflict, fight against climate change, arms control, nuclear agreement with Iran, or many international conventions and organizations. Obviously, "This raises the question of whether a unitary 'West' still exists. Despite talk of shared values, it is unclear what those values are and to what extent they are shared" (Lo, 2020, p. 21). In a kind of "world in reverse", Trump's US has become the great antagonist of economic liberalism, multilateralism, and institutionalism, that is, the great disturber of the liberal international order.

These divergences, as well as distrust of the US leadership and credibility, have increased with the pandemic crisis. COVID-19 was a pretext for Trump to promote his nationalist and protectionist agenda "against everything and against everyone". And unlike most US partners and allies, Trump harassed the WHO, boycotted its global coordination efforts, and removed the US from this UN agency and did not place the US among the 172 countries participating in the COVAX initiative. A clear example of the poor state of relations is that Trump failed to convince his allies to hold the G7 Summit in the US in the Spring/Summer 2020, not even in an online video conference. On the other hand, the recent *"Regional Comprehensive Economic Partnership"* (RCEP) — with 15 Asia-Pacific countries, including China — and the EU–China "Comprehensive Agreement on Investment" (CAI) clearly demonstrate that the US and its allies and partners have different approaches to free trade and China, even in the pandemic crisis. This is also shown in the "Why attempts to build a new anti-China alliance will fail" (Foreign Policy, 2021). It is significant, moreover, that the signing of the RCEP and the CAI agreements occurred after Biden's victory in the US presidential elections and before his inauguration.

The divergences are particularly deep between the United States and its European allies. Worse: Europeans' attitudes toward the US have undergone a massive change. While most Europeans rejoiced at Joe Biden's victory in the elections, they do not think he can help America make a comeback as the pre-eminent global leader; they no longer trust America to defend Europe; and they express little solidarity with the US if it became involved in a conflict with other great powers. These are the key findings of a pan-European survey of more than 15,000 people in 11 countries[1] commissioned by the European Council on Foreign Relations (ECFR) published in January 2021 (Krastev & Leonard, 2021). Across the 11 countries covered by the ECFR's poll, 60% of respondents believe that the US political system is completely or somewhat broken, evaluate the EU and/or their own countries' systems much more positively than that of the US, and look to Berlin rather than Washington as the most important partner; 32% agree that, after voting for Trump in 2016, Americans cannot be trusted and only 27% disagree with this statement (most strikingly, 53% of German respondents said that the American electorate cannot be trusted); at least 60% in every surveyed country (and an average of 67% across all 11 countries) believe that they cannot always

---

[1] The United Kingdom, Sweden, Portugal, Poland, Netherlands, Italy, Hungary, France, Spain, Denmark, and Germany.

rely on the US to defend them and therefore need to invest in European defense — interestingly, 74% of British respondents hold this view (a higher share than in any other national group), and two-thirds of respondents thought the EU should develop its defense capacities.

Europe's unwillingness to side with the US also comes out in respondents' views on a conflict between the US and Russia: 59% of respondents want their country to remain neutral; in no surveyed country would a majority want to take Washington's side, and just 23% hold the view that their country should side with the US in such a scenario. Also, there is the dramatic shift in the Europeans' perception of US power *vis-à-vis* China: 60% of respondents think that China will become more powerful than the US within the next ten years — a view shared by 79% in Spain and by 72% in Portugal and Italy (*Ibid.*, p. 8). On the other hand, the ECFR's poll shows that, in today's Europe, there is no dream of a return to a bipolar world in which the West would face off against China and its allies as it once did against the Soviet Union: at least 50% of respondents in every surveyed country would like their government to remain neutral in a conflict between the US and China (*Ibid.*, p. 17). Hence, as stated by Krastev & Leonard, "Even as Biden seeks to overturn the isolationism and unpredictability of the Trump administration, he will be hampered by policies that made America seem volatile, selfish, and weak" (*Ibid.*, pp. 22–23).

Tensions have also increased between European countries/NATO Allies. The quarrels and suspicions between Turkey — increasingly less secular and democratic and more Islamist and autocratic — and its European allies (and the US) have been worsening, especially since the attempted coup in 2016 and also in the face of Ankara's cyclical threats to "turn on the tap" of refugees to Europe and Turkish politics in Syria. These tensions rose in the pandemic context, also due to Turkey's testing of S-400 missiles purchased from Russia and its unilateral stances in Libya, in the Eastern Mediterranean, or in the second Nagorno-Karabakh war. For its part, the UK's exit from the EU disappointed the other 27 member states, which were angry at the support given by the Trump administration to this process. Brexit is indeed a game-changer in Europe, having profound repercussions for the EU and the transatlantic relations. And the pandemic crisis not only hampered the EU–UK Trade and Cooperation Agreement obtained at the "last minute" at the end of December 2020, but also created new frictions between Brussels and London over mutual access to the first vaccines produced in the territories on both sides. Meanwhile, leaders such as the Hungarian Prime Minister Viktor Orbán appear to have more in common with authoritarian rulers than with their counterparts in the EU. In fact, nationalism and "illiberal democracies" have flourished in Europe, and the pandemic crisis has created a new pretext for its expansion.

On the other hand, COVID-19 has highlighted the flimsiness of EU solidarity: when the pandemic hit Europe, EU member states did not act together or in solidarity but unilaterally, closing borders, suspending free movement, stipulating measures individually, competing for the purchase of protective materials, etc., in a logic of "each one for himself" and without any coordination. After the sovereign debt crisis and the migratory crisis, the pandemic crisis once again underlined the European Union's disunity. Associated with this, the EU saw its touted "attractiveness" and "normative power" hindered, again being unable to lead or to be a decisive voice in the overall management of the pandemic, that is, missing an excellent opportunity to assert itself as a relevant international actor and world power in the face of the "absence" of the US.

Paradoxically, the pandemic crisis has also sparked new lines of cohesion in the EU: learning from initial mistakes, greater coordination between member states in the second and third waves of the pandemic; the launch of the "pharmaceutical strategy" and the rapid progress toward achieving the "European Health Union"; centralized management of the negotiation, acquisition and equitable distribution of vaccines among member states; and the approval of a recovery plan to help repair the economic and social damages caused by the coronavirus pandemic that contemplates the largest stimulus package ever financed through the EU budget (a total of €1.8 trillion will help rebuild a post-COVID-19 Europe). Nonetheless, the dispute over the so-called Next Generation EU fund, the Multiannual Financial Framework, and the rule of law mechanism with Hungary and Poland highlight the conflict between "illiberal" and liberal tendencies in the EU. At the same time, the slow arrival of vaccines has led several European countries to criticize the centralized management of the European Commission and to launch a race for vaccines available beyond the framework negotiated by the EU. And, more broadly, as Charles Grant (2020) stated, the shift in influence from EU institutions to national governments — already visible pre-coronavirus — has accelerated and threatens to widen political, economic, and cultural fissures across Europe.

True, President Biden is trying to repair the much damage done by Trump and constantly repeats the United States commitment under his Presidency to work with "our closest friends — Canada, Mexico, the UK, Germany, France, NATO, Japan, South Korea, Australia — to begin reforming the habits of cooperation and rebuilding the muscle of democratic alliances that have atrophied over the past few years of neglect" (Biden, 2021b). However, the breakdown of transatlantic consensus and growing European divisions, as mentioned by Bobo Lo (2020, p. 22), "highlight a more fundamental problem. The principles that have hitherto distinguished and sustained the modern West — the rule of law, transparency, accountability, the separation of powers — are now in question. The issue is no longer just policy disagreements or conflicting interests. At stake are the very identity, values, and purpose of the West".

8. Reinforcing a Competitive US–China Bipolarity

The pandemic crisis emerged in a context of systemic changes in world geopolitics and in the international security system. The world power structure has changed drastically since the hegemony and unipolarity of post-Cold War US *hyperpuissance* to a "uni-bi-multi-polar" configuration — in which the increasingly incomplete American supremacy coincides with the rise of several other powers (China, Russia, the EU, Japan, India…) and where the resurgent China stands out. And in a hierarchy of power in transition and under great pressure, the tendency is for US–China bipolarization (Tomé, 2016). On the other hand, the interactions between major players have evolved toward a hybrid pattern that we have been characterizing with the notion of "congagement" (combining "containment" and "engagement"), in which the main actors compete and dispute, but at the same time they also engage and cooperate, both at bilateral and multilateral levels. Likewise, the "international security complex" has become a mixed and very dense competitive, cooperative, collective, and communities' security "systems' system" (*Ibid.*). In an environment perceived as extraordinarily complex and volatile and where the course of events is uncertain, the pandemic crisis seems to have accelerated the trend of competitive bipolarity between the apparently declining (US) and emerging (China) superpowers without, however, changing the logic of "congagement" among all the major powers.

The growth of China's "comprehensive national power" has two main consequences: a natural systemic rivalry with the dominant superpower and a change in the global power structure that tends to be more bipolar. In these conditions, a reference to the "Thucydides' trap" (Allison, 2017) or the classic dilemma of "hegemonic transitions" is inevitable. The competitive logic between the US and China is fueled by the many differences, divergences, and disputes involving trade issues, human rights, technology, Taiwan, or South China Sea. COVID-19 is neither the source nor the cause of competition between the US and China, but it has exacerbated tensions and frictions that have existed for years, in an environment aggravated by the assertiveness of Xi Jinping's China, the hostile anti-China rhetoric of the Trump administration, and the campaign for the 2020 American presidential elections. The year 2020 even seemed to indicate a less tense phase in US–China relations, given the "phase one" trade agreement established in January 2020 that apparently ended the "trade war" between the two countries that had been going on since 2018. However, the pandemic has raised the stakes. Far from China and the United States joining forces to meet COVID-19 common threat, there was a desperate sequence of accusations: "Beijing has sought to evade responsibility for the original outbreak and its early lack of transparency by highlighting its subsequent success in bringing the pandemic under control, contrasting this to the mismanagement and record death toll in the United States. And, the Trump Administration has attacked Beijing for causing the pandemic and then covering it up … hitting China hard and often, and ensuring that Beijing is held responsible for the suffering of the American people" (Lo, 2020, p. 12). In an attempt to be re-elected, Trump escalated and instrumentalized "demonization" of China to deflect criticism and hide his own mistakes. But the fact is that the perception of China as the main strategic rival has become relatively consensual in the US in the midst of the pandemic crisis, with China being the almost exclusive foreign policy topic of the Trump and Biden campaigns in the presidentials. And also, for Joe Biden, China represents a "special challenge" and "the United States does need to get tough with China" (Biden, 2020).

In a context of crisis, geopolitical rivalries are more likely to intensify than to abate, and the pandemic crisis seems to confirm this *dictum*. In the first year of the COVID-19 pandemic, US–China frictions accumulated over trade disputes (Washington and Beijing not only expressed lack of interest in pursuing negotiations toward "phase 2" of a broad trade agreement but also cyclically threatened to impose new economic sanctions), the Taiwan question (the US sold Taiwan weapons worth US$620 million in 2020, and in retaliation, China announced sanctions against the US arms giant Lockheed Martin), human rights (namely, the American denunciation of massive arrests and forced labor of Muslim Uighurs in the Chinese province of Xinjiang, with Beijing imposing sanctions against US congressmen and senators), technological disputes (increasing American restrictions on Huawei and other Chinese technology and communication companies, in addition to the fierce increase in American pressure on their allies not to accept Chinese 5G), or the South China Sea — where, to the growing militarization and Chinese presence, the US responded with a significant increase in Freedom of Navigation Operations (FONOPs), alongside constant incidents between Chinese and American ships and aircrafts in the South China Sea. In addition, in response to the new Chinese National Security Law imposed on Hong Kong, the US announced sanctions against Chinese and Hong Kong officials and the two chambers of Congress unanimously approved the Hong Kong Autonomy Act, ending the special economic and commercial status that the US had granted until then to that Special Administrative Region of China. There are also unprecedented symbolic developments never seen since the establishment of bilateral diplomatic relations in 1979, such as the ban on entry into the US by CCP members or the orders to close the Chinese Consulate in Houston and the US Consulate in Chengdu. At the same time, China and the US have turned the UN, the WHO and the WTO, as well as the South China Sea, the "Indo-Pacific" and virtually all regions of the world, into real "battlegrounds" (Tomé, 2020). To a certain extent, the competitive side toward China remains with the new American administration: "we'll also take on directly the challenges posed by our prosperity, security, and democratic values by our most serious competitor, China. We'll confront China's economic abuses; counter its aggressive, coercive action; push back on China's attack on human rights, intellectual property, and global governance" (Biden, 2021b).

This competitive escalation in a pandemic crisis environment leads many to see a "new/second cold war". However, bipolarity does not necessarily mean conflict between the two powers. And in addition to competition, the China–US relationship also has a cooperative facet in a very broad and diverse agenda. Moreover, the world and the international system are completely different and much more complex than during the Cold War; China is not "USSR 2.0" (starting with the fact that the basis for its resurgence is primarily economic); the rivalry between China and the US is not primarily of a military nature; the level of China's involvement with the US and also with all US allies is too deep; there are many new risks and challenges that are truly global and concern everyone; and the US allies' widespread perception of China is not of an "enemy". Gone is the "iron curtain".

China represents a powerful challenge, but the US and its allies and partners' adaptation to the "China factor" cannot be based on obsolete conceptions and strategies rather on the skilful balance between cooperation and competition (Tomé, 2019). Biden recognizes this, for which reason his stance is quite different from that of Trump: "The most effective way to meet that challenge is to build a united front of U.S. allies and partners to confront China's abusive behaviors and human rights violations, even as we seek to cooperate with Beijing on issues where our interests converge, such as climate change, nonproliferation, and global health security" (Biden, 2020). And as President of the United States, he reaffirms that "we are ready to work with Beijing when it's in America's interest to do so. We will compete from a position of strength by building back better at home, working with our allies and partners, renewing our role in international institutions, and reclaiming our credibility and moral authority, much of which has been lost" (Biden, 2021b). For his part, the more confident Chinese President and Secretary General of the CCP says: "we should stay committed to international law and international rules instead of seeking one's own supremacy … to consultation and cooperation instead of conflict and confrontation … China is on course to finish building a moderately prosperous society in all respects … As China enters a new development stage … China will continue to take an active part in international cooperation … China will continue to implement a win-win strategy of opening-up … China will continue to promote a new type of international relations … Let us all join hands and let multilateralism light our way toward a community with a shared future for mankind" (Xi, 2021).

9. Further Erosion of the Liberal International Order

The liberal international order is routed on a concept of a "rules-based order", multilateralism through international organizations, a certain sharing of sovereignties and responsibilities to find common solutions to common problems, political liberalism meaning liberal democracy (as opposed to authoritarianism and self-"democracy with national features"), open market economies and free trade (as opposed to protectionism and economic nationalism), free navigation of the seas (as opposed to practices of *mare nostrum/mare clausum*), access free-for-all to "global commons", recognition of the legitimacy of different international actors, and on a conception of human rights that implies the safeguarding of individual freedom, human dignity and respect for minorities and ethnic, religious and cultural diversity (as opposed to a human rights conception rooted only in certain economic rights). The liberal order was built, promoted, and cherished by the "West", becoming "universal" at the end of the Cold War, always sustained by the US supremacy and leadership. However, it faced its greatest crisis since the end of the Cold War. Liberalism is in retreat around the world, and the liberal order is contested and disputed again. It went backwards under the pressure of sovereigntist powers (such as China and Russia, but not only) and the expansion of authoritarianisms, nationalisms, protectionisms, populisms, and "illiberal democracies".

In contrast, the old Westphalian order has re-emerged, in which a conventional concept of sovereignty prevails; the state is the only legitimate actor; there is the absolutization of "non-interference in internal affairs" principle; the cult of areas of influence; the indifference to oppressive governments; the resolution of disputes only through direct negotiations or the imposition of will by one of the parties (refusing mediation and arbitration processes carried out by international courts); and an international order that results only from the balance of power among great powers. In fact, the liberal and Westphalian international orders have always coexisted since the last 100 years, and it was over the Westphalian order that the liberal one was built, and then it expanded after the Cold War. But the point is that in the last few years, the international order has become less liberal and more Westphalian.

For the reasons explained in the previous points, the erosion and retreat of the liberal international order precedes the pandemic crisis, but COVID-19 accentuated this trend: countries have acted out of a restricted and selfish notion of their own interests and not of international standards or shared values; nationalism gains space away from internationalism and multilateralism; the same goes for protectionism in the face of free trade or authoritarianism regarding political liberalism. In many ways, the pandemic is emblematic of the liberal order crisis. On the other hand, this crisis favored China's and Russia's attempts to subvert the liberal order, each in its own way and highlighted the West's ambivalences in the equation between principles and practice.

Whereas China has been the biggest beneficiary of the post-Cold War order, Russia considers itself to be its main victim. At least, this is the Moscow narrative since Vladimir Putin's rise to power in 1999. Consequently, not only "the liberal idea has become obsolete" (Putin, 2019) but Russia has sought to replace the liberal order with a "truly multipolar" system that reflects the realities of the 21st century. In practice, this means confronting and dividing the West, ending the hegemony of the United States, and promoting much greater influence for other great powers, especially Russia and China. In reality, what Putin is really interested in is reviving the old concert of the great imperial powers (Tomé, 2018). The pandemic crisis in no way changed these Russian purposes. On the contrary, Putin's failure to manage Russia's pandemic crisis has resulted in his lowest popularity in two decades. And the combination of lockdowns and falling oil and natural gas prices on the world market has seriously damaged the Russian economy. But COVID-19 has had little effect on Russian foreign policy, except to reinforce its perception of American decline, division between Westerners and international disorder. On the other hand, the pandemic led Russia to embark on the "vaccine race", claiming that its vaccine (Sputnik V) was the first allegedly effective against the coronavirus — announcement made even before the test's decisive "phase three". With the world's attention focusing on the pandemic and the US–China dispute, Russia has maintained a relatively lower profile than it has maintained since Trump's presidential victory. As before, strategic flexibility is key. The partnership with China remains the cornerstone of Russia's international policy, but Putin has kept his options open. And in the context of a pandemic, he never tired of expressing Russian interest in improving his involvement with the US, namely by agreeing to the extension of the New Strategic Arms Reduction Treaty (New START) without conditions — extension signed when President Biden was already at the White House.

Beijing's view and approach to the international order is not entirely consistent with Moscow's. China resurgence placed it at a higher level in the relationship with Russia and gradually brought it closer to the superpower US level, so President Xi Jinping leads China in a "new era" when the goal is to restore Chinese centrality and to lead the reform of the global governance system. The multipolarity rhetoric became instrumental for Beijing in an increasingly bipolar world power structure. That is why the leaders of the CCP also pragmatically keep China's options open, including the articulation with the US, the "other" superpower, in the management of global affairs and wherever it is possible to identify common interests. The contradictions between Moscow and Beijing do not harm, until further notice, their relationship, which has increased since the Russian annexation of Crimea in 2014 and the subsequent tensions between Russia and the West. They cooperate not because they are members of an "Autocratic International" but because they consider it to serve their respective geopolitical, strategic, and economic purposes. And Russian and Chinese interests coincide in much of what is essential for both: Russia has armaments and energy resources that China needs, and China is a fabulous customer for Russian energy and armaments that are essential for Moscow's budget; mutual cooperation is essential to stabilize Central Asia; and both are very committed to limiting the exercise of American power; divide the West and the "league of democracies"; and suppress or exclude liberal political influences internally in international organizations and in the international order. Both, China and Russia, believe that the great powers have certain natural rights, including regional spheres of influence, as well as the instrumental absolutization of the Westphalian principle of "noninterference in internal affairs". China and Russia, each in its own way, promote a kind of "embedded revisionism" in the international organizations that they are part of with the western powers. And their perspectives are consistent on more specific issues, such as the idea of the "sovereign internet".

An increasingly assertive China and a revisionist Russia are therefore two of the main contributors to the erosion of the liberal international order. They flagrantly challenge the assumptions of that order: threatening their neighbors, exporting authoritarianism, subverting democratic processes, minimizing the international rules to which they are bound, and shaping multilateral institutions to their interests. In addition, the Sino–Russian partnership has a multiplier effect in other regions and with other governments, eroding the liberal order and the global primacy of the US and the West. COVID-19 has not disturbed strategic cooperation between China and Russia and has even contributed to both the crisis of the liberal order and the expansion of the anti-liberal agendas of Beijing and Moscow.

On the other hand, Western governments — the main creators of the liberal international order — have not lived up to the values underlying a liberal order, including due to the aforementioned "polarization of the West". In addition to internal divisions, in Europe there has been an expansion of "illiberal democracies", such as Hungary and Poland, not to mention Turkey. An "illiberal" evolution, to say the least, characterizes other cases in the world, such as the Philippines, India, South Africa, or Brazil. And in particular, the Trump administration's stance has undermined America's credibility, leadership, and moral authority. Aware of this, Joe Biden has tried to underline the difference from his predecessor, restoring the "normal" premises of US foreign policy: "we must start with diplomacy rooted in America's most cherished democratic values: defending freedom, championing opportunity, upholding universal rights, respecting the rule of law, and treating every person with dignity... Though many of these values have come under intense pressure in recent years... to unite the world in fighting to defend democracy, because we have fought for it ourselves... to begin restoring American engagement internationally and earn back our leadership position, to catalyse global action on shared challenges... when we host the Summit of Democracy early in my administration to rally the nations of the world to defend democracy globally, to push back the authoritarianism's advance" (Biden, 2021b). It is too early to realize the impact that this turn but the American Administration will have on the international order. But the recovery from the global pandemic and economic crisis will be a decisive test for America's leadership ability, and subsequently, for the recovery (or not) of a more liberal international order.

10. Final Remarks

About a year after COVID-19 was declared a pandemic, and although we are still in the middle of the crisis and therefore do not know all its consequences, it is possible to identify multiple impacts of the pandemic crisis on international politics. At the outset, as we have seen, the existing data shows that the best or worst performance of countries in managing the pandemic is not the result of either the level of national wealth or the type of political regime. However, as the inoculation of societies progresses, and in parallel, the effects of the crisis/economic recovery are more felt, the differences between rich and poor countries worsen. On the other hand, the pandemic crisis has again served as a pretext for autocratic regimes to reinforce their repressive arsenals, while many democratic societies have seen some of their inherent freedoms limited or even violated. In addition to the reinforcement of authoritarianism, a second effect of the pandemic crisis confirms another trend that was already ongoing: the expansion of nationalism and the erosion of multilateralism and internationalism, precisely in a context that would advise the exact opposite. Even so, there are countless examples of the humanist spirit of solidarity and generosity, and there are very positive developments, such as the extraordinary collaboration between transnational scientific communities or international initiatives, such as COVAX, which allows us to maintain expectations that international solidarity will overcome national selfishness.

The emergence of the new coronavirus and its rapid expansion, together with the difficulties of global production and distribution chains in meeting the urgency of protective materials and medical equipment, again raised the question of *hyperglobalization*. But like other previous phases and crises, the tendency is for globalization to survive COVID-19, albeit with adjustments due to the need to guarantee "national reserves" of certain essential goods. And what is clear once again with this pandemic is that globalization needs more and better regulation to be fairer. On the other hand, the pandemic crisis seems to reinforce Asia-Pacific's centrality in world economy, due to a better performance in the management of the pandemic and the economic situation compared, mainly, to Europe and North America.

Likewise, the pandemic crisis seemed to accelerate a more Sino-centric globalization and the perception of China as an emerging superpower — which is still paradoxical, considering that COVID-19 emerged in China, and therefore, the CCP regime was unable to prevent it from becoming a global pandemic. The reality is that, in the context of the pandemic crisis, China emphasized a more assertive stance that was already in existence. These circumstances were instrumentalized by President Trump to escalate the demonization of China, trying to conceal his own mistakes in the tragic management of the pandemic in the US. Trump's America was "first" but only regarding the number of dead and infected by COVID-19, which contributed to Trump's defeat and Biden's victory in the American presidential elections. In addition, the failure in the internal management of the pandemic and in the leadership of the world in a global crisis, and the extreme polarization of American society, favors the perception of decline in the US and again raises questions about its position in the international system. On the other hand, COVID-19 is not the cause of disputes between the US and China, but the Chinese assertiveness and a more hostile American stance in the context of the pandemic crisis have accentuated the dynamic of competitive bipolarity between the declining and emerging superpowers. However, the pandemic crisis does not seem to alter the previous pattern of behaviours and interactions between the main international actors (including the US and China, and also Russia, the EU, Japan, India, and others) that we characterize as "congagement", that is, simultaneously containment and engagement.

The pandemic crisis also accentuated two other previous major trends: the polarization of the "West" and the crisis of the liberal international order. Transatlantic divergences, disunity, and lack of coordination between European countries reappeared when the pandemic hit Europe and North America. Here too, national populism became evident. On the other hand, Western countries returned to exhibiting practices that are not consistent with the principles of the liberal order. In particular, Trump's "America First" was the contradiction of the very idea of liberalism. These aspects, together with the decline of the US and the erosion of multilateralism and internationalism, contribute decisively to the retreat of the liberal international order that the West does not seem capable of stopping. Western leaders must therefore do more to end the inconsistencies between liberal principles and "illiberal" practices. The most convincing argument of liberalism, and of a liberal order, is to prove that it is more effective and more humane than any other alternative. In contrast, the pandemic crisis seems to favor the perspectives and interests of the most sovereigntist powers, mainly Russia and China, both contrary to the liberal order and active contributors to the re-emergence of the old Westphalian order. COVID-19 does not distinguish between democratic societies and autocratic regimes, or between rich and poor, and the same can be said of the environmental and climate crisis. But the pandemic crisis highlights the need for more international "order" to face the greater "disorder" caused by the crises. The question faced by the international order is what the main actors make of it because it has always been dependent on the powers that guarantee and shape it. Much still depends on the power and ability of the United States, but it is not certain — far from it — that the "normalization" of American foreign policy under President Biden halt the retreat of the liberal order. And if the liberal international order is in crisis, it is hard to imagine what a more Chinese–American world order will look like.

The discernible impact of COVID-19 on international politics so far demonstrate that the pandemic crisis underlined and accelerated trends that already existed, at the same time that it triggered dynamics that may redefine world geopolitics and international order — thus validating our argument presented from the beginning. However, the outcome of the pandemic crisis is uncertain — uncertainty is, after all, another effect of a crisis. A return to the *status quo ante* is impossible, but several future scenarios are possible, some better than others. In an international system that was already volatile and fluid, the pandemic crisis added disorder and uncertainty. And we are lost in transition...

References

Allen, J. (2020). The History of COVID-19 Will Be Written by the Victors, in *Foreign Policy* Analysis — How the World Will Look After the Coronavirus Pandemic, March 20, 2020.

Allison, G. (2017). *Destined for War: Can America and China Escape Thucidides's Trap?* Boston: Houghton Mifflin Harcourt.

BBC News (2021). *Covid Vaccine: WHO Warns of "Catastrophic Moral Failure"*, 18 January 2021, https://www.bbc.com/news/world-55709428 (Accessed on 05.02.2021).

Biden, Jr., J. R. (2020). Why America Must Lead Again. Rescuing U.S. Foreign Policy After Trump in *Foreign Affairs*, March/April 2020.

Biden, Jr., J. R. (2021a). *Inaugural Address by President Joseph R. Biden, Jr. Washington, D.C., The United States Capitol, January 20, 2021*. The White House, https://www.whitehouse.gov/briefing-room/speeches-remarks/2021/01/20/inaugural-address-by-president-joseph-r-biden-jr/ (Accessed on 24.01.2021).

Biden, Jr., J. R. (2021b). *Remarks by President Biden on America's Place in the World. U.S. Department of State Headquarters Harry S. Truman Building Washington, D.C. February 4, 2021*. The White House, https://www.whitehouse.gov/briefing-room/speeches-remarks/2021/02/04/remarks-by-president-biden-on-americas-place-in-the-world/ (Accessed on 05.02.2021).

Burns, N. (2020). In Every Country, We See the Power of the Human Spirit, in *Foreign Policy* Analysis — How the World Will Look After the Coronavirus Pandemic, March 20, 2020.

CIVICUS (2020), *Civicus Monitor 2020. People Power under Attack*, https://findings2020.monitor.civicus.org/ (Accessed on 04.02.2021).

EIU — The Economist Intelligence Unit (2020). *Rich Countries Will Get Access to Coronavírus Vaccines Earlier than Others*, 18 December 2020, https://www.eiu.com/n/rich-countries-will-get-access-to-coronavirus-vaccines-earlier-than-others/ (Accessed on 04.02.2021).

EIU — The Economist Intelligence Unit (2021), *Democracy Index 2020*. January 2021.

Erçetin, Ş. Ş. & Açıkalın, Ş. N. (Eds.) (2020). *Chaos, Complexity and Leadership 2018. Explorations of Chaotic and Complexity Theory.* Amsterdam: Springer International Publishing.

Farrell, H. & Newman, A. (2020), "Will the Coronavirus End Globalization as We Know It? The Pandemic Is Exposing Market Vulnerabilities No One Knew Existed" in *Foreign Affairs*, March 16, 2020.

Foreign Policy (2020). *Analysis — How the World Will Look After the Coronavirus Pandemic*, March 20, 2020.

Foreign Policy (2021), *FP Editors' Picks,* January 27, 2021.

Fukuyama, F. (2020). The Pandemic and Political Order. It Takes a State, in *Foreign Affairs*, July/August 2020.

Gavi — The Vaccine Alliance website, *COVAX Explained*, https://www.gavi.org/vaccineswork/covax-explained (Accessed on 05.02.2021).

Grant, C. (2020). Coronavirus is Pushing the EU in New and Undesirable Directions, *Centre for European Reform*, 15 May 2020, https://www.cer.eu/insights/coronavirus-pushing-eu-new-andundesirable-directions (Accessed on 03.02.2021).

Guterres, A. (2020). United Nation's *Secretary-General's Remarks to the General Assembly on His Priorities for 2020*, 22 January 2020, https://www.un.org/sg/en/content/sg/statement/2020-01-22/secretary-generals-remarks-the-general-assembly-his-priorities-for-2020-bilingual-delivered-scroll-down-for-all-english-version (Accessed on 01.02.2021).

Ikenberry, G. J. (2020). Democracies Will Come out of Their Shell, in *Foreign Policy* Analysis — How the World Will Look After the Coronavirus Pandemic, March 20, 2020.

IMF — International Monetary Fund website, *Datamapper — World Economic Outlook (October 2020)*, https://www.imf.org/external/datamapper/NGDP_RPCH@WEO/OEMDC/ADVEC/WEOWORLD (Accessed on 06.02.2021).

International Idea-Institute for Democracy and Electoral Assistance (2020). *Taking Stock of Global Democratic Trends Befores and During the COVID-19 Pandemic.* The Global State of Democracy (GSoD) In Focus Special Brief, 9 December 2020. Online (access 05.02.2021), url: https://www.idea.int/publications/catalogue/global-democratic-trends-before-and-during-covid19?lang=en (Accessed on 05.02.2021).

Işyar, Ö. G. (2008). Definition and Management of International Crises, in *Perceptions*, Winter 2008, pp. 1–49.

Krastev, I. & Leonard, M. (2021). *The Crisis of American Power: How Europeans See Biden's America*. European Council on Foreign Relations (ECFR) Policy Brief, January 2021.

Lipscy, P. Y. (2020). "COVID-19 and the politics of crisis" *International Organization,* 74 (Supplement), December 2020, E98–E127.

Lo, Bobo (2020). *Global Order in the Shadow of the Coronavirus: China, Russia and the West*. Lowy Institute Analysis, July 2020.

Lowy Institute website (2021). *Covid Performance Index. Deconstructing Pandemic Responses*, https://interactives.lowyinstitute.org/features/covid-performance/ (Accessed on 04.02.2021).

Mahbubani, K. (2020). "A More China-Centric Globalization" in *Foreign Policy* Analysis — How the World Will Look After the Coronavirus Pandemic, March 20, 2020.

Nye, Jr. & Joseph S. (2020). "American Power Will Need a New Strategy" in *Foreign Policy* Analysis — How the World Will Look After the Coronavirus Pandemic, March 20, 2020.

O'Neil, Shannon K. (2020). "Lower Profits, but More Stability" in *Foreign Policy* Analysis — How the World Will Look After the Coronavirus Pandemic, March 20, 2020.

Oxford Learner's Dictionaries website, *Crisis*, https://www.oxfordlearners dictionaries.com/definition/english/crisis_1 (Accessed on 02.02.2021).

P.R.China (2019). *China's National Defense in the New Era*. Ministry of National Defense of the People's Republic of China, July 24, 2019.

Putin, V. (2019). Interview with the "Financial Times", 27 June 2019. Kremlin http://en.kremlin.ru/events/president/news/60836 (Accessed on 05.02.2021).

Schake Kori (2020). "The United States Has Failed the Leadership Test" in *Foreign Policy* Analysis — How the World Will Look After the Coronavirus Pandemic, March 20, 2020.

Tomé, L. (2016). Complex systems theories and eclectic approach in analysing and theorising the contemporary international security complex. In Ş. Ş. Erçetin & H. Bagci (Eds.), *Handbook of Research on Chaos and Complexity Theory in the Social Sciences*, pp. 19–32. IGI Global/Springer.

Tomé, L. (2018). Geopolítica da Rússia de Putin: Não é a União Soviética, mas gostava de ser… (Putin Russia's geopolitics: Not the Soviet Union, but it world like to be...) in *Relações Internacionais (International Relations), 60,* 69–99.

Tomé, L. (2019). "Região Indo-Pacífico: O factor China e motivações geopolíti-cas" (Indo-Pacific Region: The China factor and geopolitical motivations) in *Nação e Defesa nº (Nation and Defense No), 151,* 66–100.

Tomé, L. (2020). "Geopolítica Mundial em contexto de Pandemia: EUA vs China" (World Geopolitics in a Pandemic Context: US vs China) in *IDN Brief especial — A Nova (Des)Ordem Mundial: Efeitos da Pandemia (The*

New World (Des)Order: Effects of the Pandemic), 5 August 2020. Lisboa, National Defense Institute, pp. 8–9.

Tomé, L. & Açıkalın, S. N. (2019). Chapter 1. Complexity theory as a new lens in international relations: System and change. In S. Ş Erçetin & N. Potas (Eds.), *Chaos, Complexity and Leadership 2017. Explorations of Chaos and Complexity Theory*, pp. 1–15. Netherlands: IGI Global/Springer.

Transparency International (2021). *Corruption Perceptions Index (CPI) 2020*, January 2021, https://www.transparency.org/en/cpi/2020 (Accessed on 03.02.2021).

WHO — World Health Organization website, *COVAX: Working for Global Equitable Access to COVID-19 Vaccines*, https://www.who.int/emergencies/diseases/novel-coronavirus-2019/situation-reports (Accessed on 05.02.2021).

WHO — World Health Organization website, *Covid-19 Situation Report. Coronavirus disease (COVID-19) Weekly Epidemiological Update and Weekly Operational Update*, https://www.who.int/emergencies/diseases/novel-coronavirus-2019/situation-reports (Accessed on 05.02.2021).

Worldometers.Info (2021). COVID-19 *Coronavirus Pandemic. Reported Cases and Deaths by Country or Territory,* Last updated: February 08, 2021, 15:06 GMT, https://www.worldometers.info/coronavirus/ (Accessed on 08.02.2021).

Xi Jinping (2017). *Report at the 19th National Congress of the Communist Party of China (CPC)* on October 18, 2017. Available in Xinhuanet, http://www.xinhuanet.com/english/special/2017-11/03/c_136725942.htm (Accessed on 02.02.2021).

Xi Jinping (2021). Special Address by Chinese President Xi Jinping at the World Economic Forum Virtual Event of the Davos Agenda, 25 January 2021. Available in *Xinhuanet*, http://www.xinhuanet.com/english/2021-01/25/c_139696610.htm (Accessed on 02.02.2021).

Chapter 5

Effects of COVID-19 on Healthcare Service Delivery: Focus on Otolaryngology and Speech and Language Pathology Services

Mariam KAVAKCI

*Department of Speech and Language Therapy,
Ankara Yıldırım Beyazit University, Ankara, Turkey*

mariamkavakci@gmail.com

Abstract

COVID-19 has impacted many aspects of life, quickly spiraling into a global health threat since it was first reported in late 2019. Its impact on the healthcare sector was catastrophic, causing mass panic in hospitals and medical centers worldwide. The otolaryngology and speech and language pathology fields, which both involve a high risk of exposure to the virus, were forced to adopt novel measures to protect providers and patients from the deadly disease. This chapter discusses the impact and consequences of the COVID-19 pandemic on otolaryngology services, speech and language pathology services, general patient care, and medical education.

1. Introduction

It would not be an understatement to say that the fate of the world is hanging in the balance. As of February 2021, the total number of confirmed cases globally for the novel coronavirus was nearly 107 million according to United Nations estimates. Over 190 countries have reported cases of the coronavirus disease with the death toll climbing up to 2.3 million in 2021. These figures are astonishing when one considers that there are about 75 nations with a population less than the total reported deaths of the coronavirus disease. Some nations have been hit harder than others by the virus. For example, in February 2021, the United States had 483,200 deaths resulting from the coronavirus disease, followed closely by Brazil at 234,945 deaths (Statista, 2021).

The variance in these numbers has been linked to many different reasons. In the United States, a strong claim has been made for ignorance and defiance by the government's administration and Brazil's cases are believed to have been mainly contributed by political propaganda and poor response policies in place (Filho, 2020). While it remains true that the pandemic is yet to subside, adjustments have to be made to keep moving forward with educational, vocational, and social life activities.

The impact of the pandemic has been felt on many levels and continues to influence many decisions that people make socially, economically, politically, and environmentally. Different institutions are experiencing the adverse impacts of the current pandemic. One example is the hospitality industry, which subsequently affects the economy of different nations. Notably, the new coronavirus regulations require people to stay indoors. Countries are closing down their beaches and public parks to ensure that social interaction is kept to a minimum. International borders are being closed, national events are being broadcasted without attendants, and governments are being criticized in regard to how they are responding to the pandemic.

One of the hardest hit domains remains the healthcare sector. The pressure to find a vaccine has been building up since the outbreak of the virus, while different branches within the sector tried to cope with providing medical services to patients. Healthcare institutions are facing unique challenges due to the nature of the virus. Because the virus spreads through respiratory droplets, procedures that put the physicians and healthcare staff in direct contact with these droplets significantly increase their risk of contracting and spreading the virus. Notable examples of these procedures are those carried out otolaryngology evaluations and treatments by doctors, and in speech, language, and swallowing evaluations and treatments by speech and language pathologists (SLPs).

Aside from increased risk of exposure to patients' respiratory droplets, the virus impacts the healthcare sector in many other ways. Patient care has taken a different turn, and medical education is also seeing reforms. Some of the changes could be foreseen, but others were less expected. In both cases, what stands out the most is the abrupt dependence on technology. The virus has forced many people to stay away from facilities that break social distance regulations and put individuals in a position to contract or spread the virus. Therefore, virtual consultations, evaluations, and classrooms have become standard practice since the spread of the virus began. This change can be viewed as a positive or negative one. On the one hand, switching over to a world of virtual services was already on the horizon, and the pandemic only served to hasten this process. On the other hand, many institutions were not prepared for such a drastic shift. The consequences of these changes continue to be experienced with significant implications for the future of healthcare services. The purpose of this chapter is to analyze each one of these aspects, specifically how the virus has affected (a) otolaryngology procedures, (b) SLP services (c) general patient care, and (d) the future of medical education.

2. Otolaryngology Procedures During COVID-19

The COVID-19 pandemic struck the world so suddenly that healthcare institutions across the world were initially caught off guard and overwhelmed with the gravity of work. Many adjustments had to be made to accommodate the changes necessary to combat the dangers of the virus. The precautionary measures needed to reduce the spread of virus have been especially critical in the otolaryngology branch, owing to the procedures that require close doctor–patient contact (Ghulam-Smith *et al.*, 2020). Because the virus is transmitted between people through respiratory droplets about 5–10 μm in diameter (World Health Organization, 2020c), physicians, nurses, and clinicians in otolaryngology clinics who are exposed to mucus, saliva, and other bodily fluids are among the most at-risk groups within healthcare. Furthermore, the upper airway has a high viral load, exposing otolaryngologists to more risk than other professions who also do invasive procedures (Kulcsar *et al.*, 2020). As such, otolaryngology clinics have had to make drastic modifications to their practices to ensure safety from the virus while also maintaining patient-centered, quality care. Patients, on the other hand, want to have their healthcare needs met but are afraid of entering healthcare facilities. For instance, the elderly tend to skip their medical appointments and delay doctor visits. The result of this has been an exacerbation of different otolaryngology conditions.

The new changes to healthcare provision have been difficult for both providers and receivers. The impact of COVID-19 on physicians and the challenges they face has been thoroughly discussed on the international platform. Among the most urgent problems for patients that need to be addressed are the delays in receiving a diagnosis, which is a critical first step in the administration of care (Ghulam-Smith *et al.*, 2020). With the new restrictions, healthcare facilities have to find a way to ensure that patients remain safe. It is especially problematic when about 80% of people who have contracted the coronavirus disease are asymptomatic (Kulcsar *et al.*, 2020). Therefore, facilities are forced to cut back on the number of procedures that they have to perform per day.

The first death recorded for a medical practitioner was an otolaryngologist on January 20, 2020 (Kulcsar *et al.*, 2020), a testament to how much risk the profession carries. Even though more people are now quarantining and following social distancing rules, the anxiety associated with contracting the virus remains. This is especially pronounced in otolaryngology clinics. For example, in Wuhan, during a procedure that requires an endoscope to pass through the patient's nose termed endonasal video-assisted hypophysectomy (Dubey & Munjal, 2014), 14 patients were infected with COVID-19 (Kulcsar *et al.*, 2020). This became a common trend in Wuhan, and especially with otolaryngologists due to the interventional nature of their procedures. After hearing about these types of situations, many patients make the assumption that they are better off staying at home than attending an otolaryngology appointment that may result in them contracting the deadly virus.

3. Effects on Quality of Life

A combination of the fear of contracting the coronavirus disease during otolaryngology procedures and delayed intervention build up to other issues that affect the quality of life for the patients, especially the elderly. According to statistics from the World Health Organization (2020b), approximately a third of the population aged 65 years and above have a hearing loss disability. The number stands at 432 million adults with hearing loss in an age-matched total population of 466 million people in the world. This situation is further complicated by the fact that individuals in this age range are more severely impacted by the virus compared to their younger counterparts. As the Centers for Disease Control and Prevention (2020) reports, about eight deaths out of ten are people aged 65 years and above. Therefore, when choosing between staying isolated to prevent being infected with the deadly virus and taking a risk by going to a hearing check appointment, it is not difficult to imagine why elderly patients would forgo the latter. Unfortunately, this scenario significantly impacts spoken communication skills, which has become a crucial element in the society during this period where social isolation threatens individuals' quality of life.

Moreover, prolonged isolation in elderly patients with and without hearing loss increases the possibility of developing cognitive impairments such as dementia (Gurgel *et al.*, 2014). Other conditions such as chronic suppurative otitis media (CSOM), a global health problem, may lead to a decreased hearing in children if the treatment is delayed. Chronic suppurative otitis media affects about 31 million people every year, 22.6% of whom are children under the age of five years (Hunt *et al.*, 2017). These children may fail to acquire appropriate speech patterns and may develop language impairments. Delayed intervention in such cases severely affects the quality of life for children and their families. Telemedicine and protective gear, which are meant to protect people from contracting the coronavirus disease, have also contributed to reducing the quality of life for many patients. Individuals with autism spectrum disorder (ASD), who have documented difficulties with facial recognition (Wolf *et al.*, 2008), may have an exacerbation of their difficulty with identifying faces due to the use of masks. Patients with hearing loss who rely on lip-reading may also have challenges due to face masks (Goldin *et al.*, 2020).

Despite the importance of receiving therapy and treatments for otolaryngologic conditions, many patients opt to stay away from healthcare facilities due to the high-risk environment, evidence that the pandemic has adversely impacted services even in this important branch of healthcare.

4. Interventions and Lasting Impact

The risk of viral contamination for healthcare workers has proven to be high owing to the invasive nature of the procedures performed during evaluation and treatment. Patients have chosen to stay in their homes as per government regulations. Those who opt to visit healthcare facilities, such as otolaryngology clinics, are required to wear personal protective equipment (PPE). While PPE have helped reduce the spread of the coronavirus disease, a few disadvantages are present. For example, the physician's vision is limited by protective gear around their eyes, complicating performance of sensitive procedures involving the nasal and oral cavities (Liu *et al.*, 2020). Despite the limitations, one cannot ignore the importance of PPE in helping prevent spreading of the virus as will be discussed in the following section.

Personal Protective Equipment (PPE): Protective gear comes in many forms. For patients visiting healthcare facilities, a face mask is a necessity. Masks help protect individuals by reducing exposure to respiratory droplets and decrease the chances of the virus spreading from one person to another. Like patients, clinicians also require protection but for longer periods of time. The first step is taken by minimizing physician–patient interaction to when it is completely necessary. The second step is to wear appropriate protection when coming into contact with a patient. Such protection includes scrubs and all accompanying protective clothing, such as gloves, a flexible face shield, high protection mask, goggles, and a frontal headlight to improve vision (Benito *et al.*, 2020, Farneti *et al.*, 2020). Some secondary measures, which have also become part of common practice, include regular cleaning of surfaces and hands, avoiding decongestants and anesthetics in the form of sprays, and performing procedures in a negative pressure room with the lowest possible number of people. These interventions have become part of regular practice due to the COVID-19 pandemic. There are also other feasible alternatives to performing risky procedures more safely (Farneti *et al.*, 2020). This is possible with the use of technology as will be discussed next.

Telehealth: A highly recommended measure against the coronavirus during otolaryngology procedures is performing evaluations via telehealth. Telehealth is a form of delivering patient care while avoiding the physical interaction between the healthcare provider and consumer. It is done remotely, either via telephone or a video call.

Telehealth is not a new concept. According to Hofstetter *et al.* (2010), the implementation of telehealth in Alaska has been in the works for several years. However, it would be erroneous to assume that all healthcare facilities were prepared for such a change. Telehealth involves remotely attending to a patient's needs. While this ensures that both parties remain safe from contamination through physical interaction, it requires previous telehealth experience to conduct a reliable evaluation online. Clinical application also remains a major challenge in situations where video connection is difficult to establish. For patients with tracheostomies or laryngectomies who have respiration, voice, and speech production difficulties, the challenge of communicating is exacerbated over the internet or telephone. The same is true for patients who have other speech, language, and cognitive-communication impairments. Furthermore, technology is not always familiar tool to the elderly population which poses another challenge. Elderly adults may require assistance with establishing remote access to their doctor's office via a computer. Despite these barriers, there are signs of an increase in the number of weekly scheduled telehealth visits (Kasle *et al.*, 2020). In as much as the implementation of telehealth poses a challenge, there appears to be hope for the future.

5. Speech and Language Pathology Services

The highly contagious nature of the coronavirus disease and the resulting mortality rates have caused mass panic around the world. The Middle East respiratory syndrome (MERS) and severe acute respiratory syndrome (SARS) are two examples of diseases that posed a major threat to the regions in which they occurred (Tohidast *et al.*, 2020). The difference between previous outbreaks and the current pandemic is that COVID-19 has spread uncontrollably to the extent that governments and institutions did not have adequate time to prepare for it. The ensuing panic resulted in irrational actions by some members of the public. Several governments have thus ordered that people quarantine themselves in their homes, which has had serious social and economic repercussions.

Similar to otolaryngology services, the speech and language pathology field has also been impacted by COVID-19 in several ways. In the United States, speech and language therapy services are provided in hospitals, private clinics, rehabilitation centers, nursing homes, and schools. While there are different models of delivering therapy for those with speech, language, and swallowing impairments, all of them include close patient–clinician contact. Importantly, effective speech and language therapy delivery relies heavily on face-to-face interaction with the therapist (Tohidast *et al.*, 2020). The social distancing requirement that people should stay at least three feet apart to prevent respiratory droplets from passing from one person to another (Rose, 2020) is counterproductive from a therapeutic perspective. As such, speech and language therapy has been impacted by the social distancing limitations that have come about due to the introduction of new governmental regulations geared toward reducing the spread of the coronavirus disease. Additionally, the use of masks limits the amount of visual cueing provided by the SLP. It is well documented that children, including those with phonological disorders, benefit from seeing the clinician's mouth during therapy (de Castro & Wertzner, 2009; Lalonde & Holt, 2015). Based on this analysis, the delivery of speech, language, and swallowing therapies have been affected negatively by the COVID-19 pandemic.

6. Case Study: Dysphagia Evaluation and Treatment

While the delivery of speech and language therapy has been discussed in several studies, this section focuses on another type of impairment treated by SLPs that has been most negatively impacted during the pandemic. Dysphagia is a medical term for swallowing difficulties (National Health Service, 2020). These difficulties, which are diagnosed and treated by SLPs, may be caused by several factors. Dysphagia may occur in isolation or secondary to another condition such as a stroke, dementia, traumatic brain injury, or neurodegenerative diseases. Patients with cancer, gastroesophageal reflux disease, or developmental and genetic conditions may also have dysphagia (National Health Service, 2020).

According to Adkins *et al.* (2020), dysphagia affects one in six people. Despite its common occurrence, many people fail to seek treatment even when the condition is treatable. If left untreated, dysphagia can lead to further complications such as aspiration pneumonia and even death (Marik & Kaplan, 2003). One of the most common challenges and problems developed by dysphagia patients is food entering into the airway, thus blocking the flow of air to the lungs and consequently leading to choking. People who frequently have this type of experience often limit their eating and drinking out of fear of choking, which in turn results in malnutrition and dehydration. A patient's quality of life is significantly reduced as a consequence of not being able to enjoy meals or spend time with others in social gatherings involving food. Dysphagia is also very prevalent in elderly adults residing in nursing homes.

It occurs in 25 to 70% of people admitted to these facilities (Fong *et al.*, 2020). Unfortunately, COVID-19 has made it very difficult to provide services for patients with swallowing disorders in these types of settings.

Dysphagia rehabilitation requires a team approach. In nursing homes, for example, SLPs are responsible for the evaluation and treatment procedures while nurses monitor the patient during their daily meals and report to the SLP about any issues that may arise. In hospitals, a multidisciplinary team combining several healthcare staff including SLPs, nurses, otolaryngologists, and gastroenterologists may work together to manage the dysphagic patient (Miles *et al.*, 2020; Namasivayam-MacDonald & Riquelme, 2020). Unfortunately, the multidisciplinary interaction necessary to evaluate and treat these patients optimally has also been impacted by COVID-19, posing yet another challenge to delivering quality healthcare services.

In standard practice, SLPs work in close physical contact with patients during the evaluation and treatment of dysphagia. The chances of aerosol emissions in these situations are very high. Evaluation occurs in two ways: instrumentally and non-instrumentally. The SLP usually begins with a non-instrumental evaluation, also known as a clinical swallow evaluation (CSE). In medical settings, the CSE is typically conducted bedside and includes cognitive-communication assessment, oral-motor examination, and swallowing trials with food and liquids of different consistencies (Fong *et al.*, 2020). These processes are what Bolton *et al.* (2020) refer to as aerosol-generating procedures and expose the SLP to an increased risk of viral contamination.

The risk is even more during nstrumental dysphagia evaluations including the videofluoroscopic swallow study (VFSS) and flexible endoscopic evaluation of swallowing (FEES; Brodsky & Gilbert, 2020). The VFSS is a procedure used by speech pathologists in observing what happens in the oropharyngeal phases of swallowing when a dysphagia patient is swallowing foods or liquids. In the FEES procedure, a flexible endoscope is passed through the patients nose to see what happens when the patient swallows foods or liquids. These procedures are also considered aerosol-generating and thus need to be conducted with extra caution. Due to the strong association between respiration and swallowing mechanisms, COVID-19 patients frequently require VFSS or FEES, especially after extubation from mechanical ventilation. Since the patient cannot wear a mask during the presentation of food and liquids for testing in either of these procedures, both the patient and clinician are at increased risk of viral contamination.

From this vantage point, one begins to realize just how much the coronavirus pandemic has affected healthcare services. Clinicians have no choice but to find alternatives to the standard way of conducting risky procedures such as those performed by SLPs (Brodsky & Gilbert, 2020). One alternative is to administer the non-instrumental CSE via telehealth. In this case, the clinician can safely evaluate the patient's swallowing skills. For example, dystussia (i.e., disordered cough) is risky to evaluate in-person due to exposure to aerosol droplets. However, the cough is a critical component of the examination in order to determine the patient's level of risk for choking (i.e., patients who have an adequately strong cough have a better chance of clearing out anything that might escape into their airway). To assess for dystussia during the CSE, patients are asked to cough voluntarily as strong as possible. Due to the risks involved, this variable can be evaluated much more safely via telehealth compared to in-person evaluation. Recently, researchers have begun to formulate guidelines for the telemanagement of dysphagia (Malandraki *et al.*, 2021) that may serve as a roadmap for SLPs in the future.

7. Solutions and Long-Term Impact in Speech and Language Therapy Delivery

After analyzing the negative impacts of COVID-19 on speech and language therapy services with a special focus on dysphagia, it is important to analyze how the current practice has adapted to these limitations. Many facilities have closed down, and the risk of performing house calls for both clinicians and their patients is still present. Medical practitioners are thus being forced into the field of telepractice (Tohidast *et al.*, 2020). This field, however, brings about the need for several policy changes, which may change the way SLPs operate. One of the immediate changes is that face-to-face interactions will be reduced to when it is absolutely necessary. This necessity is brought about by the fact that speech, language, and swallowing therapy procedures put both patient and clinician at risk as discussed in the previous section. A policy change in this regard means that part-time SLPs will be eligible for reimbursement for services offered via telepractice (Haque, 2020). Before the coronavirus pandemic, reimbursement would only be received for services provided on-site.

Additionally, some facilities are setting up "One Stop" clinics where different parts of the hospital have minimum interaction with each other (Iyengar *et al.*, 2020) to prevent spreading of the virus within the facility.

Another consideration in healthcare that will need reinforcement is the security department. With many physicians relying on telehealth, software systems used by facilities will need to be upgraded to ensure protection of patient information (Haque, 2020). This may be overlooked in facilities that rely on paper-based filing systems that do not utilize information systems technology.

Along with these changes, SLPs have to align themselves with the required social distance precautions to prevent contracting the virus. During in-person sessions involving invasive procedures, where social distancing is almost impossible to achieve, PPE is the best form of protection. Regardless of whether or not the patient has tested positive for the virus, PPE must be utilized. Unfortunately, a shortage of PPE challenges this requirement and hence the implementation of SPACES — Sharing Patient Assessments Cuts Exposure for Staff — by the British Thoracic Society (Zaga *et al.*, 2020). This practice reduces the number of people that come into contact with the patient but ensures that interdisciplinary practice is reinforced. The sudden need to adjust and adhere to these new measures continues to present a great challenge during the pandemic. However, each of these steps is likely to become standard practice in healthcare facilities in the post-COVID era.

8. General Patient Care

The definition of general patient care has been elusive even among healthcare professionals. According to Yorke (2016), many healthcare professionals define patient care depending on the field they operate in. One definition put forward by professionals who have been operating for less than three years is that patient care is engaging in tasks that patients cannot do for themselves. Some of those tasks include, but are not limited to, providing physical care for the patient. This definition implies that patient care is acting on behalf of a patient, for instance, in a nursing home where the elderly can no longer physically function without the aid of an assistant. Examples of these functions include eating, toileting, and ambulation.

A different group of professionals working in the intensive care unit defines patient care as monitoring and operating the medical equipment that supports the lives of patients under their care. More experienced physicians believe that patient care extends outside the boundaries of medical services. In this context, patient care refers to the interaction between a healthcare provider and consumer that is focused on the patient's curing, healing, and/or comfort restoration (Yorke, 2016). These interactions may be, for example, a pre-op meeting with the patient to give them a sense of reassurance about the procedure, pain management, or recovery. This interaction is a part of patient care that is not found in every department of healthcare. Therefore, patient care, similar to nursing care according to Segen's Medical Dictionary (2012), is the all-encompassing act of providing comfort to a patient while they are under the care of a physician.

This analysis of the meaning of patient care shows that it has to be considered in relation to certain goals such as improving quality of life, ensuring safety, alleviating symptoms, and providing interdisciplinary services (Yoke, 2016). This section considers the impact of the COVID-19 pandemic on patient care.

The first significant impact of the pandemic is on providing care in healthcare. The pandemic has struck fear into the hearts of many professionals, as the number of medical practitioners contracting the virus continues to rise. Schwirtz (2020) contends that the situation in New York grows worse by the day, with more than 200 frontline workers having fallen sick by the end of 2020. Much of this has been brought about by the scarcity of commodities that were once in plenty — PPE, gloves, gowns, shields, respirators, masks, and goggles. The mass panic caused by misinformation led to stockpiling of PPE by the public, thereby leaving many healthcare workers at risk of not having enough protection (Boškoski *et al.*, 2020). In addition to panicking as a result of the scale of the pandemic, healthcare workers are also left in fear of working without PPE. Medical staff in Italy have expressed their shock at how rapidly the situation is aggravating (Médecins Sans Frontières, 2020). Indeed, a large majority of medical professionals have never seen a pandemic of this scale. Hospitals are flooding with patients who want to be tested, with some already in critical condition. Majority of resources have been directed to dealing with the COVID-19 patients such that other patients have been neglected. In a press release early in June, the World Health Organization (WHO) noted that the prevention and treatment of noncommunicable diseases has severely declined due to the pandemic (World

Health Organization, 2020a). Many patients with cancer, diabetes, heart disease, and other conditions are not receiving adequate patient care since most efforts are being directed to managing COVID-19 patients.

Aside from the overload of work, shortage of staff, and emotional burnout, the coronavirus pandemic has affected patient care by disrupting healthcare services on a global scale. Many governments ordered an immediate lockdown of all nonessential services once the WHO declared COVID-19 as a pandemic. These measures, along with social distancing and use of PPE, were aimed at preventing the spread of the coronavirus disease. These sudden measures led to the collapse of many job sectors and mass panic. One example of the impact of COVID-19 on general patient care is in the prenatal department. Prenatal care is important since it helps mothers and their unborn children to remain healthy throughout the pregnancy period. Expecting mothers are typically advised to go for a checkup at least once a month before 28 weeks and twice a month between 28 and 36 weeks, after which the checkups should be weekly (Cohut, 2020). These services have been interrupted as a result of the restrictions during lockdown. Even when they have the opportunity, pregnant mothers do not always choose to visit a healthcare facility due to the existing risks. Allotey *et al*. (2020) note that pregnant women or recently pregnant women are less likely to manifest symptoms of the virus but are more likely to end up needing intensive care as compared to other women. Given the situation with COVID-19, expecting mothers may be afraid that visiting a doctor for a checkup is riskier than trying to cope with their pregnancy alone.

While some are opting out of their regular appointments, the number of visits to healthcare facilities due to medical emergencies unrelated to COVID-19 is on the rise. For example, according to Selesnick (2020), the number of people coming in with fractures has gone up tremendously. With so much time on their hands, people have taken up projects within their homes as a way to keep themselves busy. Besides, the number of injuries from falling, hammering, and other construction-related injuries is increasing. In one hospital, the number of people in need of hand surgery due to fractures is on the rise (Selesnick, 2020). However, many of these patients do not go in for follow-up appointments with their doctors. People appear to weigh the benefits of therapy against the risk of entering a hospital during the COVID-19 pandemic and decide to opt out of their appointments. It is no surprise that many facilities are turning to telehealth as a solution to such problems.

Aside from the negative impacts, the coronavirus pandemic continues to force some institutions into changes that they did not anticipate. While some of these changes are a burden initially, they improve and streamline the provision of patient care in the long run. One advantage is the increased focus on the sharing of information. With the current situation forcing healthcare practitioners to interact with patients, the flow of information has become a crucial element of institutions across the world. For example, a COVID-19 dashboard built by Johns Hopkins University has seen an uptake of daily requests from 200 million in January 2020 to 1.2 billion in March 2020 (Taghipour & Kumar, 2020). This is a positive trend that will place a wealth of knowledge at the reach of healthcare professionals. Physicians and clinicians must be well informed about current trends in the healthcare field and the coronavirus pandemic has facilitated this process through the creation of information-sharing platforms.

Fortunately, civilians also appear to be taking medical advice more seriously. Individuals have taken it upon themselves to share the burden of patient care by heeding to the advice of those with medical expertise by self-isolating, staying at home, using PPE in public, maintaining safe social distance, and performing routine hygiene procedures such as washing hands regularly and sanitizing. Adherence to these recommendations has become a communal task which eases the burden on healthcare professionals. Public appreciation for healthcare professionals has also increased significantly as a result of the COVID-19 pandemic (Taghipour & Kumar, 2020).

9. Impact of COVID-19 on Medical Education

The coronavirus pandemic is an unprecedented event. Many people living in these uncertain times have never experienced such a massive disruption to their daily routines as has been seen with the COVID-19 pandemic. So far, this chapter has discussed these disruptions with specific branches of health care under the microscope. However, it would be naïve to assume that life for up-and-coming medical professionals will continue as normal. The medical student's path is more or less set out for them, and they know what to expect as they progress through years of medical school; they commit their time to theoretical studies, then in their final year, they are engaged in the practice of actualizing their theoretical knowledge on placement (Samaraee, 2020). This practice of taking part in clinical and non-clinical studies is a crucial step in introducing medical students to the rigors of healthcare. However, the COVID-19 pandemic has undone this chain, and the future of students, especially those in their final year of medical studies, hangs in the balance. Samaraee (2020) analyzed this situation from a disaster management perspective to safely get through the pandemic or at the least to minimize its damages. The steps that the author proposes are mitigation, preparedness, response, and recovery. He stipulates that these steps are essential tools for any disaster management program.

The situation during the COVID-19 pandemic is that medical students in their final year cannot take part in their normal clinical training, while those in earlier stages of their education are forced to stay at home since many governments across the world have shut down educational institutions to try and manage the coronavirus pandemic. Fortunately, education systems were already adapting to a new age — an age of technology. Indeed, learning programs have been incorporating technology for a while now with examples of successful applications in medical and laboratory settings. Furthermore, learning curriculums have been personalized with students no longer having to travel to a physical setting. Virtual classrooms have facilitated learning anywhere at any time. Nevertheless, it is still necessary for students to interact and learn in actual classrooms and lecture halls. This aspect of learning which has been disrupted due to the coronavirus pandemic presents a barrier to learning.

The act of social distancing has forced many institutions to shut down since it is not always feasible to meet the social distancing requirements. This means that group sessions, especially clinical instruction that requires a group setting, cannot be carried out. One solution has been to reformulate pre-clerkship programs into an online format that students can use while off campus grounds. Technology has become the backbone of medical studies and virtual learning has become the preferred mode of learning during the COVID-19 pandemic.

Students in their final year of medical school are especially disadvantaged since they need hands-on clinical practice to apply their theoretical knowledge and gain confidence to work in the field. However, this structure increases students' risk of being infected with the virus and spreading it to others. Clerkship programs that have been very effective in the past and have been passed down through decades of medical education are now under threat. This model of education also faces challenges due to the COVID-19 pandemic.

In the past, medical students were called upon to help manage disasters by helping out in medical facilities. Examples of such events include floods, forest fires, and other disasters (Rose, 2020). During these times, medical students were able to apply their work to a crisis. However, the coronavirus pandemic presents a different challenge. While short-staffed hospitals in many regions means that there is room for students to come and assist, it also means that there are fewer facilitators able to spare their time to guide these students. Many healthcare professionals, especially nurses, admit that the work they are doing is physically demanding and mentally exhausting (Covert, 2020). It is not surprising that healthcare workers in Belgium were outraged when a decree was passed to allow unqualified healthcare professionals to work as nurses during the COVID-19 pandemic (Mathers, 2020). Opponents argue that nursing skills are not easily transferable to other healthcare professionals. In this sense, having medical students perform a nurse's duties may cause other unexpected problems. Logistical issues present another challenge. It may not be feasible to train medical students in this difficult climate where even the most well-trained doctors are struggling. Furthermore, many healthcare institutions are barely coping with the new technological advances required to deal with patients. It would be very time-consuming to try to operate an unfamiliar system during these difficult times.

10. Conclusion

This chapter has highlighted how the coronavirus pandemic has impacted different branches of the healthcare sector with a special focus on otolaryngology and speech and language pathology services. The COVID-19 pandemic has completely changed how people interact with each other, how healthcare professionals approach the delivery of patient care, and finally it has reshaped the future of medical practices and clinical education. Looking back at the points addressed in this chapter, some things stand out and dovetail the various topics discussed. The nature of the coronavirus pandemic has forced people to practice social distancing and self-isolation. These practices have become a normal part of people's lives, forcing them to alternate ways of interaction. Social distancing requires that people rely heavily technology, with healthcare also taking to this trend. Initially, isolation proved to be a challenge causing patients to cancel medical appointments. With the introduction of telemedicine, more patients are booking appointments with their physicians and clinicians virtually. This is a positive trend since it solves the problem of physical interaction and pushes the healthcare sector in a safer direction. The same can be said for medical education. Institutions are changing their pre-clerkship programs to a virtual system that is compatible with students' schedules. In this sense, the future of healthcare provision and medical education look positive.

The increasing number of people in hospitals, however, continues to be a risk factor for healthcare professionals. Otolaryngologists, nurses, and SLPs continuously put themselves at risk to try and deliver the best form of care possible. To protect themselves from the coronavirus disease, they require high levels of protection. PPE have become a necessity for all practitioners, which has its advantages and disadvantages. For example, face masks are proving to be a problem for people who have hearing difficulties and rely on visual cues for understanding speech, and face shields blur the vision of the physicians as they carry out sensitive procedures. These forms of protections are geared toward keeping everyone safe but in some ways are proving to be a nuisance.

An analysis of the impact of COVID-19 on healthcare would be incomplete without a discussion of where the field is headed post the pandemic. This chapter has already pointed out some areas in which the pandemic is shaping the future, especially in regards to technology. However, patient care is also quickly evolving. With the advent of new methods and scientific advances, there is a visible improvement in patient care. Risk factors, preventative measures, and vaccinations are being researched all around the world. Given this undeniable effort, the pandemic has also forced civilians into appreciating just how much healthcare workers do. Videos of celebrities and political figures applauding the efforts of frontline workers have surfaced. Restaurants, despite having a drop in sales, are offering free food to workers at their respective facilities. Most importantly, civilians are taking patient care and healthcare seriously. People are opting to stay at home, avoid unnecessary trips, and protecting themselves to stay healthy and ease the burden on healthcare workers. Healthcare workers on the other hand are improving their interdisciplinary collaborations. Information sharing has gone up drastically as countries across the world exchange information to find the best way to deal with the virus. The proliferation of research on COVID-19 is also helping physicians adopt new techniques to deal with the challenges that arise due to the pandemic and contributing positively to performance in the healthcare sector. In this context, the COVID-19 pandemic appears to be pushing medical practice in the right direction.

References

Adkins, C., Takakura, W., Spiegel, B. M. R., Lu, M., Vera-Llonch, M., Williams, J., & Almario, C. V. (2020). Prevalence and characteristics of dysphagia based on a population-based survey. *Clinical Gastroenterology and Hepatology, 18*(9), 1970–1979, https://doi.org/10.1016/j.cgh.2019.10.029.

Allotey, J., Stallings, E., Bonet, M., Yap, M., Chatterjee, S., Kew, T., Debenham, L., Llavall, A. C., Dixit, A., Zhou, D., Balaji, R., Lee, S. I., Qiu, X., Yuan, M., Coomar, D., van Wely, M., van Leeuwen, E., Kostova, E., Kunst, H., & Thangaratinam, S. (2020). Clinical manifestations, risk factors, and maternal and perinatal outcomes of coronavirus disease 2019 in pregnancy: Living systematic review and meta-analysis. *BMJ, 370*, m3320, https://doi.org/10.1136/bmj.m3320.

Benito, D. A., Pasick, L. J., Mulcahy, C. F., Rajasekaran, K., Todd-Hesham, H., Joshi, A. S., Goodman, J. F., & Thakkar, P. (2020). Local spikes in COVID-19 cases: Recommendations for maintaining otolaryngology clinic operations. *American Journal of Otolaryngology, 41*(6), 102688, https://doi.org/10.1016/j.amjoto.2020.102688.

Bolton, L., Mills, C., Wallace, S., & Brady, M. C. (2020). Aerosol generating procedures, dysphagia assessment and COVID-19: A rapid review. *International Journal of Language and Communication Disorders*, https://doi.org/10.1111/1460-6984.12544.

Boškoski, I., Gallo, C., Wallace, M. B., & Costamagna, G. (2020). COVID-19 pandemic and personal protective equipment shortage: Protective efficacy comparing masks and scientific methods for respirator reuse. *Gastrointestinal Endoscopy, 92*(3), 519–523, https://doi.org/10.1016/j.gie.2020.04.048.

Brodsky, M. B. & Gilbert, R. J. (2020). The long-term effects of COVID-19 on dysphagia evaluation and treatment. *Archives of Physical Medicine and Rehabilitation, 101*(9), 1662–1664, https://doi.org/10.1016/j.apmr.2020.05.006.

Centers for Disease Control and Prevention. (2020). *Older Adults and COVID-19*. CDC, https://www.cdc.gov/coronavirus/2019-ncov/need-extra-precautions/older-adults.html.

Cohut, M. (2020). The Effect of the COVID-19 Pandemic on Primary Healthcare Worldwide. *Medical News Today*, https://www.medicalnewstoday.com/articles/how-the-pandemic-has-affected-primary-healthcare-around-the-world.

Covert, B. (2020). Women Fighting COVID-19 Are Underpaid and Overworked. *The Atlantic*, https://www.theatlantic.com/health/archive/2020/04/women-fighting-covid-19-are-underpaid-and-overworked/609934/.

de Castro, M. M. & Wertzner, H. F. (2009). Influence of sensory cues on the stimulability for liquid sounds in Brazilian Portuguese-speaking children. *Folia phoniatrica et logopaedica: Official organ of the International Association of Logopedics and Phoniatrics (IALP)*, *61*(5), 283–287, https://doi.org/10.1159/000235661.

Dubey, S. P. & Munjal, V. R. (2014). Endoscopic endonasal transsphenoidal hypophysectomy: Two hand versus four hand technique: Our experience. *Indian Journal of Otolaryngology and Head and Neck Surgery: Official Publication of the Association of Otolaryngologists of India*, *66*(3), 287–290, https://doi.org/10.1007/s12070-014-0703-9.

Farneti, P., Sorace, F., & Tasca, I. (2020). Personal protective equipment for ENT activity during COVID-19 pandemic. *European Archives of Oto-Rhino-Laryngology*, *277*(10), 2933–2935, https://doi.org/10.1007/s00405-020-06177-3.

Filho, A. (2020). Coronavirus: How Brazil became the second worst affected country in the world. *The Conversation*, https://theconversation.com/coronavirus-how-brazil-became-the-second-worst-affected-country-in-the-world-141102.

Fong, R., Tsai, K. C. F., Tong, M. C. F., & Lee, K. Y. S. (2020). Management of dysphagia in nursing homes during the COVID-19 pandemic: Strategies and experiences. *SN Comprehensive Clinical Medicine*, 1361–1365, https://doi.org/10.1007/s42399-020-00464-0.

Ghulam-Smith, M., Choi, Y., Edwards, H., & Levi, J. R. (2020). Unique challenges for otolaryngology patients during the COVID-19 pandemic. *American Academy of Otolaryngology — Head and Neck Surgery (United States)*, 1–3, https://doi.org/10.1177/0194599820954838.

Goldin, A., Weinstein, B.E., & Shiman, N. (2020) How do medical masks degrade speech perception? *Hearing Review*, *27*(5), 8–9.

Gurgel, R. K., Ward, P. D., Schwartz, S., Norton, M. C., Foster, N. L., & Tschanz, J. T. (2014). Relationship of hearing loss and dementia: A prospective, population-based study. *Otology & neurotology: Official publication of the American Otological Society, American Neurotology Society [and] European Academy of Otology and Neurotology*, *35*(5), 775–781, https://doi.org/10.1097/MAO.0000000000000313.

Haque, S. N. (2020). Telehealth Beyond COVID-19. *Psychiatric Services*, appi.ps.2020003, https://doi.org/10.1176/appi.ps.202000368.

Hofstetter, P. J., Kokesh, J., Ferguson, A. S., & Hood, L. J. (2010). The impact of telehealth on wait time for ENT specialty care. *Telemedicine Journal and E-Health: The Official Journal of the American Telemedicine Association*, *16*(5), 551–556, https://doi.org/10.1089/tmj.2009.0142.

Hunt, L., Mulwafu, W., Knott, V., Ndamala, C. B., Naunje, A. W., Dewhurst, S., Hall, A., & Mortimer, K. (2017). Prevalence of paediatric chronic suppurative otitis media and hearing impairment in rural Malawi: A cross-sectional survey. *PloS One*, *12*(12), e0188950–e0188950, https://doi.org/10.1371/journal.pone.0188950.

Iyengar, K., Mabrouk, A., Jain, V. K., Venkatesan, A., & Vaishya, R. (2020). Learning opportunities from COVID-19 and future effects on health care system. *Diabetes and Metabolic Syndrome: Clinical Research and Reviews*, *14*(5), 943–946, https://doi.org/10.1016/j.dsx.2020.06.036.

Kasle, D. A., Torabi, S. J., Savoca, E. L., Judson, B. L., & Manes, R. P. (2020). Outpatient otolaryngology in the era of COVID-19: A data-driven analysis of practice patterns. *Otolaryngology — Head and Neck Surgery: Official Journal of American Academy of Otolaryngology-Head and Neck Surgery*, *163*(1), 138–144, https://doi.org/10.1177/0194599820928987.

Kulcsar, M. A., Montenegro, F. L., Arap, S. S., Tavares, M. R., & Kowalski, L. P. (2020). High risk of COVID-19 infection for head and neck surgeons. *International Archives of Otorhinolaryngology*, *24*(2), e129–e130, https://doi.org/10.1055/s-0040-1709725.

Lalonde, K. & Holt, R. F. (2015). Preschoolers benefit from visually salient speech cues. *Journal of Speech, Language, and Hearing Research: JSLHR*, *58*(1), 135–150, https://doi.org/10.1044/2014_JSLHR-H-13-0343.

Liu, M., Cheng, S.-Z., Xu, K.-W., Yang, Y., Zhu, Q.-T., Zhang, H., Yang, D.-Y., Cheng, S.-Y., Xiao, H., Wang, J.-W., Yao, H.-R., Cong, Y.-T., Zhou, Y.-Q., Peng, S., Kuang, M., Hou, F.-F., Cheng, K. K., & Xiao, H.-P. (2020). Use of personal protective equipment against coronavirus disease 2019 by health-care professionals in Wuhan, China: Cross sectional study. *BMJ*, *369*, https://doi.org/10.1136/bmj.m2195.

Malandraki, G. A., Arkenberg, R. H., Mitchell, S. S., & Malandraki, J. B. (2021). Telehealth for dysphagia across the life span: Using contemporary evidence and expertise to guide clinical practice during and after COVID-19. *American Journal of Speech-Language Pathology*, 1–19. Advance online publication, https://doi.org/10.1044/2020_AJSLP-20-00252.

Marik, P. E. & Kaplan, D. (2003). Aspiration pneumonia and dysphagia in the elderly. *Chest*, *124*(1), 328–336, https://doi.org/10.1378/chest.124.1.328.

Mathers, M. (2020). Coronavirus Belgium: "Outraged" Medics Turn Their Backs in Protest at PM's Handling of Pandemicnt. *The Independent*, https://www.independent.co.uk/news/world/europe/coronavirus-belgium-medics-protest-hospital-sophie-wilmes-a9519686.html.

Médecins Sans Frontières. (2020). Coronavirus COVID-19 Brings Challenges to Developed Healthcare Systems. *MSF*, https://www.msf.org/new-approach-public-health-big-change-needed-fight-covid-19.

Miles, A., Connor, N. P., Desai, R. V., Jadcherla, S., Allen, J., Brodsky, M., Garand, K. L., Malandraki, G. A., McCulloch, T. M., Moss, M., Murray, J., Pulia, M., Riquelme, L. F., & Langmore, S. E. (2020). Dysphagia care across the continuum: A multidisciplinary dysphagia research society taskforce report of service-delivery during the COVID-19 global pandemic. *Dysphagia*, https://doi.org/10.1007/s00455-020-10153-8.

Namasivayam-MacDonald, A. M. & Riquelme, L. F. (2020). Speech-language pathology management for adults with COVID-19 in the acute hospital setting: Initial recommendations to guide clinical practice. *American Journal of Speech-Language Pathology*, 1–16, https://doi.org/10.1044/2020_ajslp-20-00096.

National Health Service. (2020). Dysphagia (Swallowing Problems) — Illnesses & Conditions. *NHS*, https://www.nhsinform.scot/illnesses-and-conditions/stomach-liver-and-gastrointestinal-tract/dysphagia-swallowing-problems.

Rose, S. (2020). Medical student education in the time of COVID-19. *JAMA — Journal of the American Medical Association*, *323*(21), 2131–2132, https://doi.org/10.1001/jama.2020.5227.

Samaraee, A. Al. (2020). The impact of the COVID-19 pandemic on medical education. *British Journal of Hospital Medicine*, *81*(7), 1–4, https://doi.org/10.12968/hmed.2020.0191.

Schwirtz, M. (2020). Nurses Die, Doctors Fall Sick and Panic Rises on Virus Front Lines. *The New York Times*, https://www.nytimes.com/2020/03/30/nyregion/ny-coronavirus-doctors-sick.html.

Segen's Medical Dictionary. (2012). Nursing Care | Definition of Nursing Care by Medical Dictionary. *Farlex*, https://medical-dictionary.thefreedictionary.com/nursing+care.

Selesnick, H. (2020). Don't Cancel Crucial Doctor's Appointment Due to Coronavirus. *Miami Herald*, https://www.miamiherald.com/living/health-fitness/jock-doc/article241754746.html.

Statista. (2021). Novel coronavirus (COVID-19) deaths by country worldwide. In *Statista*, https://www.statista.com/statistics/1093256/novel-coronavirus-2019ncov-deaths-worldwide-by-country/.

Taghipour, D. & Kumar, V. (2020). 9 Ways coronavirus changed treating patients. *ABC News*, https://abcnews.go.com/Health/ways-coronavirus-changed-treating-patients/story?id=70336461.

Tohidast, S. A., Mansuri, B., Bagheri, R., & Azimi, H. (2020). Provision of speech-language pathology services for the treatment of speech and language disorders in children during the COVID-19 pandemic: Problems, concerns, and solutions. *International Journal of Pediatric Otorhinolaryngology*, *138*, 110262, https://doi.org/10.1016/j.ijporl.2020.110262.

Wolf, J. M., Tanaka, J. W., Klaiman, C., Cockburn, J., Herlihy, L., Brown, C., South, M., McPartland, J., Kaiser, M. D., Phillips, R., & Schultz, R. T. (2008). Specific impairment of face-processing abilities in children with autism spectrum disorder using the Let's Face It! skills battery. *Autism Research: Official Journal of the International Society for Autism Research*, *1*(6), 329–340, https://doi.org/10.1002/aur.56.

World Health Organization. (2020a). COVID-19 Significantly impacts health services for noncommunicable diseases. *WHO*, https://www.who.int/news-room/detail/01-06-2020-covid-19-significantly-impacts-health-services-for-noncommunicable-diseases.

World Health Organization. (2020b). Deafness and hearing loss. *WHO*, https://www.who.int/news-room/fact-sheets/detail/deafness-and-hearing-loss.

World Health Organization. (2020c). *Modes of Transmission of Virus Causing COVID-19: Implications for IPC Precaution Recommendations*, https://www.who.int/news-room/commentaries/detail/modes-of-transmission-of-virus-causing-covid-19-implications-for-ipc-precaution-recommendations.

Yorke, D. (2016). Patient care: What is it? *Journal of Patient Care*, *02*(02), 4598, https://doi.org/10.4172/2573-4598.1000e101.

Zaga, C. J., Pandian, V., Brodsky, M. B., Wallace, S., Cameron, T. S., Chao, C., Orloff, L. A., Atkins, N. E., McGrath, B. A., Lazarus, C. L., Vogel, A. P., & Brenner, M. J. (2020). Speech-language pathology guidance for tracheostomy during the COVID-19 pandemic: An international multidisciplinary perspective. *American Journal of Speech-Language Pathology*, *29*(3), 1320–1334, https://doi.org/10.1044/2020_AJSLP-20-00089.

Chapter 6

International Law During and After the COVID-19 Crisis: Does Achieving a True International Cooperation Impossible Without a Structural Shift?

Onur URAZ

International Public Law Department,
Hacettepe University Law School, Ankara, Turkey

onururaz@hacettepe.edu.tr

Abstract

This chapter examines whether the lack of cooperation and coordination in the fight against COVID-19 emerges from some deficiencies in the international legal framework or if there exists a deeper structural problem that requires a much more fundamental change that goes beyond the boundaries of law. This question primarily stems from the writings of Slovaj Žižek, who argues that the ongoing crisis exposed the structural problems inherent to the existing liberal–capitalist order and may ultimately prompt a new form of "communism". This chapter consists of three main parts following the introduction. In part two, Žižek's arguments are presented to the reader. Part three summarizes the international legal framework that governs the fight against the pandemic. The fourth and final part of the chapter offers a critical analysis of the international legal framework in the light of Žižek's criticisms. Here, it is ultimately argued that while both legal reforms and a structural change are needed for better global cooperation in responding to the global needs and threats, rather than liberalism, we should challenge the rising nationalism and the sacralized state sovereignty.

1. Introduction

The possible effects of the ongoing COVID-19 crisis have led to much debate in a variety of fields, including legal studies. Legal scholars and practitioners have been discussing the issues, such as how the disruption caused by the pandemic will affect international commercial disputes and economic system (Bradlow, 2020) or rules on immigration (Wadhia, 2020); can China be held accountable for the pandemic (Kraska, 2020; Lahmann, 2020; Mazzuoli, 2020; Klein, 2020); or whether the pandemic will significantly change the legal culture (Bradley & Halfer, 2020). While the concerns and debates on these matters have undeniable merit and importance, this chapter aims to focus on one particular issue: whether the lack of sufficient international cooperation and coordination in dealing with the COVID-19 crisis simply stems from some deficiencies in the international legal framework and subordinate status of the second-generation rights or from a deeper structural problem which requires a more fundamental change that extends beyond the limits of law.

This question mainly stems from philosopher Slovaj Žižek's argument that the pandemic may ultimately have a positive effect since it has exposed the lack of cooperation and ability of collective action of the ruling liberal–capitalist order in the face of such an imminent threat against the well-being of the entire humanity (Žižek, 2020). According to Žižek, this revelation may incite a demand for what he provocatively calls "communism", by which he refers to a global organization or a form of cooperation that can limit and regulate the market as well as the sovereignty of nation-states in favor of enhancing the social and economic welfare of individuals (*Ibid.*).

This chapter scrutinizes the posed question in three main steps. The second part explores Žižek's philosophical account and its argument that the COVID-19 crisis should prompt a structural shift, as the existing world order is inherently ineffective in responding to global threats like COVID-19 (another example would be the environmental hazards we have been facing). The third part lays out the existing international legal framework utilized in the fight against COVID-19. The final part, by using the criticisms posed by Žižek as a stepping stone, offers an over-all analysis and questions whether the insufficiency of international legal instruments and institutions emerges from a structural problem that requires us to rethink the fundamental pillars and assumptions of the "liberal" system or stems from drifting away from the fundamental values of it.

2. Žižek's Critique: From the COVID-19 Pandemic to a New Form of "Communism"?

When the Cold War was over and Francis Fukuyama declared the "end of history", one of the emerging narratives was a hope for an unprecedented international unity and cooperation underpinned by the liberal ideals. It was assumed that the Soviet bloc had been the main obstacle to the "liberal dream", and once it collapsed, the future would be mostly bright. As we all witnessed during the past three decades, the liberal hope for global unity and the capitalist promise of global prosperity faded away on various fronts. We live in an era where various proxy wars continue, international terrorism has become a more common threat than ever, and the global south and the third world countries are minimally benefited from the triumph of the "free world". Nevertheless, one may have thought that the dream of unity could at least have been realized in the face of global threats, like an environmental disaster or a pandemic. Yet global reactions against the COVID-19 crisis and the threat of global warming appear to prove that even in such extreme circumstances that threaten the entire humankind, the post-Cold War international order has failed to ensure acting with coherence and unity.

From the beginning of the outbreak, Žižek has been vocal about the crisis, and it took less than four months for him to publish a book on the subject. There is no doubt that Žižek capitalizes on the crisis "to peddle his philosophical speculations concerning a re-branded communism" (Gunkel, 2020). Yet there appears nothing wrong with such an approach given that the structural shifts usually occur at the times of global crises, and there is perhaps no better time for an intellectual to advance his/her call for the direction of such a structural shift. Žižek mainly argues that the structural deficits of the prevailing liberal–capitalist order and the danger of nationalist populism have been exposed by the virus. This kind and scale of exposure might, according to Žižek, pave the way for a "new form of communism", by which he refers to a form of global cooperation, which whenever it is needed, controls and regulates the market economy and limits the sovereignty of states (Žižek, 2020).

To begin with his critique of liberal–capitalist order, Žižek, in his humorous style, considers the pandemic as "a kind of 'Five Point Palm Exploding Heart Technique' [a reference to the popular movie Kill Bill] on the global capitalist system — a signal that we cannot go on the way we have till now, that a radical change is needed (Žižek, 2020). "For him, the entire discourse of 'going back to the normal' is misleading. Instead of waiting for things to go back to "normal", we must question the "normal" and ask "Whose normal is this? What interests does it serve? And how does asking about a return to normal normalize exceptional expressions of power and control in which we have always and already been complicit?" (Gunkel, 2020). The pandemic thus provides an opportunity to confront "normal", because it highlights the consequences of structural problems inherent to "normal" in their extremes.

By "normal" Žižek refers to a system driven by market mechanisms. According to him, "[a]s the world-wide epidemic develops, we need to be aware that market mechanisms will not be enough to prevent chaos and hunger (Žižek, 2020)". The global response to the crisis appears to confirm this observation. From a socioeconomic viewpoint, the pandemic has more severely affected the lower classes and underdeveloped countries compared to the developed nations, which further highlighted the deeply rooted inequality of the existing world order. As Žižek notes, while working from home or in isolation is a viable option for certain classes, those who work in sweatshops, fields, stores, medical, and other services do not have the same opportunity (*Ibid.*). In the same vein, the mainstream media and governments became more and more concerned with the effects of the pandemic on the "market" rather than the lives of ordinary individuals (*Ibid.*).

The World Health Organization (WHO), which was established to ensure effective collective responses against global health hazards, particularly epidemics, has also struggled. The WHO was slow to publicly recognize the severity of the situation. Its recommendations have been constantly ignored by the states. Weaknesses stem from the lack of funding and dependency on voluntary donations have been exposed and ultimately led the US to blame the WHO for protecting Chinese interests (Hathaway & Phillips-Robins, 2020a). Despite the rapidly developed COVAX project, the capitalist/nationalist DNA of the global order has led to a race of nations and companies to find an effective vaccination.

Donald Trump's alleged offer of $1 billion to CureVac to secure a vaccine "only for the United States" is one of the most extreme examples in this context (Bennhold & Sanger, 2020).

While several vaccines are now invented and available, the WHO Director-General noted at the early stages of the vaccine distribution that "39 million vaccine doses had been given in 49 richer states — but one poor nation had only 25 doses" (BBC, 2021a). It appears then, while we are in the same boat against the COVID-19 virus, some hold the priority in the rescue process. While each of these issues requires a lengthy examination, which goes beyond the limits of this chapter, when they are considered together, it is hard to deny that the existing global order has severely failed in safeguarding much-needed international cooperation — even in the face of a common threat.

In addition to this critique, Žižek argues that the pandemic has also highlighted how fragile and delusive is the suggestion that global liberalism has been on its way to becoming a common ideal. Rather, the pandemic accelerated the already (re)growing authoritarianism and populist nationalism, and connectedly, problems such as fake news, conspiracy theories, and xenophobia. Leaders with authoritarian tendencies like Bolsonaro, Orban, or Trump used the emergency situation to target minorities and undermine the opposing press (Pozen & Scheppele, 2020). Trump and Bolsonaro particularly relied on unscientific ideas to downplay the situation and to pose as "strong men". Furthermore, rather than genuine international cooperation, "every country for itself" stances are now prevailing with "bans on exports of key products such as medical supplies, with countries falling back on their own analysis of the crisis amid localized shortages and haphazard, primitive approaches to containment" (Žižek, 2020).

Yet from Žižek's viewpoint, the pandemic has nevertheless revealed the ineffectiveness and dangers of nationalist populism and ideas upholding full state sovereignty simply because, for any country to be saved from COVID-19, some form of global coordination and collaboration is necessary. Those countries whose governments denied the scientific facts and international cooperation for bolstering nationalist sentiments or state sovereignty (most notably Brazil) have more significantly suffered from the pandemic. Thus, according to Žižek, "the present crisis demonstrates clearly how global solidarity and cooperation is in the interest of the survival of all and each of us, how it is the only rational egotist thing to do" (Žižek, 2020).

That said, while discussing the situation in China, Žižek makes it clear that liberal–capitalist order should not be perceived as the ultimate value that needs to be supported and defended against these rather dangerous tendencies. Even though he somewhat praises the highly coordinated reaction of China in its fight against the pandemic, he admits that if the Chinese system was not an oppressive one and Li Wenliang, the doctor who first discovered the pandemic, was not tried to be silenced, the present crisis might have been evaded. He nevertheless notes that

> "[t]here should be more than one voice in a healthy society, [...] but this urgent need for other voices to be heard does not necessarily mean Western-style multiparty democracy, it just demands an open space for citizens' critical reactions to circulate. The chief argument against the idea that the state has to control rumors to prevent panic is that this control itself spreads distrust and thus creates even more conspiracy theories. Only a mutual trust between ordinary people and the state can prevent this from happening" (Žižek, 2020).

It must be pointed out, however, even if we accept Žižek's argument that the mutual trust between the state and its citizens is the only way to avoid both the oppression of citizens' critical reaction and circulation of manipulative rumors, he offers no mechanisms to ensure and check this trust relationship. It can also be argued that, despite all its deficits, Western-style liberal democracies provided the most effective "open space" for their citizens.

Overall, then, Žižek emphasizes that even though global crises like the ongoing pandemic requires a form of global cooperation, the liberal–capitalist world order and market mechanisms failed in fulfilling this requirement, which was in fact, one of their primary promises. Instead, market mechanisms have led to a race for more profit through the development of the vaccine as well as the "us first" approach at the national level. Similarly, the crisis prompted some further nationalist populism, which impeded the effective response to the pandemic. For Žižek, this situation may and should induce what he provocatively calls a new form of "communism". By this, he does not refer to "the 'old-style' states of the 20th century, he tells us, but the necessity for a "global organization that can control and regulate the economy as well as limit the sovereignty of nation-states when needed, and a coordinated shift away from the market" (Žižek, 2020).

Žižek claims that despite all the drawbacks stemmed from the afore-mentioned reactions, the situation obliged governments and global actors to offer some "collective" solutions. He points out the mobilization of state resources to pay wages, nationalization of services, such as the temporary nationalization of railways in the UK, or directing industrial productions, such as forcing private companies to work for collective healthcare objectives by the Trump government (Žižek, 2020).[1] Žižek further notes that

> "[m]easures that appear to most of us today as 'Communist' will have to be considered on a global level: coordination of production and distribution will have to take place outside the coordinates of the market. One should recall here the Irish potato famine in the 1840s that devastated Ireland, with millions dead or compelled to emigrate. The British state retained their trust in market mechanisms, exporting food from Ireland even when vast numbers were suffering. We must hope that a similar brutal solution is no longer acceptable today" (Žižek, 2020).

Žižek's conclusion and his call for "communism" are obviously ideologically driven and their merits can easily be contested. However, the facts and criticisms Žižek relied on while building his argument are far from being challengeable. For an international lawyer, his account presents some questions to be examined. First, to what extent the existing international legal framework that governs the fight against the pandemic could be blamed for the lack of cooperation and coordination. And if there exists an inadequacy, is this a structural failure of the liberal–capitalist world order and thus it is unsalvageable without a structural shift or a failure of executive bodies and merely requires a better application? Second, is this crisis the conclusive proof that first-generation rights can only be fully enjoyed if they come hand-in-hand with second-generation rights? If so, is the existing international legal framework sufficient to respond to this need? Before giving some answers to these questions, however, the relevant international legal framework should be examined.

---

[1] He sees stirrings of this in the massive mobilization of state resources to pay private sector wages, nationalize services, and direct industrial production.

3. International Legal Framework that Governs the Fight Against the Pandemic

There are two things certain about the pandemic we are facing. It has a multidimensional nature, which means it affects several levels of society on a variety of issues; and it recognizes no borders, which demands a collective response. For both reasons, international law plays (or should have played) a central role in the global fight against the pandemic since it requires states to take certain actions to detect, prevent, and cure the virus (Hathaway *et al.*, 2021). Yet, as it should be clear by now, the role international law has played through its institutions satisfied very few. International law and its institutions were arguably required to achieve three major objectives in the face of this crisis, namely (1) ensuring the global coordination for prevention and detection, (2) collectively developing and fairly distributing a cure, and (3) protecting the vulnerable groups against the ill-effects of the crisis. International law has seemingly failed, at least to a certain extent, on each front, which calls forth the question of whether the institutions of international law suffered from the shortcomings of their legal framework or bad governance.

Regarding the first two objectives, the WHO, a specialized institution of the United Nations with a mandate in issues of global health, and the International Health Regulations (IHR), the main legally binding rules for the cross-border spread of diseases, have been the main subject of controversy. The WHO has a long normative history, as the idea of crafting a shared framework for coordinating responses against the spread of diseases dates back to 1851 (von Bogdandy & Villarreal, 2020a). A group of states, mostly European, came together to create a framework "to harmonize measures taken by states against international trade and travel" since the "disparities between the measures adopted by states were disrupting commercial activities" (*Ibid.*). The initiative was ultimately unsuccessful as some states "were simply unwilling to cave in to their police powers to confront outbreaks" (von Bogdandy & Villarreal, 2020a)'. Of course, diseases were seen as like natural disasters in the 19th century and thus less responsibility was publicly ascribed to states. Nevertheless, what appears interesting about this early attempt from almost two centuries ago is that, just like today, states were more concerned about their commercial activities and national sovereignty compared to the well-being of individuals.

In the early 20th century, the precursors of the WHO, namely the American Health Organization and the *Office Internationale d'Hygiène Publique*, were established (von Bogdandy & Villarreal, 2020a). The emergence of the consensus over the establishment of global institutions after the Second World War has led to the formation of the WHO, which entered into force in 1947 by superseding the *Office Internationale d'Hygiène Publique* (*Ibid.*). The WHO Constitution expresses that the institution aims "directing and coordinating authority on international health work" and gives a direct mandate to the institution in the fight against pandemics. The WHO constitution also endows some powers to the institution (Gostin, Habibi & Meier, 2020). Articles 21 and 22 of the constitution "stipulate the competence to issue regulations binding for all the member states without national ratification procedures. This represents a truly atypical feature in the landscape of international organizations" (von Bogdandy & Villarreal, 2020a). The World Health Assembly can enact binding regulations by a majority vote of its present and voting members. States who dissent can opt-out of such regulations. Von Bogdandy and Villarreal stresses that this somewhat unique nature of the WHO,

> "shows enormous trust in technical rule-making fostered by experts, technocrats and diplomats. Consequently, it is all the more detrimental to its authority if the WHO is accused for acting, or failing to do so, due to reasons not strictly related to health. The long-standing criticisms due to 'politicization' — broadly understood — and of regulatory capture resonate in public fora. Examples include complaints by the United States government about the WHO's direct intervention in healthcare policies in Palestine and past clashes with the pharmaceutical industry over the Model List of Essential Medicines in 1977. Whenever its decisions are perceived publicly as anything other than technical, their legitimacy becomes contested" (von Bogdandy & Villarreal, 2020a).

Over the years, the WHO has led the fight against both communicable and non-communicable diseases and achieved some success in coordinating efforts and informing communities against diseases like smallpox. However, things have changed since the 1970s. The WHO was affected by the Cold War and its actions started to be considered ideologically favoring one side over the other (Fidler, 2020). Furthermore, mismanagement of health crises brought criticisms. The most notable of these crises was the HIV/AIDS epidemic of the 1980s. "The WHO's deficient response, as well as the absence of any international instrument dealing with such a novel disease, led to an epiphany. The creation of a separate agency specializing in this issue, UNAIDS, was seen as an open critique of the WHO, as it is an issue that fell within its core mandate" (von Bogdandy & Villarreal, 2020a).

Even though the WHO has conservatively used its mandate of creating new binding norms under articles 19 (conventions) and 21 (bylaws) of its constitution and has been criticized for this conservative approach (von Bogdandy & Villarreal, 2020a; see also Taylor & Habibi, 2020; Michael *et al.*, 2014; Lawrence *et al.*, 2015), there are nevertheless several regulations issued by the WHO. The most important of these is the International Health Regulations (IHR), adopted in 1969. However, the early IHR was only limited to cholera, plague, and yellow fever diseases, which was significantly limiting its applicative impact (Gostin *et al.*, 2020). In 2005, the IHR was radically revised and the limitation pertaining to the diseases abandoned. The revision was pioneering, at least on paper, due to that it "was meant to usher an era of rules-based disease surveillance and response, where state sovereignty gives in to shared goals of the international community" (von Bogdandy & Villarreal, 2020a). According to article 2 of the IHR,

> "[t]he purpose and scope of these Regulations are to prevent, protect against, control and provide a public health response to the international spread of disease in ways that are commensurate with and restricted to public health risks, and which avoid unnecessary interference with international traffic and trade".

One obvious peculiarity about this article is that while there is an explicit reference to international traffic and trade, any reference to human rights is missing. Although respect to human rights and freedoms listed as a principle that should be respected in the implementation of the IHR, it can be argued that the protection of human rights in the fight against diseases must be specified as one of the objectives, particularly when it is considered that the WHO constitution is also missing such an explicit reference.

The IHR prescribes a global system in the fight against infectious diseases and draws the minimum and maximum limits for states regarding the measures that they may take in such circumstances. A central element of the IHR system is its global surveillance and reporting mechanism. The problem is that since the WHO is not capable of collecting information on a global scale, it heavily relies on domestic authorities, which makes the system vulnerable to be manipulated by states. While articles 9 and 10 of the IHR stipulate that the WHO can take "other reports" into account as well, the IHR, as it is, gives an undeniable priority to the state reports. There are also not sufficient safeguarding mechanisms when a state denies cooperation. The only concrete provision of the IHR is that when a state denies cooperation, information from other reports will be shared with the other states.

The reporting and surveillance system gain particular importance in the context of article 6 of the IHR. Article 6 provides the main "weapon" of the WHO against the pandemics, which is declaring "Public Health Emergency of International Concern" (PHEIC). The WHO Director-General has the ultimate competence for declaring a PHEIC.[2] Once a PHEIC is declared, all states are required to be ready for containment, e.g., active surveillance, early detection, isolation, contact tracing, and prevention, as well as sharing full data with the WHO. In other words, such a declaration puts some concrete responsibilities on states, yet recommendations are still not legally binding (see article 1 of the IHR) unlike conventions or bylaws.

According to article 6, a PHEIC should be declared in an extraordinary event, which "1. constitutes a public health risk to other states through the international spread of disease (broadly defined as 'any illness or medical condition, irrespective of origin or source, that presents or could present significant harm to humans') and 2. potentially requires a coordinated international response" (see also Gostin *et al.*, 2020).

---

[2] "Although the authority to declare a PHEIC rests in the WHO's Director-General, the procedure involves further expertise. Under article 48 of the IHR, before he/she can declare a PHEIC, the Director-General must summon an Emergency Committee" *Ibid.*, p. 12. According to article 12 of the IHR, in considering declaring PHEIC, the WHO Director-General may take into account the following: (1) information provided by the state party within whose territory an event is occurring, (2) advice from an *ad hoc* technical expert group known as the Emergency Committee, (3) scientific principles, available scientific evidence, and other related information, and (4) an assessment of the risk to human health, of the risk of international spread, and of the risk of interference with international traffic.

Article 6 requires states to inform the WHO within 24 hours "all events that might constitute a public health emergency of international concern" (von Bogdandy & Villarreal, 2020a). Thus, if a state party fails to inform[3] or misinforms the WHO this may lead to the responsibility of that state. Indeed, this has become one of the main points of controversies as to the COVID-19 crises, as China has been blamed by the US for hiding information and violating its obligations.[4] As is observed by Gostin *et al.*,

> "One of the principal IHR reforms in 2005 sought to allow WHO to take account of non-state ('unofficial') sources of information, recognizing that governments are often reluctant to notify WHO of novel pathogens within their borders; however, this innovation was ineffective in the early days of the COVID-19 outbreak, as Chinese authorities repressed health workers, scientists, and civil society in December 2019 [...]. (As the IHR does not provide WHO with the authority to investigate events independently, the IHR requirement for WHO to verify reports received from non-state sources with the relevant state dismantled an additional channel through which WHO could have received the necessary information.)

> [...] Even after China notified WHO about this coronavirus outbreak, the IHR failed to facilitate WHO's rapid declaration of a PHEIC, delaying global preparations for a pandemic response. With inadequate

---

[3] As Gostin *et al.* noted "SARS emerged in Guangdong, China in late 2002, but China did not inform WHO of this emerging threat — as SARS was not one of the three diseases covered by the IHR. China's delay in accurately reporting the SARS outbreak — compounded by the use of domestic legal restrictions inconsistent with public health practice — drew widespread international condemnation, raising calls for WHO action. With SARS highlighting the weaknesses of international law to control for infectious disease, the international community committed with remarkable speed to updating the breadth, scope, and notification obligations under the IHR" (Gostin *et al.*, 2020).

[4] For a similar comment "China first notified the WHO of a cluster of novel coronavirus-like infections on December 31, 2019, but the disease had been circulating in Wuhan for several weeks before that. Yet throughout December, the Wuhan authorities had insisted that the situation was under control. Local police had accused several people who posted on social media about the outbreak of spreading 'rumors' and the city's medical authorities had barred a doctor from speaking publicly about patients suffering from a SARS-like disease. Subsequent assessments by the US intelligence community have reportedly concluded that Wuhan authorities played the decisive role in covering up the initial spread of the virus, keeping central party officials in the dark" (Hathaway *et al.*, 2020a).

reporting and a split in expert opinion, WHO Director-General Tedros Adhanom Ghebreyesus convened an Emergency Committee on three occasions in late January 2020 to advise on the declaration of a PHEIC, as the Committee continued to find that it was 'too early' and that there were 'a limited number of cases abroad'" (Gostin *et al.*, 2020).

According to Gostin *et al.*, the potential economic consequences of a PHEIC declaration as well as the risk of inciting extremely nationalist responses made the WHO reluctant (Gostin *et al.*, 2020).

The events after the deceleration of the PHEIC regarding COVID-19 has proved the accuracy of these concerns since states applied severe restrictions, even against the recommendations of the WHO.

This brings us to the other central element of the IHR system to confront pandemics, which is the WHO recommendations. Article 18 lists series of measures that the WHO may recommend to states, including retaining infected individuals in isolation, executing complementary screening procedures in ports, or applying travel bans. States are expected to adhere to these measures recommended by the WHO. Article 43 allows states to apply additional measures than those recommended by the WHO; however, such measures should satisfy the criteria established in article 43(3).[5] Moreover, these further measures should be reported to the WHO, and the higher degree of restrictiveness should be justified by the evidence. The following parts of the IHR largely include provisions that specify the limits of the restrictions and how they should be applied (von Bogdandy & Villarreal, 2020a). The aim of these is mainly to protect passengers and merchants against the overly restrictive applications of states.[6] However, the IHR is merely a secondary law of the WHO and has

---

[5] Article 43(3): "[…] states parties shall base their determinations upon: (a) scientific principles, (b) available scientific evidence of a risk to human health, or where such evidence is insufficient, the available information including from WHO and other relevant intergovernmental organizations and international bodies, and (c) any available specific guidance or advice from WHO".

[6] "The IHR includes public health measures that a state can take to prevent the spread of a disease. In that sense, the IHR contains mandatory limitations of health measures the state parties can take. Limitations are established to ensure adequate health protection with respect to basic human rights and a minimal hindrance to international traffic. Generally, the state parties cannot request invasive health checks, vaccination or other prophylaxis as a condition of admitting travelers to their territory, nor a state party can request any health documents, other than those provided for under these Regulations or in recommendations

no effective enforcement mechanisms. Therefore, even though it is binding for the member states, the IHR is rarely directly applicable in domestic legal systems, which lessens its effect on the lives of ordinary individuals (*Ibid.*).

Moreover, as noted by Fidler, "the search for a vaccine exposed how states have not crafted an international legal framework for critical aspects of pandemic response — the sharing of pathogen samples and the need for equitable access to pharmaceutical interventions" (Fidler, 2020). Indeed, when the COVID-19 pandemic broke out, and it appeared that a vaccine could be the most efficient response, the WHO had to find an *ad hoc* solution and thus commenced the COVAX (COVID vaccination) initiative. COVAX is not an organization or agreement in its technical sense but rather a partnership between the WHO and two international groups — the Gavi, the Vaccine Alliance and the Coalition for Epidemic Preparedness Innovations (CEPI). The project aims for the equitable distribution of vaccines by acting as a platform that supports the research, development, and manufacturing of a wide range of COVID-19 vaccine candidates and provides an equitable global distribution (Barkley, 2020).

The initiative is now supported by 186 countries. Participants are divided into two categories. First, there are self-financing countries who are required to effectuate upfront payments for their doses.[7] As is noted by von Bogdandy & Villarreal,

> "For high-income countries, COVAX represents a vehicle for their global solidarity, but also for their national interest. Since it is not known which vaccine candidates will ultimately receive regulatory approval, nor what their price will be, self-financing states increased their chances by participating in COVAX, considering its big portfolio of potential vaccines" (von Bogdandy & Villarreal, 2020b).

The second group is the funded states, which consists of low to middle-income states and their doses will be paid by the World Bank and other donors, such as the Bill and Melinda Gates Foundation (von Bogdandy & Villarreal, 2020b). Therefore, the COVAX initiative

---

issued by WHO (article 35 of the IHR). The IHR also prescribes the measures the state parties can apply on ships, aircraft, goods, and containers" (Mladenov & Spaic, 2020).

[7] Also, COVAX's pricing mechanism is set so richer countries pay a premium to subsidize poorer countries.

ultimately aims to make series of international agreements to obtain vaccines and facilitating them by ensuring equal distribution. Accordingly, COVAX expressed its aim to provide two billion vaccine doses by the end of 2021 and ensuring at least twenty per cent of populations are vaccinated. However, COVAX is moving forward much slower than planned. While it was planning to deliver 100 million doses by the end of March 2021, less than 40 million doses were delivered. Also, the WHO Director-General stressed that, as of April 2021, "[o]n average in high-income countries, almost one in four people have received a COVID-19 vaccine. In low-income countries, its one in more than 500" (BBC, 2021b).

Apart from the fact that COVAX emerged as an *ad hoc* solution, which highlights the unpreparedness of the global system against such health crises, it primarily relies on the goodwill and voluntary participation. In other words, states, companies, and other contributors could have refused to join. International law contains no explicit provision to impose an obligation on states in such circumstances. In fact, article 12 of the ICESCR requires states to take essential steps for "[t]he prevention, treatment, and control of epidemic… and other diseases". As is well known, however, the ICESCR deals with the protection of second-generation rights, which are heavily violated during the COVID-19 crisis, and due to the contested nature of these rights and their effectively subordinate status, they are not absolute. This means while all states have the same absolute responsibility in protecting the first-generation rights of their citizens under the ICCPR, article 2 of the ICESCR requires states to take necessary action to protect and enhance the second-generation rights of their citizens "progressively" and "to the maximum of its available resources". Similarly, the Maastricht principles on extra-territorial obligations of states in the area of economic, social, and cultural rights obliges every state to realize such rights "to the maximum of its ability". Consequently, second-generation rights, including the rights to health, work, education, do not have an absolute nature.

4. Can Revising the International Legal Framework Salvage the Problems?

Having summarized the relevant international legal framework, we can now revisit the research question in the light of Žižek's criticisms. It should be evident from the previous part that the international legal framework fails in ensuring cooperation and coordination as well as in protecting the rights of individuals in emergency situations. In order to present some ideas about a solution, one must first identify the source of the problems. In our case, to begin with the problem of lack of sufficient cooperation and coordination, it appears logical to focus on the reasons for the WHO's failure. For Alvarez, there are five of them.

The first of these is sticking with a state-centered approach. As is noted by Alvarez,

> "WHO officials, appointed by states and accountable to them, are reluctant to resort to the nonstate sources of information that the revised IHR allow them to use, much less use that information to challenge what states report to the organization.

> In the absence of other checks on what states report and the measures they take in response to pandemics […], changing the overly deferential stance of the organization to its most powerful members (including but not only China) will require hard work and the selection of WHO officials with backbone and principles" (Alvarez, 2020).

Moreover, albeit states are no longer the only financial source for the WHO, it still relies on them. Moreover, it operates with half of the budget of the United States Centers for Disease Control and Prevention and only twenty per cent of its annual budget comes as guaranteed contributions for general operations, while the rest is voluntary donations that are usually devoted to particular projects (Hathaway & Phillips-Robins, 2020b). It is thus clear that this dependency of the WHO "puts it in an extremely difficult position when it comes to criticizing the actions of individual countries and ultimately poses a threat to the survival of the agency and consequently to global health" (Mladenov & Spaic, 2020).

Against this background, the organization is blamed by Trump for covering up the spread of coronavirus to protect China's interests (Taylor & Habibi, 2020).[8] Similarly, the Japanese Deputy Prime Minister

---

[8] In reality, however, "even after China reported the cluster of cases on December 31, the WHO took a full month to declare a 'Public Health Emergency of International Concern', the IHR's official international alert. That delay reflected, in part, China's decision to prevent health care workers, scientists, and reporters from speaking publicly about an outbreak of SARS-like illnesses in December, and even after acknowledging the cluster of

sarcastically renamed the organization as the "Chinese Health Organization" (Hathaway & Phillips-Robins, 2020b). For the WHO to stop being a venue for political strife between states, organizational reform is obviously needed. Such reform should aim to reduce the de facto reliability of the WHO to states and ensure its autonomy, both financially and politically. Expectedly, this chapter is not the first one that made such a suggestion (Gostin *et al.*, 2020). The question is whether the states support any such reform that will help to achieve greater coordination and cooperation.

It hardly seems so but not because of liberalism or capitalism, as even a diehard capitalist would be supporting cooperation in the face of global threats such as this. Indeed, the COVID-19 crisis has significant ill effects on international trade. From the author's viewpoint, the states will be reluctant because, at their core, they are largely refusing to internalize global liberalist ideals — even the Western democracies — and held on to the Westphalian idea of sovereignty and nationalism. Trump's 2019 statement to the UN General Assembly is striking in this respect, where Trump stated that the "future does not belong to globalists. The future belongs to patriots. The future belongs to sovereign and independent nations who protect their citizens, respect their neighbors, and honor the differences that make each country special and unique" (Trump, 2019). Trump is no longer the US president, but these ideas globally persist on a significant scale and as long as they persist true global cooperation will be unlikely.

The second reason Alvarez put forward for the failure of the WHO is the reliance on the soft law and that the organization has no teeth against the sovereign power of the states, let alone the non-binding recommendations, even the binding instruments of the WHO stipulates no real sanction for disobedience. As Alvarez notes, the "absence of 'name and shame' techniques, much less sanctions of any kind, for WHO members that ignore or openly defy their legal obligations under the IHR is a problem that needs fixing" (Alvarez, 2020). Similarly, Fidler draws attention to the lack of international legal obligation that can effectively ensure sample sharing and equitable access by stressing the lack of cooperation from China in sharing samples of SARS-CoV-2 for surveillance and countermeasure (Fidler, 2020).

---

infections on December 31, to decline for weeks offers from the WHO and the US Centers for Disease Control to send teams of experts to Wuhan" (Taylor & Habibi, 2020).

Indeed, the COVID-19 crisis raised the question of whether the WHO is properly equipped to achieve its object. Benvenisti, answering in the negative, stresses that the organization lacks the necessary authority. For Benvenisti, the organization was established with the assumption that the improvement of global health was the shared goal of all nations and that fighting disease and thus the primary challenge was seen as ensuring proper expert coordination (Benvenisti, 2020). Yet the COVID-19 crisis proved that the problem does not lie in the experts of the WHO and lack of their coordination, but the lack of political cooperation.

> "The WHO's efforts to combat the pandemic have been plagued by competing economic, political, and social demands — conflicts that render coordination difficult and cooperation impossible. [...] Seeking to protect their citizens, states are primed to take defensive action, such as underreporting outbreaks or closing their borders preemptively. At the same time there are also domestic conflicts of interest, as powerful lobbies weigh in to steer national and global health policies in their favor" (Benvenisti, 2020).

A very important distinction between cooperation and coordination is drawn by Benvenisti. Accordingly, the WHO constitution defines the task of the organization as managing global coordination to eradicate the disease by promoting knowledge about them "through a set of rules based on medical expertise. In this foundational model, politics are sidelined" (Benvenisti, 2020). Yet global health management demands more than technical cooperation. It also requires political cooperation. "Cooperation problems are usually mired by the fact that despite common goals, it is strategically advantageous for every actor to 'cheat'" (*Ibid.*). Indeed, this was arguably the underlying motivation of the Chinese government while avoiding sharing information. Hence, as Benvenisti notes, "to facilitate cooperation, it is not enough to set the rules. Instead, it is crucial to set up enforcement mechanisms to ensure compliance" (*Ibid.*).[9] However, due to

---

[9] He further notes that "the management of global health poses both types of problem. Health is a coordination game because actors need to know what the health risks are and the correct ways to treat the disease in question. A global body can reduce health risks by identifying pathogens and disseminating information about the most effective ways to remedy them. It can also resolve coordination problems for those active within states, e.g., by providing useful information to civil society activists seeking to curb the inordinate

the underlying presumption of the WHO, sufficient monitoring and enforcement tools are not endowed to the organization.

Benvenisti also observes that the WHO activism during the SARS pandemic triggered states to reassert their sovereignty by revising the IHR in 2005. To begin with, states imposed some further restrictions to the Director-General's autonomy. According to Benvenisti, this conclusion stemmed from a fundamental disagreement.

"[D]eveloped states wanted the WHO to have greater access to non-state-based information about impending health risks but limited author-ity to censure their protective measures; while developing countries insisted that the WHO remain dependent on information only they would provide, and demanded more accountability from states blocking trade. The outcome was an agreement to 'reify member states' sover-eignty" (Benvenisti, 2020).

He stresses that the revised IHR even undermined the coordination ability of the WHO by imposing that the organization now has to consult with a source states before exercising its powers. As is already mentioned, sharing information with other states is also possible only in exceptional circumstances. Also, the obligation of revealing the identity of indepen-dent sources has a hindering effect on obtaining information from non-state sources (Benvenisti, 2020).

Another important issue is that the control of the WHO over the health measures taken by states is very little as the COVID-19 crisis proved. Indeed, many states disregarded the WHO recommendations (such as the one against travel restrictions) and also implemented some severe

---

political power of lobbies such as tobacco companies, or big pharma companies. But global health also poses a set of interstate cooperation problems, as states have different capabilities and vulnerabilities that shape their responses to health risks. These differences create externalities, as one state can impose risks on another: often, states conceal out-breaks to avoid becoming 'the target of other states' costly [trade] barriers'. Furthermore, scarcity problems plague the attainment of global health goals particularly in times of pandemics as states may hoard medical equipment, profiteer off in-demand resources, and limit their export. As much as nations want other nations to get rid of their illicit weapons while clandestinely keeping stocks of their own, some states would wish their neighbors to eradicate domestic causes of diseases while they keep pushing their farmers to clear forests and get even closer to virus-bearing animals" (Benvenisti, 2020).

measures.[10] As article 43 of the IHR reflects, the states can implement more intrusive and restrictive measures only when there exists no reasonable, less restrictive alternative with a similar effect. Once again, however, the WHO has no power to monitor and sanction power over a state other than asking for a revision of a measure. During the ongoing crisis, some measures like travel bans or lockdowns have been justified in retrospective, more restrictive measures the reasonability of which are questionable is applied by some states and the WHO had no weight whatsoever on these kinds of applications. Once again it appears evident that the lack of power of the WHO is a result of states' obsession with protecting their sovereign rights. As is noted in Gostin *et al.*, "the rise of nationalism has undercut the global solidarity envisaged under the IHR, which requires states to adopt a common and shared responsibility to 'collaborate … to the extent possible'. […] states have reverted to isolationist policies, geopolitical competition, and global neglect" (Gostin *et al.*, 2020).

The third reason that Alvarez mentions is the inflexibility of a PHEIC declaration (Alvarez, 2020). This is a technical problem that can be solved through revising the IHR. The WHO was blamed for being late in its PHEIC declaration as to the ongoing crisis, while in some early cases it was also blamed for making the declaration prematurely or even unnecessarily. However, the fact that the IHR stipulates a binary system puts the WHO in a tough position since it is either a PHEIC or nothing. A more nuanced system with more options that can more accurately reflect the risks could allow the WHO to act easier and encourage states to provide more accurate information.

Moreover, the process of declaring a PHEIC lacks the necessary transparency. While the Director-General holds the ultimate authority, according to article 48 of the IHR, he/she first needs to summon an Emergency Committee, which is composed of experts in the field. Experts are selected from a roster created by the WHO Director-General in consultation with states. Once the Committee is set, it advises the Director-General, but he/she is not obliged to follow this advice. So far, this scenario has not occurred, as the expert views have a de facto weight in the WHO. The problem is, however, while the selection of the committee already lacks sufficient transparency, its decision-making process draws even more criticism on this front because "the Emergency Committee

---

[10] One common criticism is that, in retrospect, state measures of flight restrictions and border closures proved to be effective. This has also harmed the trust against the WHO.

always speaks in 'one voice'. No individual dissents may be reflected in the statements" (von Bogdandy & Villarreal, 2020a).

The fourth reason for Alvarez is an absence of institutionalized mechanisms for cross-regime collaboration. As he notes,

"like many challenges facing UN system organizations, global health threats raise questions of the prioritization and/or harmonization of distinct parts of international law. [...] [B]lack letter international legal doctrine is woefully underdeveloped when it comes to resolving when, for example, the individual or collective 'fundamental' right to health needs to give way to other human rights or needs to be given priority, along with the right to life" (Alvarez, 2020).

As is already mentioned, this a reflection of a broader problem in international law. While the governmental responses to the pandemic have raised concerns about the civil and political, (given that the state of emergency used for travel restriction, curfews, technological surveillance, delay of election, and so on) (Gostin *et al.*, 2020),[11] it also particularly highlighted the tension between first- and second-generation rights. As Quintana & Uriburu note, international law provides much more effective tools to protect civil and political rights from authoritarian measures taken in the fight against the pandemic. Yet, due to the aforementioned subordinate status of the second-generation rights, less-effective tools are devoted to their protection (Quintana & Uriburu, 2020).

What the COVID-19 crisis has shown is, however, that enjoyment of first- and second-generation of rights go hand-in-hand. Indeed, the right

---

[11] That being said, the ongoing crisis and emergency situation nevertheless led to the violation of the first-generation rights as well (Bradley & Helfer, 2020). As is noted by Gostin *et al.*, "Governments rapidly instituted domestic stay-at-home orders, closed businesses, banned public gatherings, and even erected cordon sanitaires (guarded areas where individuals may not enter or leave (WHO praised China's containment efforts as 'ambitious, agile, and aggressive', yet it has since tempered its enthusiasm for such restrictions on individual liberties.) Even as evidence increasingly points to the need for widespread testing, contact tracing, and physical distancing, with transparent governance and public participation in health decision making, governments are increasingly using such states of emergency as pretext for widespread abuses of human rights and subversive attacks on democratic governance" (Gostin *et al.*, 2020, p. 379).

to health as a second-generation right now becames essential for the fulfil-
ment of the right to live. On this point, one must agree with Žižek in that
the overly libertarian ideology that advanced primarily by the US is condemned to fail in the face of the pandemic. This does not entail, of course,
a complete divorce from a liberal way of thinking. However, a more modest version of such ideology must be advanced in future to drift away from
treating differently to those inherently connected two generations of
rights. Similarly, Bennoune observes that

> "COVID-19 'vividly illustrates the importance of the indivisibility and
> interdependence of all human rights'. A pandemic requires nothing less
> than a pan-normative approach. This means actually taking into consid-
> eration the range of rights: civil, cultural, economic, political, and social,
> while also recognizing what the HRC has termed the centrality of the
> right to life. It will also be essential to take as seriously the issue of
> accountability for willful violations of economic, social, and cultural
> rights, as of civil and political rights, during the pandemic" (Bennoune,
> 2020).

Fifth and finally, Alvarez identifies the heavily technocratic nature of
the WHO as a reason (Alvarez, 2020). There is growing consensus that
when experts play bureaucratic roles, their organizations have problems
with governance, as it requires a different kind of expertise. Due to the
foundational presumption attached to the WHO's establishment, this very
fact was overlooked. However, the technocratic design of the WHO
makes it vulnerable both against the political manipulations of states and
assessing the political consequences of its certain actions. As Alvarez
notes, "the WHO's singular reliance on public health professionals may
cause it to be less nimble with respect to reasonable state measures that
are not (yet) backed by rigorous testing or peer-reviewed studies but
which are warranted by the precautionary principle" (*Ibid.*). Such a problem requires a legal reform in the composition of the WHO.

Having laid out these reasons, what can be said about the questions
posed in the early parts of the chapter and to what extent can we agree on
Žižek's arguments. To give a very straightforward answer, in the light of
the arguments so far, one can conclude not only a legal reform but also a
structural change that extends beyond the law is needed in order to better
respond to the needs of humanity in moving forward. However, I am
doubtful that a new form of "communism" should be strived for (Koshy,

2020).[12] This is not to deny that the capitalist DNA of the international order, which is also reflected in the legal documents, has an important role in the problems we are facing now. However, liberalism does not entail brutal capitalism. Rather, it can exist together with conscious capitalism or welfare state as an economic ideology.

From the author's point of view, the pandemic revealed something else, which is that, at the international level, liberalism has never truly established. As Carl Schmitt famously remarked, a state of emergency is the moment that shows who in a state actually is the sovereign. If we translate this idea to the international value systems, the ongoing global state of emergency crystallized that nationalism and sovereignty are the main values upheld in international legal order. In a study that supports this idea, Danchin *et al.* identify what they called the "patriotism paradox" as one of the main reasons that add to the international legal order's failure in efficiently tackling the pandemic. The term denotes the practice of populist governments seeking "to strengthen their national sovereignty by disengaging from global treaty regimes and international organizations. Yet by doing so, they diminish their very sovereign capacity to project externally and protect internally their most basic national values and interests (Danchin *et al.*, 2020)". Thus, in a way, they are not only harming the international order but also themselves.

All in all, it is hard to deny that a legal reform and a structural shift that goes beyond law are much needed to ensure global cooperation, better protection of the rights of individuals, and better response to pressing global needs and threats. What stands in the way is not, however, unlike

---

[12] From a different perspective, Yohann Koshy criticizes Žižek's account by noting that "though this is interesting, it's an image of communism that lacks a central scene: the fate of the working class. In the global south, where most of the world's laborers live, millions find themselves desperate and immediately without income. In countries where there are fewer ventilators than cabinet members, where social distancing in crowded slums is impossible, where debt repayments to western creditors are set to rise, where there are no powerful central banks to issue bonds that investors will trust, Žižek's 'communism' means little. And contrary to his sketch of the situation in Israel, reports show Palestinians are worried about coronavirus overwhelming the West Bank after one sick laborer was 'unceremoniously dumped' at the border by Israeli police. Israel has also linked the political conditions of returning captured soldiers to any future coronavirus-aid to Gaza, Reuters reports. It turns out the logic of domination trumps even the rationalism of 'biological' solidarity" (Koshy, 2020).

what Žižek claims, liberal thinking. Rather it is rising nationalism and sacralized state sovereignty that prevents the realization of true global liberalism, which if it can fully flourish one day, may lead to the realization of a much more effective global cooperation — particularly, if it can be divorced from a brutal form of capitalism.

References

Alvarez, J. E. (2020). The WHO in the age of the coronavirus. *American Journal of International Law*, *114*(4), 578–587, https://doi.org/10.1017/ajil.2020.70.

Barkley, S. (2020). COVAX Explained, https://www.gavi.org/vaccineswork/covax-explained.

BBC (2021a). Covid vaccine: WHO warns of "catastrophic moral failure", https://www.bbc.com/news/world-55709428.

BBC (2021b). Coronavirus: WHO chief criticises "shocking" global vaccine divide, https://www.bbc.com/news/world-56698854.

Bennhold, K. & Sanger, D. (2020). U.S. Offered "Large Sum" to German Company for Access to Coronavirus Vaccine Research, German Officials Say, *NY Times*, https://www.nytimes.com/2020/03/15/world/europe/cornonavirus-vaccine-us-germany.html.

Bennoune, K. (2020). "Lest we should sleep": COVID-19 and human rights. *American Journal of International Law*, *114*(4), 666–676, https://doi.org/10.1017/ajil.2020.68.

Benvenisti, E. (2020). The WHO — Destined to fail?: Political cooperation and the COVID-19 pandemic. *American Journal of International Law*, *114*(4), 588–597, https://doi.org/10.1017/ajil.2020.66.

Bradley, C. & Helfer, L. (2020). Introduction to "the international legal order and the global Pandemic". *American Journal of International Law*, *114*(4), 571–577, https://doi.org/10.1017/ajil.2020.72.

Bradlow, D. & Park, S. (2020). A global liathan emerges: The federal reserve, COVID-19, and international law. *American Journal of International Law*, *114*(4), 657–665, https://doi.org/10.1017/ajil.2020.62.

Danchin, P. G., Farrall, J., Rana, S., & Saunders, I. (2020). The pandemic paradox in international law. *American Journal of International Law*, *114*(4), 598–607, https://doi.org/10.1017/ajil.2020.69.

Fidler, D. P. (2020). To fight a new coronavirus: The COVID-19 pandemic, political herd immunity, and global health jurisprudence. *Chinese Journal of International Law*, *19*(2), 207–213, https://doi.org/10.1093/chinesejil/jmaa016.

Gostin, L. O., Habibi, R., & Meier, B. M. (2020). Has global health law risen to meet the COVID-19 challenge? Revisiting the international health regulations to prepare for future threats. *The Journal of Law, Medicine & Ethics, 48*(2), 376–381. DOI:10.1177/1073110520935354.

Gunkel, D. (2020). Deconstructing the panic of pandemic: A critical review of Slavoj Žižek's pandemic! COVID-19 shakes the world. *International Journal of Zizek Studies, 14*(2), 1–6.

Hathaway, O. & Phillips-Robins. A. (2020a). COVID-19 and International Law Series: WHO's Pandemic Response and the International Health Regulations, available at, https://www.justsecurity.org/73753/covid-19-and-international-law-series-whos-pandemic-response-and-the-international-health-regulations/.

Hathaway, O. & Phillips-Robins. A. (2020b). COVID-19 and International Law Series: Reforming the World Health Organization Series: WHO's Pandemic Response and the International Health Regulations, https://www.justsecurity.org/73793/covid-19-and-international-law-series-reforming-the-world-health-organization/.

Hathaway, O. A., Lim, P., Phillips-Robins, A., & Stevens, M. (2021). The COVID-19 pandemic and international law (March 29, 2021). *Cornell International Law Journal, 54*(2), *SSRN*, https://ssrn.com/abstract=3815164; http://dx.doi.org/10.2139/ssrn.3815164.

Klein, N. (2020). Can China be sued for COVID-19? *East Asia Forum*, https://www.eastasiaforum.org/2020/05/18/can-china-be-sued-for-covid-19.

Kraska, J. (2020). China is legally responsible for COVID-19 damage and claims could be in the trillions, *War on the Rocks*, at https://warontherocks.com/2020/03/china-is-legally-responsible-for-covid-19-damage-and-claims-could-be-in-the-trillions

Koshy, Y. (2020). Pandemic! by Slavoj Žižek review the philosopherprovides his solution, *Guardian*, https://www.theguardian.com/books/2020/apr/23/pandemic-by-slavoj-zizek-review-the-philosopher-provides-his-solution.

Lahmann, H. (2020). Does China really owe the world trillions of dollars? Lawfare, https://www.lawfareblog.com/does-china-really-owe-us-trillions-dollars-reparations-covid-19-light-bosnian-genocide-judgment.

Lawrence, G., Sridhar, D., & Hougendobler, D. (2015). The normative authority of the World Health Organization, *129 Public Health*, 855. DOI:10.1016/j.puhe.2015.05.002.

Mazzuoli, V. (2020). State responsibility and COVID-19: Bringing China to the international court of justice? *International Law Blog*, https://internationallaw.blog/2020/05/15/state-responsibility-and-covid-19-bringing-china-to-the-international-court-of-justice.

Mladenov, M. & Spaic I. (2020). Legal Framework of the World Health Organization Activities During Covid-19 Pandemic, CIP–Cataloging in publication Library of Matica srpska, Novi Sad 3, 25.

Pozen, D. & Scheppele, K. (2020). Executive underreach, in pandemics and otherwise. *American Journal of International Law*, *114*(4), 608–617, https://doi.org/10.1017/ajil.2020.59.

Quintana, F. J. & Uriburu, J. (2020). Modest international law: COVID-19, international legal responses, and depoliticization. *American Journal of International Law*, *114*(4), 687–697, https://doi.org/10.1017/ajil.2020.65.

Taylor, A. L. & Habibi, R. (2020). The collapse of global cooperation under the WHO international health regulations at the outset of COVID-19: Sculpting the future of global health governance. *American Journal of International Law Insights*, *24*(15), 15, available at, https://www.asil.org/insights/volume/24/issue/15/collapse-global-cooperation-under-who-international-health-regulations.

Trump, D. (September 24, 2019). Remarks to the 74th Session of the UN General Assembly, https://www.whitehouse.gov/briefings-statements.

von Bogdandy, A. & Villarreal, P. (2020a). International Law on Pandemic Response: A First Stocktaking in Light of the Coronavirus Crisis, Max Planck Institute for Comparative Public Law & International Law (MPIL) Research Paper No. 2020-07. http://dx.doi.org/10.2139/ssrn.3561650.

von Bogdandy, A. & Villarreal, P. (2020b). The Role of International Law in Vaccinating Against COVID-19: Appraising the COVAX Initiative, Max Planck Institute for Comparative Public Law & International Law (MPIL) Research Paper No. 2020-46. http://dx.doi.org/10.2139/ssrn.3733454.

Wadhia, S. S. (2020). Immigration in the time of COVID-19. In K. Pistor, (Ed.), *Law in the Time of Covid-19*, https://scholarship.law.columbia.edu/cgi/viewcontent.cgi?article=1239&context=books.

Žižek, S. (2020). *Pandemic! COVID-19 Shakes the World*. New York: O/R Books, https://doi.org/10.2307/j.ctv16t6n4q.

Chapter 7

COVID-19: An Existential Crisis of Liberal International Order and the US Leadership

Çağatay ÖZDEMİR

*Department of Political Science and International Relations,
Altinbas University, Istanbul, Turkey*

cagatayozdemir38@gmail.com

Abstract

Following the end of World War II, the West under the US leadership constituted the liberal international order. In recent years, this liberal order has already been suffering from a series of threats and its reliability has also been criticized by many scholars. However, the spread of the COVID-19 pandemic has amplified the interrogation of the existing US-led liberal international order. It has had serious implications on the world's political, economic, and social fabric. Instead of international solidarity and coordination, selfishness and self-centeredness have become prominent in different parts of the world since the onset of the pandemic. In this regard, this chapter addresses the principal foundations of the dominant liberal international order and discusses the effects of COVID-19 on them. The chapter analyses the leadership role of the US during pandemic, the response of multilateral institutions, the degree of international cooperation, and rising political tendencies in the Western world.

1. Introduction

The COVID-19 pandemic is considered one of the most destructive worldwide events since World War II. It is a global crisis in human history and has such far-reaching effects that no country can remain indifferent (Walt, 2020a). The pandemic recognizes no borders and it has made states more skeptical about unrestrictive movement of people. All countries closed their borders to prevent the spread of the virus and international traveling has become difficult. In addition, COVID-19 has triggered xenophobia and racism, which are already existing in many parts of the world. Opponents of immigration have taken the opportunity of the pandemic to implement rigid controls and confined people by prohibiting immigration (BCC News, 2020a).

The United Nations Secretary-General Antonio Guterres argued that "COVID-19 is the greatest test that we have faced together since the formation of the United Nations. This human crisis demands coordinated, decisive, inclusive, and innovative policy action from the world's leading economies" (United Nations, 2020). Since the emergence of the pandemic, individual countries have worked in isolation, instead of international cooperation, coordination, and collaboration. Selfishness and self-centeredness became very common in various countries in different parts of the world. In this regard, from the onset of the unprecedented COVID-19, many countries and international institutions were unsuccessful in containing and managing the crisis. The lack of investment in public health care and inability to take right measures contributed to the extension of crisis.

Existing liberal international order under US leadership was already in jeopardy. Before the pandemic, a great power rivalry between the US and China was present. Relations between the Western world and Russia was weakening. The UK already decided to leave the EU. Hence, COVID-19 has had a triggering effect regarding the questions and debates about the existing liberal international order. It threatens all aspects of human activity, qualifying as one of the most challenging global crises of the post-war era. Accordingly, this chapter argues that the COVID-19 pandemic poses a challenge to the main functioning mechanisms of the US-led liberal international order, which was already faced with a series of threats. The chapter will first examine the principal foundations of the liberal international order after World War II. Then, it will proceed by analyzing the response of multilateral institutions to the COVID-19 crisis, the degree of international cooperation, the role played by the US during the pandemic, and rising political tendencies in the Western world. In the final section, there will be concluding remarks which also strive to evaluate the effect of the COVID-19 on changing dynamics of the current liberal international order.

2. Elements of Liberal International Order

Orders are essential for modern international systems (Mearsheimer, 2019). "Order" is described by Mearsheimer as "an organized group of international institutions that help govern the interactions among the member states" (Mearsheimer, 2019, p. 9). The relations between states are administered by orders in an interdependent world (Keohane, 1984). Orders are significant to regulate state interactions in various areas encompassing economic, environmental, military, and health issues. Hence, the aim of international orders is to facilitate cooperation between states. According to Mearsheimer, liberal international orders can emerge solely in unipolar systems in which the regime of the leading state is based on liberal democracy (Mearsheimer, 2019). In addition, a significant number of other liberal democracies should exist in the system. The main aim of these liberal democracies, particularly the leading state, is to spread democracy around the world and establish effective international institutions. In this regard, liberal international order is expected to be free of war and provide prosperity for its members (*Ibid.*).

According to Mearsheimer (2019), establishing a liberal order necessitates three main tasks. First, it is necessary for significantly expanding the membership in the institutions that made up the Western order (Mearsheimer, 2019). Second, in order to strengthen free trade and capital markets, it is necessary to build an open international economy. Third, it is important to spread liberal democracy across the globe and this aim was adopted by both the US and its European allies.

Although scholars of international relations have made various interpretations of liberal international order, it is agreed that the existing liberal international order was established under the leadership of the US after World War II. It rests on various significant foundations: the US leadership, emphasis on values including democracy and respect for human rights, the principle of multilateralism and international cooperation. As it is argued by Ikenberry, the US and its partners created a multifaceted and emanating international order, strengthened by free market economy, multilateral institutions, cooperation, and democratic solidarity (Ikenberry, 2018). The US-led Western liberal order is "a hierarchical order with liberal characteristics" (*Ibid.*, 2011, p. 8). Both World War II and the Cold War were significant for the US to constitute a liberal international order.

In this regard, the US appeared as the "first citizen" of this order by having a leadership role to support the alliances, to stabilize the world economy, to strengthen cooperation, and to champion "free world" values (Ikenberry, 2018). The US utilized its post-war position to manage the establishment of international order. The West under the US leadership established multilateral organizations involving the United Nations (UN), the World Bank, the International Monetary Fund (IMF), and the General Agreement on Tariffs and Trade (GATT) that became the World Trade Organization (WTO) in 1995.

The post-Cold War period created under American leadership was considered a kind of "security community". In this regard, liberal internationalism became not only more universal in terms of its principles but also more connected to American-led political order (Ikenberry, 2011). The US put forward the rules and institutions, strengthened security cooperation, and managed the world economy. It constituted security partnerships, like NATO, and an American organization, Bretton Woods system was also created as a new global monetary system.

Liberal international order under the US leadership was constituted on open multilateral trade. According to Ikenberry (2018), the general logic of liberal internationalism is based on "openness". The economic foundation of the liberal international order has relied on promotion of peace and prosperity by free trade, open market, and globalization. Hence, exchange and trade are integral for modern society. Accordingly, open international order strengthens economic development and furthers share of knowledge and technology, which brings states together. The US worked to reach an open global economy and took initiatives to open the world economy by establishing institutions such as GATT and WTO.

Transatlantic relations have also had a significant role in the establishment of liberal international order. After World War II, transatlantic relations were strengthened. The UN was established in order to promote peace globally and to facilitate international cooperation economically, socially, and culturally. Although these initiatives were taken, a power struggle between the US and the Soviet Union emerged. The power struggle especially took place in Europe in this bipolar world (Trachtnberg,

1999). Hence, the character of transatlantic relations was based on cooperation in collective security. After the collapse of the Soviet Union, transatlantic relations were transformed since European countries thought that they do not need to be dependent on the US regarding security issues (Henriksen, 2017). Transatlantic relations faced with challenges especially during Iraq War after September 11. The US and European countries pursued different policies during this period. Although some problems occurred in different periods, in general it can be argued that transatlantic relations have had a positive characteristic in liberal international order. The US supported European integration from the beginning and promoted the development of prosperity and stability in Europe for the preservation of liberal international order (Smith, 2008).

When the Cold War came to an end and the Soviet Union dissolved, the US appeared to be the most powerful country in the world. It was considered the leading state to pursue a foreign policy based on establishing an international order on the basis of liberal principles (Mearsheimer, 2018). Liberal ideology, underlying democratic values and norms, sprawled to other countries previously not included in the "free world".

Accordingly, the "unipolar moment" arose and various impediments resulted from security competition between great powers were disappeared (Krauthammer, 1991). President George H. W. Bush underlined in 1990 that "There is no substitute for American leadership" (Bush, 1990). Eastern enlargement process of NATO was considered by Mearsheimer as a good example of the strengthening of the liberal international order under the US leadership (Mearsheimer, 2014). The main goal of this expansion was to integrate Eastern European countries into the "security community" of Western Europe (Mearsheimer, 2019). Deputy Secretary of State Strobe Talbott stated in 1995 that "Enlargement of NATO would be a force for the rule of law both within Europe's new democracies and among them…, it would 'promote and consolidate democratic and free market values'" (Talbott, 1995, pp. 27–28).

Besides US leadership, another basis of the liberal international order was the principle of multilateralism which rests on international cooperation and management of international relations with multilateral organizations. After the end of World War II, multilateralism became significant in world politics. Rules and institutions promote cooperation and provide capacities for states to make good on their domestic obligations (Ikenberry, 2018). According to John Gerard Ruggie, multilateralism is based on an institutional form coordinating behavior among three or more states according to "generalized principles of conduct" (Ruggie, 1993, p. 571). Ruggie's definition of multilateralism involves three bases: indivisibility, nondiscrimination, and "diffuse reciprocity" (Ruggie, 1993). According to Caporaso, multilateralism includes cooperative actions and "not all cooperation is multilateral, but all multilateral activities include cooperation" (Caporaso, 1992, p. 603). In addition, Robert Keohane defines multilateralism as "the practice of coordinating national policies in groups of three or more states, through *ad hoc* arrangements or by means of institutions" (Keohane, 1990, p. 731). He also describes multilateral institutions as multilateral arrangements based on consistent set of rules and considers these institutions in terms of international regimes or bureaucratic organizations (*Ibid.*, 1990).

In this regard, international institutions established under the principle of multilateralism and international cooperation have an important role in maintaining the liberal international order. They can have an effect on state behavior and regulate the state (Acharya, 2006). Moreover, they make essential transformations legitimate and peaceful (*Ibid.*). Multilateralism underlines international cooperation and regulation of international relations. As the Cold War came to an end, multilateral institutions became more prominent regarding the maintenance of international order. For instance, NATO and the EU expanded their memberships after the Cold War. The WTO was created in 1995, and G-20 played a vital role in developing significant responses to various challenges the world economy has faced. When more and more countries participated in those multilateral institutions, political and economic globalization process was stimulated. In this regard, East Asian, Eastern European, and Latin American countries made democratic transition and became integrated into the world economy (Ikenberry, 2018).

The liberal international order has also been supported by shared values and principles. Under the dominant power of the US, the main norms of liberal international order were considered "universal" which are expected to be embraced by different countries. Both the US and its Western liberal-democratic partners aimed to protect a cohesive liberal order by promoting shared values and norms, including respect for human rights and democracy. The power of the US in terms of economy and military capacity facilitated to provide an international system of relative peace and security and constituted the rules of a liberal international order (Gilpin, 1981). In this regard, in order to maintain the liberal order, the US and other Western-oriented liberal democracies have promoted shared values. From Woodrow Wilson to Barack Obama, the US presidents have assumed that democracies have a peculiar capacity to cooperate (Ikenberry, 2018). In the Cold War period, the free world was considered as a community of shared fate (Ash, 2004). Hence, as it is argued by Ikenberry, liberal international order under US leadership was basically a "democratic alliance" to promote a shared liberal-democratic political environment (Ikenberry, 2018).

Although liberal international order has been dominant in world politics for a long time, both the US leadership and the sustainability of the existing liberal international order have become increasingly questionable in today's world. The 2008 global financial crisis undermined the key aspects of international liberal order. Economic conditions of workers and middle-class citizens in the Western world deteriorated (Ikenberry, 2018). Hence, the liberal order lost its image as the provider of economic security and protection. In addition to the financial crisis, the election of Trump as the US President has contributed to the erosion of the liberal international order. During President Donald Trump's period, the US withdrew from various treaties, including the Joint Comprehensive Plan of Action, the Paris Agreement on climate change, and the Treaty Open Skies (Rej, 2020). Moreover, he abandoned negotiations of multilateral trade and investment agreements, including the Trans-Pacific Partnership (TPP) and Transatlantic Trade and Investment Partnership (TTIP), and renegotiated the North American Free Trade Agreement (NAFTA) (Baker, 2017). In addition, transatlantic relationship cracked in Trump's era. When Trump was elected as the US President, German Chancellor Angela Merkel stated that Europe should not be dependent on the US, and she said that Europeans "really must take their fate into their own hands" (Farrell, 2017). Trump considered international institutions including the EU as "obsolete" during the 2016 campaign (Parker, 2016). In this regard, the US was so critical toward liberal international order during Trump's period that, according to some scholars, during Trump's term, the US abandoned its leadership role in this liberal international order (Patrick, 2017).

The rise of China and Russia also challenged the US-led international liberal order. As it is argued by Stephens, the rising China and Russia have threatened the US-led successful liberal-democratic model (Stephens, 2015). These two powers have different view of international system compared to that of the Western world. Both rising powers keep themselves at a distance from the international community since it is too dominated by

Western powers for them (Grant, 2012). Russia and China have supported each other in terms of economic, military policies, and within international institutions such as the UN Security Council (Mearsheimer, 2019). In this regard, the increasing influence of China and Russia is turning the existing liberal international order into a multipolar world. In addition, BRICS countries (Brazil, Russia, India, China, and South Africa) are challenging the Western dominance. The relative significance of these countries has increased promptly over the last two decades. While the contribution of BRICS to global economy rose from 16% during the 1990s to around 30% during 2000–2008, the corresponding contribution of the G7 countries dropped from 70% to around 40% (O'Neill & Stupnytska, 2009). It is approximated that the combined share of global GDP of BRICS to be around US$69.34 trillion, which will transcend that of the G7 by around US$11.42 trillion in 2045 (Mostafa & Mahmood, 2015).

Although international organizations have played a pivotal role in the perpetuation of liberal values in the international order, the trust and reliability on them are diminishing in recent years. For example, the UN Security Council was already under pressure to reform. In addition, while the US has retreated many parts of the multilateral order created after World War II, China's role is intensifying in international institutions. Beijing is pushing its civil servants to the center of the UN institutions, which determines global standards for air travel, telecommunications, and agriculture (Trofimov *et al.*, 2020).

COVID-19 is the latest challenge to the liberal international order, which is in peril. It has propelled a new phase of questioning the survival of the liberal international order. International responses to COVID-19 aggravated the current crisis of the liberal world order. Liberal values, multilateral institutions, and US leadership have appeared to be incapable of dealing with pandemic. Hence, COVID-19 reveals the contradictions within the existing international order, and the Western world has turned out to be incompetent in the struggle with the virus.

3. The Impact of COVID-19 on International Liberal Order

Especially in the early stage of the pandemic, struggling with the scarcity of medical equipment, such as surgical masks and sanitation products, each country in the world handled this problem on its own. During this stage, there was also a lack of a coordinated international response to the pandemic in the means of supplying medical ventilators. In contrast to the main missions of the multilateral institutions, the coronavirus pandemic revealed that they are not functional any more for the global order, stability, and common good, which has made the roles of international organizations controversial. In addition, the hegemony of the US has become a highly controversial topic since it was unsuccessful in providing a leadership role and a transatlantic alliance during the fight with COVID-19 pandemic. Hence, the US, under Trump administration, prioritized national interests over international collaboration. The other impact of the COVID-19 pandemic on international liberal order is the rise of populist and far-right political movements in the West. There is an increase in support for far-right parties across Europe due to pandemic fatigue. These domestic movements are also believed to influence international cooperation negatively.

3.1. *Lack of international cooperation*

Although it is expected that the battle against global health concerns require joint strategies and collective effort, individual practices and territorial measures of the countries during the COVID-19 pandemic have become very common. As it is argued by Basrur and Kliem, if international organizations were effective in developing a collective response to the pandemic, nations would not have prioritized their own interests over common interests (Basrur & Kliem, 2021). On the other hand, in combating a common enemy, the countries' nationalist response trends toward putting their own interests first, blocking international cooperation, and preventing an effective joint response. In this regard, these approaches, observed amid the pandemic, have characterized international relations as self-centered and lacking in collaboration.

The pandemic has revealed the unwillingness of the countries to cooperate with each other when it comes to their own interests. For example, EU countries did not help or give an immediate response to Italy when it asked for medical equipment in its fight against the spread of the virus. Leaving Italy's request for medical equipment through the EU Civil Protection Mechanism unanswered has shown the unwillingness of the other member states to help (Herszenhorn & Wheaton, 2020). When there is no intention to cooperate and no international authority to coordinate the fight and bring synergy during a global health crisis like COVID-19, mask wars, raised prices for ventilators, export bans, and national vaccination campaigns can be regarded as inevitable (Brown & Susskind, 2020, pp. 67–68).

Amidst the pandemic, Germany decided to launch trade restrictions for personal protective equipment in order to secure its own needs. Germany's decision to ban the export of personal protective equipment after France's decision to produce them was criticized for sabotaging the collaborative spirit of the EU (Herszenhorn & Wheaton, 2020). These individual decisions can be evaluated as examples of an increasing trend to protect the national community first in case of an emergency or scarcity. On the other hand, EU member states were unable to enjoy the right of traveling across the Europe since the capitals established border barriers. Besides European countries, many countries chose to impose lockdowns, travel bans, and border restrictions, which are thought to be effective at restraining the pandemic. However, studies show that countries tend to take external precautions like border restrictions rather than internal ones such as social distancing since they aimed to express that domestic public is more cared for (Kenwick & Simmons, 2020, p. 40–41). As a result, these restrictions, which reveal that nations prioritize their community, damage international cooperation and coordination.

During the COVID-19 pandemic, the US has been expected to play a dominant role in strengthening international cooperation to fight with the pandemic. However, under the Trump administration, it has been blamed for keeping ventilators, masks, and other medical supplies within the country through imposing trade barriers or outbidding in the market for equipment, which were originally ordered by and headed to other countries (BBC News, 2020b). The US's reaction to protect its citizens by ignoring the other countries' needs of masks and medical supplies has been criticized even by US officials (Toosi, 2020). Trump administration has also been reluctant to cooperate with emerging powers like China. Since there has been a great power rivalry between two states, international cooperation has not become possible between them. They accused each other regarding the emergence of the pandemic. While China blamed US army personnel for bringing the virus to Wuhan (Myers, 2020), Trump maintained phrasing the virus as the "Chinese virus" and argued that it had been designed in a laboratory (BBC News, 2020c). The Trump administration's self-interested approach in the battle against pandemic has once again shown that international cooperation can be easily ignored during an unprecedented global crisis.

3.2. *Dysfunctional international institutions*

Liberal international order necessitates international organizations which are crucial to form cooperation among states. However, during the COVID-19 pandemic, the WHO has been criticized for not alerting the global society on time and accused of misleading the countries with wrong statements. The WHO, which describes itself as "the directing and coordinating authority on international health within the United Nations system" (WHO, 2021), has been found incapable of handling the COVID-19 pandemic throughout the world. Its leading role in fighting the global disease has become the main target of critics (Winsor, 2020). On March 11, 2020, when the WHO Director-General Dr. Tedros Adhanom Ghebreyesus gave a media brief and declared that COVID-19 could be characterized as a pandemic (WHO Twitter post, 2020), it was regarded as a late call by many experts. The WHO was also criticized for its contradictory statement that there was no transmission of the COVID-19 from person to person and for its misleading advice that travel restrictions were not recommended in the first place (BBC News, 2020d).

Donald Trump and many other world leaders (Hernández, 2020) denounced the WHO for being under the control of China and accused the WHO of taking biased actions (Buranyi, 2020). The Trump administration even decided to terminate relations with the WHO and conveyed the notice of withdrawal to the UN (Cohen *et al.*, 2020). In other words, during the crisis, the reliability of the organization was debated by many leaders, particularly by Trump. They claimed that the WHO, under the influence of China, had cooperated with the Beijing administration to conceal the facts about COVID-19 (Rauhala, 2021). Furthermore, they also stated that the graveness of the virus was undermined by the WHO and China, so they are equally responsible for the outbreak of this global crisis. Despite the dubious accuracy of such claims, these statements resulted in questioning the reliability of the WHO. In the following period, international society started to question the efficiency of the WHO regarding its failure to take necessary precautions to prevent the spread of the virus. Thus, these developments have contributed to the skepticism about the validity of the current liberal international order.

The EU is another multilateral organization where a strong global cooperation and solidarity was unable to be established during the pandemic. With 27 member countries, the EU is an economic and political supranational organization which aims to ensure "social, economic, and territorial solidarity" in the European continent (europa.eu, 2021). Although it represents an economic and social zone, the COVID-19 pandemic showed that it was not ready to fight a global health crisis jointly. Hence, it can be stated that the EU was unable to develop collaborative mechanisms and take joint actions while dealing with the pandemic.

As the country which was hit hardest by the pandemic in Europe, Italy was the first to impose COVID-19 restrictions, such as lockdowns and travel bans. When Italy asked for personal protective equipment, EU partners were not eager to assist and most of the time they were too late to respond (Momtaz, 2020). After Italy's call for assistance, the other countries started to realize the severity of the outbreak and began to consider their own conditions (Herszenhorn & Wheaton, 2020).

During the coronavirus outbreak, EU countries handled the problems with the help of their own mechanisms. It can be stated that the EU's battle against COVID-19 was not a united one, it was more of a sum of individual actions of the member countries. Furthermore, the EU was especially criticized for not taking the necessary precautions and being ill-prepared to defend against the outbreak. Neither national governments nor the EU had any records regarding the medical supply and staff they possessed (Herszenhorn & Wheaton, 2020).

COVID-19 cannot be described only as a health crisis; it also has devastating effects on national economies. Especially Italy, Spain, and France have had a hard time in dealing with the economic effects of the coronavirus outbreak. The EU's response to this economic crisis was found insufficient, since the Union considered it as a fiscal crisis and should be solved by national policies (Rohac, 2020). It assumed that national fiscal measures are needed for combating the economic crisis; thus, a Union-wide response could not be developed.

Furthermore, EU has been criticized for being too slow in delivering the vaccines to the member states. It is argued that the UK has been able to make deals with the vaccine makers with the advantage of the Brexit (BBC News, 2021). Since the UK is not subject to EU regulations, it could stay out of the bureaucracy and move fast. On the other hand, the Union was incapable of satisfying the public in terms of the reliability of the AstraZeneca vaccine, which caused lower vaccination rates (Cendrowicz,

2021). This points out that EU has difficulties in building trust in its policies and actions. Although the EU tried to establish a crisis management system which carries out the search and the procurement phases of the vaccination process, it seems that the system does not work properly, so that the countries still have doubts (Rankin, 2020). It can be inferred from these cases that the EU has been incapable of developing a holistic strategy to overcome the COVID-19 crisis. As a result, European synergy has weakened and lost its collaborative power.

3.3. *Decline of the US leadership and acceleration of the existing transatlantic differences*

The COVID-19 outbreak has become part of discussions on the future of liberal international order, led by the US, and uncertain transformation of transatlantic relations. Especially, the deepening fractures in liberal order and distrustful atmosphere in transatlantic ties had worsened with the Trump administration's foreign policy choices. According to Duran, the debate on the impact of the Trump administration — retreated the US from the position of a global leader with the motto of "America First" — on international order and the predictions on the outcome of the pandemic are persisting. Actually, the management of the pandemic which is based on self-sufficiency policies of states is closely related with President Trump's inability to lead the fight against the COVID-19 pandemic and his incapacity for diplomacy (except accusing China) are seen as new signs of "the collapse of liberal world order" (Duran, 2020). Furthermore, some scholars presented that the economic outcome of the pandemic and political failure of Trump administration in responding to the crisis became a serious existential threat to the liberal order. For example, Kaplan claimed that the pandemic has paved the way for serious issues for the US economy, which was built on free trade and market understanding of capitalism. The liberal international order, constructed after World War II, is on the verge of the devastation. As a result of Washington's reluctance to lead, international organizations could not coordinate necessary measures to respond to the outbreak (Kaplan, 2020).

Furthermore, the pandemic has brought a serious economic burden on the shoulders of the US citizens, so internal matters became the main focus point of Trump administration, which had affected the liberal order adversely. On the other hand, the pandemic also has created a significant opportunity for some states to strengthen their positions in the international system. In this context, Kaplan said that it is argued that China and Russia will obtain an apparent advantage at the end of the COVID-19 outbreak because of Washington's position. The economic capacity of Beijing means it can stand on the burden of economic challenges and its political structure has given a suitable environment to apply debatable measures. On the other hand, the Moscow administration had formed a self-supporting economic structure to limit the impact of economic sanctions, so it was not caught unaware of the catastrophic effects of the pandemic (Kaplan, 2020). Therefore, it can be claimed that Russia and China will be more prepared and more competitive in the international system to compete with the US after the pandemic. At the same time, the US will have to face new challenges to sustain liberal order alongside the adverse consequences of COVID-19.

In addition, the performance of the EU in this period should be examined in order to make a comprehensive analysis of transatlantic relations and liberal international order. Considering ineffectiveness and incapability of international organizations to fight against COVID-19, the EU had to face a tough test. After the European debt crisis, the pandemic became the most severe political and economic challenge for the EU and its member states, which has spurred discussions on the future of the EU. In this context, the lateness of the EU, a supranational organization model, to respond to the crisis, the lack of a proper mechanism in the EU structure to fight against the crisis, national security prioritization of the EU members, and the problematic image of unity within the EU due to the closure of national borders are remarkable (Aydın, 2020). In this context, EU member states tried to find solutions to ease their economic burden since the precautions to prevent the spread of COVID-19 has paved the way for a financial crisis for them. Member states had tried to form a European solution within the EU in spite of infrastructural weakness of the European Union. For instance, within this framework, leaders of EU member states could not find a common ground on the idea of "corona bonds", a financial instrument to recover from economic devastation of member states due to the pandemic (Herszenhorn et al., 2020). It was a clear example for EU member states to comprehend the capacity of the Union to deal with the outbreak. At the same time, a crisis does test not only the response capability of an actor but also its durability against challenges. After Brexit, it may be said that the confidence and will of member states in terms of its success in the fight against the pandemic and the degree to which the burden is eased will determine the future of the EU. At the end of the day, EU leaders had assessed this meeting as an opportunity to express the Union's unity. However, it made diversities among members more apparent because of current and previous problems of the EU. Particularly, the reluctant stance of EU members to come to Italy's assistance in terms of medical supplies has paved the way for serious disputes among the member states (*Ibid.*, 2020). Furthermore, discussions on the old problems have revealed that some EU member states were commencing to rake up the past, so COVID-19 may have serious political consequences for the EU in the long run. At that point, Aydın expressed that it should be noted that the existence of the EU after the crisis will be determined within the context of its contribution and effort to overcome ongoing economic crisis and to transform member states' economies. The success of EU in abovementioned issues will contribute to the evolution and continuation of the EU. Otherwise, it will cause more weakening of the Union (Aydın, 2020).

In balance, the direction of international liberal order and the future of global leadership of the US were being questioned after a long time in order to make a comprehensive analysis of the next international system before the pandemic. Therefore, existence of transatlantic ties and liberal world order were significant parts of these debates, so the pandemic has added new aspects and new variables to them. On the one hand, the continuation of the US's retreat policy and the reluctant stance to lead the global community to fight against COVID-19 has strengthened suspicious views about liberal international order and the willingness of the US to lead the system. On the other hand, poor performance of the EU and "every man for himself" perspective of member states have damaged the unity norm of the EU. Therefore, it could be stated that political and economic results of the pandemic may incite debates on exiting the Union in some member states. Under any circumstances, alternatives for liberal international order will be discussed loudly to reshape the post-pandemic world, so while transatlantic relations weaken gradually, states will seek to form new partnerships in the recovery process.

In this regard, transatlantic relationship is at risk of being further deteriorating with the pandemic. After the emergence of COVID-19, Trump decided to implement travel ban against European countries on March 11, 2020 without consulting with any European officials (BBC News, 2020e). In addition, transatlantic relations were negatively affected because of the US decision to stop funding the WHO. High Representative of the Union for Foreign Affairs and Security Policy Josep Borrell criticized the suspension of funds (Reuters, 2020). Similarly, German Foreign Minister Heiko Maas considered Trump's decision to halt funding the WHO as "throwing the pilot out the plane" (DW, 2020). In this regard, the COVID-19 has made top state officials on both sides of the Atlantic more inward-looking while they are combating with its negative ramifications.

3.4. *Populism and the rise of far-right political movement in the West*

The existing order has already deteriorated with the rise of more protective and more isolationist policies in the world. COVID-19 probably accelerated this process by increasing the implementation of policies based on self-help understanding (Aydınlı, 2020). The effects of the pandemics were not limited to international level, so it has started to create significant consequences for local politics and societies. Particularly, economic problems and increasing number of impoverished people due to COVID-19 outbreak have turned into a political challenge for European leaders. In this context, increasing populism and strengthening far-right political movements in the Western states became the most apparent result of the pandemic. Muddle & Wondreys (2020) stated that the pandemic was turned into a political leverage by many far-right parties in the opposition that criticized the performance of their administration in fighting against COVID-19. At the beginning, their criticisms were based on ineffective and late response of their governments. Subsequently, quarantine and lockdown decisions of governments were criticized by far-right parties by emphasizing democratic and constitutional concerns (Muddle & Wondreys, 2020). In this framework, these parties have preferred to use a discourse based on the freedom of speech and the rule of law, so they could channelize the anger or the disappointment of people against the governments.

At the same time, COVID-19 has given an enormous opportunity to far-right parties to exploit the fears of the masses. In other words, it can be said that the far-right has assessed the COVID-19 pandemic as an opportunity to trigger masses of people who could be impressed by conspiracy theories. For instance, the anti-vaccination movement is very active in Germany where people regularly organize protests against the measures aimed at fighting against COVID-19 (TRT World, 2020).

Furthermore, there are many variables which determine the political structure of European states in the near future; however, far-right parties, which instrumentalized xenophobia as a political tool, will make an effort to exploit the sufferings of the masses caused by the outbreak. In this context, the effect of the pandemic on far-right movements and its outcomes for European politics in the long run are not still at the final point. Regarding Trump's electoral loss, it should be noted that far-right parties in Europe are more capable of using the crisis as political leverage in a sophisticated way (*Ibid.*). In the same vein, Muddle & Wondreys emphasized that the debate about the far-right and the pandemic should be examined more carefully. In general, the far-right is aware of the possible outcomes of the pandemic and has not faced unintended political consequences, so the far-right could preserve its public image (Muddle & Wondreys, 2020).

In the light of these, European far-right political parties have a strong ideological background and enough political experience to produce different discourses on unsuccessful attempts of governments to fight against the outbreak or undemocratic decisions in terms of quarantine policies. At the same time, it could be argued that the solution proposals of these parties will be limited to discursive debates. On the other hand, regarding political trends in Europe, far-right political parties may achieve their political goals by using their ideological and reductive discourses, if European leaders cannot succeed in finding comprehensive remedies to cure outcomes of COVID-19.

4. Conclusion

The unprecedented COVID-19 pandemic can be regarded as one of the most challenging crises of the post-war liberal international order, which had a deep impact on the international cooperation and world politics. While fighting against a global pandemic indicates a critical necessity for international cooperation, it can be argued that countries have implemented policies inconsistent with the liberal international order. Although the US was expected to have an effective leadership role from the onset of the pandemic, it has been reluctant to take responsibility to take a leading role and to promote multilateralism in order to deal with the crisis.

In this regard, the COVID-19 pandemic has caused serious debates on the future of the current liberal order. Particularly, regarding recent discussions on the existence of liberal order, political, social, and economic consequences of this outbreak have turned into a significant determiner in order to understand potential transformation of the international system. At that point, increasing uncertainties in the current international order with the pandemic complicates the interpretations of the future of the existing order. As it is argued by Walt (2020b), states will evaluate the COVID-19 pandemic as another cause to restrain globalization. COVID-19 and its severe consequences demonstrated the capacity of states to find comprehensive solutions in fighting against the pandemic. Hence, contrary to the principal foundations of liberal international order, states and multilateral organizations have made an effort to minimize liabilities and burdens by limiting their responsibilities and the scope of their relations with one another (Walt, 2020b). Although the US-led liberal international order was established on the basis of strengthening international cooperation and multilateralism, states and societies preferred unilateral and self-help solutions as the only way to solve the crisis.

In this context, domestic consequences of COVID-19 may present unexpected alterations in the Western states regarding strengthening far-right political movements. Weakening liberal order and ineffectiveness of international organizations have created a suitable environment for the nationalist and state-centric discourses of these political groups. Therefore, far-right politicians have tried to exploit the suffering of the masses, which is the focal point of their discourse. In the long run, it could be said that severe outcomes of the outbreak may cause significant changes in European politics. Particularly, rising extremist political thoughts may have more supporters and get a better position in their states' political field as a result of COVID-19. On the other hand, it should be noted that the future of European political structure will be determined by European leaders in terms of their economic and political success to ease the burden on the masses.

In the final analysis, in modern history, the structure of international order usually has been determined by great turning points such as WWII or the end of Cold War. The rise and fall of ideologies and great powers have been shaped in this context that determined our world's political, economic, and social structure. Regarding COVID-19, it is too early to assess precise impact of its consequences on world politics. However, it should be said that international order has been experiencing a significant structural change. In this frame, the outbreak and its severe outcomes on states and societies will accelerate the transformation of international order and define its contour in the long run. At the same time, the pandemic will pave the way for people to begin questioning existing state–society relations. Therefore, the transformative effect of the pandemic at domestic and international levels will be debated for a long period of time.

References

Acharya, A. (2006). Multilateralism, sovereignty and normative change in world politics. In E. Newman, R. Thakur & J. Tirman (Eds.), *Multilateralism Under Challenge? Power, International Order, and Structural Change*, pp. 95–118. Tokyo: United Nations University Press.

Ash, T. G. (2004). *Free World: America, Europe, and the Surprising Future of the West*. New York: Random House.

Aydın, M. (2020). COVID-19 ve Uluslararasi Düzen. In *Covid Sonrası Küresel Sistem: Eski Sorunlar Yeni Trendler*, pp. 40–44. Ankara: T. C. Dışişleri Bakanlığı Stratejik Araştırmalar Merkezi (Ministry of Foreign Affairs Center for Strategic Research).

Aydınlı E. (2020). *Salgınlar ve Uluslararası Sitemin Dayanıklılığı. In Covid Sonrası Küresel Sitem: Eski Sorunlar, Yeni Trendler,* pp. 35–39. Ankara: T. C. Dışişleri Bakanlığı Stratejik Araştırmalar Merkezi (Ministry of Foreign Affairs Center for Strategic Research).

Baker, P. (2017). Trump Abandons Trans-Pacific Partnership, Obama's Signature Trade Deal. Retrieved April 4, 2021, from *The New York Times*, https://www.nytimes.com/2017/01/23/us/politics/tpp-trump-trade-nafta.html.

Basrur, R. & Kliem, F. (2021). Covid-19 and international cooperation: IR paradigms at odds. *SN Social Sciences*, 1(7), 1–10.

BBC News (April 22, 2020a). Coronavirus: US green cards to be halted for 60 days, Trump says. Retrieved March 12, 2021, from https://www.bbc.com/news/world-us-canada-52377122.

BBC News. (April 4, 2020b). Coronavirus: US accused of 'piracy' over mask 'confiscation'. Retrieved March 15, 2021, from https://www.bbc.com/news/world-52161995.

BBC News. (May 1, 2020c). Coronavirus: Trump stands by China lab origin theory for virus. Retrieved March 30, 2021, from https://www.bbc.com/news/world-us-canada-52496098.

BBC News. (July 8, 2020d). Coronavirus: What are President Trump's charges against the WHO? Retrieved April 9, 2021, from https://www.bbc.com/news/world-us-canada-52294623.

BBC News. (March 12, 2020e). Coronavirus: Trump suspends travel from Europe to US. Retrieved April 9, 2021, from https://www.bbc.com/news/world-us-canada-51846923.

BBC News. (April 7, 2021). Covid: What's the problem with the EU vaccine rollout? Retrieved April 12, 2020, from https://www.bbc.com/news/explainers-52380823.

Brown, G. & Susskind, D. (2020). International cooperation during the COVID-19 pandemic. *Oxford Review of Economic Policy*, 36(1), 64–76.

Buranyi, S. (April 20, 2020). The WHO v Coronavirus: Why It Can't Handle the Pandemic. Retrieved March 18, 2021, from *The Guardian*, https://www.theguardian.com/news/2020/apr/10/world-health-organization-who-v-coronavirus-why-it-cant-handle-pandemic.

Bush, G. H. W. (1990). Address before a Joint Session of the Congress on the Persian Gulf Crisis and the Federal Budget Deficit. Retrieved March 18, 2021, from *George H.W. Bush Presidential Library & Museum*, https://bush41library.tamu.edu/archives/public-papers/2217.

Caporaso, J. A. (1992). International relations theory and multilateralism: The search for foundations. *International Organization*, 46(3), 599–632.

Cendrowicz, L. (February 24, 2021). *Why Is the EU Running into So Many Difficulties with its Covid Vaccine Campaign?* Retrieved March 20, 2021, from *The Guardian*, https://www.theguardian.com/commentisfree/2021/feb/24/eu-covid-vaccination-difficulties-anti-vaxxers.

Cohen, Z., Hansler, J., Atwood, K., Salama, V., & Murray, S. (July 8, 2020). Trump Administration begins Formal Withdrawal from World Health Organization. Retrieved April 5, from *CNN*, https://edition.cnn.com/2020/07/07/politics/us-withdrawing-world-health-organization/index.html.

Duran, B. (2020). Koronavirüs Sonrası Yeni Bir Dünya Düzeni Mi, Düzensizliği Mi? In *Covid-19 Sonrası Küresel Sistem: Eski Sorunlar, Yeni Trendler (Global System after Covid-19: Old Problems, New Trends)*, pp. 29–34. Ankara: Dışişleri Bakanlığı Stratejik Araştırmalar Merkezi (Ministry of Foreign Affairs Center for Strategic Studies).

DW. (April 16, 2020). Germany's Angela Merkel backs WHO after Donald Trump Cuts Funding Over Coronavirus. Retrieved April 5, 2021, from https://www.dw.com/en/germanys-angela-merkel-backs-who-after-donald-trump-cuts-funding-over-coronavirus/a-53156070.

European Union (EU) Official Website (2021). The EU in Brief, Retrieved April 8, 2021, from European Union, https://europa.eu/european-union/about-eu/eu-in-brief_en.

Farrell, H. (May 28, 2017). Thanks to Trump, Germany Says It Can't Rely on the United States. What Does That Mean? Retrieved March 19, 2021, from *Washington Post*, https://www.washingtonpost.com/news/monkey-cage/wp/2017/05/28/thanks-to-trump-germany-says-it-cant-rely-onamerica-what-does-that-mean.

Gilpin, R. (1981). *War and Change in World Politics*. Cambridge: Cambridge University Press.

Grant, C. (February, 2012). Russia, China and Global Governance, *Centre for European Reform*. Retrieved March 23, 2021, from Carnegie Endowment for International Peace: https://carnegieendowment.org/files/Grant_CER_Eng. pdf.

Henriksen, T. H. (2017). *Cycles in US Foreign Policy since the Cold War*. California: Palgrave Macmillian Press.

Hernández, J. C. (May 29, 2020). *Trump Slammed the W.H.O. Over Coronavirus. He's Not Alone*. Retrieved March 25, 2021, from *The New York Times*, https://www.nytimes.com/2020/04/08/world/asia/trump-who-coronavirus-china.html.

Herszenhorn, D., Barigazzi, J., & Momtaz, R. (March 27, 2020). *Virtual Summit, Real Acrimony: EU Leaders Clash over 'Corona Bonds'*. Retrieved March 29, 2021, from *Politico*: https://www.politico.eu/article/virtual-summit-real-acrimony-eu-leaders-clash-over-corona-bonds/.

Herszenhorn, D. M. & Wheaton, S. (April 7, 2020). How Europe Failed the Coronavirus Test. Retrieved April 4, 2021, from *Politico*, https://www.politico.eu/article/coronavirus-europe-failed-the-test/.

Ikenberry, G. J. (2011). *Liberal Leviathan: The Origins, Crisis, and Transformation of the American World Order*. Princeton, NJ: Princeton University Press.

Ikenberry, G. J. (2018). The end of liberal international order? *International Affairs*, *94*(1), 7–23.

Kaplan, R. (April 18, 2020). *Why the Pandemic Should Transform the Way America Thinks about War*. Retrieved March 14, 2021, from The Washington Post, https://www.washingtonpost.com/opinions/2020/04/08/why-pandemic-should-transform-way-america-thinks-about-war/.

Kenwick, M. R. & Simmons, B. A. (2020). Pandemic response as border politics. *International Organization*, *74*(1), 36–58.

Keohane, R. O. (1984). *After Hegemony: Cooperation and Discord in the World Political Economy*. Princeton, NJ: Princeton University Press.

Keohane, R. O. (1990). Multilateralism: An agenda for research. *International Journal*, *45*(4), 731–764.

Krauthammer, C. (1990/1991). The unipolar moment. *Foreign Affairs*, *70*(1), 23–33.

Mearsheimer, J. J. (2014). Why the Ukraine crisis is the West's Fault: The liberal delusions that provoked Putin. *Foreign Affairs*, *93*(5), 77–89.

Mearsheimer, J. J. (2018). *The Great Delusion: Liberal Dreams and International Realities*. New Haven: Yale University Press.

Mearsheimer, J. J. (2019). Bound to fail: The rise and fall of the liberal international order. *International Security*, *43*(4), 7–50.

Momtaz, R. (March 14, 2020). Germany to Send Face Masks to Italy to Help Deal with Coronavirus. Retrieved March 21, 2021, from *Politico*, https://www.politico.eu/article/germany-to-send-face-masks-to-italy-to-help-deal-with-coronavirus/.

Mostafa, G. & Mahmood, M. (2015). The rise of the BRICS and their challenge to the G7. *International Journal of Emerging Markets*, *10*(1), 156–170.

Muddle, C. & Wondreys, J. (December 17, 2020). Unlike Trump, Europe's Far-Right Leaders Haven't Been Damaged By The Pandemic. Retrieved March 18, 2021, from *The Guardian*, https://www.theguardian.com/world/commentisfree/2020/dec/17/trump-europe-far-right-pandemic-covid-19-us-presidents.

Myers, S. L. (March 13, 2020). China Spins Tale that the US Army Started the Coronavirus Epidemic. Retrieved March 30, 2021, from *The New York Times*, https://www.nytimes.com/2020/03/13/world/asia/coronavirus-china-conspiracy-theory.html.

O'Neill, J. & Stupnytska, A. (2009). The Long Term Outlook for the BRICs and N-11 Post Crisis. *Goldman Sachs Global Economic Paper No. 192*, Retrieved March 28, 2021, from Goldman Sachs, New York, NY, https://www.goldmansachs.com/insights/archive/brics-at-8/brics-the-long-term-outlook.pdf.

Parker, A. (April 2, 2016). *Donald Trump Says NATO Is 'Obsolete', UN Is 'Political Game'*. Retrieved March 21, 2021, from The New York Times: https://www.nytimes.com/politics/ªrst-draft/2016/04/02/donald-trumptells-crowd-hed-be-ªne-if-nato-broke-up/.

Patrick, S. M. (2017). Trump and world order: The return of self-help. *Foreign Affairs*, *96*(2) (March/April), 52–57.

Rankin, J. (April 1, 2020). *Coronavirus Could be Final Straw for EU, European Experts Warn*. Retrieved March 12, from The Guardian: https://www.theguardian.com/world/2020/apr/01/coronavirus-could-be-final-straw-for-eu-european-experts-warn.

Rauhala, E. (March 30, 2021). WHO Chief, U.S. and Other World Leaders Criticize China for Limiting Access of Team Researching Coronavirus Origins. Retrieved April 1 2021, from *The Washington Post*, https://www.washingtonpost.com/world/who-wuhan-tedros-lab/2021/03/30/896fe3f6-90d1-11eb-aadc-af78701a30ca_story.html.

Rej, A. (November 23, 2020). United States Formally Exits Open Skies Treaty. Retrieved April 4, 2021, from *The Diplomat*, https://thediplomat.com/2020/11/united-states-formally-exits-open-skies-treaty/.

Reuters. (April 15, 2020). EU 'Deeply Regrets' Trump's Cut to WHO Funding, says Usnjustified. Retrieved April 4, 2020, from https://www.reuters.com/article/us-health-coronavirus-trump-eu/eu-deeply-regrets-trumps-cut-to-who-funding-says-unjustified-idUKKCN21X1E0.

Rohac, D. (March 16, 2020). Coronavirus Could Break the EU. Retrieved March 31, 2021, from *Politico*, https://www.politico.eu/article/coronavirus-covid19-public-health-crisis-could-break-the-eu-european-union/.

Ruggie, J. G. (1992). Multilateralism: The anatomy of an institution. *MIT Press*, *46*(3), 561–598.

Ruggie, J. G. (1993). Multilateralism: The anatomy of an institution. In J. G. Ruggie (Ed.), *Multilateralism Matters: The Theory and Praxis of An Institutional Form*, pp. 3–50. New York: Columbia University Press.

Smith, M. (2008). The USA and the EU. In M. Cox and D. Stokes (Eds.), *US Foreign Policy*, pp. 219–238. Oxford: Oxford University Press.

Stephens, B. (2015). *America in Retreat: The New Isolationism and the Coming Global Disorder*. New York: Sentinel.

Talbott, S. (1995). Why NATO Should Grow. *New York Review of Books*, pp. 27–28.

Toosi, N. (April 4, 2020). US Cast as Culprit in Global Scrum Over Coronavirus Supplies. Retrieved March 20, 2021, from *Politico*, https://www.politico.eu/article/coronavirus-united-states-cast-as-culprit-in-global-scrum-over-supplies/.

Trachtnberg, M. (1999). *A Constructed Peace, the Making of the European Settlement 1945–1963*. Princeton, NJ: Princeton University Press.

Trofimov, Y., Hinshaw D., & O'Keeffe, K. (September 29, 2020). How China is taking over international organizations, one vote at a time. Retrieved March 30, 2021, from *The Wall Street Journal*, https://www.wsj.com/articles/how-china-is-taking-over-international-organizations-one-vote-at-a-time-11601397208.

TRT World. (December 18, 2020). *Europe's Far-Right Parties Make Headway Amid Covid-19 Pandemic*. Retrieved March 18, 2021, from TRT World: https://www.trtworld.com/magazine/europe-s-far-right-parties-make-headway-amid-covid-19-pandemic-42480.

United Nations (2020). United Nations Secretary-General Launches Plan to Address the Potentially Devastating Socio-Economic Impacts of COVID-19. (March 31, 2020). Retrieved March 14, 2021, from *United Nations: Press Releases*, https://unhabitat.org/sites/default/files/2020/04/sg_press_release_march31_2020_final10am.pdf.

Walt, S. M. (2020a). *The Global Order After COVID-19*. Retrieved March 12, 2021, from Institute for Security Policy (ISP) Working Paper: https://www.institutfuersicherheit.at/wp-content/uploads/2020/06/ISP-Working-Paper-Stephen-M.-WALT-The-Global-Order-After-COVID-19.pdf.

Walt, S. M. (March 9, 2020b). *The Realist's Guide to the Coronavirus Outbreak*. Retrieved March 20, 2021, from Foreign Policy: https://foreignpolicy.com/2020/03/09/coronavirus-economy-globalization-virus-icu-realism/.

Winsor, M. (August 15, 2020). *Timeline: WHO's Response to the Coronavirus Pandemic and the Ensuing Controversy.* Retrieved March 22, 2021, from abcNews: https://abcnews.go.com/Health/timeline-response-coronavirus-pandemic-ensuing-controversy/story?id=71690767.

World Health Organization (WHO) Official Twitter Account. (2020). *Twitter post 11 March 07:16 pm.* Retrieved March 24, 2021, from https://twitter.com/WHO/status/1237774421307228160.

World Health Organization (WHO). (2021). *Our Values.* Retrieved March 24, 2021, from WHO: https://www.who.int/about/who-we-are/our-values.

Chapter 8

Can We Stop and Listen Now?

Helena BELCHIOR-ROCHA[*,‡] and
Rosário MAURITTI[†,§]

*Department of Political Science and Public Policy,
ISCTE-Lisbon University Institute, Lisbon, Portugal*

†*Department of Sociology, ISCTE-Lisbon University Institute,
Lisbon, Portugal*

‡*helena_rocha@iscte-iul.pt*
§*rosario.mauritti@iscte-iul.pt*

Abstract

The objective of this chapter is to present, in a systematic way, the most recent data that shows the general consequences of the situation experienced in our country (Portugal), since the beginning of the Contingency Plans — COVID-19, focusing on the impact felt in higher education institutions and in the analysis of requirements and challenges to be faced by higher education and its institutions. Thus, in order to find effective ways of acting on the effects of this crisis / challenge, in a proactive way, re-learning a critical attitude to understand the constant societies crises, with which we are currently struggling, our proposal is to prepare students to face unexpected and increasingly frequent situations. Although in addition to the specific knowledge of each area, associate transversal, transferable and soft skills, to articulate with interdisciplinary teams, promoting their adaptation and resilience, inner-self-knowledge, empathy, social responsibility awareness and recover the fundamental value of BEING.

1. Introduction

Undoubtedly, March 2020 will forever be known in the educational community as the month when almost all schools and universities in the world were closed. Due to the pandemic, governments have instituted school and university closures. According to UNESCO,[1] by the end of March, 185 countries had implemented closures, affecting 90% of the world's students. The speed of these closures and the rapid transition to distance learning allowed very little time to plan or reflect on both potential challenges and potential opportunities.

The rush to change to distance learning has brought some associated risks. The worst way to learn is to sit passively and listen, and this was the way that many students experienced online education during this period. Some say there is something magical in the face-to-face connection that unites teachers and their students in a classroom and that in a distance learning environment, this personal interaction is very difficult to replicate.

Blackman[2] described the pandemic as a chance to use digital tools to make higher education more accessible: "an opportunity to reach out, open up access, and really show what higher education can do in a crisis like this" (Blackman, 2020). In a recent interview, he highlighted "In online education, the difficult part is not technology … it is teaching. Most university professors don't know how to involve students in online learning environments. They do this, but they were not trained to do so" (*Ibid.*). They were not evaluated for that.

It is not surprising that some students who use online education during the pandemic have a bad experience and say, "It has been terrible". Bad experiences with online learning during the pandemic can make it difficult to accept good use of this model later. However, these bad experiences are important for learning what works and what doesn't.

Beyond the health crisis, the COVID-19 pandemic affected and had an impact on the entire human condition and on the economic, social, and political systems. These circumstances lead the human being to accept uncertainties, ambivalences, and contradictions present in the system, which reminds us of Morin when he said in an interview "it is necessary to regroup knowledge in order to seek an understanding of the universe"

---

[1] https://en.unesco.org/.
[2] Tim Blackman Vice-chancellor of The Open University (United Kingdom).

to go beyond what "is established as lawful and true knowledge" and to carry out a constant exercise of questioning what is evident and accepting the limits of our thinking and uncertainties. Based on the premises made by Morin (2001) about the knowledge necessary for the education of the future, an analysis was developed with a methodological support in bibliographic research and secondary statistical data.

2. The Impact of COVID-19 — General Consequences

Our contemporaneity, marked by the project of building a global world, is confronted with challenging in social, political, and economic issues; therefore, it is essential to return to trust in Man, in his capacities, in his communicative potential, in understanding and acceptance of the Other. The moment we live in is not compatible with rigid ways of thinking about the world; change is not achieved by repeating the same mistakes. Until now, few things were pitied with slowness, the speed of the world was too fast, we ran out of resources, and the challenges faced by contemporary societies in which the political, economic, and social paradigms were constantly changing and simultaneously with a heavy cultural inheritance, are facing a hybrid present and a future of unknown dimensions: a virus.

> "Nobody can rely, today, on his claim to knowledge, on an undoubted evidence or on a definitely verified knowledge. Nobody can build his knowledge on a certain rock. My research on Method starts, not from the mainland, but from the soil that collapses" (Morin, 1998).

In Portugal (COVID-19: Report of Health General Direction), until today, the number of cases confirmed were 796,339, recovered 696,916, active 83,526, deaths 15,897 — we are a small country with 10,286,300 resident population.[3]

The impact of COVID-19, according to a recent study realized by a team of academic researchers (Magalhães *et al.*, 2020), show that part of the concerns of the Portuguese lies in social inequalities and poverty as consequences of the health crisis; forms of social discrimination, particularly in relation to older people; the impact on the younger ones of being

---

[3] https://www.pordata.pt/Portugal.

away from school; and the political consequences of the pandemic, particularly with regard to civil liberties and the future of the European project. Many also express more diffuse, but no less intense concerns: the lack of control over their own lives with increased uncertainty and unpredictability, the decrease in the quality of family and interpersonal relationships, and the loss of a lifestyle (travel, life "outside home", enjoying the city). Another fact was the question of trust in information; young people rely less on information channels than older people, and in this second wave, the theme addressed was the family tensions arising from confinement. One in five respondents reported that they experienced more moments of family tension during confinement than before. This was more frequent among the youngest (16–24) and those who are studying and less among respondents aged 45–54 years.

The increase in family tensions was also more frequent in single-parent households; a single parent and the child, in households composed of an extended family, couples with children, parents, in-laws, grandparents, grandchildren, etc., and in households made up of several people without a nucleus co-workers, friends, or cousins. Finally, the increase in tension within families is also associated with changing routines and the difficulty in dealing with restrictions caused by confinement.

One of the respondents' main concerns about the future is the "economic situation of the country", followed by the "public health situation" and "uncertainty about when we will be back with family, friends, and colleagues".

In another recent study, Costa (2020) alerts us to social justice issues and threats to the democratically organized human existence that the intensification of inequalities is generating, even more in an extraordinary situation of linked crises, pandemic, economic, and social.

3. Challenges of Higher Education Institutions

The consequences of COVID-19 in higher education has recently been studied around the world. Pereira (2020) reports several of them as is the case of "the massive and extremely rapid transfer of face-to-face work to a telework regime; the disruption and restructuring of teaching activities at all levels; the cancellation, suspension, or postponement of a large number of scientific events and processes (such as conferences or evaluation and audits); the interruption or disruption of research work due to higher levels of illness and anxiety, the closure of universities, restrictions on mobility, more intense and complex loads of care for the most varied types of dependents and less favorable working conditions (for example, with less access to technologies, books, and other materials, with more distractions and less capacity of multi-tasking, in confined spaces shared with others); outbreaks of dismissals and freezing of hires and career advancement; changes in academic calendars and calendars for applications, execution, or evaluation of scholarships and research projects; changes in the number of students applying for courses, with an impact on university budgets; the reduction or redirection of funding available for certain activities or scientific areas". It is a fact that they are consequences and transformations common to several universities in the world, but all assume different manifestations and intensities in each context, institution, or area of knowledge.

In Portugal students enrolled in higher education in 2019 were 126,345 and in 2020, 133,322 (PORDATA/DGEEC/ME-MCTES) — about 5.5% more, but in our university, we had an increase in the number of enrollments from 1490 students in 2019/2020 to 2510 in 2020/2021, an almost 40% increase. COVID-19 launched us all into a massive pedagogical experiment, forcing the adoption and evaluation of new approaches like never before: synchronous delivery (where students and teachers must be involved at the same time) versus asynchronous delivery (where they are not); social media versus traditional media; multimedia versus written work; and home learning material versus labor commercial learning material.

In addition to this need for pedagogical creativity, there is a different way of assessing the effectiveness of learning. We usually defend that the primary responsibility must be to focus on students and their learning, this being the most important criterion for deciding whether pedagogical approaches are successful. So, this becomes even more important when teachers and students are not sitting in the same space, when face-to-face informal feedback between student and teacher does not happen.

The pandemic is not only a time of change for educational technology, but also for pedagogy, and the challenges of the transition to distance learning must encourage universities to put more resources into teacher training to teach better. This is a time for higher education to collectively challenge all types of ingrained practices, because as Morin (2001) warned, with so many changes happening in the contemporary society, the act of looking at education today cannot be in an isolated or decontextualized way. It was intended to grant to society students who predominantly dominated theoretical knowledge and strictly technical procedures, but today's society presents other requirements and has already presented them long before, evident in the first of the seven knowledge postulated by Morin (2001): "The blindness of knowledge: the error and the illusion" referring to the knowledge that the individual has and that must include learning from the mistakes we have been making. It is in this sense that we defend the importance of investing in studies on science, paradigms, in order to reflect on the blindness of knowledge, the risks of error and illusion; train to develop the ability to welcome the new and be prepared for uncertainty; build questions that make it possible to review the conceptions of the world, of society, of education and rethink teacher education considering subjectivity; educate to change attitudes toward knowledge and interpersonal relationships; dialogue with the other; invest in methodologies that allow students to perceive and position themselves, become aware of what they are and what they think; use methodologies to seek to reflect on "how we are constituted and who we are"; break with the fragmentation of knowledge; educate reason and emotion so that the student develops autonomy of thought and interpretation of reality, with the focus of valuing the student as a rational, human, and creative being.

The fifth knowledge "Facing uncertainties" (Morin, 2001) talks about uncertainty when dealing with "knowledge" may seem a paradox, since predominantly, educational institutions are intended to teach only the conceptual and scientific "certainties". But as time goes by, it has noticed the emergence and rise of what is unexpected and for which we were not prepared and these uncertainties can be taught in the light of the historical process of humanity. Another of Morin's (2001) seven knowledges, the sixth, concerns "teaching understanding"; this issue was mentioned because the author said that "we do not teach how to understand each other", in this context we speak of a sense of empathy, identification, and human communication as a fundamental element.

However, a society characterized by intense individualism emerged, gained strength more and more, giving voice to many aspects related to self-centeredness. Understanding, in this perspective, is not just for the other, but includes the individual with oneself, since self-analysis is also configured as necessary, and this is possible with the teaching of soft skills. The role of education should be centered on a process of a globalized society, living with information technologies, without forgetting the human condition.

The transformative effects of higher education are well understood in the sector and in society. There are links between university education and more innovative societies but a deeper commitment to social justice. That said, universities around the world are under pressure to justify their existence, be more accessible, and to find ways to be more inclusive on different knowledges and experiences.

There is also "a need for governments and institutions to rethink their models of professional development, recognizing that the skills acquired by a student are as important as knowledge, and that in terms of teaching, opportunities should be provided to incorporate teaching skills such as problem-solving development, collaboration, creativity, and communication. Furthermore, these competences cannot be taught in isolation, but must be present in the curriculum as part of teaching practices" (Belchior-Rocha, 2020).

Thus, each educational institution must pay attention when carrying out its planning: understand its technological infrastructure, the knowledge of its teaching staff, the number of face-to-face classes that students may have, whether the model adopted will be more face-to-face or online, and countless other factors, practically all of them with some implication in the area of health and future contingent situations.

4. Technology as an Ally, Not a Protagonist

The development of technological solutions for creation of new forms of teaching has seen multiple innovations in the recent years, some of which have a positive impact on students. Today, through the internet, you can easily access games and exercises for learning, interactive content for teachers to use, or even digital platforms that are authentic schools in the virtual world. Therefore, due to the challenges that the COVID-19 pandemic is placing, dozens of educational resources (paid or free) have been referred to as alternatives in newspapers, by official bodies (such as the Ministry of Education), or by UNESCO, encouraging teachers and students to explore distance learning.

The initiative makes sense, in this context of emergency and social isolation, it was the only viable solution to, almost immediately, provide students with a kind of continuity of learning. But, if the solution is possible, how effective is it? There are still many doubts in the scientific communities about the effectiveness of distance learning in terms of learning, especially when compared to classroom teaching. Some even argue that distance learning is a weak substitute for classroom teaching. Of course, its effectiveness varies depending on several factors, from the preparation of the teacher for distance learning to the specific profile of the student. It is these details and the responses on this issue that require reflection on what this implies for the present and the future.

According to an opinion survey of students from universities and institutes in Portugal about the pandemic and the education system, the majority of students (59.4%) said that they felt hampered by distance learning in relation to classroom teaching. Four out of ten students admitted to feeling higher levels of anxiety because of confinement, while 18.4% did not feel any changes in behavior. More than eight out of ten students (83.6%) of those who complain about distance learning accumulate feelings of apathy, anxiety, isolation, and unrest — a situation that is shared by 58.3% of those who say they are in a globally favorable situation.

Among students who are not satisfied with the current teaching situation, there is a 44% decrease in participation, while among other students the decrease is 15%.

Students admit that they are concerned with the final assessment and complain about the workload (60.2%), also feel that they are also less interested in classes now, with emphasis on those who feel disadvantaged with distance learning (only 26.6% say the level of interest remains).

Almost two-thirds of students do not know families of colleagues without access to computer equipment or the Internet at home, but among students who say they are in a globally unfavorable situation, 38.3% say they know at least up to five families unable to ensure non-classroom teaching.

Although these results may seem negative, we have to think that technologies are present in all moments of our life, this involves everything from social use to daily practices resulting from the transformations that happen through human socialization. For Kenski (2010) "… the convergence of information and communication technologies for the configuration of a new technology, digital, caused radical changes". The changes occurred by the technologies in teaching and learning processes made it possible for several researchers to become interested in the theme and carry out studies in the area, such as Kenski (2010), Almeida & Prado (2009), Belloni (2010), Buckingham (2010), and Rossato (2014). Most of these studies question the ease of access to information and how it is being worked on in pedagogical practice. They also inquire about the new possibilities of teaching and learning since contemporary students are also known as digital natives. They state that information and communication technologies has transformed social interactions and access to information, but they also presented relevant considerations about new ways of teaching and learning that are emerging through the interaction between the real and the virtual. Our students are immersed in a digital context, inserted into a digitalized society in which information and communication technologies are present in the organization and functioning of their everyday lives, so besides the pandemic situation we must include them in the teaching and learning process, although we emphasize that there is still an abyss regarding the use of information and communication technologies in social life and in education.

Outside the university, students use this technological universe, but we still find restrictions on its use in pedagogical practice and in the learning pattern.

There is still a small number of empirical researches on this subject, when compared to opinion articles, and it is therefore necessary in any future scientific work to avoid prejudices or opinions without any scientific basis.

Let us not forget that digital natives are causing a rupture not only in the labor and consumption market but in society as a whole. Furthermore, because this generation is more connected, attentive, concerned with needs (environment, social, and others), the job market will have to find a way to fit them and universities have to respond. Thus, those who know how to deal with the wishes of this generation end up adapting better to a new reality.

For digital natives, the way of thinking and acting can hardly be framed within the mental schemes of a digital immigrant (where teachers are inserted). Digital natives develop a thought based on a cognitive structure that works in "parallel" and that is not sequential.

In this digital context, Prensky (2012) stated that "... technology, rather, is an extension of our brains; it's the new way of thinking. It's a new solution we humans have created to deal with our difficult new context of variability". As can be seen, the digital immigrant has a whole set of references that do not fit in this digital context for the reason of having developed a set of routines and mental schemes throughout their life where linearity and sequentially constituted their references.

Once more this is not new, Castells (2005) came to introduce and discuss the concept of network society as being a social structure based on networks that are operated by the technologies that generate, promote the processing and diffusion of information from the knowledge accumulated in the different nodes of these networks. It is in this "web of networks" that the synergies leading to the generation of knowledge are centered and where the opportunities for creativity and innovation are contextualized. In this sense, cyberspace came to configure a new reality, a digital reality, where everyone can connect and interact between the different nodes of the network, in a more flexible and more adaptable logic that can provide new and more efficient possibilities due to the ability to be able to "decentralize" whenever it proves to be convenient and necessary.

As is still stated by Castells (2005), network communication manages to cross and transcend borders, becoming global, making the human and social organization increasingly integrated, and at the same time, dependent on these digital networks with all advantages and disadvantages associated with it. In order to be able to take advantage of cyberspace, digital skills must be possessed that allow an appropriate use and interaction in this digital context. In other words, whoever is in an info-exclusion situation is no longer able to take advantage of this reality, and as such, is no longer socially included.

Another issue that has been talked about a lot is security: a survey carried out by the Cybersecurity Observatory of the National Center for Cybersecurity (CNCS) with the support of the General Directorate of Education (DGE) on the aspects experienced by the teaching community in the first period of confinement (2nd semester of 2019/2020) reveals that 81% said "they have not experienced any type of cyber threat", of the few existing cases the most verified was "third party intrusion in videoconference class" (11%), malicious software (5%), unauthorized recording of the class (3%), and phishing/smishing (3%) (Observatório de Cibersegurança Centro Nacional de Cibersegurança, 2021).

The positive side of this huge experience is that many different blended learning approaches are being tried, tested, and used more and more. We know that the most engaging learning experiences are those that are most interactive, that face-to-face learning is better than 100% online learning. But the future requires that teaching/learning processes combines online teaching and classroom interaction with traditional teaching methods. It is based on the best of both worlds. After having done 100%

online during this pandemic, we can think of a balanced combination of classroom and online learning. Teachers are innovating and experimenting with online tools and may want to continue teaching online as a result of all of this, which is really promising.

We know that online teaching will not replace face-to-face teaching in the long run, but as already mentioned, more important is pedagogy, that is, approaches to facilitate learning that capitalize on the opportunities presented by technology. This is a time for higher education to challenge its collective view on all kinds of ingrained practices. It is a time to introduce more creative flexibility in higher education.

For each assumption underlying the way universities are run, the question must be: Is what we are doing today really up to the standards of the future?

Knowing the technological limitations resulting from some equipment that equips universities, the inadequate training of some teachers, we believe that the use of the internet in a safe and controlled way is, even today, a topic of great discussion and with many gaps.

Aware of the mission of preparing students to live in the information and communication society, generated by flows, we agree that there are several challenges that are posed to today's schools, because as Silva (2006) says: "they are the models that become out of place in the face of society's requests, are the audiences that change, the techniques and technologies that have developed quickly, the skills that teachers are asked to evolve".

In this society we have to educate ourselves to get to know information, but educating implies having a vision of the future and for that to happen, we have to think in the long term.

5. Educating for Uncertainty, Complexity, Unforeseen, and Ambiguity

Currently, we live in a paradigm that prevails in all spheres of public life and in which there is a subjective change in the way man sees his future. No longer with the security of the past but with the discouragement that the uncertainty of the unknown and the risk provoke. However, today, in the context of globalization, risk is something that is totally open; it is no longer limited to traditional risks, but it also covers all aspects of human life.

It is this dimension that gives it a character that is new, since in the past, man lived and overcame risk, finding the confidence that allowed him to overcome this dichotomy and simultaneous complementarity between risk and trust, which contributed to the progress of humanity. However, in a constantly changing world, traditional forms of trust (in those closest to us) have been dissolved. Currently our lives are influenced by unknown and distant people, and we are losing "the ontological security founded on the continuity of our personal identity and which is rooted in the constancy of the surrounding social and material environments" (Giddens, 2004).

The first half of 2020 was the scene of unprecedented abrupt disruptions in all social layers. The pandemic quickly introduced changes that passed through everyone's lives, directly affecting all sociability spaces. In the face of so many changes and restructuring, questions and uncertainties emerge in everyday experiences. Social, economic, and political relations will undergo post-pandemic changes; with universities, it will be no different. These are collective and socialization spaces where the perception of the multidisciplinary nature of knowledge must be transmitted, as well as a vision of transversal multiculturalism, in a world that, due to its evolution in communications, has become increasingly interdependent, with all resulting socio-political consequences.

It is important to deepen skills associated with aptitudes and attitudes, to develop personal and interpersonal skills, such as critical spirit, autonomy, leadership, group and team work, communication, and as delicate as it is difficult, the emotional control, particularly when thinking about the labor market world and social life in a context of uncertainty. The development of this type of skills must be present in the curriculum.

The remote experience gave us insights that will be useful in the present/future, such as the importance of thinking about face-to-face activities that really are different for students. This moment should be used to work closely with students, to clarify doubts, to make exchanges, more in-depth discussions, and those activities in which the teacher really needs to be close or that were limited to be performed at a distance. In addition, it is important to think of activities that really make sense. The face-to-face moment needs to be rich and valuable.

Thus, since the university is a privileged space for social interactions, the expectation is that, in a post-pandemic scenario, both relationships and the spaces themselves will be affected and therefore should be rebuilt, articulating possible paths for a post-pandemic context, rethinking the use of technologies, pedagogical methodologies, socio-emotional relations, collaboration between the university and society. It is essential that students understand their role in the future of society and how they intend to make their contribution.

We believe that teachers and students will value each other more intensely, and the university will have its role consolidated as a learning, socializing, and communication environment if the student finds teachers who care about their integral education.

6. Citizenship, Resilience, and Sustainability

The principle of responsibility "deals with a central theme for the physical and spiritual survival of humanity", the search of an ethics for the technological civilization. From an ontological point of view, Hans Jonas (1985) returns to questions about the relationship between being and duty, cause and purpose, nature and value. It seeks to overcome the subjectivism of values to ground the contemporary man's duty to be. Certain transformations in our capabilities, he says, have brought about a change in the nature of human action. And since ethics has to do with acting, the modified nature of human acting also imposes a change in ethics.

It does not criticize traditional ethics, it just shows that it did not, nor could it have, rules for the entirely new modalities of technological power since it has always analyzed human action aimed at "acting closely". His concern was limited to discussing the "quality of the momentary moral act" and not the prediction or the weather of future generations now threatened by technical progress (Jonas, 1985).

It is a reflection on the ethics of limits, care, renunciation, forecasting, prevention, anticipation of risks, in view of the possibility of technological effects leading the planet to unforeseeable consequences.

Technologies have introduced actions of such an unprecedented order of magnitude, with such new objects and consequences that the framework of ancient ethics can no longer fit them. In traditional thinking, the presence of man in the world was a primary and indisputable fact, from which came every idea of duty regarding human conduct. Now, that presence has itself become an object of duty, the duty to preserve the world and preserve the conditions of that presence.

The object of analysis will be the magnitude of the consequences of the potentialized technological processes that affect the action (behave), part of the observation that "if the nature of the action has changed, there must also be changes in ethics" (Jonas, 1985).

Jonas (1985) draws attention to the exaggerations of the limitless power of modern technology, defends the existence of an ethic for the world of nature, and declares that the phenomenon of life needs to be put back in its place of honor.

The new principle of responsibility will have as its concrete object of understanding the possibility of indefinite perpetuation of humanity in the future, which may be compromised by the degradation of environment and that humanity is facing the "threat" of the new powers that go beyond legislation and moral prescriptions. It is this vacuum that needs to be filled by reflection, an ethical void that is, for Jonas, "the void of the current relativism of values" (Jonas, 1985).

The power of technology has become a threat because its consistency is associated with the idea of "promise, utopia, success, and well-being" (Jonas, 1985). Utopia accompanies the technique because it reveals power, omnipotence, and domination. Successes and breakthroughs "have affected human nature itself" where "fear" and "danger" raise the possibility of catastrophe. Therefore, if man has "power" and if this was made possible by the advancement of scientific knowledge, ethics based on the doctrine of being makes room for saying "no" to "not being", and this means "yes to life". For Jonas (1985), the world is vulnerable, nature is vulnerable as well as human life. Faced with vulnerability, the only way out is care and responsibility. In taking care of present generations, we will also be taking care of future ones.

The social and environmental imperatives require a civilizational change for the survival of humanity associated with an ethical and rights paradigm; in this sense, the education of the future must be not only a digital education but essentially an environmental one. Future generations will need a thorough understanding of environmental resources and how to manage them. In addition to knowledge about the digital culture in which they are inserted. Creating a dialogue between these two types of knowledge — digital and environmental — seems to be the great challenge for the education of the post-pandemic future. COVID-19 is not just a health problem; it is also an environmental problem. As new viruses begin to emerge in the ecosystem and overpopulated models of society, with large agglomerations becoming the epicenter of transmission outbreaks, a new organization of society, urban space and a new education of citizens are needed.

We must train individuals capable of solving complex problems, think creatively, and have cognitive flexibility, focusing on socio-emotional skills. They must become able to collaborate with machines and new technologies, not compete with them, and to connect more and more with reality, proposing solutions to the current problems of society. The university must prepare students with curiosity and the skills to learn their whole lives, teaching them to think globally, so that they are able to respond and contribute to the construction of a more egalitarian and constantly changing society.

Without a doubt, our normality will be different, with great care in terms of physical distance and the recommended hygiene and health measures. It was clear that the link is very important for both the mental and social health of the students, and therefore the focus will be on the human dimension and its perpetuation.

7. Final Considerations

At a time when the new coronavirus has infected more than 111 million people worldwide and around 3 million have died, the governments of several countries — including Portugal — are beginning to think about the lack of continuity and the recovery of the economy, it is natural for them to arise several doubts. What will change and what will remain the same?

With so many uncertainties, projecting what education will look like from now on is complex, and perhaps the only certainty we have is that education will definitely not be the same after this period. The pandemic has brought numerous challenges to education, together with the need for adaptations, reflections, but at the same time, it has enabled learning opportunities in different directions.

We are left with the feeling that higher education is increasingly distant from the reality that students will face, from their needs, works far from the time we are living in, that knowledge is out of focus in contemporary time, that methodologies are inadequate, and that in the classroom, actions seem insufficient for education to fulfill its role of developing knowledge, so that students become citizens capable of living in their present and future times.

This leads us to the duty to think about future generations, who will be the work force. Work, or whatever it will become, has a growing centrality in the issues surrounding the model of society that we will have (and wish) in the future.

The society is now a place, not only different, but profoundly more unequal. The social structure is at risk, and the new reality forces us to look at the world in a different way. From the simplest to the most structuring things, in a short period we had to learn to reinvent ourselves, as professionals, as parents, as educators, as workers, as companies, as humanity. Stop and see that the complexity and unpredictability of the world will continue and no one is prepared.

The challenge of educating for uncertainty is to realize that all knowledge is also provisional, of course it has given and will give us bases, but it needs updating; therefore, the best or worst ability to adapt to a society forced to change is at stake today.

We can no longer retreat, the question that arises is no longer "What can I get from the world?" but "How can I give, cooperate, and participate in the world?" This implies a commitment with the other, to ourselves, that can bring a knowledge capable of building the future of education, that has already started and is moving.

Among the main legacies that will be left after this period, and certainly, will bring important impacts, we highlight: the immersion in digital culture, the use of new technologies, added to the possibility of teachers to expand their teaching strategies, creating interesting and attractive classes, as well as the planning of new and different possibilities of interaction.

New challenges are foreseen, especially when we think about how we will reconnect with people after so much time of isolation, how we will organize our physical spaces on returning to school, how we will take care of the emotional issues and feelings that such a worrying situation brings.

By inserting digital tools in the student's learning process, this strategy will be more consistent with the state of the art of education. The students of this century, the digital natives, are immersed in the virtual world, but we must not forget that, not always with the skills and knowledge necessary to identify their risks and opportunities. It is in this digital space that the language itself, the form of expression, the interactions, and mainly, the information sources. In this sense, teachers have a crucial role in the reform that is taking place, insofar as they are the holders of knowledge.

The new pedagogical proposals, the training content, and the model for sharing and transmitting knowledge will be successful to the extent of their commitment. Institutions must recognize this role of teachers and provide the means to enable reform to succeed. Governments must necessarily provide the legal framework as well as incentives to move forward in modernizing and updating their higher education system.

The theme of digital citizenship will become central to pedagogical projects due to the relevance of considering training for critics, placing in pedagogical projects the valorization of scientific culture and its crucial role in life and on the planet, as well as the importance of making structural the issue of socio-environmental sustainability in all stages and cycles of studying, to take as an emergency issues about how we are taking care of the climate, our planet, and its inhabitants.

Thus, in order to find effective ways of acting, in order to act on the effects of this crisis/challenge, in a proactive way, in re-learning a critical attitude that contributes to a constructive reading of societies, of the crisis (or crises) with which these are currently struggling, our proposal is to prepare students to face unexpected and increasingly frequent situations, and in addition to the specific knowledge of each area, associate transversal, transferable and soft skills, can articulate with interdisciplinary teams, promote their adaptation and resilience, inner-self-knowledge, empathy, social responsibility awareness and recover the fundamental value of being.

If there is a sector that must become an example, it is education in general, and the higher education system in particular, so it would be essential to put a strategy for transforming the education system in one of the principal priorities, as a whole, which projects us toward a future, although being uncertain, will occur and only the most prepared can face it. Recalling a phrase from Peter Drucker, "The best way to predict the future is to create it".

It is our future that we are dealing with, not with vested interests, nor with pressure to keep everything as if the world had stopped.

Ending with a sentence by Morin, in his last interview published on January 1, 2021, with almost 100 years of age he said, "We must learn that in history the unexpected happens and will happen again".

References

Almeida, M.E.B. & Prado, M.E.B.B. (2009). Integração tecnológica, linguagem e representação. (Technology integration, language and representation), http://midiasnaeducacao-joanirse.blogspot.com/2009/02/integracao-tecnologica-linguagem-e.html (Accessed on October 5, 2020).

Belchior-Rocha, H., Mauritti, R., Paiva Monteiro, J., & Carneiro, L. (2020). 21st Century Skills and Digital Skills, are one and the same thing? *Edulearn20 Proceedings*, pp. 2752–2758. DOI:10.21125/edulearn.2020.0831.

Belloni, M. L., (2010). Mídia-educação e Educação a Distância na formação de professores. (Media education and distance education in teacher training). In: Mill, D. R. S. & Pimentel N. M. (orgs). Educação a distância: desafios contemporâneos. (Distance education: Contemporary challenges). São Carlos: eduFSCar.

Blackman, T. (2020). A Panel Explores What Higher Education Could Look Like in a Post-Coronavirus World, https://diverseeducation.com/article/176361/ (Accessed on January 7, 2021).

Buckingham, D. (2010). Cultura digital, educação midiática e o lugar da escolarização. Educação e Realidade. (Digital culture, media education and the place of schooling. Education and Reality). 35(3), pp. 37–58, http://www.seer.ufrgs.br/index.php/educacaoerealidade/article/view/13077/10270 (Accessed on September 7, 2020).

Castells, M. e Cardoso, G. (2005). A Sociedade em Rede — Do conhecimento à Ação Política. (The Network Society — From Knowledge to Political Action). Lisboa: Imprensa Nacional-Casa da Moeda Observatório de Cibersegurança Centro Nacional de Cibersegurança (2021) Relatório de Cibersegurança e Ensino a Distância Resultados de inquérito à comunidade docente (Cybersecurity and Distance Learning Report Faculty Community Survey Results) — janeiro (January) 2021, p. 8, https://www.cncs.gov.pt/content/files/inquerito_ciberseg_ensino_dist_cncs_dge.pdf (Accessed on February 4, 2021)

Costa, A. F. da (2020). Desigualdades Sociais e Pandemia (Social Inequalities and the Pandemic) in Carmo, Renato Miguel do; Inês Tavares; e Ana Filipa Cândido (orgs.) (2020), Um Olhar Sociológico sobre a Crise Covid-19 (A sociological look at Covid-19 Crisis) em Livro (in book), Lisboa, Observatório das Desigualdades, CIES-Iscte, https://www.observatoriodasdesigualdades.com/2020/11/29/umolharsociologicosobreacovid19emlivro/Primeira edição: novembro de 2020. ISBN: 978-972-8048-58-7 DOI: 10.15847/CIESOD2020 covid19 (Accessed on January 10, 2021)

COVID-19. Report of Health General Direction (DGS), https://covid19.min-saude.pt/wp-content/uploads/2021/02/355_DGS_boletim_20210220.pdf (Accessed on January 22, 2020).

Giddens, Anthony. (2004). Sociologia. (Sociology). Lisboa. Fundação Calouste Gulbenkian, 4ª edição (Lisbon. Calouste Foundation Gulbenkian, 4th edition), p. 64.

Jonas, H. (1985). The imperative of responsibility. In search of an ethics for the technological age. Chicago: University of Chicago Press. ISBN-10: 0226405974.

Kenski, V. M. (2010). Novas tecnologias: o redimensionamento do espaço e do tempo e os impactos no trabalho docente. (New technologies: The resizing of space and time and the impacts on teaching work). Revista Brasileira de Educação (Education of Brazil). N.8, p. 57–71.

Magalhães, P., Lopes, R.C., Adão e Silva, P. (coord.) (2020). O Impacto Social da Pandemia (The Pademic Social Impact). Estudo ICS/ISCTE Covid-19 — Dados da 2ª Vaga Junho, p. 3, 5.

Morin, E. (1998). O método: As ideias. (The method: The ideas), Porto Alegre: Sulina, p. 31.

Morin, E. (2001). Os sete saberes necessários à educação do futuro (The Seven Knowledge Necessary for the Education of the Future), São Paulo: Cortez/ Brasília: Unesco, p. 19, 79, 93.

Observatório de Cibersegurança Centro Nacional de Cibersegurança (2021). Relatório de Cibersegurança e Ensino a Distância Resultados de inquérito à comunidade docente — janeiro (Cybersecurity Observatory National Cybersecurity Center (2021). Cybersecurity and Distance Learning Report Survey results to teaching community — January), p. 8, https://www.cncs.gov. pt/content/files/inquerito_ciberseg_ensino_dist_cncs_dge.pdf (Accessed on February 4, 2021).

Pereira, M. do Mar. (2020). A Pandemia na Academia: Fazer e Transformar o trabalho científico em tempos de Covid-19 (Pandemic in Academia: Doing and Transforming Scientific Work in Covid-19 Times) in Carmo, Renato Miguel do; Inês Tavares; e Ana Filipa Cândido (in Carmo, Renato Miguel do; Inês Tavares; and Ana Filipa Cândido) (orgs.) Um Olhar Sociológico sobre a Crise Covid-19 (A sociological look at Covid-19 Crisis) em Livro (in book), Lisboa, Observatório das Desigualdades (Lisbon, Observatory of Inequality), CIES-Iscte, https://www.observatorio-dasdesigualdades.com/ 2020/11/29/umolharsociologicosobreacovid19emlivro/ novembro de 2020, ISBN: 978-972-8048-58-7, DOI: 10.15847/CIESOD2020covid19 (Accessed on January 10, 2021).

PORDATA/DGEEC/ME-MCTES, https://www.pordata.pt/Portugal/Alunos+matri culados+pela+1.%c2%aa+vez+no+ensino+superior+total+e+por+%c3%a1re a+de+educa%c3%a7%c3%a3o+e+forma%c3%a7%c3%a3o-1037 (Accessed on December 26, 2020).

Prensky, M. (2012). *From Digital Nativesto Digital Wisdom: Hopefulessays for 21st Century Learning*. Thousand Oaks: Corwin.

Rossato, M. (2014). A aprendizagem dos nativos digitais. (The learning of digital natives). In A. Mitjáns Martínez, & P. Álvarez (Orgs.), O sujeito que aprende: diálogo entre a psicanálise e o enfoque histórico-cultural. (The learning subject: Dialogue between psychoanalysis and the cultural-historical approach), pp. 151–178. Brasília: Liber Livro.

Silva Adelina Maria Pereira da (2006). Processos de ensino-aprendizagem na Era Digital. (Teachng and Learning processes in the Digital Era). Universidade Aberta, p. 7, http://www.bocc.ubi.pt/pag/silva-adelina-processos-ensino-aprendizagem.pdf (Accessed on December 3, 2020).

Chapter 9

Pandemic Process and Differences in Learning Approaches

Dilek İLHAN-BEYAZTAŞ[*,‡] **and Nuray SENEMOĞLU**[†,§]

*Erzincan Binali Yıldırım University, College of Education,
Department of Primary School Education, Erzincan, Turkey*

†*Hacettepe University, College of Education,
Department of Educational Sciences, Ankara, Turkey*

‡*dilekilhanbeyaztas@gmail.com*
§*n.senem@hacettepe.edu.tr*

Abstract

This study aims to determine and compare the learning approaches adopted by education faculty students before and during the pandemic in terms of various variables. In this study, the survey method, one of the quantitative research designs, was used to reveal the learning approaches adopted by faculty of education students in the face-to-face and distance education processes. The research group consists of 307 students enrolled in first and third grades in the Faculty of Education at Erzincan Binali Yıldırım University. In order to determine the learning approaches preferred by pre-service teachers, the "Learning Approaches and Study Skills Scale" developed by Tait *et al.* (1998) and adapted to Turkish by Senemoğlu (2011) was employed. As a result of the research, it was determined that the mean scores of deep and strategic learning approaches of students in both distance and face-to-face education with respect to various variables (gender, grade level, department, and access to the internet) were higher than the mean scores of the surface learning approach. In addition, although the mean scores of deep and strategic learning approaches in both face-to-face and distance education were high, it was concluded that these mean scores significantly decreased when switching from face-to-face education to distance education and that the scores of the surface learning approach increased significantly.

1. Introduction

Learning is the change that takes place in human disposition and capacity within a certain period of time, which cannot be attributed only to the growth process (Gagné, 1985, p. 2). This change takes place in a process that cannot be addressed within the boundaries of the school and can take place at any moment of life. Biggs (1979) discusses this process in three stages: input, process, and output. The input variable refers to the program content and other characteristics in the context of teaching, the process variable refers to the specific methods/approaches used in selecting and learning the information coming from the input, and the output variable refers to the qualitative and quantitative results of performance (Biggs, 1979). The learning process, which is also related to the input and output stages, develops as a result of the interaction between the teaching and the student. Students entering the teaching process interpret their own prejudices, orientations, and expectations. These elements, which will guide the actions of the students, encompass the cognitive behaviors to be displayed depending on the task itself as well as the executive cognitive activities that focus on the learning process. At this stage, the element that guides the students' behaviors by interpreting the learning task is the learning approaches adopted by the students (*Ibid.*, 1996).

Learning approach is defined as the change of intention and behavior in the way the learner works toward the learning task depending on the learner's perception of their context (Entwistle, 1991; İlhan-Beyaztaş & Senemoğlu, 2015). Learning approaches, within the scope of the perception of the current situation and the intention displayed, are classified as deep learning, surface learning, and strategic learning.

The deep learning approach is an individual's desire to perform the task that he/she has undertaken with an intrinsic motivation in a meaningful and appropriate way (Biggs, 2001; Biggs & Tang, 2007; Curzon, 2004). Accordingly, deep learning is an approach where learners (i) associate their previous knowledge and experiences with new knowledge, (ii) investigate the basic elements and principles underlying the subject to be learned, (iii) make logical and critical discussions on these elements and principles using available evidence, and (iv) observe and evaluate the development in the level of understanding while learning (Entwistle, McCune, & Walker, 2001).

The surface learning approach is the intention of the individual to fulfill the task he/she has undertaken with an extrinsic motivation (Biggs, 2001; Curzon, 2004) and with a low level of effort (Biggs & Tang, 2007). Accordingly, in this learning approach, learners memorize the content without understanding (Biggs, 2001), accept ideas passively giving little thought to their applications (Curzon, 2004), focus only on "key issues/ points" that they consider important, perceiving them as separate pieces disconnected from each other without approaching the learning task as a whole (Curzon, 2004; Biggs & Tang, 2007).

The strategic learning approach, on the other hand, is an approach that uses one of the superficial and deep learning approaches depending on the quality of the assessment process by dealing with the task that the individual has undertaken in a success-oriented manner (Entwistle, 1995; Newble & Entwistle, 1986). Accordingly, it is an approach where the individual pays attention to the assessment criteria effectively, studies according to the teacher's preferences, effectively manages their time and efforts, and controls the effectiveness of the methods of studying by setting the appropriate environment for study in order to be successful or to get a high grade (Entwistle, 1995; Entwistle, McCune, & Walker, 2001). Thus, it is seen that the learner follows different paths with different intentions in the process of deep, superficial, and strategic learning approaches.

Having reviewed the literature, it is seen that different perspectives have emerged regarding the factors that affect learning approaches. The biggest reason for this is that learning approaches are not a static characteristic of students. These approaches can change with changes in students' perception of the learning task and behaviors exhibited by teachers and administrators (Prosser & Trigwell, 1999). It is stated that, in particular, the academic environmental factors, such as the context in which teaching and learning take place (Huddleston & Unwin, 2008), teaching method, teacher's open stance toward students, perception of teaching and learning (Dart *et al.*, 2000), access to information (Gaff *et al.*, 1976), and individual characteristics (student's perception of competence, understanding of learning, interest, and prior knowledge) affect students' approaches to learning (Dart *et al.*, 2000).

Research on the factors affecting learning approaches is still ongoing. However, there are no findings yet on the extent to which sudden and extensive changes in the education process affect learning approaches. As it is known, the first COVID-19 case was reported in the Wuhan region of China in 2019, and in March 2020, the World Health Organization declared a worldwide pandemic. Because of the COVID-19 pandemic, 192 countries (covering 91.4% of the number of students enrolled in schools worldwide) had to temporarily close schools (UNESCO, 2020). With the closure of schools, alternative ways of imparting education were tried, and the distance education method was adopted predominantly. Distance education has led to a decrease in the time spent by students on learning, an increase in stress level, and a decrease in learning motivation (European Commission, 2020). However, in this day and age, focus has been on the production, use, and management of information, emphasizing the information society. In this context, the information society rewards individuals who find, process, produce, and create the right information and asserts that these activities can only be managed by individuals who have obtained effective learning and acquired high-level thinking skills. The learning approaches that affect the quality of learning, especially the deep learning approach, are effective in the acquisition of the stated qualifications. However, no study has been found to show the extent to which students' learning approaches are affected during the current pandemic. Within this scope, this study aims to determine and compare the learning approaches adopted by education faculty students before and during the pandemic in terms of various variables. The following questions will be answered within the scope of the research:

1. What are the learning approaches students adopt in face-to-face and distance education?
2. Is there a difference between the learning approaches students adopt in face-to-face and distance education?
3. Considering different variables (gender, grade level, department, internet access), what are the learning approaches students adopt in face-to-face and distance education and is there any difference between their learning approaches?

2. Method

2.1. *Research model*

In this study, the survey method, one of the quantitative research designs, was used to reveal the learning approaches adopted by students of the faculty of education in the face-to-face and distance education processes.

2.2. *Study sample*

The sample for the study consists of first and third grade students currently enrolled in Erzincan Binali Yıldırım University, Faculty of Education, who participated in the study on a voluntary basis. The data of the study were collected from the students studying at the education faculty with a measurement tool prepared in digital space. A total of 324 students participated in the study and 14 outliers affecting normality distribution were removed from the dataset and analyses were made using the data from 307 students. Information on the study group is presented in Table 1.

2.3. *Data collection tool*

In order to determine the learning approaches preferred by pre-service teachers, the "Learning Approaches and Study Skills Scale" developed by Tait *et al.*, (1998) and adapted to Turkish by Senemoğlu (2011) was

Table 1.   Descriptive characteristics of the study sample.

	Variable	**N**
Department	Primary education	124
	Pre-school education	65
	Turkish education	81
	Primary school mathematics education	37
Gender	Female	242
	Male	65
Grade	1	183
	3	124
Internet connection	Yes	269
	No	38

employed. The scale consists of four parts including 67 items, all of which are 5-point Likert. The first part of the scale consists of 6 items that measure perceptions of the participants toward the concept of learning, the second part consists of 52 items for determining learning approaches, the third part consists of 8 items that measure their preferences for different types of lessons and teaching, and the fourth part of the scale consists of an item that determines how successful students find themselves regarding all assessment results. In this study, the second part of the scale was used. The second part of the scale consists of three sub-dimensions under the headings of the deep, superficial, and strategic approaches to learning. The deep learning approach dimension consists of seeking meaning, associating ideas, using evidence, and dealing with thoughts; strategic learning approach dimension consists of organizing studying, time management, assessment awareness, monitoring success and efficiency; and surface learning approach includes items that measure lack of purpose, memorization without associating, commitment to the program, and fear of failing. Cronbach's alpha coefficients of the measurements based on the Turkish version of the scale vary between 0.71 and 0.81 for the whole scale and sub-dimensions (Senemoğlu, 2011). Cronbach's alpha coefficients of the scale were reported to be 0.86 for the deep learning approach dimension, 0.88 for the strategic learning approach dimension, and 0.70 for the surface approach to learning (*Ibid.*).

2.4. *Data analysis*

In this research, descriptive statistics (mean, standard deviation) scores were calculated based on the learning approaches scores preferred by the students using the SPSS software. Before descriptive statistics were calculated, the total score averages of the deep and surface learning approaches were converted to a 100-point scale, using ratio and proportion calculation, in order to make a comparison between the data, since the number of items related to the sub-dimensions of the scale were not equal (deep: 16 items, strategic: 20 items, and surface: 16 items of learning approaches).

In order to compare the scores of the students regarding the learning approaches adopted in face-to-face and distance education, *t*-test statistics were used in dependent groups.

3. Findings

The first sub-problem of the research is: "What are the learning approaches students adopt in face-to-face and distance education?" In this context, descriptive scores related to the students' level of preference for learning approaches are presented in Table 2.

When Table 2 is examined, it is determined that the mean score of the students regarding the strategic and deep learning approaches in both face-to-face and distance education is above the expected mean score (60.00), while the mean for the surface learning approach is below the average in face-to-face education but above the average score in distance education. Further, the highest mean score in face-to-face education is the score of the strategic learning approach, while the mean of the deep learning approach in distance education is high. In addition, the mean of the surface learning approach was found to have a higher value in distance education. The kurtosis and skewness coefficients were calculated to determine whether or not the scores of the students' learning approaches exhibit a normal distribution. Accordingly, the skewness coefficients for the strategic, deep, and surface learning approaches in face-to-face education were found to be between -1.153 and 0.114, while the kurtosis coefficients were between 1.059 and 1.839. In distance education, the skewness coefficients for strategic, deep, and surface learning approaches were found to be in the range between -0.119 and 0.840, while the kurtosis coefficients were between -0.044 and 1.036. The fact that the coefficient of skewness is smaller than 3 and the kurtosis coefficient is smaller than 10 (Kline, 2016) indicates that the data meet the normal distribution criteria.

Table 2. Descriptive statistics regarding learning approaches adopted by students in face-to-face and distance education.

Education Type	Learning Approaches	n	$\overline{X}/100$	ss	Skewness	Kurtosis
Face-to-face education	Deep	307	78.97	12.08	−0.830	1.492
	Surface	307	59.01	10.38	0.114	1.059
	Strategic	307	81.43	11.68	−1.153	1.839
Distance education	Deep	307	72.02	14.37	−0.840	1.013
	Surface	307	63.43	11.76	−0.119	−0.044
	Strategic	307	71.06	11.76	−0.826	1.036

Table 3. Comparison of the arithmetic mean scores of students regarding learning approaches in face-to-face and distance education.

Learning Approaches	n	Face-to-Face Education		Distance Education		t	p
		$\bar{X}/100$	ss	$\bar{X}/100$	ss		
Deep	307	78.97	12.08	72.02	14.37	9.12	.00
Surface	307	59.01	10.38	63.43	11.76	−7.47	.00
Strategic	307	81.43	11.68	71.06	11.76	12.63	.00

The second sub-problem of the study is "Is there a difference between the learning approaches that students adopt in face-to-face and distance education?" In this context, t-test analysis was conducted in dependent groups in order to compare the scores of the students regarding the learning approaches adopted in face-to-face and distance education. The findings regarding the analysis are given in Table 3.

When Table 3 is examined, it is seen that the mean score of the students regarding the strategic and deep learning approaches in distance education decreased compared to the scores obtained in face-to-face education, while the mean score regarding the surface learning approach increased. Examining whether the differences between the mean scores are statistically significant or not, it is seen that the mean scores of the strategic and deep learning approaches are statistically significant in favor of face-to-face education measurement, while the mean scores regarding the surface learning approach are significant in favor of distance education measurement.

The third sub-problem of the study was "What are the learning approaches that students adopt in face-to-face and distance education with respect to various variables (gender, grade level, department, access to internet, tools used in distance education), and is there a difference between the learning approaches?" In this context, descriptive scores and score comparisons are included under separate subtitles for each variable.

3.1. *Comparison of students' learning approaches according to the gender variable*

With respect to the gender variable, the scores regarding the learning approaches students adopted in face-to-face and distance education and

Table 4. Comparison of students' arithmetic mean scores regarding learning approaches in face-to-face and distance education with respect to the gender variable.

Gender	Learning Approaches	n	Face-to-Face Education		Distance Education		t	p
			$\overline{X}/100$	ss	$\overline{X}/100$	ss		
Male	Deep	242	78.64	12.34	72.25	13.62	7.855	.00
	Surface	242	59.51	10.37	64.36	11.39	−7.321	.00
	Strategic	242	81.56	11.73	71.66	13.13	10.994	.00
Female	Deep	65	80.19	11.05	71.17	13.62	4.596	.00
	Surface	65	57.13	10.27	59.96	12.57	−2.274	.02
	Strategic	65	80.98	11.57	68.81	17.58	6.346	.00

the results of the *t*-test analysis of the dependent groups carried out through comparison of the scores are presented in Table 4.

When Table 4 is examined, it is seen that the mean score of the strategic and deep learning approaches adopted in distance education for both female and male students decreased compared to the mean score obtained in face-to-face education, while the mean score for the surface learning approach increased. Examining whether the differences between the mean scores are statistically significant or not, it is seen that the mean scores of the strategic and deep learning approach are significant in favor of the face-to-face learning approach for both female and male students, while the mean scores for the surface learning approach are significant in favor of distance education.

3.2. *Comparison of students' learning approaches with respect to the grade level variable*

With respect to the grade level variable of the students, the mean scores of the learning approaches adopted in face-to-face and distance education and the results of the *t*-test analysis in dependent groups used in the comparison of the mean scores and are given in Table 5.

When Table 5 is examined, it is seen that the mean score of the strategic and deep learning approach adopted in distance education for both first grade and third grade students decreased compared to the mean score obtained in face-to-face education, while the mean score for the surface

Table 5. Comparison of students' arithmetic mean scores regarding learning approaches in face-to-face and distance education with respect to the grade level variable.

Grade Level	Learning Approaches	n	Face-to-Face Education		Distance Education		t	p
			$\overline{X}/100$	ss	$\overline{X}/100$	ss		
1.Sınıf	Deep	183	78.72	12.67	73.33	13.57	6.104	.00
	Surface	183	59.03	11.04	63.20	12.14	−5.592	.00
	Strategic	183	82.04	12.01	72.84	13.11	8.995	.00
3.Sınıf	Deep	124	79.23	11.19	69.95	15.29	6.878	.00
	Surface	124	58.90	9.39	63.65	11.22	−4.873	.00
	Strategic	124	80.42	11.11	68.31	15.32	8.897	.00

learning approach increased. Examining whether the differences between the mean scores are statistically significant or not, it is seen that the mean score of the strategic and deep learning approaches is significant in favor of the face-to-face learning approach for both first grade and third grade students, while the mean score for the surface learning approach is significant in favor of distance education.

3.3. *Comparison of the learning approaches of students according to the department variable*

Table 6 shows the scores of the learning approaches adopted by the students in face-to-face and distance education and the results of the *t*-test analysis in dependent groups used in the comparison of the scores according to the variable of the department students' study.

When Table 6 is examined, it is seen that the mean scores of the students who study in four different departments regarding the strategic and deep learning approaches adopted in distance education decreased compared to the mean score obtained in face-to-face education, while the mean score for the surface learning approach increased. Examining whether the differences between the mean scores are statistically significant or not, it is seen that the mean scores of the strategic and deep learning approaches for students studying in four different departments are significant in favor of face-to-face education measurement, while the mean scores regarding the surface learning approach are significant in

Table 6. Comparison of students' arithmetic mean scores regarding learning approaches in face-to-face and distance education with respect to the department variable.

Department	Learning Approaches	n	Face-to-Face Education		Distance Education		t	p
			$\overline{X}$/100	ss	$\overline{X}$/100	ss		
Primary school education	Deep	124	79.24	11.02	71.42	12.92	7.148	.00
	Surface	124	58.98	9.69	65.64	11.01	−7.06	.00
	Strategic	124	82.29	9.80	69.63	13.35	10.342	.00
Pre-school education	Deep	65	79.36	13.05	72.48	15.22	3.856	.00
	Surface	65	61.13	12.93	65.11	12.22	−2.751	.00
	Strategic	65	81.73	12.78	72.36	14.77	4.962	.00
Turkish education	Deep	81	79.29	12.62	73.61	14.68	4.144	.00
	Surface	81	57.76	9.67	60.98	11.42	−3.563	.00
	Strategic	81	80.67	13.00	73.32	13.79	5.115	.00
Primary school mathematics education	Deep	37	76.68	12.75	69.76	16.79	2.450	.01
	Surface	37	58.10	8.80	58.41	12.04	−0.177	.86
	Strategic	37	79.70	12.56	68.59	16.36	3.899	.00

favor of distance education mean scores except for primary school mathematics education.

3.4. *Comparison of students' learning approaches according to internet access variable*

Scores of the learning approaches adopted by the students in face-to-face and distance education and the results of the *t*-test analysis in dependent groups made through the comparison of the scores according to the availability of the internet are given in Table 7.

When Table 7 is examined, it is seen that the mean score of the strategic and deep learning approaches adopted in distance education decreased compared to the scores obtained in face-to-face education, while the mean score regarding the surface learning approach increased, even with or without internet access. Examining whether the differences between the mean scores are statistically significant or not, it is seen that the mean scores of the strategic and deep learning approach are significant in favor of the mean score obtained in the face-to-face learning for

Table 7. Comparison of students' mean scores regarding learning approaches in face-to-face and distance education with respect to the internet access variable.

Internet Access	Learning Approaches	n	Face-to-Face Education		Distance Education		t	p
			$\overline{X}/100$	ss	$\overline{X}/100$	ss		
Yes	Deep	269	79.00	11.85	72.22	14.28	8.539	.00
	Surface	269	58.86	10.18	63.19	11.79	−6.770	.00
	Strategic	269	81.55	11.31	71.46	14.13	11.699	.00
No	Deep	38	78.78	13.75	70.59	15.13	3.217	.00
	Surface	38	60.03	11.81	65.09	11.57	−3.268	.00
	Strategic	38	80.65	14.16	68.23	14.59	4.757	.00

students with and without internet access, while the mean scores for the surface learning approach are in favor of distance education.

4. Discussion

In the light of the findings, it was determined that the mean scores of deep and strategic learning approaches of students in face-to-face education with respect to various variables (gender, grade level, department, and access to the internet) were higher than the mean scores of the surface learning approach. The literature also supports this finding (Biggs, 1987; Ekinci, 2008; İlhan-Beyaztaş, 2014; İlhan-Beyaztaş & Senemoğlu, 2015; Senemoğlu, 2011; Watkins & Hattie, 1981). Based on the findings regarding distance education, it was determined that students adopted learning approaches similar to face-to-face education. In the studies conducted by Harper & Kember (1986, 1989) and Richardson (2005), it was found that the mean scores of the students' deep and strategic learning approaches, in both distance and face-to-face education, are higher than the mean scores of the surface learning approach.

Perhaps one of the most interesting findings of the research is that, although the mean scores of deep and strategic learning approaches in both face-to-face and distance education were high, it is concluded that these mean scores significantly decreased when switching from face-to-face education to distance education and that the scores of the surface learning approach increased significantly. When the literature is examined, it is observed that the studies on learning approaches were mostly conducted on different study groups (Harper & Kember, 1986; Köymen, 1992; Richardson, 2005); however, there are no comparisons of the learning approaches adopted by the same study group in face-to-face and distance education. This study obtained an important finding by comparing face-to-face and distance education in the context of learning approaches involving the same study group. Accordingly, when the literature is examined, it is seen that learning approaches can change according to the student's perception of the process or task he/she is involved in. In particular, factors such as the context in which the teaching and learning process takes place (Huddleston & Unwin, 2008), perception of teaching and learning (Dart *et al.*, 2000) and access to information (Gaff *et al.*, 1976) influence the learning approaches adopted. Teacher–student, student–student, and student–material interactions, all of which constitute the most important source of effective learning in face-to-face education, are replaced by a virtual interactive environment in distance education. This virtual environment created may have caused the intrinsic motivation of the students toward the learning task to decrease (European Commission, 2020). Also, learning approaches are influenced by factors such as in-class activities and extracurricular activities employed for the lesson, the availability of places for students' interests, the individual care/attention provided to students, and the teachers' level of understanding of their students (Gaff *et al.*, 1976). In this context, although the scores of deep and strategic learning approaches in distance education are higher than that of the surface learning approach, the decrease in their mean scores in distance education compared to face-to-face education can be attributed to the failure of the virtual environment to meet the specified factors. Another striking finding of the study is the change that took place in the ranking regarding the deep and strategic approaches to learning. In this respect, when the findings are considered, it is seen that the mean scores of the strategic learning approaches of the students in face-to-face education with respect to various variables (gender, grade level, department, and access to the internet) are higher than the mean scores of the deep learning approach in distance education, whereas the mean scores of deep learning approach in distance education were found to be higher than the mean scores of the strategic learning approach. Based on the literature reviewed, it is apparent that there is a positive relationship between both deep and strategic learning approaches and self-regulation skills (Heikkilä & Lonka, 2006; Heikkilä *et al.*, 2011; Magno, 2009). However, these studies do not cover a crisis period, like a pandemic. With the COVID-19 pandemic, the closure of schools and the rapid transition to distance education caused students to reduce their time spent on learning, raised their stress, and lowered their motivation to learn (European Commission, 2020). In this respect, the decrease in the mean scores of the strategic learning approach can be linked to the particular fact that the students who achieve their goals by enacting self-regulation skills have been adversely affected by the pandemic and have had difficulty in managing the process. Thus, a decrease was observed in the mean score of the strategic learning approach.

In this age of the fourth industrial revolution, individuals are expected to utilize problem-solving, critical thinking and creativity skills. These skills can be developed by individuals who approach the learning process with an intrinsic motivation under all circumstances, seek the nature of knowledge, and learn in depth. Although the pandemic negatively affects the learning process and its quality, it has also served as an opportunity for showcasing the deficiencies in the current process. In line with the findings of the study, it is recommended to create learning environments that foster teacher–student, student–student, and student–material interactions in order to achieve the desired quality of learning, especially in distance education. Accordingly, it is also recommended that teachers integrate activities that will enable students to gain the nature of knowledge in distance education. In addition, it is recommended that teachers, who are primarily responsible for conducting the distance education environment in an interactive way, should be given the necessary in-service training to enable them to apply information technologies more effectively.

The limitation of this study is that it is carried out by collecting quantitative data from a small study group. It is particularly recommended to conduct large-scale qualitative studies on how students perceive the compulsory distance education process during the pandemic and how these perceptions affect their learning approaches. Thus, it is expected that insights will be gained on how the education systems, to be developed in the future, should be shaped, and the efforts to create a more comprehensive infrastructure can be accelerated by examining the effects of the pandemic on the education process in greater depth.

References

Biggs, J. B. (1979). Individual differences in study processes and the quality of learning outcomes. *Higher Education, 8*(4), 381–394, https://doi.org/10.1007/BF01680526.

Biggs, J. B. (1987). Student approaches to learning and studying. *Melbourne: Australian Council for Educational Research.*

Biggs, J. B. (1996). Approaches to learning of Asian students: A multiple paradox. In J. Pandey, D. Sinha, & ve D. P. S. Bhawuk, (Eds.), *Asian Contributions to Cross-Cultural Psychology*, pp. 180–200. New Delhi: Sage Publications.

Biggs, J. B. (2001). Enhancing learning: A matter of style or approach? In Sternberg, R. J. & Zhang, L. F. (Eds.), *Perspective on Thinking, Learning, and Cognitive Styles*, pp. 73–102. London: Lawrence Erlbaum Associates, Inc.

Biggs, J. B. & Tang, C. (2007). *The Society for Research into Higher Education Teaching for Quality Learning at University.* USA: McGraw Hill.

Curzon, L. B. (2004). *Teaching in Further Education an Outline of Principles and Practice.* New York: Continuum.

Dart, B. C., Burnett, P. C., Purdie, N., Boulton-Lewis, G., Campbell, J., & Smith, D. (2000). Students' conceptions of learning, the classroom environment, and approaches to learning, *The Journal of Educational Research, 93*(4), 262–270, https://doi.org/10.1080/00220670009598715.

Ekinci, N. (2008). *Üniversite öğrencilerinin öğrenme yaklaşımlarının belirlenmesi ve öğretme-öğrenme süreci değişkenleri ile ilişkileri* (Determining the learning approaches of university students and their relations with the variables of the teaching-learning process), Unpublished doctoral dissertation, Hacettepe University, Ankara.

Entwistle, N. J. (1991). Approaches to learning and perceptions of the learning environment introduction to the special issue. *Higher Education, 22*, 201–204, https://doi.org/10.1007/BF00132287.

Entwistle, N. J. (1995). Frameworks for understanding as experienced in essay writing and in preparing for examinations. *Educational Psychologist, 30*(1), 47–54, https://doi.org/10.1207/s15326985ep3001_5.

Entwistle, N., McCune, V., & Walker, P. (2001). Conceptions, styles, and approaches within higher education: Analytic abstractions and everyday experience. In Sternberg, R. J. & Zhang, L. F. (Eds.), *Perspective on Thinking, Learning, and Cognitive Styles*, pp. 103–136. London: Lawrence Erlbaum Associates, Inc.

European Commission (2020). The likely impact of COVID-19 on education: Reflections based on the existing literature and recent international datasets. Retrieved from: https://ec.europa.eu/jrc/en/publication/likely-impact-covid-19-education-reflections-based-existing-literature-and-recent-international.

Gaff, J. G., Crombag, H. F. M., & Chang, T. M. (1976). Environments for learning in a Dutch university. *Higher Education, 5*, 285–299, https://doi.org/10.1007/BF00136450.

Gagné, R. M. (1985). *The Conditions of Learning and Theory of Instruction.* USA: Holt, Rinehart and Winston, Inc.

Heikkilä, A. & Lonka, K. (2006). Studying in higher education: Students' approaches to learning, self-regulation, and cognitive strategies. *Studies in Higher Education, 31*(1), 99–117, https://doi.org/10.1080/03075070500392433.

Heikkilä, A., Niemivirta, M., Nieminen, J., & Lonka, K. (2011). Interrelations among university students' approaches to learning, regulation of learning, and cognitive and attributional strategies a person oriented approach, *High Education, 61*, 513–529, https://doi.org/10.1007/s10734-010-9346-2.

Harper, G. & Kember, D. (1986). Approaches to study of distance education students. *British Journal of Educational Technology, 17*(3), 212–222, https://doi.org/10.1111/j.1467-8535.1986.tb00510.x.

Harper, G. & Kember. D. (1989). Interpretation of factor analyses from the approaches to studying inventory. *British Journal of Educational Psychology, 59*(1), 66–74, https://doi.org/10.1111/j.2044-8279.1989.tb03077.x.

Huddleston, P. & Unwin, L. (2008). *Teaching and Learning in Further Education Diversity & Change*, Cornwall: Routledge Taylor & Francis Group.

İlhan-Beyaztaş, D. (2014). Başarılı Öğrencilerin Öğrenme Yaklaşımları ve Etkili Öğrenmeye İlişkin Önerileri (Successful Students' Learning Approaches and Effectiveness Advice on Learning). Unpublished doctoral dissertation, Hacettepe University, Ankara.

İlhan-Beyaztaş, D. & ve Senemoğlu, N. (2015). Başarılı Öğrencilerin Öğrenme Yaklaşımları ve Öğrenme Yaklaşımlarını Etkileyen Faktörler (Learning of Successful Students Factors Affecting Approaches and Learning Approaches). *Eğitim ve Bilim (Education and Science Journal), 40*(179), 193–216, http://dx.doi.org/10.15390/EB.2015.4214.

Köymen, U. S. (1992). Comparison of learning and study strategies of traditional and open learning-system students in Turkey. *Distance Education, 13*, 108–117, https://doi.org/10.1080/0158791920130109.

Newble, D. I. & Entwistle, N. J. (1986). Learning styles and approaches. Implications for medical education. *Medical Education, 20*, 162–175, https://doi.org/10.1111/j.1365-2923.1986.tb01163.x.

Magno, C. (2009). Self-Regulation and approaches to learning in English composition writing. *Tesol Journal, 1*, 1–16.

Prosser, M. & Trigwell, K. (1999). *Understanding Learning and Teaching the Experience in Higher Education.* London: The Society for Research into Higher Education & Open University Press.

Richardson, J. T. E. (2005). Students' perceptions of academic quality and approaches to studying in distance education. *British Educational Research Journal, 31*(1), 7–27, https://doi.org/10.1080/0141192052000310001.

Senemoğlu, N. (2011). College of education students' approaches to learning and study skills. *Education and Science, 36*(160), 65–80.

Tait, H., Entwistle, N. J., & McCune, V. (1998). ASSIST: A re-conceptualization of the approaches to studying inventory. In Rust C. (Ed.), *Improving Students as Learners*, pp. 262–271. Oxford: Oxford Brooks University.

United Nations Education Scientific and Cultural Organization (2020). *COVID-19 Educational Disruption and Response*. Retrieved from https://en.unesco.org/covid19/educationresponse.

Watkins, D. & Hattie, J. (1981). The learning processes of Australian university students: Investigations of contextual and personological factors. *British Journal of Educational Psychology, 51*, 384–393, https://doi.org/10.1111/j.2044-8279.1981.tb02494.x.

Chapter 10

The Future of the European Union Under the Shadow of the COVID-19 Crisis

Mustafa Nail ALKAN[*,‡] **and Bora Berkan ALKAN**[†,§]

*Department of International Relations,
Ankara Hacı Bayram Veli University, Ankara, Turkey*

†*Department of Peace Research and
International Relations, University of Tübingen, Tübingen, Germany*

‡*nail.alkan@hbv.edu.tr*
§*boraberkanalkan@gmail.com*

Abstract

The COVID-19 crisis, which radically changed all the habits of humanity, started a new era in relations between European states. The European states and the EU institutions, working in the light of the principles of solidarity and cooperation since the Second World War, suffered greatly with this health crisis. This period, which resulted in the diminishing of cooperation and their states to pay more attention to their national interests, faltered in European solidarity. At this point, the study will address the problems experienced in the economic, political, and health fields. In addition, in the light of these problems, the course of the relations between the European Union states in the post-COVID-19 period will be discussed.

195

1. Introduction

In the first days of 2020, no one could foresee that a global pandemic would be a part of our lives in a devastating manner. Assumptions were that COVID-19 emerged during the last months of 2019 and had begun to spread throughout to world. This spread has had political, economic, and social effects in Europe as well as in other parts of the world. As the pandemic is a major incident, it has also more considerable impacts than any other minor events have. When we contemplate Europe and the European Union (EU), it is obvious that the continent faces another significant impact from COVID-19 other than the aspect of health: political alternation.

After the Second World War, the whole continent was damaged and searching for a new beginning. The idea of a politically and economically unified Europe arose in this period and gradually had become a core element of European political environment. Year by year, the concept of multilateralism has been penetrating the states, and the entire notion came to be called the EU. The principle of this organization lies in the supranationalism which can be defined as states that have transferred their powers to a superstructure. In the case of the EU, as a matter of fact in the unique case of the EU, member states are expected to convey some responsibilities in several fields such as monetary policies, custom regulations, negotiating with a non-member third party, and health strategies. At the end of the day, the borderless Europe had been formed so that the citizens of the EU members can travel or live in whichever country they want to. It was no longer the border between the member states that mattered, but the EU's border with other states. In the meantime, the idea of nationalism has been almost retired, and the importance of nation states in Europe has been weakened.

2. A Challenging Threat to the Settled European Order

After the system of the EU started to operate, it can be said that it is the first time the union is facing such a challenge. It will also be marked in history as an important detail that this pandemic emerged at a time when anti-EU sentiments in the Union were rising. Therefore, the response of the EU to the pandemic has had critical significance. The question of whether the EU has been successful during the pandemic is still up for debate and will perhaps be discussed over the years. However, there is a fact: the anti-EU view and skepticism of member states and citizens have increased significantly. To evaluate the reasons behind this change of mind correctly, the reactions of both the EU and member states, the policies, and the facts should be determined.

In January 2020, Europe was widely unaware of what was going to happen in the next month. Frankly, it can be said that the spread of the COVID-19 had a slow pace until February. Then Italy, particularly the Lombardy region, was confronted with traumatic days. Increasing numbers of cases in the region caused people to move away from that area and thus spread the virus to other regions. Similarly, the number of cases increased in other countries, and the whole world had to go into an emergency. The increase caused both the EU member states and the non-EU countries to close their borders. During this period, only medical supplies were allowed to be transported. Thus, the customs controls were relaunched after 25 years of free movement, which was provided by Schengen regulation (Opiłowska, 2020). Despite these initial measures, the situation had worsened and the EU's first serious test against the pandemic started in Italy. The needs of the country for fighting the virus, such as medical equipment, masks, and medical gear, were not met. Moreover, with the dramatic increase in the number of cases, there were not enough intensive care units left in hospitals, especially in Lombardy region. In this case, Italy naturally sought assistance from the EU and its member states, which are geographically and politically close to each other. In stark contrast to this expectation, Italy's borders with the Schengen area were closed. The lack of response from the member states started a new era of tension within the Union. To be more specific, with the huge acceleration of cases in March, there was a huge need for masks and medical gear. At that time, Italy was importing masks from Germany; however, the increase of cases made Germany make the decision of banning the export of masks (Hall *et al.*, 2020). Blocking of the masks by Germany left Italy in a desperate position. Furthermore, mechanisms of the EU and the other member states did not respond to the call from the Italian government requiring aid. Consequently, the EU itself was starting to be questioned in Italy. The principle of solidarity was becoming meaningless. Let alone sending masks as aid, even the products purchased by Italy were confiscated at the border. Because of the border closure, transportation among states was minimal and this left Italy helpless. The reason why member states did not help was the desire to protect their own citizens instead of other member states' citizens. It should be noted that such an action is completely against the fundamental element of multilateral solidarity of the EU. Figure 1 shows that 57% of the citizens of the member states are not satisfied with the cooperation of the states with each other during the pandemic period (European Parliament, 2020a).

Besides the problem of medical equipment aid, there was also a problem on the economic aspect. Since the government of Italy wanted to stop the spread of COVID-19, the national lockdown process was initiated. It meant that all businesses, small or large, would have to shut down. Its effects on the economy were enormous: Many people were unemployed, and businesses were unable to pay their expenses. To overcome this, Italy requested economic aid from the EU and member states. However, states left Italy alone with its destiny. Without exception, all member states with or without a good economy left the request for assistance unanswered. The anti-EU ideas in Italy started to rise after these negative responses were made by the EU member states which were totally against the core culture of the EU. At the same time, it should be noted that with the decision taken on March 22, 2020, the EU Commission provided economic

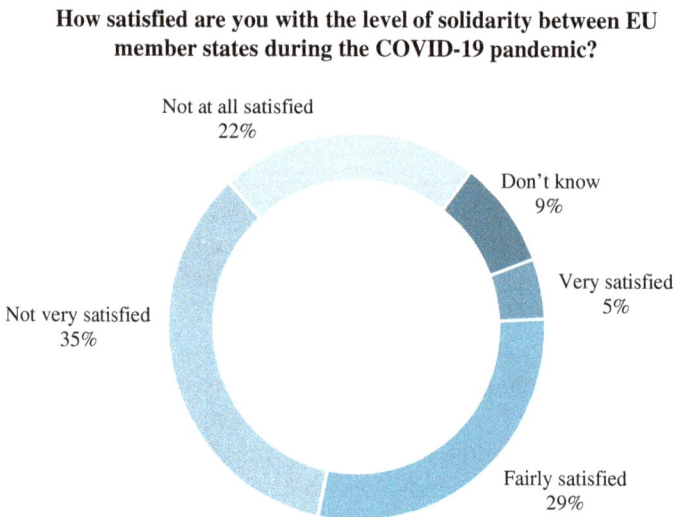

How satisfied are you with the level of solidarity between EU member states during the COVID-19 pandemic?

Not at all satisfied
22%

Don't know
9%

Very satisfied
5%

Not very satisfied
35%

Fairly satisfied
29%

Figure 1.   View of citizens on EU solidarity.

Source: European Parliament (2020).

aid to Italy to produce medical equipment (European Commission, 2020). Leaving aside the assistance of the EU, no state has put into practice the principle of cooperation, which is one of the most important principles on which the Union is based. For instance, countries which have good economic conditions, such as Netherlands and Germany, were slow to respond to Italy's calls. At the end of the day, the approach of the member states to the situation has caused Italy to reconsider the EU itself and showed that it should prioritize its own interests rather than the EU's.

Italy is not the only case that has started to question the EU. As in the rest of the world, all over Europe, the war over masks started. States began to seize masks bought by other countries. The existing global economic order, which leans into multilateral cooperation, interdependent and integrated economies, suddenly halted. The international system turned to a kind of race among countries whose aim was the seizure of medical equipment before other countries. Similarly, the EU members that have been integrated not only economically but also in many other fields had to act on their own. The example of Italy happened again in many countries that had difficulty fighting COVID-19. Requests for aid were not welcomed by states, but EU governing bodies made efforts to finalize them. As we think about questioning the EU, we can clearly advocate that the EU administrative bodies are not being criticized, but the states that were not inclined to assist. The member states initiated national policies and bypassed the EU decision mechanisms. This weakened the EU's organs, and the decision-making process was stalled by the individual actions of the states.

3. Beginning of an Era of Political Loneliness

The efforts of states to formulate individual policies and to prioritize their own people have been an important building block of this process since the beginning of the pandemic. Nevertheless, the EU endeavored to work independently from member states' policies. The Union, which emphasized the calls for cooperation, joint solution, and dialogue, tried to draw the states in line with the spirit of the EU. Despite all these attempts, there are situations where the EU itself is criticized. First, the decision about the closure of borders was not welcomed by most of the countries in the Union. This caused a lot of losses in business and trade. Second, the EU bodies were condemned for acting slowly at the beginning of the crisis. To elaborate, the late response of the EU Commission to Italy would be a compelling example. Even the president of the Commission during this period, Ursula von der Leyen, apologized for this mistake (Engman, 2020). Although the EU has shown a more unifying and successful image in the later stages of the pandemic, the individual movements of the members have always been a problem. When the COVID-19 vaccines were developed, the EU took on a huge responsibility for the provision and distribution of vaccines. This creates the third point of criticism toward the EU. In fact, a vaccine distribution strategy that is accessible to every state has been adopted rather than a vaccine strategy that made states compete, like for past diseases like swine and bird flu (van Schaik *et al.*, 2020).

However, facts and expectations do not always come true. Once the vaccines were ready for use, EU governing bodies ordered a sufficient initial purchase for member states' populations. Although this initiative can be considered successful, when it comes to the procurement and distribution process of vaccines, we can conclude that the EU has failed. The delayed and defective rollout of the vaccines available caused EU states to fall behind in vaccination. The EU is seen as mainly responsible for the occurrence of this situation. According to a survey by Spiegel, 42% of the participants state that after the procurement process, the perception of the EU has significantly deteriorated (Der Spiegel, 2021). Moreover, the same survey also revealed that 50% of the respondents think the image of Ursula von der Leyen has worsened.

The individual acts of the states, the attitude away from the cooperation between the EU members, and the criticism of the EU on many issues prove that the pandemic will have a significant impact on the EU integration. The effects of the pandemic on the EU can be categorized under several points.

4. Rising in Value: Nation-States and Nationalism

The first and perhaps the most remarkable impact of COVID-19 on the EU is that nation-states have regained their importance. In previous crises, like the 2008 Economic Crisis, states tried to overcome the processes by adhering to Union policies rather than individual movements. In contrast, during the COVID-19 crisis, states have ignored applying the policies of the EU and started to act individually. The reason is that, when it comes to vital issues, the state and its citizens would want to rely on only each other. While member states primarily strive to save the lives of their citizens and give them priority, citizens of the country also want to be helped by their government and rely solely on them for vital matters. It is easier for states to access a crisis-qualified workforce and citizens are more likely to believe in their own leaders (Martin, 2020). This can be explained by the citizenship bond. Since other states will also act with this instinct, the spirit and principle of solidarity within the Union will be shelved. When we think of the COVID-19 crisis, we can see that the state and citizens are acting in exactly this context. Decisions were taken and applied by the nation-states instead of the Union. The first signs of this situation showed itself in the case of Italy. While Italy was seeking aid from the Union, they were left to themselves and it started a crisis moment reaction, in which states only thought about themselves, far from helping each other. This ended up with Italy having to rely on itself and its relations to other countries, instead of relying on the EU members or relations with them. Another example of states' steps away from coordination would be Germany's unilateral closure of its border with France without providing comprehensive information (Mason, 2020). These movements, given as examples, prove that the importance of national state policies has increased and reveal that central governments rather than the EU administration are getting stronger again.

Member nation-states gave priority to national decision-making mechanisms, especially since they could not get support from the organization in the early stages of the pandemic. In this context, states in need of assistance, especially economically, made demands from other states without paying attention to the EU mechanism. At this point, China's assistance to many states, including Italy, is an important example. China's aid in economic and health equipment was greater than the aid provided by EU states to each other. Consequently, states realized that, in such a crisis, they had to take responsibility for their external relations rather than rely on the EU. Furthermore, states closing their borders reaffirm the importance of nations. Each member country has to care about its own citizens. A Europe without borders is losing its reality. At the end of the day, this is a sign of the rise of nationalism.

In parallel with the gaining importance of nation-state policies, the increase in nationalism and populist movements is another effect of the pandemic on the EU. The rise of nationalist ideology had increased especially after the 2008 Global Economic Crisis and the refugee crisis. The decline in household incomes, the cheap labor of refugees, and the decline in employment and welfare due to the 2008 crisis were factors that brought people closer to nationalist thinking. Similarly, the COVID-19 process has led to the spread of this thought. As stated in the previous paragraph, the strengthening of the role of nation-states within the EU also finds a response among citizens too. The EU's delay in both medical and economic aid, the organization's slowness in decision-making processes, lack of solidarity and the fact that this is a factor in the spread of the pandemic in Europe drove people to hold a protective nationalist approach against external influences. After states isolated themselves, every citizen had to trust their own country. Neither the EU nor any other entity could help them. This environment also affected the political environment. Particularly in Hungary and Poland, practices that are far from the general democratic understanding of the EU attracted attention (Leigh, 2020). In particular, the Hungarian Parliament gave Viktor Orbán the authority to declare a state of emergency for an indefinite period. This authority also paved the way for him to make regulations that could harm liberal values, such as press freedom and human rights. Governments with this mentality, which have made decisions far below EU standards in the areas of rule of law, human rights, and democracy, show that the populist approach has gained strength. In addition, far-right populist parties are on the rise, not only in these countries, but across Europe. It will be predictable that this rise will be more dramatic with the pandemic process. In such a health crisis, the EU's inadequacy in the medical aid, economic support, and vaccine procurement process caused the citizens of the member states to support rather than oppose the nationalist policies of the governments. According to a research, 54% of respondents support the policies applied by their national governments, displayed in Figure 2 (European Parliament, 2020a).

It is a possible outcome that states and peoples support more nationalist policies after the experiences they have gained from this process. Thus, instead of waiting for the approval of other countries, states will prioritize reaching the resources they need with their own efforts and policies. This shows that, when EU solidarity is considered, the culture of cooperation established in the EU will be in danger in consequence of the COVID-19 crisis.

**Do you support your national government policies during
COVID-19 crisis?**

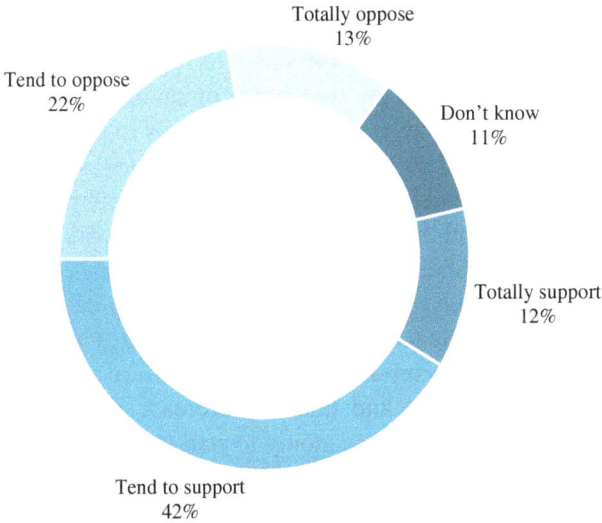

Figure 2.   Support of the national government policies.

Source: European Parliament (2020).

5. On the Brink of an Economic Crisis

The other effect of the pandemic on the EU and its members is economic. We need to examine this situation from two points of view. First, in addition to the increase in the political nationalist segment within the countries, the state administrators in office also turned toward policies that we can describe as economically protective. When the first request of aid from Italy was not accepted by the member states of the EU, the international relations between the members turned into a selfish game for the members again. The economic request of the country was not responded to because other governments were also considering that in such a pandemic they would need money more than ever to afford the expenses of the country. As we discussed before, political nationalism reflected on economic decisions too. Germany's blocking of mask exports, France's seizing of medical products purchased by other countries and sabotaging their removal from its territory would be persuasive examples. In addition to these, failure to provide economic assistance between states, export restrictions on medical products, and closing borders are practices related to protective economic policies.

While this political approach constitutes one leg of the economic effects, the other leg consist of the facts. The economic difficulties experienced do not make it possible for states to regain strength in the short term. States were torn between the choice of saving either the people or the economy. Based on the responsibility of states to protect their people, workplaces, restaurants, shopping malls, and businesses were closed, and the economy stopped suddenly. This has led to the bankruptcy and closure of many businesses and the unemployment of many workers. The support of the EU to its member states has been slower than expected. In this environment, where the member states did not help each other, the EU governing bodies announced their support packages with a delay and could not take any pre-emptive action. The closure of workplaces, the increase in unemployment and thus the decrease in household income caused a domino effect on the economy to start a decline. As an impact of these, the annual economic growth of the countries was also affected. Considering the economic data, the figures show that the worst fall in the history of the EU took place. The projections show that the GDP of EU members in 2020 fell by a dramatic rate of 6.4% compared to 2019 (Eurostat, 2020a). This decline is even greater than the 2008–2009 period when the global economic crisis was experienced — the GDP of EU countries fell by 4.9% in 2009. Considering this rate from today's economic perspective, the contraction experienced in 2020 is clearly much deeper in terms of impact. If the continuity or long-term effects of this decline remain negative, some EU members will fall into recession as a possible result.

If we look at the problem from another perspective, some of the businesses were closed to ensure social distancing, and some switched to working from home. As a result, lower income also played a key role in increasing unemployment. While the unemployment rate measured in October 2019 was 6.6%, this increased to 7.6% in the same month of 2020, and the youth unemployment rate increased from 15% in 2019 to 19% in 2020 (Eurostat, 2020b). The emergence of such gaps in the economy required the support of governments. Thus, governments had to reduce their investments in many areas and shift their investments to the distressed sectors and the field of medical product production. Although it is intended to reduce the damage in this way, the wound caused by the crisis is the kind that will be felt for many years.

In such a chaotic environment, states demanded the EU to step in and offer support packages. Even when countries needed assistance, disagreements arose among members over the use of aid mechanisms, which raised questions about the extent of European solidarity. First, the European Central Bank (ECB) announced a €750 billion package for governments and companies (Robert Schuman Foundation, 2020). But a continuous flow was required and the issue of using the European Stability Mechanism, which was created to provide support in times of crisis, occurred and a conflict between states stood out on whether to use the mechanism. At this point, we should mention the term of corona bonds that emerged in this period too. For EU financial institutions to support the public debt of the states, the idea of providing money flow to the states with the use of bonds was discussed. However, disagreement among the governments once again appeared. While the states of Italy, France and Spain, which were heavily affected by the pandemic, demanded the use of these bonds for cash support, states such as Germany, the Netherlands and Finland opposed this situation. (Engman, 2020). Although there was a reason behind this opposing, not to take responsibility for another state's public debt, the lack of economic solidarity within the EU was noteworthy. If we leave aside the differences of opinion, the balance between the state and the market has begun to shift in favor of the state. This conflicts with European integration, which argues for a low degree of government intervention in the market. Instead of directing the markets and transferring money to a certain area, the aid funds provided by the EU will ensure that this balance is not disturbed.

Finally, we need to mention the plan announced by the EU governing bodies in the later stages of the pandemic. In June 2020, the economic recovery plan was announced by the European Commission. This plan was named Next Generation, and content covering the years 2021–2027 and amounting to 750 billion euros will be provided (Celi *et al.*, 2020). With its grants and loans, the plan will be used to repair the economic flows of states. Considering the function of aid, it would not be wrong to say that it is similar to the Marshall Plan made to European states after World War II. In other words, billions of Euros of support have been provided with grants and loans in the Next Generation plan and with the ECB to awake the Europe from its weary position.

It is obvious that the pandemic has seriously damaged the multilateral economic system. Considering the European continent, the announced aid packages will not ensure that the system is not completely affected, and the wound caused by COVID-19 in the economic field will perhaps continue for many years. It would not be wrong to foresee that we will experience many problems such as economic recessions, increases in unemployment and decreases in income. Another important result of this will be that states, after this experience, will turn to national investments instead of multilateral investments. States realized at the beginning of the pandemic that they had to rely only themselves. Such a path will be followed in order to identify important sectors and support the national system in times of crisis, and this will possibly make them act as protectionist in economic policies. In short, the consequences of the pandemic in the economic field of the EU are that the members are as far from cooperation as they are in the political phase. This deepens the question of the EU's function.

6. Perception of the EU

As we mentioned before, during the pandemic process, the policies followed by the member states were criticized rather than the EU. However, there are still situations where the perception of the EU is negatively affected. For instance, Sweden acted separately from EU policies in the management of the pandemic process. Sweden adopted a national policy, and the EU's reaction to this situation was insufficient. Allowing such a move has been one of the events that negatively affected the perception of the EU. Another negative case was that no action was taken despite the undemocratic decisions of Hungarian Prime Minister Orban. The EU, which has remained silent in the face of these decisions that are incompatible with European values, has compromised its principles and this was not welcomed. In addition, the EU administration, which is expected to take faster steps in pandemic management, failed in this expectation. The last problem was in the vaccine procurement process. The slow EU supply and distribution of vaccines is being viewed as an important lapse. These are all factors that cause the perception of the EU to deteriorate. When the attitudes of EU members far from cooperation are added to these, we can see that the idea and function of the EU has begun to be questioned.

However, even though these negativities pushed the European people to question it, they could not give up the idea of the EU. It is a fact that there are also advantages provided by the EU. Citizens of member states continue to support the EU at this point. And even they think that the

How did the COVID-19 crisis change your perception toward the EU?

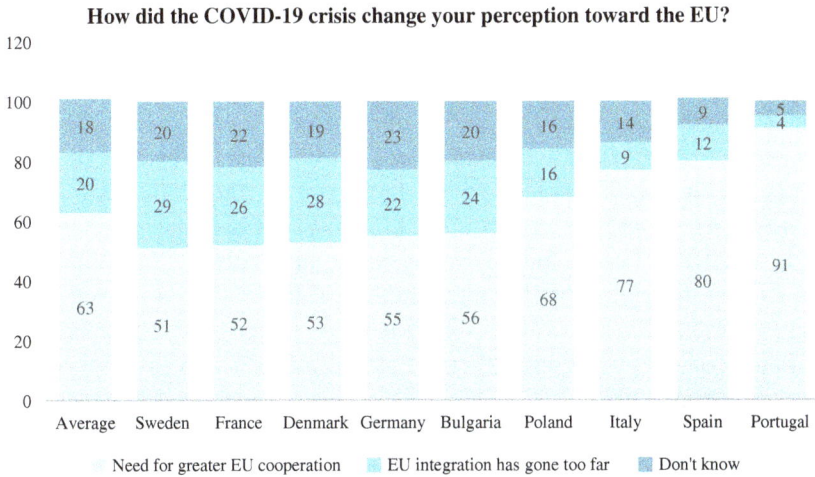

Figure 3. The need of cooperation in the EU.

Source: European Council on Foreign Relations.

actions of the EU, which we consider wrong, stem from the problems created by the member states. According to research, the portion of those who think that more cooperation is required to prevent such mistakes from repeating is determined as 63% across Europe, displayed in Figure 3 (Dennison & Zerka, 2020).

As we can see from the figure, the number of people who think that the cooperation within the EU should increase even more is too high. This shows us that during the pandemic period, it is necessary to apply to the EU again to make up for the shortcomings caused by the EU. We can conclude that the impact of the pandemic on the EU in this sense will mean more cooperation in the future. In this period, when states pursue national policies, more cooperation cannot be expected in the short term, but it will not be a surprise to expect an increase in EU integration in the medium and long term.

7. Shifting Balances

Although there is a negative picture for the EU, it would not be realistic to foresee a disaster scenario. The idea that the EU would dissolve will not go beyond conspiracy theories. The reality is that there has been a process in which balances have to be re-established within the EU. The departure of Chancellor Merkel in Germany, who has acted as a pioneering character both economically and politically for years, will create a power vacuum within the EU. At this point, the objectives of the President of France Emmanuel Macron are to be more active in EU policies and to place France in the position vacated by Germany as the dominant power. Another factor that is as important as the power transition environment in the EU between France and Germany in the new balance that will occur is the rising far-right populist movement in Europe. Populist movements mainly criticize EU integration. This ideology, which has an upward trend in many countries, including France, can lead us to an impasse in the functioning and decisions of the EU. While diplomats discussing that the EU's capacity to cope with crises can increase with deeper integration, the EU skeptic's views should not be ignored.

At the same time, there is a change of balance in international relations. For the EU to become a global actor in this new era, the problems inside the EU should be resolved and the cooperation environment should be restored again. When the challenges in domestic policy are eliminated and the EU is able to act as one, the Union will also be a part of the geopolitical shifts happening in the world. When the global conjuncture is evaluated, we should first mention the United States of America (USA). The USA's protectionist policies intensifying with the pandemic and its distancing from the multilateral global system reveal that the role of the country on a global scale has decreased. It is a fact that President Donald Trump, who was in office at the beginning of the pandemic period, had an influence on politics. However, it is unclear whether Joe Biden, who took office at the beginning of 2021, will bring the United States back to its former power in the international system after the negative effects of COVID-19. In addition, the tensions between the EU and USA, which is one of the most important partners of the EU, during the Donald Trump period has deteriorated relations. It is expected that transatlantic bilateral relations, with Joe Biden's administration, will be re-established in the post-COVID-19 period. The importance of the Biden administration for multilateral cooperation will be decisive for the EU on a global scale, especially in terms of economy and security.

Considering the global actors, China should be taken into consideration as a priority. Making a name for itself during the COVID-19 crisis, China aims to increase its geopolitical influence in the new period. China, which gave false information to the world at the beginning of the epidemic, has missed the chance of preventing a great pandemic. However, the successful recovery from the first wave of the epidemic and its return to normal life much faster than other countries make China advantageous in the post-COVID-19 period. The Chinese economy, which was already threatening the economic power of the USA before the pandemic, will become stronger in the new period.

While other countries are still fighting the virus, China's recovery of its economy and having significant advances in economic power, access to markets and domination will cause the balances to change in favor of China in the post-COVID-19 world. China sending aid to many parts of the world during this period is also critical in terms of diplomacy and political visibility. To be more specific, responding positively to EU countries in need of help made the perception of China change positively. The striking point here is that the USA followed national policies and the EU remained inadequate on a global scale due to internal problems during the pandemic. In the international system, where these two actors cannot play a decisive role, it should be underlined that China fills the political and economic gap created (Rogg, 2020).

When we consider the geopolitical effects that may occur in terms of the EU, it has been observed that as inter-state solidarity decreases, especially in times of crises, the idea of an organization that encompasses all of Europe loses sheen. This does not mean that the idea of the EU has collapsed, but we should not be far from the idea that states can establish regional organizations, especially with states that are geographically and politically close. In the EU foreign policy, the desire of the organization to become a global actor continues. But this is not an easy event, and the EU needs to make some progress in order to consolidate its place in world politics. The two most important factors for this have been identified as being a pioneer in technology field and providing political stability and affluence to neighboring regions (Martin, 2020). For the EU to become a more effective actor, it must gain a position that has a voice and a leading position both within itself and in the events taking place around it.

Finally, we need to include the international relations scenario that is expected to occur in the post-COVID-19 period. Actors will determine their future and the course of the international system as the economic recovery takes place. Russia and China, whose relations with European states increased during the pandemic period, are getting stronger at this point. On the other hand, it is expected that the relations between the USA and the EU, which have been partners for many years, will improve. In such a situation, instead of choosing between the USA and China, the EU may draw a path away from both actors. Explained by the term strategic distancing, this possible scenario argues that the EU will determine its own strategy and remain with neither China nor the USA (European Parliament, 2020b). The reason why such a scenario is likely to happen is because of the EU's desire to become a global actor. As a global actor, it is necessary to be able to work with states from all parts of the world, not just with a specific party. How far the EU can achieve this in the post-COVID-19 period will continue to be a matter of curiosity.

8. Conclusion

The effects of this epidemic, which penetrated every region of the world without exception, left deep scars in Europe as in all continents. The health, economic, political, and social problems caused by COVID-19 have taken over the entire body of the EU. Just as the disease harms the human body, it has similarly harmed EU functioning. From the policies implemented by states almost ignoring each other to the failure of the EU to take action, everything has caused the organization to mismanage this crisis. The states, which act against the European values and act in accordance with the national interests with the panic created by the chaotic environment, weakened the EU during the pandemic. When we think in the short term, these policies of the states have shown us that the EU, which is a multilateral organization, will face difficulties in terms of functionality. In addition to this, European skeptical far-right and nationalist formations, which are on the rise all over Europe and even in the European Parliament, will also have negative effects on the EU. But at the end of the day, the need for the EU, which has been criticized in terms of vaccines and reactions, will not decrease. Member states will need more money flow than mutual aid in order to revive their economies. This can be achieved with the packages announced by the EU institutions. For this reason, no state will easily break away from adhering to the EU structure. We have to admit that every crisis opens up EU integration for discussion. But this does not mean that the EU is being abandoned. Of course, there will be those who criticize every institution, government, and policy, the important thing here is the quality of the criticism. Constructive criticism is needed in this sense in order to come out of such a global crisis stronger. In the post-COVID-19 era, the EU and, of course, member states, who want to become a global actor, will not miss such an opportunity. States that do not have the capacity to become global actors individually can realize their ideals under the roof of an organization and reach a respectability accepted in every region of the world. What needs to be done for this is to put an end to the problems within the organization and to come together. Therefore, it can be predicted that this situation may change in the medium and long term after the negative effects of the pandemic on the EU in the short term. It is up to the EU states to cope with crises and become a stronger actor. Maybe there is no specific medicine that can cure the COVID-19 disease yet, but the remedy for the EU to turn the COVID-19 crisis in its favor is clear: to back each other and provide more cooperation.

References

Celi, G., Guarascio, D., & Simonazzi, A. (2020). A fragile and divided European Union meets Covid-19: Further disintegration or "Hamiltonian moment"? *Journal of Industrial and Business Economics*, *47*(3), 411–424, https://doi.org/10.1007/s40812-020-00165-8.

Dennison, S. & Zerka, P. (June 29, 2020). Together in Trauma: Europeans and the world after Covid-19. *European Council on Foreign Relations*, https://ecfr.eu/publication/together_in_trauma_europeans_and_the_world_after_covid_19/.

Der Spiegel. (February 11, 2021). *Ansehen der EU leidet massiv wegen Impfstoffbeschaffung*, https://www.spiegel.de/politik/ausland/umfrage-ansehen-der-eu-leidet-massiv-wegen-impfstoffbeschaffung-a-06324c7a-b3be-4284-b226-3382756eb394.

Engman, M. (April 2020). In the wake of Covid-19: Troubled waters ahead for the European union. *Institute for Security and Development Policy*, https://isdp.eu/publication/in-the-wake-of-covid-19-troubled-waters-ahead-for-the-european-union/.

European Commission. (March 22, 2020). *State Aid: Commission Approves €50 Million Italian Support Scheme for Production and Supply of Medical Equipment and Masks during Coronavirus Outbreak*, https://ec.europa.eu/commission/presscorner/detail/en/IP_20_507.

European Parliament. (June 2020a). Uncertainty/EU/Hope — Public opinion in times of COVID-19. *Public Opinion Monitoring Unit within the DG COMM of the European Parliament*, https://op.europa.eu/s/oNqM.

European Parliament. (September 2020b). The Geopolitical Implications of the COVID-19 Pandemic, https://doi.org/10.2861/526114.

Eurostat. (February 2, 2020a). GDP Down by 0.7% in the Euro Area and by 0.5% in the EU [Dataset]. *Eurostat*, https://ec.europa.eu/eurostat/documents/portlet_file_entry/2995521/2-02022021-AP-EN.pdf/0e84de9c-0462-6868-df3e-dbacaad9f49f.

Eurostat. (December 2, 2020b). Euro Area Unemployment at 8.4%, https://ec.europa.eu/eurostat/documents/portlet_file_entry/2995521/3-02122020-AP-EN.pdf/3b4ec2e2-f14c-2652-80bd-2f5e7c0605c2.

Hall, B., Johnson, M., & Arnold, M. (March 13, 2020). Italy wonders where Europe's solidarity is as coronavirus strains show. *Financial Times*, https://www.ft.com/content/d3bc25ea-652c-11ea-b3f3-fe4680ea68b5.

Leigh, M. (December 14, 2020). Relaunch or Disintegration? What Covid-19 Means for the Future of Europe. *EUROPP*, https://blogs.lse.ac.uk/europpblog/2020/12/14/relaunch-or-disintegration-what-covid-19-means-for-the-future-of-europe/.

Martin, É. A. (2020). COVID-19 reveals Europe's strategic loneliness. *Istituto Affari Internazionali, 40*, 1–21, https://www.iai.it/sites/default/files/iaip2040.pdf.

Mason, A. (2020). Europe's future: The impact of Covid-19 on populism. *International Development Research Network*, 1–10, https://static1.squarespace.com/static/5e8ce9ff629cbb272fd0406f/t/5eb56553639d684c20bb3241/1594895757037/Europe%27s+Future.pdf.

Opiłowska, E. Ż. (2020). The Covid-19 crisis: The end of a borderless Europe? *European Societies, 23*(sup1), 589–600, https://doi.org/10.1080/14616696.2020.1833065.

Robert Schuman Foundation. (April 6, 2020). *The European Union and the Coronavirus*, https://www.robert-schuman.eu/en/european-issues/0553-the-european-union-and-the-coronavirus.

Rogg, M. (2020). COVID-19: The pandemic and its impact on security policy. *PRISM*, 54–67, https://doi.org/10.2307/26918234.

van Schaik, L., Jørgensen, K. E., & van de Pas, R. (2020). Loyal at once? The EU's global health awakening in the Covid-19 pandemic. *Journal of European Integration, 42*(8), 1145–1160, https://doi.org/10.1080/07036337.2020.1853118.

Chapter 11

The COVID-19 Pandemic: New Normal and New Terrorism

Selim KANAT

Department of International Relations,
Süleyman Demirel University, Isparta, Turkey

selimkanat@yahoo.com

Abstract

This study is a qualitative assessment written to analyze the possible effects of the COVID-19 pandemic on international terrorism. In the first part of the study, the effects of the COVID-19 pandemic on social life and living habits were tried to be codified by supporting concrete data. In this context, the concept of "new normal", which is used to describe the life model that will emerge after the pandemic, has been tried to be explained by highlighting some features. In the second part of the study, the concept of "new terrorism", which was considered as perhaps the biggest danger to the security of states and humanity before the COVID-19 danger, was emphasized. It has been evaluated how international terrorism, which has differentiated with the effect of the globalization process experienced in the post-Cold War period and defined as new terrorism, is affected by the COVID-19 pandemic and the concept of the "new normal" created by this pandemic. As a result of this evaluation, three results have been reached. The first of these is that in the period defined as the new normal, income distribution inequalities will increase all over the world, which will increase poverty in fragile states and feed radical Islamic terrorism. The second is that the increasing digitalization with the COVID-19 pandemic will affect the methods of terrorist acts in the form of digitalization. The third is that the habit of keeping the physical distance gained with the COVID-19 pandemic in the new normal life will transform the types of actions, and this will reduce the attacks' methods such as bombing, suicide attacks, hostage taking in terrorism actions compared to the past.

1. Introduction

The COVID-19 pandemic can be considered as a serious threat to the whole of humanity, which is accepted to have emerged in China at the end of 2019 and spread all over the world in about two years, causing the death of millions of people despite all the measures and the possibilities of modern medicine. While we wonder how this pandemic, which has occupied the world agenda for more than a year, can be ended, on the other hand, there is an uncertainty about what the world will be like after the pandemic is over.

Combating the unknown is both the aim and responsibility of science. In this context, academic interest around the world has focused on the COVID-19 pandemic. Many scientists in many fields from medicine, economics, political science and international relations, education, business, and informatics have tried to do scientific research and publish their contributions to solve the mystery of the COVID-19 pandemic. When we examine the Web of Science archive, we can see that as of April 2021, 116,000 research reports have been published all over the world on COVID-19. While approximately 40,000 of these articles were written in the field of social sciences, 870 scientific publications were made in the field of international relations (WOS, 2021a). Considering that every scientific activity originates from curiosity and need, we can say that these publications indicate the unknown created by the COVID-19 pandemic and how much this unknown is wanted to be understood.

We can also say that a similar effort focuses on the concept of "new normal" emerging after the pandemic. The term "new" in this context can be accepted as a reflection of the belief that our social life will change after the pandemic. Although the changes that occur in our lives with the COVID-19 pandemic are not as much as the disease itself, it is among the subjects that have been researched. Although most of the publications on the new normal are in the field of medicine, studies have also been conducted in areas such as economics, business, education, and tourism (WOS, 2021b).

The evaluation of the new normal life in terms of social sciences will probably increase in the future. It is an expected result that many things in life we will experience after the pandemic will be different than before. Because, under the current conditions, the effects that occur in social life are likely to affect our lives. Based on this assumption, this study aims to contribute to the emerging literature by trying to analyze the effects of the new normal life on international terrorism.

The main question of this research is, "What effects will the new normal life have on international terrorism?" This effect is the main hypothesis to be tested in the research that international terrorism will become a more serious threat in the new normal, especially for developed states. Depending on this main research question, what kind of terror wave humanity will face in the new normal life should be considered as a sub-research question. The hypothesis to be proved regarding this question is that radical Islamist terrorism will rise further.

A qualitative approach has been adopted in answering these research questions and testing hypotheses. In addition, this study has strived for a conceptual basis. In this qualitative approach, literature review and comparative case studies can be specified as the main data collection methods. In this data collection process, efforts were taken for case studies and numerical data to be collected as scientific evidence to support the hypotheses.

In line with the objectives, the effects of the COVID-19 pandemic on social life and social relations were discussed in the first part of the study. The concept of "new normal", which defines the changes likely to occur after the epidemic, is explained in this section. Afterward, the content of the term "new terrorism" was discussed and the effects of the COVID-19 pandemic on the new terrorism concept were discussed.

2. COVID-19 Pandemic and New Normal

The COVID-19 pandemic is the biggest pandemic of our age so far. However, over the past century, Spanish flu (1918–1919), Asian flu (1957–1958), Hong Kong flu (1968–1969), and swine flu (2009) can be described as other serious pandemics that affected humanity. The most serious of these was the Spanish flu. We do not know the true dimensions of this pandemic both due to the censorship applied by the states on the press during the years of World War I and the medical and technical inadequacies following the pandemic. However, it is known that approximately one out of every three people in the world had the disease and approximately 50 million people died (Spinney, 2017). However, the pandemic and its effects in collective memory fell behind that of the First World War. As states learn from the war, only individual tragedies are remembered from the Spanish Flu (Whiting, 2020).

With the effect of the First World War during the period of Spanish flu, it affected the poorest people of the societies, who had to work long hours, the most disadvantaged in accessing health services, crowded in relatively small houses, and who were not well-nourished (Spinney, 2017). When the effects of World War I on the world economies were added to these effects, poor, developing countries felt the burden of the pandemic more. However, it would be more correct to say that the markets experienced a fluctuation rather than a sharp decline due to the extraordinary conditions created by the First World War. However, although not as serious as the Spanish flu, the Dow Jones suffered serious depreciation in the second half of 1957 due to the 1957–1958 Asian flu, a smaller pandemic that killed an estimated one million people (Pinsker, 2020). The situation was similar for Britain, with some factories and mines closed, the government distributed ten million pounds of sickness relief money (Jackson, 2009). The Hong Kong flu, also known as the 1968 Flu Pandemic, caused nearly one million deaths worldwide (Cockburn, *et al.*, 1969). Approximately one month after the outbreak occurred, there was an epidemic whose effect was limited with the invention of the vaccine. Apart from these epidemics, humanity has faced many epidemic diseases, large and small.

After nearly 100 years of success in the fight against global pandemics since the 1918–1919 Spanish flu pandemic, COVID-19 threatens all humanity as a challenge to modern medicine and social life. Despite all measures to combat the pandemic, more than 140 million active cases and more than 3 million deaths have occurred worldwide as of April 19, 2021 (WHO, 2021). With these rates, the COVID-19 outbreak is the second largest epidemic after the Spanish flu since the 19th century (Cirillo & Taleb, 2020).

The term used for predictions about the world after COVID-19 is the "new normal" expression. This term, which has been widely used in academic circles, also emphasizes the belief that nothing will be as it was before the pandemic. Although it is difficult to predict the medium- and long-term effects of the pandemic, it is possible to say that it has increased at least three things in our social life as far as we can observe for everyone. Accordingly, the COVID-19 pandemic has increased poverty, digitalization, and physical distance between people.

As in previous pandemics, the economic effects of COVID-19 are also global. It can be said that there are two reasons for this: pandemics affect all states at different rates and the second is that trade and markets are integrated (Jorda *et al.*, 2020). According to a projection made on the data of the pandemics that took place in the 20th century, in a pandemic in which 1.4 million people lost their lives, the global loss corresponds to 0.8% of the global gross national paroduct (GNP) (McKibbin & Sidorenko, 2006). This corresponds to approximately US$670 billion in 2020 GNP. Considering that the number of deaths due to the COVID-19 outbreak has already exceeded three million, the economic loss is estimated to be much more serious. It would not be correct to say that this is an assumption valid only for COVID-19. Before this epidemic, the negative effects of epidemics on economies were observed. With the pandemic, global income inequality is increasing. This increase may be described as a further acceleration of income inequality, which increased with post-Cold War globalization. With each passing time, rich become richer while poor become poorer in the world. In the world, the income difference between the rich and the poor is increasing, in a way, poverty is spreading. On the basis of this is the globalization of the economy, the blurring of the national economic boundaries that prevent the wealthy segments of society from gaining more profit. Global capital, which is no longer bound by national borders, gains more. The global income distribution distortion increases the income gap between the north and south economically.

When we look at the geography of poverty, it is possible to see that Muslim states are predominantly among the underdeveloped southern states. Therefore, it is likely that Muslim countries will be more affected by the economic inequality that has deepened in the global income distribution with the effect of the COVID-19 pandemic. The basis of this claim lies in the fact that seven of the top ten most vulnerable states, according to the list of "fragile states" used to describe the states with the highest probability of being driven into internal disturbances and collapse, are states with a dense Muslim population. In 2020, the number of Muslim states was only one among the top 30 states with the highest economy with the strongest standard of living, in other words, the lowest rate of vulnerability (Fund For Peace, 2020a). Four of the five states whose vulnerability increased the most between 2010 and 2020 are again Muslim states (De Latour, 2020). This situation can be interpreted as the COVID-19 pandemic affecting the economy of Muslim states more. In the new normal life, the states most likely to be dragged into internal turmoil due to economic difficulties are Muslim states numerically.

Another effect of COVID-19 is that it increases the physical distance between people. During the pandemic period, people are forced to live physically farther from each other than they were in the past. All over the world, states have declared curfews at various times and take measures that increase and protect the physical distance. Many things are now being done "remotely", where the physical distance made collectively and together compared to the past has disappeared. With the opportunities provided by technology, people can receive education remotely from their homes, they can shop, participate in concerts, theater plays, academic artistic events, and even work remotely as far as their profession allows. In this case, increasing the physical distance in the society means a decrease in crowds. This changing lifestyle during the epidemic period is expected to continue in the new normal after the pandemic at certain rates. Although the new is not normally as much as it was at the time of the epidemic, it is likely that we will continue to live farther from each other than our old lives.

The pandemic has increased both the physical distance between people in the society and the physical distance between societies in the international environment. In this process, states have diverged from each other in terms of policies, and international cooperation has decreased. When we look at the management of the pandemic and vaccination process, we can see that international cooperation is decreasing; instead, anti-integration nationalist ideas are on the rise. The first measure taken by states during the pandemic period was to close their borders to other states to reduce international mobility. This attitude continues with regard to vaccination. In a supranational organization such as the European Union, there are differences in access to vaccines between states. Regarding pandemic management and vaccination, every state keeps its distance from other states and acts in a nationalist manner in vaccination. Rich countries are selfish in accessing vaccines. For example, Canada strives to procure a number of vaccines about ten times its population size (Ciesle & Eliassen 2020). From this point of view, nationalism in the face of the new normal globalization brings with it separation instead of international integration.

Another effect of the global pandemic has been the increase in digitalization in social life. People all over the world are experiencing the digitalization, that should have likely taken place over decades, almost as once because of the pandemic. This is actually a process triggered by the need for people to perform their jobs remotely under pandemic conditions. Students and educators who had to continue their education remotely had to have and master distance education technologies. For example, those who could not go to banks for their financial affairs had to use digital banking facilities. During the epidemic period, smart mobile phones have turned into a tool for the governments to fight the disease. Applications downloaded to smart phones were used to monitor patients during the epidemic period. On the other hand, people who could not socialize by mixing with the crowds during the epidemic period started to prefer socializing through digital media. It is possible that the new normal life becomes much more digital than the old.

It is possible to say that the new normal has many more effects than increasing poverty, distance between people, and digitalization. However, this study does not only aim to focus on how our new normal life will be, but also aims to explain what kind of effect terrorism will face in the new life. Therefore, focusing on the new normal and terrorism issue at this point would be a more in line with the aim of the study.

3. New Normal and New Terrorism

The term new terrorism is a term used to describe the new form that terrorism has taken as a result of the transformation it has undergone after the Cold War. The term used for about 30 years has a dynamic structure, not a static one. It can be said that terrorism has undergone its last major transformation with the effect of the end of the Cold War. The September 11 attacks, on the other hand, can be considered as one of the biggest case studies of the new terrorism.

One of the effects of the end of the Cold War on terrorism has been the elimination of terrorism from the revolutionary left ideology and the rise of radical religion since 1979 that has become the main character of terrorism. Rapaport classified the transformation of terrorism over the years as four waves. He emphasized that the revolutionary left terrorism wave that dominated the Cold War, which was the third of these four waves, ended with the end of the Cold War and that the religious wave came in the post-Cold War period (2013). However, radical religious terrorism increases its effectiveness in the post-Cold War period. One of the sources that fuel this increase is the increasing income inequality and poverty with globalization in the post-Cold War period. If we look at the countries where terrorist organizations are active today, it is possible to see this reality.

It is possible to use the term "fragile states" for countries most affected by income inequality. Because one of the important indicators of fragility is that income inequality is high in these countries (Brock *et al.*, 2012). In these states, besides the society living in poverty, the states have lost their authority (OECD, 2013). Poverty results from the disruption of governments in these states without performing the simplest public services. Public services fail, the state falls short of protecting the rights of its citizens, cannot ensure security, and public authority disappears. In regions where state authority has weakened or disappeared, local authorities similar to medieval overlords emerge, and these elites begin to fill the lost state authority (Stepputat, 2007).

These states become virtually safe havens for both criminal and terrorist organizations (Beehner, 2018). The fact that the poor section of the society is most severely affected by the COVID-19 pandemic causes these poor people to see involvement in crime and terrorism as a logical alternative as a way out of their deep impossibilities (Schneckener, 2003). In areas where state authority is absent, terrorist organizations sometimes cooperate with local elites and turn these places into centers for themselves. Local people living in poverty, hunger, and insecurity also join or at least support the organization in order to survive or to live in better conditions to some extent (Minkiewicz, 2017). When evaluated from this point of view, poverty stands out among the sources that global terrorism feeds on. Considering that income inequality and poverty will increase all over the world with COVID-19, it is possible to say that terrorism will rise in the new normal in the future.

If we accept that the negative economic impact of the COVID-19 pandemic will be mostly on the poor, fragile states, if we remember that the majority of the most vulnerable states in the world are Muslim states, it will be possible to say that radical Islamic terrorism will rise in the new normal period. It is possible to say that the vulnerability of Iraq was effective in the emergence of ISIS even before the impact of COVID-19 (Ibrahimi, 2020). After the Cold War, terrorist organizations such as Al-Qaeda, Boko-Haram, ISIS, etc., which are considered global threats, are fundamentalist organizations and countries such as Afghanistan, Syria, Iraq, and Sudan are at the top of the vulnerability index (Fragile States Index, 2020). In this sense, developing policies for the fragility problems of states in the world can be seen not only as a humanitarian policy but also as a security policy (Firth & Glenn, 2015).

One of the characteristics of the new terrorism is the transformation that occurs in the methods of action. Bomb attacks, suicide attacks, hijackings, political assassinations, kidnappings, and hostage taking are among the preferred methods of terrorist acts during the Cold War. However, with the rapid development in technology after the Cold War, terrorism started to use technology in its actions. From this point of view, the new terrorism is much more technological than the old one. This situation has had two effects on terrorist acts. One of these effects is that terrorists have begun to reach destructive weapons more easily than before, thanks to technology. In addition, they were able to learn to use weapons that would require expertise more easily. Even taking advantage of technology, terrorists have started to manufacture more destructive weapons themselves. The second effect of technology on terrorist acts is that the actions themselves become technological. In the new terrorism, actions are now being carried out in the cyber world. Cyber terrorism is becoming a more serious threat to humanity every day.

The COVID-19 pandemic will likely double the growing threat potential of cyber terrorism. There are two reasons for this. The first is that people quickly join the virtual world with the new normal life. Before the epidemic, people who were not related to the virtual world and digital technologies started to use the internet at increasing rates to adapt to the conditions brought by the epidemic (Yıldırım, 2020). This situation makes the virtual world more attractive for terrorist acts because it needs crowds to perpetrate terrorist acts. The aim of the new terrorism, just like the old terrorism, is to create fear in the society through the actions taken. The second reason that cyber terrorism will increase faster than its normal course in the new normal life is the increasing physical distance between people. Another habit that the pandemic adds to our lives is the idea that it is bad to enter crowds and we should stay away from crowds. However, methods such as kidnapping, bombing, and suicide attacks, which are the classical methods of terrorist acts, are the types that are carried out in crowded environments. Crowds are the factor that increase the impact of actions and frightening in society. At this point, the decrease in physical crowds will increase the tendency of terrorists to prefer digital methods instead of such classical methods.

This transformation in new terrorism is a situation that existed in the period before COVID-19. In other words, before the epidemic, there was an increase in radical Islamist terrorism and a digitalization trend in terrorist acts. When terrorism is mentioned before COVID-19, radical Islamist terrorist organizations are the first terrorist profile that comes to mind. The rate of using technology by terrorists is increasing before the pandemic. The impact of the COVID-19 pandemic and the new normal life we are likely to experience afterwards on new terrorism is that it will accelerate this process. In other words, with the pandemic, radical Islamist terrorism will increase faster than its normal course, and cyber terrorism will be adopted as a more common method of action.

4. Conclusion

The COVID-19 pandemic is the largest epidemic to threaten humanity in the last century since the Spanish flu. Beyond killing millions of people, it also affects people's daily lives. Changes in daily life expressed with the term new normal are likely to reshape social life. Pandemic habits, which are expected to continue after the epidemic, will change and transform many concepts and phenomena related to social sciences in the medium and long term.

One of the prominent ones among these concepts that will change is the concept of terrorism. Because terrorism can be considered as the most serious security threat to humanity after the Cold War. So much so that the September 11 attacks, as the biggest terrorist attack affecting all humanity at the same time, have been used as a milestone in most academic studies and in everyday speech. The phenomenon of terrorism, which has been transforming throughout history, will perhaps experience its last transformation after the COVID-19 pandemic.

Terrorism, whose purpose is to terrorize people and realize some political goals, is directly affected by the transformations in social life and the change in people's approach to issues. So what kind of changes in social life will have an impact on terrorism? The first thing that comes to mind in this regard is the increasing income inequality with COVID-19. Because poverty, increased by income inequality, is one of the sources of terrorism. It is no coincidence that the world's poorest countries are also linked to global terrorism. Countries with poor economies and high poverty and hunger are predominantly Muslim countries. For these reasons, the COVID-19 pandemic will probably affect these Muslim states the most economically. Increasing poverty all over the world and in these states will especially feed radical Islamist terrorism. The state of Western states, with relatively low death rates and high prosperity, is likely to be exploited by radical Islamist terrorist organizations for their dark ambitions. In the new normal, it can be talked about the increasing radical Islamist terrorist acts against the Western states with high prosperity for various reasons.

Another difference that the new normal life may bring to social life is that it has increased the physical distance between people. The measures taken with the epidemic to reduce social mobility and contact have resulted in the transformation of many professions. Professions that can be done without going to workplaces have been started to be done remotely. Shopping, including grocery shopping, has begun to be made virtually. Concerts, sports competitions, culture, and art events are being digitalized. Even in tourism, contact reducing measures are implemented, which reduces the proximity of tourists with the local people. The importance of this for terrorism is that the old methods of action will gradually become meaningless. Methods such as bombings, kidnappings, and suicide attacks have been carried out for about a hundred years in terrorist acts. However, the way these actions can be frightening is if they are performed in crowds. However, the crowds will probably decrease in the new normal life compared to the old. For example, the contact with the local population will inevitably decrease due to contact reduction measures, and it will be more difficult to kidnap and take hostages of tourists. The decrease in contact and crowds will also push terrorist organizations to review the types of action. In this new period, we are likely to encounter different actions rather than classical action types. Even if it can be said that the hijackings or airport attacks will continue, the digitization of the actions in the new period may be an expected development.

This digitalization that can be expected in terrorist acts can also be considered as another difference that the COVID-19 pandemic has brought to our social life. During this period, the use of virtual technologies has increased. Even people who have nothing to do with the digital world have been forced into this world under the conditions brought on by the pandemic. Perhaps the digital transformation that will take decades is experienced in a short period of time under the conditions imposed by COVID-19. As people physically move away from each other, the virtual environment is getting crowded. This crowding, that is, people's increasingly digital footprints, will result in this area becoming increasingly attractive for terrorist acts. In the pre-COVID-19 period, people who do not have any digital accounts or identity have no reason to fear cyber terrorist attacks, and the increasing number of people who do not have information about cyber security in the virtual world with the new normal will probably result in the intensification of the activities of terrorists in this area. In the new normal, cyber terrorism is likely to rise as an increasingly feared and precautionary threat.

Apart from this evaluation based on the observations made and the data obtained, it is possible that there will be many innovations and differences that the new normal will bring to our lives. It can be said that this new life will create changes worth analyzing in terms of many fields of social sciences. However, it is highly probable that terrorism will increasingly continue to be a threat to human life and national security, as in the pre-COVID-19 period. With the increasing poverty, the fight against terrorism will become more difficult than before, and it is likely that human rights and freedoms must be respected in this struggle.

References

Beehner, L. (2018). Fragile states and the territory conundrum to countering violent nonstate actors, *Democracy and Security*, *14*(2), 101–127, DOI:10.1080/17419166.2017.140800.

Brock, L. Holm, H. H., Sorensen, G., & Stohl, M. (2012). *Fragile States Violence and the Failure of Intervention*. Cambridge: Polity Press.

Ciesle, W. & Eliassen, J. (November 25, 2020). History repeats itself: Attempts to prevent vaccine injustice have provided questionable results, https://www.investigate-europe.eu/en/2020/covid-vaccine-distribution-cepi-covax/ (Accessed on 01.04.2021).

Cirillo, P. & Talep, N. N. (2020). Tail risk of contagious diseases. *Nature Physics*, *16*, 606–613, https://doi.org/10.1038/s41567-020-0921-x.

Cockburn, W. C., Delon, P. J., & Ferreira, W. (1969). Origin and progress of the 1968–69 Hong Kong influenza epidemic, Bull World Health Organanization,

41(3–4–5): 343–348, https://www.ncbi.nlm.nih.gov/pmc/articles/PMC2427756/pdf/bullwho00220-0014.pdf (Accessed on 24.03.2021).

De Latour, J. J. M. (2020), There is No COVID-19 Here, https://fragilestatesindex.org/2020/05/10/there-is-no-covid-19-here/ (Accessed on 13.03.2021).

Firth, R. & Gleen, J. (2015). Fragile states and the evolution of risk governance: Intervention, prevention and extension. *Third World Quarterly*, *36*(10), 1787–1808. DOI:10.1080/01436597.2015.1063407.

Fragile States Index (2020), https://fragilestatesindex.org/data/ (Accessed on 03.04.2021).

Fund For Peace (2020a). Global Data, https://fragilestatesindex.org/data/ (Accessed on 13.03.2021).

Ibrahimi, S. Y. (2020). Violence-producing dynamics of fragile states: How state fragility in Iraq contributed to the emergence of islamic state. *Terrorism and Political Violence*, *32*(6) 1245–1267. DOI:10.1080/09546553.2018.1463914.

Jackson, C. (2009). History lessons: The asian flu pandemic. *British Journal on General Practice*, August 622–623, https://www.ncbi.nlm.nih.gov/pmc/articles/PMC2714797/pdf/bjgp59-622.pdf (Accessed on 23.03.2021).

Jorda, O., Singh, S. R., & Taylor, A. M. Longer-Run economic consequences of pandemics, *NBER Working Paper Series*, https://www.nber.org/system/files/working_papers/w26934/w26934.pdf (Accessed on 12.03.2021).

McKibbin, W. J. & Sidorenko, A. A. (2006). *Global Macroeconomic Consequences of Pandemic Influenza Australian National University Centre for Applied Macroeconomic Analysis*, Miscellaneous Publications February 2006, https://cama.crawford.anu.edu.au/pdf/working-papers/2006/262006.pdf (Accessed on 15.03.2021).

Minkiewicz, M. S. (2017). The problem of terrorism in fragile States of Africa. Causes and consequences of phenomenon. *European Journal of Transformation Studies*, *5*(1), pp. 48–63.

OECD (2013). *Fragile States: Resource Flows and Trends, Conflict and Fragility*, Paris: OECD Publishing, http://dx.doi.org/10.1787/9789264190399-en.

Pinsker, J. How to Think About the Plummeting Stock Market, https://www.theatlantic.com/business/archive/2020/02/coronavirus-stock-market/607216/ (Accessed on 23.03.2021).

Rapaport, D. C. (2013). The four waves of modern terror international dimensions and consequences. In Hanhimäki & Blumenau (Eds.), *An International History of Terrorism Western and non-Western experiences*. New York: Routledge Publishing.

Schneckener, U. (2003). Decline of the State as a Global Threat — Fragile States and Transnational Terrorism. *Internationale Politik*, *58*(11), 11–19.

Spinney, L. (2017). *Pale Rider: The Spanish Flu of 1981 and How It Changed The World*. New York: Public Affairs Books.

Stepputat, F. (2007). Insecurity, state, and impunity in Latin America. In L. Andersen, B. Moller, & F. Stepputat (Eds.), *Fragile States and Insecure People?* New York: Palgrave Macmillan.

Whiting, K. A science journalist explains how the Spanish Flu changed the world, https://www.weforum.org/agenda/2020/04/covid-19-how-spanish-flu-changed-world/ (Accessed on 14.03.2021).

WHO. Coronavirus (COVID-19) Dashboard, https://covid19.who.int/ (Accessed on 19.04.2021).

WOS (Web of Science) (2021a), http://apps.webofknowledge.com/Search.do?product=UA&SID=F6APItee9MiMxdccYJL&search_mode=GeneralSearch&prID=51ab1c92-95b9-4c5b-a5de-48ca80a41c05 (Accessed on 20.04.2021).

WOS (Web of Science) (2021b), http://apps.webofknowledge.com/summary.do?product=UA&parentProduct=UA&search_mode=GeneralSearch&parentQid=&qid=3&SID=F6APItee9MiMxdccYJL&&update_back2search_link_param=yes&page=4 (Accessed on 21.04.2021).

Yıldırım, O. (2020). Yeni Koronavirüs Salgını Dolayısıyla Gündeme Gelen Sosyal İzolasyon ve Gönüllü Karantina Döneminde İnternet ve Sosyal Medya Kullanımı (Internet and Social Media Usage During Social Isolation and Quarantine due to Covid-19 Era). *İletişim Kuram ve Araştırma Dergisi — Sayı 52 / Kış 2020 (Communication Theory and Research Journal No.52 Winter 2020)*, pp. 69–94, https://doi.org/10.47998/ikad.788255.

https://doi.org/10.1142/9781800611450_0012

Chapter 12

Effect of COVID-19 on Patients with Severe Mental Disorders

Esra AKYOL

Psychiatry Department, Ankara Yıldırım Beyazit University,
Yenimahalle Education and Research Hospital, Ankara, Turkey

esraakyol0121@gmail.com

Abstract

The COVID-19 pandemic severely affected the standards of life of individuals with severe mental disorders due to implementation of quarantine and personal precautions. Public health implementations of quarantine limitations, personal hygiene, and physical distance precautions target the whole population. However, the applicability of these strategies is at lower levels in some special populations, like those with schizophrenia and similar psychotic disorders and bipolar disorder diagnosis. In this respect, this chapter aims to dissect the effects of COVID-19 on patients with severe mental disorders. As a result, the management of severe mental disorders during the pandemic is a dynamic process that requires intense attention, dedication, and mutual solidarity. The impact of the pandemic imperatives on the re-evaluation and development of psychiatric treatments and approaches cannot be denied. Innovative and modifiable psychiatric interventions will play an important role in the future of psychiatry.

1. Introduction

The cause of the pandemic beginning in December 2019 in Wuhan city in Hubei state of China was identified to be the coronavirus SARS-CoV-2 (Chen Wang *et al.*, 2020; Na Zhu *et al.*, 2019). On January 13, 2020, the novel coronavirus disease (COVID-19) was defined as an infectious disease, causing respiratory tract symptoms (cough, shortness of breath, high fever). The WHO subsequently declared the first pandemic caused by coronavirus (WHO, 2020). Severe psychiatric disorders (schizophrenia and other psychotic disorders, schizoaffective disorders, and bipolar affective disorders) are chronic diseases causing disability in individuals due to destructive effects in cognitive, functional, and social skill areas. Due to the nature of these diseases, affected individuals require support in all time frames and situations and in all areas without exception. The destruction caused by these diseases in the cognitive area may be reduced with pharmacological treatment and the effect may be resolved. In a medical sense, amelioration of symptoms may be provided by pharmacological treatment. However, it is not possible to obtain satisfactory response for disruption in the functional and social skill areas by intervening with only medical treatment. For these areas, treatments must be supported with sociocultural support and psycho-skill programs.

The COVID-19 pandemic severely affected the standards of life of individuals with severe mental disorders due to implementation of quarantine and personal precautions. Patients with severe mental disorders experienced increased difficulties due to their disease in life because of quarantine and precautions, novel coronavirus disease symptoms, and the interactions between medications used for treatment with psychiatric medications.

It is unavoidable that patients with severe psychiatric disorders are affected more by the pandemic than individuals with medical diseases apart from psychiatric disorders. The rapid spread of the COVID-19 infection, one-on-one experience of deadly results, and requirements for quarantine limitations, individual hygiene, and physical distance precautions have caused pronounced distress and mental problems in all individuals, whether they have psychiatric disease or not (Cuiyan Wang *et al.*, 2020; Rubin & Wessely, 2020; Hao Yao *et al.*, 2020).

With all limitations, the messages about "no empty beds in hospitals", "coronavirus case numbers multiply three to five times", "number of dead rising", "not only old people, young people are dying", "there's no vaccine" and "the pandemic could last for years" on social media and mass communication tools increased psychological anxiety levels among people. It was unavoidable that psychiatric disorders, like anxiety disorders and depression, began to emerge after this. Additionally, quarantine precautions led all people to reduce, or in some situations even fully stop, communication with relatives. People became distant from their loved ones due to fear of disease and transmission, reduced sharing, were lonely, and felt unprotected and vulnerable to disease. The uncertainty of the pandemic led to feelings of hopelessness and lack of motivation about the future. COVID-19 stigmatization was added to the problem of stigma due to psychiatric disease.

Public health implementations of quarantine limitations, personal hygiene, and physical distance precautions target the whole population. However, the applicability of these strategies is at lower levels in some special populations like those with schizophrenia and similar psychotic disorders and bipolar disorder diagnosis. Some symptoms seen in severe mental disorders (delusions, hallucinations, disorganized behavior, cognitive impairment, and poor insight), along with sociocultural aspects like poor economic level, living in crowded environments and small houses, some being homeless and some living in care centers increase the risk of these individuals being infected with COVID-19. This widespread disease commonly affecting the whole public without regard to sociocultural or economic status and physical distancing and social isolation precautions are predicted to affect individuals with severe psychiatric disease more than anyone else (Kozloff *et al.*, 2020).

2. Overview of General Medical Status of Patients with Severe Mental Disorder

The bodily health of patients with a schizophrenia diagnosis is worse compared to the general population, with health problems resulting in more mortality or severe negative outcomes (Olfson *et al.*, 2015; Saxena & Maj, 2017).

Additionally, it is a reality that these individuals have lower socioeconomic level, limited interpersonal relationships with relatives socially, and experience more discrimination and stigmatization (Fonseca *et al.*, 2020, Cuiyan Wang, 2020; Rubin & Wessely, 2020).

However, the attendance rates at primary health services of these individuals are lower compared to general society (Bradford *et al.*, 2008). The stigmatization and discrimination lower the attendance rates for these individuals at health services. Additionally, patients cannot interpret and perceive health-related pathological situations as required by bodily sensations forming due to physical disease due to cognitive impairments sourced in their mental disease. It may be impossible for patients experiencing severe social withdrawal to benefit from complicated health services on their own and all the time (Bradford *et al.*, 2008; Fonseca *et al.*, 2020). We know schizophrenia patients have higher comorbid disease frequency compared to society, but one of the reasons for the more negative and mortal progression of these medical situations compared to the general population is probably the problems experienced with attending health services and with receiving service (Lawrence & Kisely, 2010; Saxena & Maj, 2017). It is a reality that discrimination and stigmatization delay access to health services, and increase the risk of self-harm and suicide among individuals with severe psychiatric disease (Thornicroft *et al.*, 2016).

Individuals with severe mental disorder have more frequent tuberculosis, HIV, hepatitis, pneumonia, and upper respiratory tract infections, along with urinary infections (Pankiewicz-Dulacz *et al.*, 2019). The reduction in the patients' self-care abilities due to disease may make it difficult to ensure sufficient levels of personal hygiene alone, and there is increased risk of catching infectious diseases due to inadequate personal and environmental cleaning (Fonseca *et al.*, 2020). Though they may perform personal self-care regularly and adequately from time to time, they cannot continuously maintain this organization. As a result, they require continuous external support and warnings. The increase in social and physical distance and reduction in interpersonal face-to-face communication in these quarantine periods means it is not possible for these individuals to maintain personal hygiene all the time at the same adequate level. For this reason, topics like ensuring personal hygiene, social distancing, and mask use should be repeated during psychosocial skills education in online interviews at intervals as frequently as possible (Hao Yao *et al.*, 2020).

If we look at the causes increasing the risk of COVID-19 infection for patients with severe mental disorder, they can be listed as causes due to the disease itself (poor insight, cognitive impairment, delusions, and hallucinations) and interpersonal relationship problems, disrupted and inattentive self-care, inability to fully understand the importance of infection and transmission, and delayed or no attendance at health centers due to disease causing transmission from the environment which has become a source of infection. For these reasons, after patients with severe mental disorder catch the infection, it is more difficult to both continue with psychiatric treatment and ensure adequate levels of COVID-19 infection treatment and that they abide by the requirements of quarantine. When all this data is assessed together, the reality that the best treatment is protection against catching the disease is even more important for individuals with severe mental health disorders. These individuals and the people they live with should be frequently informed about topics like COVID-19 infection-transmission, personal hygiene, physical distance, mask use, and symptoms of COVID-19 infection.

3. Problems Due To Quarantine

Ensuring persons with severe mental disorder remain at home represents a problem on its own. We only want patients to remain without social inclusion during acute attack periods and in the first days of treatment for acute attack until stabilization is ensured. During attack periods in severe mental disorders, patients must remain isolated due to delusions and hallucinations being experienced at intense levels, increased psychomotor activity, and medication side effects due to high initial doses (like loss of appetite, sedation, attention disorder, slowed thinking, and psychomotor slowing). However, when this period is over, we want patients with severe mental disorder to sustain their lives intertwined in society with social inclusion. There are many studies about ensuring social inclusion of patients with severe mental disorders. Community mental health centers have been created around the world and in Turkey to ensure healthy and sustainable social inclusion. Since the beginning of quarantine precautions in the pandemic, mental health professionals in these centers continued to hold mental and social skills education at regular intervals. Patients with severe mental disorder, and occasionally their families, are regularly given these trainings. In addition to education, busy-activities like painting, music, drama, handcrafts, sports, gardening, and animal care are available in these centers. These regular education and recreational activities ensure patients spend time in these community mental health centers and that patient relatives and caregivers spend time alone completing social activities without the patient. Quarantine precautions and social distance rules caused group education and activities to stop suddenly. Though many patients did not experience attacks in this period, disability thresholds fell, tolerance reduced, and daily life adjustment was observed to be disrupted. The disruption to day-to-day functioning, uncertainty of the process, disruption of some health services, and inability to meet basic requirements at the desired time and level was difficult for this group of patients. It is a reality that patients who spent all day at home with relatives will have relapses in interpersonal relationship problems at home, while new communication problems emerge due to being together continuously. In this period, the increased anxiety levels among all family members, emergence of friction (due to spending long periods of time together), and reopening of old accounts further increased communication problems. Noticeable negative symptoms, like withdrawal, reduced speaking, poverty of thought content, long duration to respond, occasional mutism, difficulty abiding by personal and general hygiene rules, and distracted behavior, increased friction between patient and relatives. In situations where these problems come to the fore, it is important to receive support from mental health professionals providing supportive interview services separately for both family and patient. Patients should be given responsibilities which are manageable for the patient but good for functioning within the house; this will satisfy both patient and other individuals in the home and ease their lives. Patient relatives should leave the home at least for short durations occasionally and give the patient personal space. Similarly, when permitted (in the time intervals without curfews), the patient should be mobilized outside the house and, if necessary, events should be organized for this. Short walks in the open air, short periods of shopping, and having tea/coffee in a garden or park will ensure individuals with severe mental disorder feel better.

Patients with severe mental disorder who are continuously at home during the day spend increased durations in bed, no different from healthy people. This situation may involve insomnia, and spending most time in bed during the day may lead to not sleeping at night, eating binges at night, and increased smoking and tea/coffee consumption. Later, the antipsychotic treatment dose and variety of the medication's increases. This situation may result in experiencing more of the medication's side effects. One of the side effects of medication is increased appetite. Being continuously at home, continuously eating things to waste and pass time, night time eating, appetite increase linked to increased medication dose, and immobility may result in weight gain and metabolic syndrome. Metabolic syndrome is a serious problem for patients with severe mental disorder. Schizophrenia patients have life expectancy 20 years shorter than their peers (Laursen *et al.*, 2014). This differential mortality rate is associated with increased risk of metabolic syndrome (DM, obesity, hypertension, and hypercholesterolemia) in schizophrenia patients (Bushe & Holt, 2004). For this reason, patients with severe mental disorder should be monitored seriously during the pandemic in terms of nutrition, exercise, and sleep–wake rhythm, have height–weight–waist circumference measurements at certain intervals, and not delay arterial blood pressure and blood and urine testing. Relatives and caregivers for patients with severe mental disorder should be informed about this topic. Online exercise programs may be followed during the pandemic. Online dietitian appointments may be attended.

In addition to metabolic syndrome, some comorbid diseases include DM type 2, cardiovascular system diseases, obesity, COPD, osteoporosis, hepatitis C, AIDS, and cancers (Lambert *et al.*, 2003). If the necessary care is not taken about comorbid bodily diseases in this patient group due to the sedentary lifestyle mentioned above, poor eating habits, antipsychotic medication use, uncontrolled sexual activity, reduced personal hygiene and self-care capacity, and poor cognition, or caregivers not paying attention to topics related to bodily health of patients, these comorbid diseases may have poor progression and cause the addition of new bodily diseases (Roberts *et al.*, 2018). Most of these diseases are associated with antipsychotic medication (APM) use. For example, APM increases the risk of pneumonia due to difficulty swallowing, excessive sedation, and hypersalivation (Kozloff *et al.*, 2020). Clozapine is the molecule causing most risk in relation to this topic. In addition to clozapine increasing pneumonia risk, it makes pneumonia treatment more difficult. Increased cytokines during pneumonia reduce the metabolism rate for clozapine and elevate serum levels, causing more hypersalivation and sedation secondary to clozapine. This forms a negative feedback cycle for pneumonia treatment. Additionally, due to the neutropenia and leukopenia effects of clozapine, it leads to susceptibility to infection. Arrhythmia is another risky clozapine side effect. For this reason, considering the systemic side effects of medications used for COVID treatment in patients with infection, reducing the dose of clozapine treatment is recommended as the most appropriate intervention (De Leon *et al.*, 2020). In this way, clozapine should be used as the minimum dose possible during pandemic periods, when lung infections are at the forefront. Patients with severe mental disorder using clozapine and their relatives/caregivers should be informed about neutropenia-leukopenia and possible infections. Additionally, they should be definitely informed about performing complete blood count (CBC) when they attend the nearest health facility with high fever, cough, sweating, shivering, throat pain, and flu-like symptoms. Even if neutropenia is not identified, the clozapine dose should be reduced by half in the event of this kind of infection. After infection without neutropenia, the clozapine dose should be increased to the previous level in stages (De Leon *et al.*, 2020). In the initial stages of clozapine treatment, frequent hemogram CBC tests results are required. For this reason, for patients planning to start clozapine for the first time, it may not be appropriate to start clozapine during the pandemic when transmission risk is high and limited levels of health service are available.

The comorbid disease status among schizophrenia patients and use of APM (especially clozapine) are risk factors in terms of increasing mortality rates due to COVID-19 in patients with severe mental disorder. For this reason, creation of a new treatment plan may be required for patients with severe mental disorder after careful assessment of present treatments (APM, presence of clozapine in treatment) and present comorbid diseases. Informing patients and caregivers about this topic repeatedly (over and again at certain intervals) is very important in terms of vital risks for patients.

4. COVID-19 Pandemic and Smoking Among Patients with Severe Mental Health Disorder

Among individuals with schizophrenia diagnosis, 53–75% regularly smoke (Yıldız *et al.*, 2010). McEachin *et al.* identified smoking rates similarly at 70% in bipolar affective disorder (McEachin *et al.*, 2010). Smoking increases pulmonary disease risks in healthy individuals and weakens the immune system (Leon & Diaz, 2005). Those who smoke have two times higher rates of catching coronavirus infections (Arcavi & Benowitz, 2004). In a previous MERS-CoV pandemic, those who smoked were reported to have higher death rates (Park *et al.*, 2018). The frequency of smoking and smoking-related lung diseases further increases the risk for patients with severe mental disorder who already have risk of lung infection due to antipsychotic medication. Schizophrenia patients hospitalized due to lung diseases have higher risk of requiring mechanical ventilation and intensive care and of developing acute respiratory failure (Hsiu-Nien Shen *et al.*, 2011). Our clinical experience shows that it is nearly impossible to limit or stop smoking among patients with severe mental disorder. For this reason, it is very important to ensure active protection from COVID-19.

5. Patient Treatment Management in Patients with Severe Mental Disorder During the COVID-19 Pandemic

Many hospitals stopped routine clinical services during the pandemic and were declared pandemic hospitals. Just as for many patient groups, the chances for the severe psychiatric patient group to obtain health services reduced. Hence, many hospitals reduced the number of beds in inpatient psychiatric wards and beds were transferred to COVID wards. This situation caused patients with severe mental disorder requiring hospitalization treatment to be unable to receive service. It is important that patients with severe mental disorder are able to receive regular and quality health services because, in this way, patients requiring the emergency service and inpatient wards reduce and the load on the health system is lessened (Kozloff *et al.*, 2020). Additionally, inpatient wards involve the risk of COVID-19 transmission (Yuncheng Zhu *et al.*, 2020). For this reason, first, health personnel and assisting personnel working in inpatient psychiatric clinics should be periodically trained for COVID-19 symptoms and protection methods. Importance should be given to pandemic precautions and they should be carefully applied. Before admission to the ward, patients and relatives should be trained for the COVID-19 infection symptoms and ward rules about protection; patients should have the necessary screening tests (infection tests), and symptom questionnaires and temperature readings should be taken. As can be predicted, as psychiatric patients are a special group, some rules are present in psychiatric inpatient wards. However, some changes, some new limitations, and some new flexibilities may be required for these rules during the pandemic. First, patient rooms should be organized for a single person, and if possible, should include toilet and bathroom. If this is not possible, toilet and bathroom use should be controlled, and toilet–bath hygiene and hand cleaning should be ensured without exception. Ward corridors and rooms and health personnel working areas should be regularly ventilated. Patients and personnel should use masks and pay attention to physical distance. Food and drink should not be allowed from outside the ward. Visitors should not be accepted. Patients should be allowed to use the telephone and watch television in their rooms. Acute attack stabilization should be provided rapidly, and patients should be discharged in as short a time as possible (Yıldız & Gürcan, 2020). Psychotic clinical services for severe mental disorders should continue without interruption. To prevent increasing load on ward services, maximum efficiency should be provided by clinical services with the best practices. COVID-19 precautions should be taken, and again informing psychiatric clinic workers is priority. Mask use and physical distance should be ensured, and it is important to warn patients and workers about this topic at every opportunity. Working areas should be ventilated, while small rooms that cannot be ventilated should not be used. Patients should be taken to the examination room alone and caregivers should be interviewed separately if necessary. Appointments should be limited to 15 minutes; if it is necessary to continue, the appointment should resume after ventilating the room. In terms of providing services with longer duration, telephone or online visual meeting choices should be assessed. This method will reduce transmission risk while also preventing interruption to health services. It is known that the participation rate for online video appointments in the patient group with severe mental disorder is low, but satisfaction levels are high (Hulsbosch *et al.*, 2017). Online video treatment methods are assessed as a low-cost method reducing hospitalization with experience/implementation for development of methods, like preventing psychotic attacks, ensuring treatment compliance, and coping strategies (Salzer *et al.*, 2004; Spaniel *et al.*, 2008). Pharmacological treatment of severe mental disorders is the most important rescue in the hands of mental health professionals. It is not possible for patients with severe mental disorder to live without controlling disease symptoms and medicine side effects. Whether during the pandemic or in normal situations, pharmacological treatment should definitely be specially planned individually for each patient. Patients and relatives should continue in coordination. First, for treatment of patients receiving medical treatment for a long time, with good medication compliance, stable on the medication with satisfactory life compliance, medication and treatment changes should not be made unless necessary (acute attack, newly developing medication side effect, or pharmacological interaction with COVID-19 medications). To protect this group of patients from transmission, the frequency of face-to-face interviews may be reduced; however, the online video messaging choice should definitely be assessed with the patient's acceptance. Storage injection treatment should be considered for patients with treatment compliance problems. For storage injection treatment, monthly injections or three-month injections and medications with low medication–medication interaction in terms of cardiac side effects, especially with medications used for COVID-19 treatment, should be chosen. As mentioned above, newly starting clozapine should not be a priority choice in terms of side effect profile. Hemogram monitoring and attendance at health facilities are required near the start of treatment. If patients using clozapine have hemogram results within normal limits, the interval between blood tests can be extended to three months. Patient and family/caregivers should be informed about infection findings and interventions, and emergency situation planning should be performed. Patients with COVID infection should have a treatment plan revised considering medication–medication interactions and the patient's medical and psychiatric status. In each stage, patients and relatives should be informed, and if possible, informed consent should be obtained.

6. Effect of COVID-19 Pandemic on Families/ Caregivers of Individuals with Severe Mental Disorder

Having a relative with severe mental disorder (child, grandchild, mother, father, partner, grandmother/grandfather, sibling, cousin) is a very difficult and wearing process on its own. Departures from the routine habits of life affects patients with severe mental disorder and their relatives most. Natural disasters (floods, earthquakes, tornados), fires, wars, and now the pandemic may cause serious adjustment problems in even mentally and physically healthy people. The difficulties experienced by patients will definitely be reflected in their family relationships. Quarantine precautions, anxiety, concern, uncertainty, economic difficulties, and lack of social support are very clearly experienced during the pandemic period making psychosocial interventions necessary for severe patients and relatives. First, as patient relatives experience as much uncertainty as patients, they will be relieved by having information about how to reach mental health professionals online or by telephone. They should be given information that patients will be most affected in the pandemic. In this period, being at home all together will increase interpersonal interaction and make new relationship problems and friction more pronounced. In this period, the duration for interviews between mental health professionals and families should be increased slightly, and if necessary, patient relatives/caregivers should be given pharmacological medication support. Patients and relatives independently leaving the house on the days and hours allowed by quarantine precautions, especially taking walks in the fresh air, will be very beneficial. Thus, domestic autonomy will be provided, even for a short duration, for those at home. Another difficult situation is the stage of returning to normal. Patients with severe mental disorder experience/will experience active avolition symptoms during the process of returning to normal. Patients may require occasional or repeated support for these symptoms. This situation may cause distress and anger in relatives/caregivers. Patient relatives should be informed and warned about this topic, while it is very important to support the patient. It should be emphasized that they succeeded before and will succeed again. In this period, use of social media (Instagram, Facebook, WhatsApp) by both patients and relatives increases. This situation involves the risk of patients being in contact with unsuitable people and being abused. Even in the remission period, patients with severe mental disorder may have disrupted assessment of reality from time to time and may experience loss of insight. For this reason, patient relatives should be very careful about this topic, and thus, care should be taken about informing them of solution choices in this situation. In fact, online group and individual appointments may have efficient and positive outcomes for caregivers as much as for patients. This choice should always be considered.

7. Effect of COVID-19 on Community Mental Health Centers

Perhaps reading the title in reverse is more appropriate: the effect of community mental health centers on the COVID-19 pandemic! Community mental health centers were created for patients with severe mental disorder and are mental rehabilitation centers providing patients with both medical treatment and individual and group psychotherapy services as well as psychoeducation and psychosocial skills training and busy activities. Since quarantine precautions began in the pandemic, mental social skills education was sustained at regular intervals by mental health professionals in these centers. Patients with severe mental disorder, and occasionally families, were regularly exposed to this education. In addition to education, busy activities like painting, music, drama, handcrafts, sports, gardening, and animal care are available in these centers. This regular education and busy activities allow patients to spend time in community mental health centers (CMHC) and relatives and caregivers to spend time alone and perform their own social activities without the patient. Quarantine precautions and social distance rules caused group education and activities to be stopped. In this sense, it can be easily seen that CMHCs did not function as required during the COVID-19 pandemic. It was not possible to complete activities with groups during the pandemic. However, in addition to this negative aspect of community mental health centers, they had an unrivaled advantage in terms of sustaining communication with patients with severe mental health disorder. In CMHCs, more time is spent with patients with severe mental health disorders and relatives/caregivers, with high content, more comprehensive and quality services offered. CMHCs offer mental rehabilitation services to patients with severe mental health disorders and relatives integrated with psychiatrists, psychologists, nurses, ergotherapists, and social workers. Thus, an integrated approach and mental rehabilitation solves both medication compliance, psychoeducation, and interpersonal problems and involves visible improvements in social inclusion of patients with severe mental disorder. This approach ensures many problems are solved before they begin, acute attack rates fall, hospitalization reduces, and social adjustment increases. Though group activities were limited in the pandemic, individual psychotherapy and psychoeducation continued with family therapy. Care should be taken to prevent interruption of treatment for patients with severe mental disorder through online video calls, telephone interviews, and injection treatment. When examined from this aspect, a new strategy should be to introduce more patients with diagnosis of severe mental disorder to CHMC and provide services for more patients and relatives.

8. Effect of Telepsychiatry Use for Management of Severe Mental Diseases During COVID-19

The physical distance and quarantine precautions in the pandemic made it mandatory for mental health professionals to use telepsychiatry initially. However, along with the difficulty, this also involved some convenience.

Until the pandemic, telepsychiatry practices were not widely used especially for severe mental disorders. It appears they will be used more widely after this point. It is clear that its use for creating timely and active communication between relatives/caregivers of patients with severe mental health disorders will be beneficial. It can be difficult to persuade family and caregivers to come for regular appointments during management of severe mental diseases. Psychosocial interventions may be disrupted occasionally by working, not being able to leave the house, and not being able to take time. Telepsychiatry will be a convenient practice for this and similar situations.

As a result, we can say that the management of severe mental disorders during the pandemic is a dynamic process that requires intense attention, dedication, and mutual solidarity. The impact of the pandemic imperatives on the re-evaluation and development of psychiatric treatments and approaches cannot be denied. Innovative and modifiable psychiatric interventions will play an important role in the future of psychiatry.

References

Arcavi, L. & Benowitz, N. L. (2004). Cigarette smoking and infection. *The Archives of Internal Medicine, 164*(20), 2206–2216. DOI:10.1001/archinte. 164.20.2206.

Bradford, D. W., Mimi M. Kim, Braxton, L. E., Marx, C. E., Butterfield, M., & Elbogen, E. B. (2008). Access to medical care among persons with psychotic and major affective disorders. *Psychiatric Services, 59*(8), 847–852. DOI:10.1176/ps.2008.59.8.847.

Bushe, C. & Holt, R. (2004). Prevalence of diabetes and impaired glucose tolerance in patients with schizophrenia. *Brazilian Journal of Psychiatry, 47*, S67–S71. DOI:10.1192/bjp.184.47.s67.

Chen Wang, Horby, P. W., Hayden, F. G., & Gao, G. F. (2020). A novel coronavirus outbreak of global health concern. *Lancet, 395*(10223), 470–473.

Cuiyan Wang, Riyu Pan, Xiaoyang Wan, Yilin Tan, Linkang Xu, Cyrus S. Ho, & Roger C. Ho. (2020). Immediate psychological responses and associated factors during the initial stage of the 2019 coronavirus disease (COVID-19) epidemic among the general population in China. *International Journal of Environmental Research and Public Health, 17*(5), 1729. DOI:10.3390/ ijerph17051729.

De Leon, J., Sanz, E. J., & De Las Cuevas, C. (2020). Data from the World Health Organization's pharmacovigilance database supports the prominent role of pneumonia in mortality associated with clozapine adverse drug reactions. *Schizophrenia Bulletin, 46*(1), 1–3. DOI:10.1093/schbul/sbz093.

Fonseca, L., Diniz, E., Mendonça, G., Malinowski, F., Mari, J., & Gadelha, A. (2020). Schizophrenia and COVID-19: Risks and recommendations. *Brazilian Journal of Psychiatry, 42*(3), 236–238. DOI:10.1590/1516-4446-2020-0010.

Hao Yao, Jian-Hua Chen, & Yi-Feng Xu (2020). Patients with mental health disorders in the COVID-19 epidemic. *Lancet Psychiatry, 7*(4), e21. DOI:10.1016/S2215-0366(20)30090-0.

Hsiu-Nien Shen, Chin-Li Lu, & Hsi-Hsing Yang. (2011). Increased risks of acute organ dysfunction and mortality in intensive care unit patients with schizophrenia: A nationwide population-based study. *Psychosomatic Medicine, 73*(7), 620–626. DOI:10.1097/PSY.0b013e3182280016.

Hulsbosch, A. M., Nugter, M. A., Tamis, P., & Kroon, H. (2017). Videoconferencing in a mental health service in The Netherlands: A randomized controlled trial on patient satisfaction and clinical outcomes for outpatients with severe mental illness. *Journal of Telemedicine and Telecare, 23*(5), 513–520. DOI:10.1177/1357633X16650096.

Kozloff, N., Mulsant, B. H., Stergiopoulos, V., & Voineskos, A. N. (2020). The COVID-19 global pandemic: Implications for people with schizophrenia and related disorders. *Schizophrenia Bulletin, 46*(4), 752–757. DOI:10.1093/schbul/sbaa051.

Lambert, T. J. R., Velakoulis, D., & Pantelis, C. (2003). Medical comorbidity in schizophrenia. *Medical Journal of Australia, 178*(S9), S67–70. DOI:10.5694/j.1326-5377.2003.tb05311.x.

Laursen, T. M., Nordentoft, M., & Mortensen, P. B. (2014). Excess early mortality in schizophrenia. *The Annual Review of Clinical Psychology, 10*, 425–448. DOI:10.1146/annurev-clinpsy-032813-153657.

Lawrence, D. & Kisely, S. (2010). Inequalities in healthcare provision for people with severe mental illness. *Journal of Psychopharmacology, 24*(4 Suppl): 61–68. DOI:10.1177/1359786810382058.

Leon, J. d. & Diaz, F. J. (2005). A meta-analysis of worldwide studies demonstrates an association between schizophrenia and tobacco smoking behaviors. *Schizophrenia Research, 76*(2–3), 135–157. DOI:10.1016/j.schres.2005.02.010.

McEachin, R. C., Saccone, N. L., Saccone, S. F., Kleyman-Smith, Y. D., Kar, T., Kare, R. K., Ade, A. S., Sartor, M. A., Cavalcoli, J. D., & McInnis, M. G. (2010). Modeling complex genetic and environmental influences on comorbid bipolar disorder with tobacco use disorder. *BMC Medical Genetics*, *11*, 14. DOI:10.1186/1471-2350-11-14.

Na Zhu, Dingyu Zhang, Wenling Wang, Xingwang Li, Bo Yang, & Jingdong Song (2019). A novel coronavirus from patients with pneumonia in China. *The New England Journal of Medicine, 382*(8), 727–733.

Olfson, M., Gerhard, T., Huang, C., Crystal, S., & Stroup, T. S. (2015). Premature mortality among adults with schizophrenia in the United States. *JAMA Psychiatry*, *72*(12), 1172–1181. DOI:10.1001/jamapsychiatry.2015.1737.

Pankiewicz-Dulacz, M., Stenager, E., Chen, M., & Stenager, E. N. (2019). Risk factors of major infections in schizophrenia. A nationwide Danish register study. *The Journal of Psychosomatic Research*, *121*, 60–67. DOI:10.1016/j.jpsychores.2019.04.003.

Park, J. E., Jung, S., Kim, A., & Park J. E. (2018). MERS transmission and risk factors: A systematic review. *BMC Public Health*, *18*(1), 574. DOI:10.1186/s12889-018-5484-8.

Roberts, R., Lockett, H., Bagnall, C., Maylea, C., & Hopwood, M. (2018). Improving the physical health of people living with mental illness in Australia and New Zealand. *Australian Journal of Rural Health*, *26*(5), 354–362. DOI:10.1111/ajr.12457.

Rubin, G. J. & Wessely, S. (2020). The psychological effects of quarantining a city. *BMJ*, *368*, m313. DOI:10.1136/bmj.m313.

Salzer, M. S., Tunner, T., & Charney, N. J. (2004). A low-cost, telephone intervention to enhance schizophrenia treatment: A demonstration study. *Schizophrenia Research*, *66*(1), 75–76. DOI:10.1016/s0920-9964(02)00483-8.

Saxena, S. & Maj, M. (2017). Physical health of people with severe mental disorders: Leave no one behind. *World Psychiatry*, *16*(1), 1–2. DOI:10.1002/wps.20403.

Spaniel, F., Vohlídka, P., Hrdlicka, J., Kozený, J., Novák, T., Motlová, L., Cermák, J., Bednarík, J., Novák, D., & Höschl, C. (2008). ITAREPS: Information technology aided relapse prevention programme in schizophrenia. *Schizophrenia Research*, *98*(1–3), 312–317. DOI:10.1016/j.schres.2007.09.005.

Thornicroft, G., Mehta, N., Clement, S., Evans-Lacko, S., Doherty, M., Rose, D., Koschorke, M., Shidhaye, R., O'Reilly, C., & Henderson, C. (2016). Evidence for effective interventions to reduce mental-health-related stigma and discrimination. *Lancet*, *387*(10023), 1123–1132. DOI:10.1016/S0140-6736(15)00298-6.

WHO (2020). Coronavirus disease (COVID-2019) situation reports.

Yıldız, M. & Gürcan, M. B. (2020). Covid-19 and management of schizophrenia, In B. Coşar (Ed.), *Psikiyatri ve Covid-19.1 (Psychiatry and Covid-19)*, pp. 30–34. Baskı. Ankara: Türkiye Klinikleri (Publishing. Ankara: Türkiye Klinikleri).

Yıldız, M., Yazıcı, A., & Böke, O. (2010). Demographic and clinical characteristics in schizophrenia: A multi center cross-sectional case record study. *Turk Psikiyatri Derg*, *21*(3), 213–224.

Yuncheng Zhu, Liangliang Chen, Haifeng Ji, Maomao Xi, Yiru Fang, & Yi Li (2020). The risk and prevention of novel coronavirus pneumonia infections among inpatients in psychiatric hospitals. *Neuroscience Bulletin*, *36*(3), 299–302. DOI:10.1007/s12264-020-00476-9.

Chapter 13

COVID-19 and the Clock of Globalization with Special Reference to India

KANUPRIYA

*Department of Economics and Trade Policy,
Indian Institute of Foreign Trade, Delhi, India*

kanupriya_phd16@iift.edu

Abstract

This perspective chapter discusses the nuances of the COVID-19 pandemic in the context of globalization, with special reference to India. It focuses primarily on the disruptions to the clock of globalization and the changes to be wrought in the global order in various spheres — economic, political/diplomatic, social, and environmental. Whether these changes would be beneficial for the world cannot be predicted right now. The only thing that is certain is that the world may not be the same place as it used to be. This crisis is perhaps the defining moment of the 21st century, in a manner akin to the two World Wars of the 20th century. The human race is set for an unprecedented transformation in the way it views and approaches the world. One hopes that this change shall bring the societies back in the lap of nature. However, a change otherwise may cost the world a golden opportunity to mend its ways of living. The sooner we embrace the change positively and improve our interactions with nature, the better. Only then the clock of globalization shall regain its shape, form, and cadence.

1. Introduction

Not many of us have ebullient memories of the year 2020. As this year draws to a close, and the COVID-19 pandemic rages on, a simple yet important question that comes to one's mind is whether this calamity would boost the process of globalization or set its clock back. To answer this question, it would be prudent first of all, to ponder the phenomenon of globalization versus glocalization. Put simply, globalization refers to the process of integrating economies, cultures, governmental policies, and political movements around the world. Glocalization, on the other hand, refers to the process of simultaneous occurrence of both universalizing and particularizing tendencies in contemporary economic, political, social, and cultural systems. Based on these fundamental definitions, this chapter seeks to develop the argument on COVID-19 and its relationship with the process of globalization and its constituents (economic, political, social, medical, and environmental) further (Khondker, 2005).

To set the tone for the chapter, it would be prudent to introduce the readers to the sections and themes to be discussed and debated in this piece. First and foremost, the introductory section seeks to highlight the main objective of this expose which is to elucidate the probable post-COVID-19 trajectory of the process of globalization or the clock of globalization. The next section explicates the manner in which the clock of globalization could be affected or to say, tampered with, owing to the ongoing pandemic. For the same, the complexity of the relationships between COVID-19 and the global economy — the social, political, mental health, medical and environmental ramifications — are explained and rationalized, with special reference to India. The last section concludes this study and expounds the way forward for the process of globalization post-COVID-19.

The next section discusses the impact of COVID-19 on the trajectory of the process of globalization, keeping in mind the multi-faceted nature of the latter.

2. COVID-19 and the Trajectory of Globalization — Which Way the Pendulum Swings?

2.1 *COVID-19 and the global economic trajectory*

That the crisis is having, and would have, major economic implications globally is no small fact. This section seeks to discuss the nuances of the economic impact of COVID-19 on the world economy. The manifestations of this crisis are in the form of its multidimensional impact on employment, poverty, inequality, traditional sectors such as agriculture, manufacturing, and the services sectors, and the digital economy, especially the "gig" economy. In a similar vein, trade and investment patterns too may witness a marked change, with countries trying to reduce their dependence on China and diversifying their trade partners. The global manufacturing supply chains may see a monumental shift in the years to come, with an attempt by the major countries of the world to noticeably contain the role played by China. In this regard, the recent RCEP agreement among Asia-Pacific nations led by China too shall be discussed and located in the present geopolitical-economic context, so as to lend greater credence to this chapter. The focus is on both the present and the future undercurrents of these issues, keeping in mind the dynamism of the current COVID-19 situation.

Coming from a lower-middle-income developing country like India, one could adjudge the tremendous hardships the COVID-19 pandemic has caused in the people's lives. It is the poor and the indigent who seem to have suffered the most due to the ongoing pandemic. Not only have these people lost their jobs, the struggle for daily survival seems to be an uphill task for many of them. From petty hawkers, traders, self-employed people to the small and marginal farmers, the list of those affected by the pandemic seems to be quite long.

However, it is not just the havoc caused by the pandemic to be discussed; the impact of the pandemic on different sectors of the global economy like the primary, secondary, tertiary, quaternary, and quinary sectors too must be examined. While it could be far-fetched to assume with certainty the long-term impact of the pandemic on the economy, it is nevertheless important to explicate the same in detail so as to lay a proper groundwork for future research on the same.

From a real to a policy recession, this crisis could spill itself into the financial domain, to ultimately turn into a 2008-like Global Financial Crisis. From the simplistic contractionary impulses in the real economy, thanks to disruptions in the demand and supply conditions, a prolonged recession could be the worst nightmare for any government. Coupled with this, higher interest rates relative to the "neutral" rates in the monetary policy domain could be yet another challenge for the global economy that could pull down the overall growth prospects from bad to worse. On top of that, cash flow strains for the small and medium enterprises (SMEs) and the rising bad loans or non-performing assets (NPAs) of commercial banks could yet again pose a challenge on the financial front for governments all over the world. The latter case of rising NPAs is especially true in the case of the Indian economy, which is still struggling to make a sense of the pandemic, despite the best policy efforts and actions. Most nations do not know the exact timeline of the winding down of this pandemic, so it is best to have additional financial reserves for any future eventuality. Besides, an adequate infusion of a concerted global fiscal stimulus is the need of the hour for any future recovery from the ravages of this crisis (Subramanian & Feman, 2020).

While discussing the economy, structural changes due to the pandemic cannot be ruled out at this moment. One could assume that the relative unimportance of the primary sector economy, namely agriculture and allied activities, would be a bygone phenomenon, given the condition of the other sectors. The pandemic has taught the human race a hard lesson the hard way. Old is gold, so goes the famous adage. True to the maxim, the crisis is proving to be a boon for the agricultural sector, with better-than-expected performance over the other sectors like the tertiary, quaternary, and quinary sectors. The reason lies with the disruptions in the globalization cycle due to the pandemic, the likes of which the world has never seen before. As long as the COVID-19-related uncertainty stays, the crisis is bound to have a negative impact on the structural foundations of the economies globally, possibly even defying the logic of textbook economics by reducing the relative importance of the tertiary/quaternary/quinary sectors *vis-à-vis* the primary sector. Again, this argument may or may not be right — only time could tell. However, one point is clear that COVID-19 shall transform the Global Economy like no other crisis has done before. As a continuation, the rising importance of the gig economy too must be discussed to form any meaningful opinion on the issue (Dev & Sengupta, 2020).

Going by the latest media reports in the context of COVID-19, several commentators have hailed the performance of the Indian agricultural sector. In fact, they have gone as far as labeling it the "only silver lining" in the current gloomy economic scenario (*The Economic Times*, 2020a).

This section shall, however, argue as to why that may not be the case over a longer time period. Being a non-homogeneous group, agriculture and allied activities are a set of dissimilar activities, each having its distinctive dynamics. The impact of the pandemic on the sector must therefore be separated into horticultural and food grains production activities. In this context, the horticultural sector is likely to face the brunt due to the very nature of its produce. By nature, one means perishability and consequently, a lower shelf life. On the other hand, the non-perishable nature of food grains renders it much less vulnerable to the vagaries of the pandemic. In addition to this, falling domestic and foreign demands of fruits and vegetables has hit the horticultural sector hard. Similarly, floriculture too has been adversely impacted thanks to the demand-side disruptions due to lockdowns and social distancing restrictions (Dev & Sengupta, 2020).

However, compared to other sectors, the agricultural sector is expected to be a bright spot in India amid the ongoing crisis. CRISIL expects the sector to grow at a rate of 2.5% in FY2021 (CRISIL, 2020).

As evident from the case of India, the manufacturing sector (or more broadly, the secondary sector) has been hit badly due to the pandemic due to depressed demand and output conditions. Of special mention is the micro, small, and medium enterprises (MSMEs) segment of the manufacturing sector that forms a significant share of the latter in India and plays a crucial role in providing employment opportunities, GDP, and exports. As per the Government of India statistics, MSMEs contribute 30% to India's GDP and 50% toward its industrial employment. However, being already burdened with issues like the non-availability of timely and affordable credit, this sector is hit badly due to reduced cash flows, disruptions in supply chain, shortage of migrant workers due to reverse migration to their native places, reduced demand conditions, and so forth. Even though the entire industrial ecosystem has been disrupted due to the pandemic, the MSME sector needs to be singled out for the pre-existing challenges complicating its survival in these trying times and its inability to deal with such catastrophic occurrences (Dev & Sengupta, 2020).

Coming to the tertiary or more broadly, the services sector, it must be stated that as per a KPMG report, the services sector in India and the world would be hit badly. Among the sectors receiving the brunt of the pandemic are aviation, travel, tourism, and transport. These sectors are the worst hit, not just in India but also globally. The total cumulative losses will depend on the duration and depth of the ongoing pandemic. The same report indicates that around 40 to 50 million jobs will be lost in India alone in the travel, tourism, and hospitality sectors due to COVID-19. This impact, when seen in its totality with the other major sub-sector of the services ecosystem, the banking sector, signals the arrival of a not-so-bright time ahead for the Indian economy and, on a larger scale, the global economy. World over, as the governments seek to firefight the pandemic, they are straining their fiscal reserves and putting their already burdened banking systems under stress. This does not bode well for any country (Trivedi & Beniwal, 2020).

To make matters worse, globally, there is a rise in poverty, unemployment, and economic deceleration. This is evident from some statistics. At least 50 million people all over the world are expected to slide into "extreme poverty" as a result of the pandemic. In September 2020 alone, India saw an unemployment rate of more than 6%. It is worth mentioning that the rate of unemployment went up to 24% in May 2020. This was due to disruptions in demand and supply linkages in the labor and output markets faced by companies globally. Furthermore, this even decelerated the gross value added to more than 9% for the Indian economy in that period (Statista, 2020).

Perhaps, the economically underprivileged have been hit the hardest owing to their limited access to proper healthcare and financial resources. Even though the Government of India has launched several schemes and policies to help sustain these marginalized people, the impact of the same has at best been limited, as per several experts (Walter, 2020).

Furthermore, any discussion on the economy cannot leave out trade and investment.

That the pandemic has disrupted international trade and global supply chains for goods and services is no hidden fact. While some countries, most notably China, have sought to maintain their global orientation, others, chiefly led by the US and India have sought to adopt more inward-looking policies. This is evident from India not joining the RCEP trade agreement as it deemed it a potential threat to its domestic manufacturing and dairy industries. Rather than exhorting and incentivizing the domestic players to become more competitive, such an approach to trade and global relations may not be the best way forward. An inward-looking strategy over a long term may hamper the domestic industry players from offering their customers and other stakeholders the best deal in terms of price and quality competitiveness. Autarkies are seldom good for any economy, whether big or small.

Another major economic impact of the COVID-19 crisis is on the digital gig economy. At a time when the pandemic has caused massive disruptions in the employment landscape, gig employment is gaining ground. As per a report in a leading financial daily of India, gig workers are independent contractual workers entering into flexible employment agreements with companies for on-demand work realization. This naturally raises the temporary and impermanence of these jobs, given that flexi-jobs are preferred by companies rather than full-time employees in these cash-strapped times COVID-19. This foretells the rising precarity of the jobs landscape in the coming times in the form of an absence of a steady source of income, social security benefits, and the resultant financial insecurity (Walter, 2020).

With precarity comes job dissatisfaction and hopelessness among the youth and the needy, who are already burdened with COVID-19-related challenges and complications. In the same report, it has been mentioned that almost 90% of the Indian gig workers have lost their incomes due to the pandemic. These workers were making less than US $68 for the entire month of August, 2020. Also, 47% of gig workers could not cover their expenses for a month without borrowing money. So how much dependence on the gig economy is desirable, only time could tell (*The Economic Times*, 2020b).

Thus, on the economic front, COVID-19 seems to have swung the pendulum in the direction of localized globalization, if not outright glocalization. For how long this trend continues is a matter of deeper investigation.

After the economic implications of the pandemic, discussion must center around the social effects of the crisis to better capture the nuances of the same with regard to people's daily lives.

2.2. *COVID-19 and social implications*

People wanting to revive the age-old traditions of greater face-to-face contact than merely relying on digital devices may yet be another paradoxical outcome of the social- distancing weary societies after some time. Furthermore, the world may see a rise in criminal activities, especially sophisticated digital crimes, as the educated unemployed youth stares at a bleak future in the event of job losses and pay cuts during the pandemic. Digital fraud may see an unprecedented spurt in the coming time. Also, of special mention is the condition of women that may go from bad to worse as they experience layoffs in the corporate world as well as find it difficult to juggle their tough schedules at offices and childcare at home. The lack of adequate childcare facilities at their workplace may be a major source of challenge in this respect. Furthermore, women workers near the lower rungs of the economy or in other words, the female employees of the informal sector, which includes a broad set of casual, temporary, and contractual labor, would be hit even harder, given the greater uncertainty associated with their job profiles. To muddy the waters further for women, with many sparring couples having to stay together at home during COVID-19, there is a rise in the number of domestic violence cases against females globally. This is true even for India (Kanupriya, 2020; United Nations, 2020).

Thus, the crisis has manifold impacts upon human society that may intensify further with the crisis timeline. In this regard, the pendulum of the clock of globalization seems to have shifted toward forced glocalization with local ramifications of global events.

2.3. *Political and diplomatic fallout of the pandemic*

Another very interesting, yet less discussed and debated, issue is pertaining to hyper nationalism and the rise of trivia on electronic and social media. Globally, nationalist leaders are seeking to divert the attention of unemployed youth from the core socioeconomic issues facing their countries. As populist leaders seek to stir up support for their domestic agenda, they often relegate the primary issues to the background, much to the detriment of citizens' growth and progress. The latter, despite all their literacy and education, fail to identify the populist narratives even as they seek a temporary refuge from their day-to-day challenges. Pent up anger over loss of jobs, incomes, near and dear ones to the pandemic manifests itself in the form of jingoism. This could take the form of media-driven narratives targeting imaginary "foes" with trivial issues being passed off as news of "national interest". A case in point being the coverage of Sushant Singh Rajput's death. Perhaps, at no other point in the history of Indian media and politics has a person's death been milked to such an extent. While the media persons across the aisle and politicians across the ideological spectrum sought to "use" the murder/ suicide mystery of a young, promising actor in Indian cinema, the kind of media trials/vilification his girlfriend underwent was not a matter for the fainthearted. For days and days running, the Indian media channels ran stories on the supposed "wicked nature" of young and beautiful women like the girl in focus. Even rationalists, like me, tossed aside their logic momentarily to feel sorry for the deceased and mad at the young woman. It was only later that the entire drama unfolded into a politically motivated plot to garner sympathy votes in a particular Indian state election. For four months, the Indian public was glued to their television sets and forgot about their COVID-19-related issues. Possibly, the television news offered an easy and cheap outlet for their anger and frustrations. Similar was the case with the social media or more specifically, Twitter, where a certain Indian cinema actress (namely, Kangana Ranaut) sought to hijack the late actor's death (whom she had never met) to settle personal scores with anyone and everyone from the Indian cinema. In fact, such was the Twitter barbarity of this person that all logic got drowned in the din of petty Twitter fights. In other words, there was no end to cheap stunts from different people and that sought to keep the Indian masses busy and pre-occupied during the lockdown phase (*The Tribune*, 2020).

Also, if the "nationalists" sought to divert attention from real issues, their political position was undermined in some prominent elections, cases being the outgoing US President Trump and Netanyahu in Israel. However, this does not mean that these leaders or their philosophy would weaken in the near future. On the contrary, their ideology might attract a far greater number of followers than at present. Historically, crises situations tend to precipitate greater intolerance and lesser coherence in societies (remember, Germany prior to World War II). In fact, if the Democratic party in the US fails to perform up to its "promised potential", the country might again see a Republican president in 2024, with policies not entirely different from those of Trump, even if undertaken after more deliberation and consideration. Let us not forget that Trump outperformed many of his Presidential peers in economic performance. It was the COVID-19 crisis that led to his undoing. A worse outcome for the US would be a Republican-majority Senate and a Democrat President, for this scenario could lead to stalling of any presidential agenda by the former. In other words, it would cause the much-feared policy paralysis in the world's largest economy at a time when it is needed to steer the global economic ship out of COVID-19 turbulence. This is not to be taken as an advocacy of any political party anywhere. Even the Democrats must bear a part of the blame for the rise of Trumpian politics in the US and many parts of the world. Also, Trump was an exceptional President in many aspects, and from the point of view of India, he was no less than a savior, especially with regard to his foreign policies. Speaking from an Indian citizen's perspective, the Republicans are a better option for this country. Also, their role in putting an end to slavery in the US under President Lincoln cannot be forgotten easily (one wonders though, how this very party could throw up a white nationalist in 2016). Having said that, this author prefers a moderately leaning Republican President over any radical Democrat (The Conversation, 2020).

As far as other diplomatic and political impact is concerned, a strong anti-China feeling brewing in several countries could manifest itself in the form of nations forming smaller groupings to tide over the crisis or even strengthening the existing groups to meet the challenges effectively. However, if the recent signing of the RCEP agreement is any indication, the Chinese grip over the Asia-Pacific region may continue unabated and smaller economies that otherwise criticize the Chinese political policies may be forced to accept it as their economic partner, given the prevalent compulsions of political economy. The US may or may not don the role of the global protector. It all depends upon the unfolding of the COVID-19 crisis there. If the already worse situation worsens further, then the US may be forced to retreat from the global space and focus internally, at least for a few years. In such a scenario, China may come to assume greater global prominence than at present. While the desirability or otherwise of such an outcome would only be apparent in the coming years; this author feels that the US too must act as an effective counter to the Chinese hegemony. The latter has often manifested itself in outright intimidation of smaller neighbors — a good case in point being the nations in the South China Sea. Or take the case of Sino–Indian border conflicts. Both these instances bear the distinctive imprint of the Chinese desire to rule the world as per its rules, with scant regard for the global order of the day (Jacob, 2020).

Having discussed that, in all probability, the world may start seeing the realities of a bipolar global order in the times to come. I would dub the scenario as Cold War 2.0 — Cold War because the two competing superpowers, the US and China, would want to outdo each other in economic, political/diplomatic, and cultural spheres. Each may adopt both hard and soft tactics to make nations fall in line with their agenda. Thus, a post-COVID-19 world may see greater latent friction between the US, a traditional hegemon, and China, the new kid on the block. The exact nature of this rivalry — violent or peaceful — may only become apparent in the coming future.

Thus, the phenomenon of glocalization, trying to outstrip the pace of globalization, is more apparent in the diplomatic/political domain.

The next section discusses the relationship between COVID-19 and mental health, a theme not much discoursed in the COVID-19 literature to date. The topic needs to be raised to address a very pressing concern before the world today. Mental health is probably the most invisible killer of people already burdened with COVID-19-related complications in their lives.

2.4. *COVID-19 and mental health issues*

For a moment, let us keep aside the discussion on politics/diplomacy, economics, and societies. Upon turning the attention inwards, the author found that it is mental health most deserving of a detailed explanation. A person's inner well-being translates into the outer self. During the pandemic, it is mental health that has taken the worst beating. It is partly contributed by the relative inability to roam freely in one's surroundings owing to the strict social distancing norms. While the social distancing rules have aided in keeping the spread of the pandemic in check, the same have caused an irreparable damage to the emotional health and well-being of the people. As Banerjee & Rai put it, "the pandemic has brought the hyperactive pace of modern-day society to a grinding halt. In the process it has also put an abrupt stop to the social interactions" (Banerjee & Rai, 2020).

Under these restricted conditions, individuals are being subjected to loneliness, isolation, and pangs of uncertainty of the future. This has contributed to increasing levels of depression, anxiety, insomnia, and stress disorders. This is largely in part to the unexpectedness of the crisis that did not allow people to be mentally prepared for such prolonged spells of isolation and loneliness (Banerjee & Rai, 2020). The only way out of this traumatic experience would be to reconcile with the times and take refuge in the solitude of peace and tranquility offered by the pandemic. Rather than taking the pandemic in a negative sense, the same could be transformed into an opportunity for peace and self-development. The pandemic has taught us the necessity of being in our elements all the time, a fact that humans seemed to have forgotten in the humdrum of their globalized daily existence. Forging loving bonds with one's family members, like parents, could be a solution to this situation. Yet another could involve engagement with one's hobbies like reading, writing, singing, or painting. Short walks, too, serve as a breather in these unprecedented times. In the author's personal opinion, staying away from the information overload on the social media too could help. During such times, the information regarding the pandemic only serves to feed into one's fears rather than helping one to cope with the crisis. Daily news of death tolls, the rising number of infected, and the arrival of new COVID-19 strains only seek to complicate the emotional state of human beings already reeling under the burden of the pandemic.

At last, one must not forget that no crisis is for eternity. However difficult it may be to believe, COVID-19 could end up becoming another flu strain just as influenza did some 30–40 years ago. In the end, no one should lose hope in this crisis. It is not here to stay permanently. One day it may either become too commonplace as mentioned before or may be totally wiped off from the face of this planet. One wonders as to how many people have heard of the Spanish flu of 1918. Not many, one can be assured. COVID-19 may meet a similar fate, when our future generations wonder about the very existence of such viral disease worth the name.

In this regard too, the phenomenon of glocalization seems to have overtaken globalization, at least for some time. But it is highly unlikely if it stays that way for too long.

2.5. *COVID-19 and the medical sciences*

A natural fallout of the COVID crisis has been the development and advancement in the medical sciences sector. The medical sciences are receiving a boost, especially in the areas of virology and vaccination research and development, and the field may emerge as the preferred choice of study for many a youth in the years to come.

Telehealth, mobile healthcare units, virtual health support for behavioral/mental health issues, biotechnology, especially virology, could soon become the buzzwords of the future generations.

Another notable point with regard to the medical profession is the regaining of its long-lost glory and prestige. Far from being seen as a noble profession it came to be viewed as a source for minting money by greedy doctors in the minds of the public. It was through the selfless service to humankind during the pandemic that the doctors have reclaimed some of their past magnanimity and honor.

In addition, the recent research and development efforts toward an effective COVID-19 vaccine have exposed the gaping holes in the global pharmaceutical supply chain. Given that the investments in infrastructure and storage facilities, especially ultra-cold freezing capabilities, have not kept apace that of a vaccine, the need to develop cold storage facilities has only strengthened. Thankfully, India, with its Universal Immunization Program (UIP), already has an impressive vaccine distribution infrastructure in place. All it needs is to upgrade it further to meet the exigencies of the pandemic, especially to store vaccine candidates of the likes of Pfizer, that require ultra-cold storage at — 70°C. Another crucial aspect of the supply chain is tracking the vaccine all through its transit until it is dosed. Here, a software of the likes of Electronic Vaccine Intelligence Network or e-VIN can keep track of the vaccine stocks and temperatures in the cold storage (De, 2020).

Undoubtedly, COVID-19 serves as a reminder for the global community to invest greater amounts toward health and wellness, for such pandemics may become a common occurrence in the coming future thanks to the hyper-globalized human existence.

2.6. COVID-19 and the environment

This section discusses the fallout of the pandemic on the global environment. It has been observed that the crisis has led to a visible improvement in the ecological landscape of the world, with reduced air, land, and water pollution. However, if there are some benefits, there are certain challenges too. For instance, there is an increase in medical waste generation since the pandemic spread globally. This is proving to be a major problem for the global environment and public health (Somani *et al.*, 2020; Zambrano-Monserrate *et al.*, 2020). An example could help prove this point. The initial epicenter of the disease in the world, Wuhan in China, produced more than 200 metric tons of medical waste daily during the peak of the pandemic there (*Ibid.*). This is about 150 metric tons more than pre-COVID times (*Ibid.*).

Even the Indian city of Ahmedabad reported high medical waste generation of as much as 1000 kg per day from 500 kg per day (Somani *et al.*, 2020).

Cities like New York, London, Milan, Kuala Lumpur, Bangkok, Hanoi, and Tokyo have reported similar increases, producing 150 to 300 metric tons more medical waste daily than during the pre-pandemic situation (Somani *et al.*, 2020). Hazardous waste of such magnitude and volume is posing fresh sanitary challenges before the municipal authorities globally. As the virus stays on the solid/liquid surfaces like medical waste, the waste generated from hospitals should be handled with utmost care and hygiene. Any carelessness on this front may render the populace of that locality susceptible to further infection. Thus, pollution from medical waste is a matter of concern for the global community.

A related issue is of e-commerce waste in the form of packages and plastic material that often accompanies items delivered through online shopping sites. The rise in online shopping during the pandemic has also brought its own issues for the environment in the form of rising plastic and packaging waste (Somani *et al.*, 2020).

These challenges aside, there have been certain beneficial outcomes of the COVID-19 pandemic for the global environment.

First and foremost, there is a marked reduction in air pollution and greenhouse gas (GHGs) emissions. As the economic activities, like industrial, transportation, and commercial establishments, closed during the lockdowns across the world, emission of GHGs such as carbon dioxide and nitrogen oxides came down drastically. It is estimated that the levels of air pollution came down by as much as 40 to 50% in countries like the US, China, and India. Vehicular and industrial emissions being the largest contributors to global GHG emissions, the pandemic marked a welcome respite for the human race after many years (Somani *et al.*, 2020). Similar improvements had been reported due to stoppage of flights globally during the peak of the pandemic in 2020 (*Ibid.*).

Even the author could personally feel the fresh air in the Indian city of Delhi, that saw a sudden stoppage to its vehicular movement on roads between March and September 2020. Overall, 40 to 50% reduction of $PM_{2.5}$ and PM_{10} was reported in India during its national lockdown. One fears though, if the situation after the unlock down in India since

October–November 2020 would reverse the pollution levels to pre-COVID-19 lockdown levels (Somani *et al.*, 2020).

Second, one very important positive impact of the COVID-19 pandemic on the environment is the environmental restoration and renewal, after a long period of abuse and destruction. Owing to the impressive growth of the tourism industry in this globalized era, it is estimated that annually it contributes to 8% of total GHG emissions. Besides, it also inflicts damages to places of pristine beauty and significance, such as islands, seas, beaches, national parks, mountains, and deserts. Some tourist spots in Europe and Bangladesh have spotted dolphins in seas and lakes that had since long lost their presence. This is a welcome sign. For how long it would sustain itself is a question of fate and time and most importantly, the teachings imbued by the pandemic for the human race (Somani *et al.*, 2020).

Should humanity decide to adopt its pre-COVID-19 lifestyle, one doubts if such beneficent impact could sustain itself. At least in this case, glocalization has been a welcome change.

The next section summarizes and analyses the chapter in the context of the discussion so far and seeks to locate the trajectory of globalization in the perspective of COVID-19.

3. Conclusion and Future Implications of the Study

This segment sums up the aforementioned sections with a broad overview summarizing the overall impact of the pandemic on the human societies globally, with a special reference to the Indian society.

Based on this chapter and an informed reading of the pandemic so far, it may be stated that the clock of globalization has certainly suffered severe damage in 2020. Even if the COVID pandemic is completely controlled in 2021 (highly unlikely as per this author), the pendulum of globalization might take a few more years to regain its pre-pandemic rhythm. And even if it is regained, the pre-COVID-19 trust and tempo may have been eroded to such an extent that people gradually adapt themselves to the new way of living during the pandemic times and extend the same to post-COVID-19 scenario as well. Pessimistic though it may seem, the author believes that this is the most probable outcome of the crisis. It would be foolish to think otherwise and revel in utopian thinking. Even if COVID-19 goes away, the pandemic lifestyle may be here to stay across spheres — economic, political/diplomatic, societal, and environmental. Thus, one might see the world moving toward greater globalization in the immediate aftermath of this pandemic.

The changes in the world may shape and reshape the entire human race for decades and centuries ahead. In other words, the pandemic has been the marquee event of this century, just like the World Wars of the 20th century.

As discussed in this chapter, India has been no stranger to the travesty of the pandemic and stares at monumental alterations in her domestic political/diplomatic, economic, social, and ecological landscape. Whether these changes would be good or bad, only time will tell.

To conclude, in all probability, the chapter forcefully articulates that globalization has been molded and shaped as per the need of the hour. That this trend shall have profound implications for the coming years too has been discussed and analyzed. Moreover, quite importantly, the clock of globalization has been impaired and would take years to be what it was in pre-COVID-19 years.

In the end, let us not forget the famous Buddhist adage, "only change is constant".

Maybe God saw it coming, but we humans missed it in the noise called globalization. Probably, it was God's way to teach humans a memorable lesson on the need to keep pace with nature. The sooner we learn it, the better.

References

Banerjee, D. & Rai, M. (2020). Social isolation in Covid-19: The impact of loneliness, *International Journal of Social Psychiatry*. Retrieved from: https://doi.org/10.1177/0020764020922269.

CRISIL (2020). *Quickonomics: The One Bright Spot in the Economy*. Retrieved from: https://www.crisil.com/en/home/our-analysis/views-and-commentaries/2020/06/the-one-bright-spot-in- the-economy.html.

De, A. (2020). Retrieved from: https://indianexpress.com/article/india/2020-how-years-of-trials-research-were-compressed-into-months-in-developing-a-covid-19-vaccine-7116351/.

Dev, S. M. & Sengupta, R. (2020). *Covid-19: Impact on the Indian economy*. Mumbai: Indira Gandhi Institute of Development Research.

Jacob, H. (2020). Retrieved from: https://www.thehindu.com/opinion/lead/chinas-lac-aggression-indias-obfuscation/article32546823.ece.

Kanupriya (2020). Covid-19: A socio-economic perspective. *FIIB Business Review*. Retrieved from: https://journals.sagepub.com/doi/full/10.1177/2319714520923918.

Khondker, H. (2005). Globalisation to glocalisation: A conceptual exploration, *Intellectual Discourse, 13*(2), 181–199.

Somani, M., Srivastava, A. N., Gummadivalli, S. K., & Sharma, A. (2020). Indirect implications of COVID-19 towards sustainable environment: An investigation in Indian context, *Bio Resource Technology Report*. Retrieved from: https://pesquisa.bvsalud.org/global-literature-on-novel-coronavirus-2019-ncov/resource/en/covidwho-643092.

Statista (2020). Retrieved from: https://www.statista.com/statistics/1111487/coronavirus-impact-on-unemployment-rate/.

Subramanian, A. & Feman, J. (2020). With Covid-19 crisis dealing sharp blow to struggling financial sector, revival calls for new approach. Retrieved from: https://indianexpress.com/article/opinion/columns/india-economy-npa-covid-19-arvind-subramanian-josh-felman-6400664/.

The Conversation (2020). Retrieved from: https://theconversation.com/how-covid-19-led-to-donald-trumps-defeat-150110.

The Economic Times (2020a). Retrieved from: https://m.economictimes.com/news/economy/agriculture/farming-sector-will-not-be-impacted-by-coronavirus-agriculture-minister/articleshow/75450174.cms.

The Economic Times (2020b). Retrieved from: https://economictimes.indiatimes.com/news/economy/policy/covid-19-prompts-workers-corporates-to-adopt-gig-economy/articleshow/78732156.cms?utm_source=contentofinterest&utm_medium=text&utm_campaign=cppst.

The Tribune (2020). Retrieved from: https://www.tribuneindia.com/news/editorials/stink-of-witch-hunt-145990.

Trivedi, U. & Beniwal, V. (2020). *World's Biggest Lockdown to Push 12 Million into Extreme Poverty in India*. Retrieved from: https://economictimes.indiatimes.com/news/economy/indicators/worlds-biggest-lockdown-to-push-12-million-into-extreme-poverty/articleshow/76056756.cms.

United Nations (2020). *Everyone Included: Social Impact of COVID-19*. United Nations, Department of Economic and Social Affairs Social Inclusion, https://www.un.org/development/desa/dspd/everyone-included-covid-19.html/.

Walter, D. (2020). Implications of Covid-19 for Labour and Employment in India, *Indian Journal of Labour Economics*. Retrieved from: https://doi.org/10.1007/s41027-020-00255-0.

Zambrano-Monserrate M. A., Ruanob M. A., & Sanchez-Alcalde, L. (2020). Indirect effects of COVID-19 on the environment. *Science of the Total Environment*. Retrieved from: https://www.ncbi.nlm.nih.gov/pmc/articles/PMC7169883/.

Chapter 14

The Role of High Technologies in China's Fight Against COVID-19

SHAN Qiyue

School of Social Sciences, Buenos Aires,
University of Buenos Aires, Buenos Aires, Argentina

gabriel.shan@hotmail.com

Abstract

China was the first country to fight against the COVID-19 pandemic. Not only medical guidance but also the role of high technology has been undeniably important for China's battle against the pandemic. In this respect, the first section of this chapter examines the technologies used in China's combat against COVID-19. The author aims to initiate a conversation on the alleged health–freedom dichotomy based on its consequences and contributions and to provide an interpretation of the Chinese side based on its political and cultural traditions.

1. Introduction

Since COVID-19 began to spread around the world, China had been its first epicenter on a global scale. In less than three months, the Eastern country experienced the peak of the pandemic — milder than many other Western countries — and managed to bring the virus under control with a rather low death toll, taking into account the fact that China has the largest population.

The impressive efficiency of China shown in its fight against COVID-19 is largely attributed to the use of different cutting-edge technologies, such as 5G, Big Data, artificial intelligence, etc., which allowed the government and the public health system react promptly in the prevention and treatment of the disease. However, some Western politicians or media accused the use of such technologies by the Chinese state of violating the civil rights of its people, breaching their privacy, and restricting their freedom.

This chapter begins by reviewing the technologies applied in China's fight against COVID-19. Based on its effects and contributions, the author seeks to open a dialogue on the supposed health–freedom dichotomy and offer an interpretation of the Chinese side based on its political and cultural traditions.

2. The Use of High Technologies in China's Fight Against COVID-19

2.1. *Mobilize specialized forces and accelerate scientific–technological exploration*

Since the COVID-19 outbreak in China — before it was recognized as a pandemic or an epidemic — the government of the Asian giant launched the scientific–technological race to crush the greatest health crisis since the beginning of the 21st century as soon as possible. Governmental leadership ordered corresponding forces to vehemently promote the selection of medicines and the research and development of the vaccine. The Chinese Academy of Sciences, the Academy of Military Sciences, the Chinese Academy of Medical Sciences, and the Chinese Center for Disease Control and Prevention formed the body of research, which also had the broad participation of universities, institutes, and specialized companies of the whole country. They advanced using the same strategies based on: etiology and epidemiology, detection technology and derived materials, medicine and clinical treatment, vaccine research and development, and the establishment of animal model. Thanks to these collective efforts, China extracted the strain of the virus and presented the complete genome sequence to the World Health Organization in January 2020, laying the groundwork for the improvement of healing techniques and the research and development of medicines and vaccines.

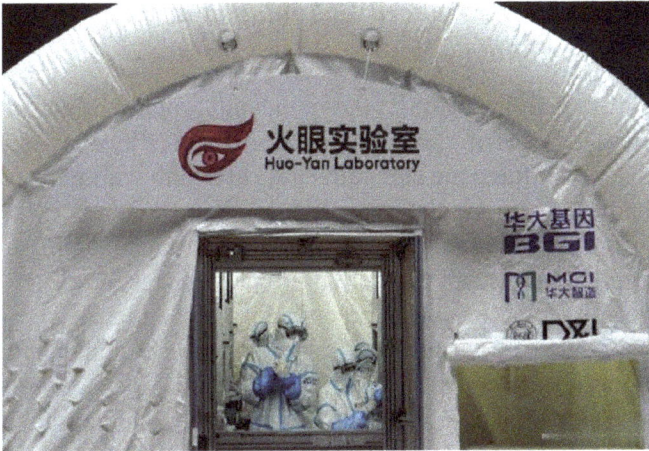

Figure 1:   Huoyan Laboratory for massive tests.

The Nucleic Acid Testing (NAT) against COVID-19 is a fundamental tool for clinical diagnosis and hospital discharge of patients, as well as lifting the close contact person from quarantine. Chinese pharmaceutical companies proceeded to the development and production of the NAT as soon as the outbreak was detected. On January 26, 2020, the National Medical Products Administration sanctioned the use of four types of NAT products developed by four Chinese companies. On February 8 of the same year, the first laboratory called "Huoyan"[1] was put into practice (see Figure 1); the lab had the capacity to diagnose ten thousand samples per day, which facilitated the identification of suspected cases and the detection among high-risk groups, relieving the pressure of clinical treatment and mitigating social distress. The first laboratory was installed in an indoor stadium in Shijiazhuang city, capital of the northern Hebei province, which took only 10 hours to be built. It was later replicated at dozens of other Chinese cities. When the disease became a pandemic, this experience was a point of reference for several countries, such as the United Arab Emirates, Brunei, and Serbia, among others.

---

[1] Huoyan, literally means "eyes of fire" in Chinese, a term that has its origin in the classic novel *The Odyssey to the West*, written in the 16th century, whose protagonist, the Monkey King, strengthened the sight of his eyes in the fire to identify the evil monsters even if they are disguised with magic of good-hearted characters.

2.2. *Apply the most advanced technologies at the front of the battle*

Throughout the fight against the pandemic, many high integrated technologies — 5G, artificial intelligence, virtual reality, etc. — were put into practice to reinforce the combativeness of health workers on the front lines of the battle. Among the new products derived from such technologies, the artificial respirator, monitor, oxygenator, negative pressure isolation ambulance, among others, were used with greater frequency.

The negative pressure isolation ambulance (see Figure 2), for example, bears the nickname "mobile N95 mask", whose fundamental difference with respect to an ordinary ambulance consists precisely in the negative pressure isolation, that is, to permanently maintain the pressure in the cabin of the vehicle lower than that of the atmosphere so that the air circulating inside the cabin cannot leave before being purified. This technology minimizes the possibility of health workers catching the virus in transport and contact with those infected people. Besides the ambulance, this technology was also used in the hospital for the inpatient rooms or for those on stretchers.

Doctors working in the hospital were equipped with other advanced technologies to facilitate diagnosis and treatment, such as the visual intercom, critical ultrasound, electronic stethoscope, portable central monitoring station, etc. Intelligent robotics integrated with 5G offered a very important reinforcing force to doctors and nurses, since in the most crucial stage of the pandemic in Wuhan — when the number of new cases grew

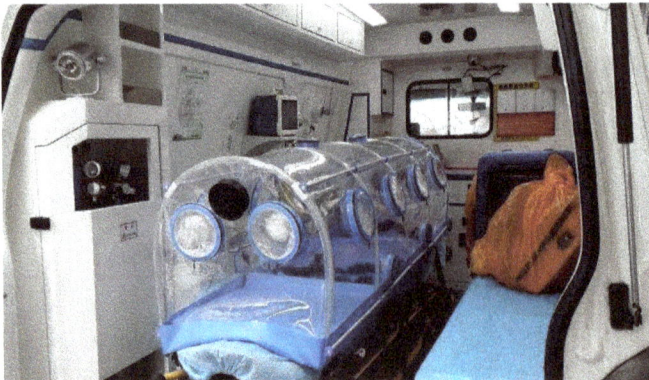

Figure 2:   The negative pressure isolation ambulance.

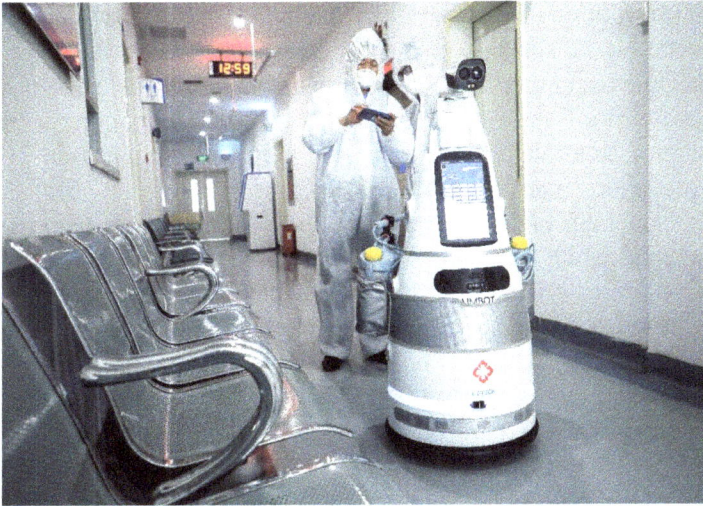

Figure 3:   Robots working in the hospitals to support the treatment.

faster — it was the robots that were in charge of guiding patients, disinfecting the environment, cleaning rooms, and distributing medicines in the hospital (see Figure 3). There were even cooking robots that prepared hot food for health workers and inpatients. They greatly reduced the human cost and the risk of human-to-human transmission, as well as significantly improving efficiency and ensuring orderliness in the hospital.

2.3. *Generalize the technology in popular prevention and control against the virus*

In March 2020, in a television interview, Dr. Li Lanjuan, a member of the Senior Group of Experts convened by the National Health Commission — equivalent to the Ministry of Health in Western countries — shared the case of the identification of an infected person. During epidemiological follow-up, the woman confessed with complete certainty that she had never visited those affected areas. After the big data review, it was discovered that she had had contact at her place of residence with at least three people from one affected province, who were at high risk of contagion. Big Data technology made it possible to follow the mobility trail of the suspected object and draw a map of the interactions he/she had established with other people, which facilitated the precise detection of the infection route and helped to cut off transmission early.

Since the beginning of the pandemic in China, all provinces turned to the Internet, Big Data, and artificial intelligence, among other advanced technologies, to locate the information of the floating population, intensifying prevention and control in their jurisdictions. The Ministry of Industry and Information Technology opened its database to provincial governments, while technology companies — for example Alibaba and Tencent — devoted themselves to the research and development of applications installed on the cell phone to make life easier for the population. An app allows you to consult the information of the train or flight that each infected person took so that other passengers may take preventive measures as soon as possible. Another collects data from hospitals authorized to treat COVID-19 in all cities. When contagion cases began to decline in the country in April, Alibaba launched a control system based on artificial intelligence for public spaces in order to neutralize the impact of the pandemic on the economy. This system integrates thermograph temperature measurement, infrared and visible radiations to intensively and precisely detect the temperature of individuals who move quickly in public spaces, so that economic activities can recover vitality with greater safety.

In the same sense, it is worth highlighting one of the most innovative measures — the implementation of the "Health QR Code" (see Figure 4) (Mazzoccone, 2021). This tool uses Big Data technology developed by Alibaba and Tencent to prevent and control COVID-19. Its massive use was immediate because these companies added this QR code to the two

Figure 4:   Health QR Code on personal mobile phone.

most used applications in China: Alipay — which is used to make online payments — and WeChat — similar to WhatsApp. This QR code works by using three colors like a traffic light. The green code allows free movement. The yellow code requires the person to stay at home for 7 days, and the red code for 14 days. Those who have these two colors must be prepared to report their situation at any time and receive unannounced checks at their homes. Once this period has elapsed, the yellow and red codes become green. The color is defined based on the places where each person was present, information that is obtained from the telecommunications companies in China. If a person is in an area with a COVID-19 outbreak or if they were with someone who has a yellow or red code, that person will have that color too. Also, all citizens have to update the QR code daily by entering body temperature.

3. Western Criticism of the Chinese Government's Technological Practices

On January 16, 2021, the famous British magazine *The Economist* published in its special column on China called *Chaguan* — *teahouse* in Chinese — an article entitled *Many in China are strikingly accepting of harsh virus controls* (Chaguan, 2021). This article began by citing the case of an office worker surnamed Zhou, resident in Beijing, who was tested positive for COVID-19 on January 10, 2021, which alarmed the government of the capital so much that it responded with a vigor that many other countries reserve for invasions in times of war.

Mrs. Zhou's trail of the last ten days in the city was quickly traced by the government through Big Data technology and made public by the official media. The revealed itinerary was so detailed that it is even known what time she visited a noodle restaurant, in addition she was traced to her work visit to Hebei province where more than 400 cases of infection had been registered so far since the beginning of this year. According to that article, "thanks to" Mrs. Zhou, almost a hundred people in close contact — family members, colleagues, even clients who had dinner at the noodle restaurant — were compulsorily quarantined for 14 days, while thousands of people who live or work near her office were subjected to the nucleic acid test. The article criticized, although implicitly, the use of personal data by the Chinese government without the permission of the citizens, which had caused so many inconveniences in their daily lives.

This was the latest example of Western media accusing the Chinese state of having violated the civil rights of its population under the excuse of fighting against the pandemic. One year ago, when COVID-19 was still at its peak in the Asian country, criticisms of this nature sounded much more explicit. Here are some more prominent examples.

Example 1: The New York Times: *China's Virus Apps May Outlast the Outbreak, Stirring Privacy Fears*

On May 26, 2020, the powerful American daily *The New York Times* published an article written by Raymond Zhong (2020b).

The article noted that despite the pandemic having gone through its worst stage in China, "the government's monitoring apps are hardly fading into obsolescence". Instead, these apps are "tiptoeing toward becoming a permanent fixture of everyday life, one with potential to be used in troubling and invasive ways".

The author added that the country's leaders have long sought to harness vast troves of digital information to govern their nation more efficiently and that it is not known whether citizens agreed with the government on collecting so much information, or how the police used the personal data provided by these apps.

Example 2: VOA: *China's Virus Tracking Technology Sparks Privacy Concerns*

On June 22, 2020, another major US media outlet, *VOA News*, posted an article written by Joyce Huang titled *China's Virus Tracking Technology Sparks Privacy Concerns* (Huang, 2020).

The article cited Charles Mok, a lawmaker and tech entrepreneur in Hong Kong, who highlighted that the biggest worry was that once this latest practice of using spatial data — referring to the "health code" — was in place it would be very difficult to take away. He also mentioned the reaction of some netizens on Weibo, a Chinese social media similar to Twitter, who complained about the deep intervention of the State in their private life thanks to advanced technologies. "Needless to say, we civilians are completely naked in front of the telecom operators", commented a netizen.

Mok confessed to VOA that the increasing tolerance of the Chinese people on the government's digital measures on the pretext of the pandemic fighting do worry him, because the Chinese government can easily find excuses in the future to extend its tracking policy for political reasons and keep tabs on political dissidents.

The author of this chapter is a Ph.D. student in social sciences at the University of Buenos Aires in Argentina, whose thesis addresses the social representations of China in the press of the South American country — specifically, in the three most important newspapers — during the period 2018–2020. The corresponding studies cover all the news about China among which the COVID-19 pandemic is an unavoidable topic. One of the most striking characteristics of the news about China published by the Argentine press was that the source was not, in most cases, direct but "imported" from the North American or European media that imposed their media hegemony on the Western hemisphere because Argentina, like other countries on the continent, did not have — nor does it have — its own correspondent in China. In this sense, studying the news in the Argentine press about the Chinese use of technology against the pandemic would be a more efficient way of knowing the positions of the Western developed countries in this regard.

For example, an article in *The New York Times*, written by Raymond Zhong and the above-mentioned, was translated into Spanish and published on the same date in *Clarín*, Argentina's best-selling newspaper (Zhong, 2020a).

Throughout 2020, *Clarín* made good use of Western sources and published a series of articles related to Chinese experiences in the use of science and technology in the fight against the pandemic, while not reserving complaints or criticisms against the impact of these on individual privacy.

Example 3: Clarín: *Control ciudadano y "big data", la fórmula de China contra el coronavirus (Citizen control and "big data", China's formula against the coronavirus)*

On March 3, 2020, the newspaper published its first article (Rodríguez-Rata, 2020), with a declared source from the Spanish newspaper *La Vanguardia*. The article began with a rather sensational phrase: "Big data watches over the Chinese".

Then, it presented two of the smartphone applications that classify citizens to "condition what to do and who to interact with". The first app presented was the well-known "health code", in three colors, which served to guide the local authorities in charge of controlling the virus on their land. The second deepened the first and allowed people to be tracked and alerted as to whether they had had a "close contact with someone infected", whose forms reminded, in the words of the author, "of the times of the Cultural Revolution undertaken by Mao Tse Tung in the 60s and 70s of the last 20th Century".

To highlight the impartiality of his position, the author did not forget to quote a senior official of the World Health Organization, who, taking into account the serious consequences for personal freedom concluded that "in a democracy they would not have been possible while the political regime there — in China — allows it".

Example 4: Clarín: *La vida en tiempos de coronavirus: Termómetros, barbijos, guantes y nuevas tecnologías (Life in times of coronavirus: Thermometers, masks, gloves and new technologies)*

On March 5, 2020, the same Clarín (2020) released another report, whose indicated source was the French Press Agency (AFP).

This article said that the "health code" system had fueled "the criticism in matters of privacy because it is based on the analysis of the movements made by the user of the application". He denounced that having this QR code was almost mandatory in several cities of the country to leave the train stations or use public transport. The AFP correspondent who visited several Chinese cities during the first months of 2020 complained about the inconvenience of such measures and believed, although he did not offer any basis, that the Chinese did not accept or comply with them voluntarily.

4. Chinese Political and Cultural Traditions Facing the Health-Freedom Dichotomy

4.1. *The "ren" (仁) concept in the art of governance prevailing for 2,000 years in China*

The long history of Chinese civilization, dating back approximately 5,000 years, has seen the birth of a great variety of thoughts and philosophies of different senses. Since the First Emperor unified the seven pre-existing kingdoms in 221 BCE creating the stamp of the territorial extension of the feudal empire that, despite the vertiginous changes of dynasties, retained its political–economic–social structure until 1911, when the last Qing dynasty was overthrown by the bourgeois revolution, there has been a philosophy that was always on the table of the highest ruler: Confucianism.

Founded by the great teacher Confucius (551 BCE–479 BCE), this philosophy designs its vision of the world around the core concept "ren". Its writing in Mandarin Chinese is 仁, which hieroglyphically means "two people". The "ren" attaches great importance to interpersonal relationships, establishing that each one has to put friendship, solidarity, and fraternity into practice when he/she comes into contact with others. A person with "ren" is one who never reserves his/her love for others. To make the "ren" be received and accepted fluently by others, the issuer must show it with more visible acts, such as trust, help, and most often, care for the fundamental rights of others.

For Confucius, the rulers of all levels should be chosen from those who have the greatest "ren", knowing how to apply the policies that most favor the well-being of the citizens. If they do not have such a virtue and make the citizens' survival difficult, these ones have the right to remove the rulers — through peaceful or violent ways — and elect others who are more competent in this sense. Therefore, the "ren" has been the value most appreciated by Chinese popular culture and consequently most sought after by the rulers throughout the thousands of years. Although all the dynasties of the Empire were characterized by their totalitarian style, the rulers could not disregard the potentially rebellious strength of the social sectors, taking into account the large population and the abundance of resources accessible to it. In this sense, an "unannounced contract" was established between the rulers and the governed people: the people voluntarily accepted the government of those by complying with their policies, paying their taxes, and respecting their authority, while those did everything possible to guarantee their rights, leading to their full exercise of well-being.

Among the rights that the rulers had to take full care of, the most fundamental was the right of survival, since in ancient times the lives of ordinary people were more vulnerable to natural challenges — drought, plague, flood, etc. — and artificial — external invasion, armed peasant uprising, organized crime, etc. —, and an effective and strong social control by the State — or the Imperial Court — was essential to give the people the desired security. If the rulers could not satisfy this fundamental right and brought about social chaos that made the population suffer, the other rights that they had managed to guarantee were not enough to compensate for that loss, because the right of survival preceded, according to Confucianism and culture Chinese people, to all other human rights.

5. The Chinese Communist Party's Attachment to the "Ren" Concept and Its Adaptation to Contemporary Governance

The Chinese Communist Party (CCP), founded in 1921 and achieved power in 1949 after some 20 years of revolution, has taken Marxism-Leninism as the matrix of its political–economic thought, but it did not ignore the traditional thoughts of China, taking into account that the social conditions of the country were very different from those of Europe and Russia. Many of the historical leaders of the CCP were experts in Confucianism but struggled to integrate the concept of "ren" into their art of government inherited from Marxism–Leninism.

In this sense, Mao Tse Tung proposed the slogan "Serve the people wholeheartedly" in 1944, which soon became one of the fundamental values of the CCP that any member of the Party, especially those who exercise public power, was obliged to fulfill. This value put the well-being of citizens in the supreme place of the Party's work and the Chinese also took as a touchstone to evaluate the work of the CCP and its performance with respect to the services offered to the people. As with their predecessors, the right to survive mattered most for the contemporary Chinese people.

This consensus came into effect on October 1, 1949, the date of the founding of the People's Republic of China, and has worked perfectly since the outbreak of the COVID-19 pandemic in the country. Both the total blockade of some cities, the compulsive use of the mask in any public space, and the mandatory quarantine for those who had close contact with the infected person, which in the eyes of many Western media constituted a serious threat to human rights, were actively accepted and complied with by the majority of citizens residing in the affected areas.

The same has happened in the case of the use of advanced technologies to track the movement of citizens and classify the risk of each one. Although these technologies have filtered into private life and markedly reduced the personal freedom, the Chinese citizens have accepted this situation, on the one hand, thanks to the high precision of these technologies that do not wrongly annoy the innocents, and on the other, due to the prevalent importance that they always give primarily to the safety of their life.

6. Conclusion

On February 4, 2021, in order to "accompany" the aforementioned article *Many in China are strikingly accepting of harsh virus controls* diffused by *The Economist*, the China Global Television Network (CGTN), a state-run media, published on its website the article by Bhakal (2021). The author Maitreya Bhakalis is an Indian commentator who writes about China, India, US, and global issues. This article noted that Americans love challenging authority; they do not like being told what to do. "Unfortunately, this concept of rejecting authority extends to authoritative expert advice too" highlighted the author.

Both articles, despite their mutual opposition, as a whole have highlighted an inescapable truth: the behaviors of the individuals of each nation are highly influenced by their respective political and cultural traditions. The reaction to the difficulties or crises such as the COVID-19 pandemic was also the result of this influence.

The Chinese do accept that the State intervenes with science and technology in their private life not because it is compulsory for them to do so but because they appreciate the right to survival as the absolute priority of human rights, in the sense that they willingly endure temporary sacrifice of other rights as long as the one who takes it away — the State in this case — guarantees that supreme right.

On the other hand, no one can reject the fact that the use of Big Data and artificial intelligence technologies by the Chinese State in the fight against the pandemic has greatly facilitated the mobility of Chinese people, in order that the economic activities and daily life continue to function normally, when COVID-19 still persists in certain parts of the Asian continent until the date of writing of this chapter. Meanwhile, other advanced technologies have been improving the effectiveness of treatment for the infected people and contributing to the development and research of medicines and vaccines. In this sense, if we weigh the advantages against the disadvantages of the interactions of the Chinese people with the science and technology used in the fight against COVID-19, it is clear that what they have gained is much more than what they have lost.

References

Bhakal, M. (February 4, 2021). Many Americans are Strikingly Tolerant of Massive COVID-19 Casualties. *CGTN*, https://news.cgtn.com/news/2021-02-04/Many-Americans-are-strikingly-tolerant-of-massive-COVID-19-casualties-XBotnJfQD6/index.html.

Chaguan (January 16, 2021). Many in China Are Strikingly Accepting of Harsh Virus Controls. *The Economist*, https://www.economist.com/china/2021/01/16/many-in-china-are-strikingly-accepting-of-harsh-virus-controls.

Clarín (March 5, 2020). La vida en tiempos de coronavirus: Termómetros, barbijos, guantes y nuevas tecnologías (Life in times of coronavirus: Thermometers, masks, gloves and new technologies), https://www.clarin.com/mundo/vida-tiempos-coronavirus-termometros-barbijos-guantes-nuevas-tecnologias_0_5zyDfRQZ.html.

Huang, J. (June 22, 2020). China's Virus Tracking Technology Sparks Privacy Concerns. *VOA News*, https://www.voanews.com/covid-19-pandemic/chinas-virus-tracking-technology-sparks-privacy-concerns.

Mazzoccone, D. (January 27, 2021). ¿Cómo China pudo controlar la pandemia? (How China was able to control the pandemic?) *Página (page) 12*, https://www.pagina12.com.ar/319725-como-china-pudo-controlar-la-pandemia.

Rodríguez-Rata, A. (March 3, 2020). Control ciudadano y "big data", la fórmula de China contra el coronavirus (Citizen control and "Big Data", China's formula against the coronavirus). *Clarín*, https://www.clarin.com/mundo/control-ciudadano-big-data--formula-china-coronavirus_0_yiM2jHUu.html.

Zhong, R. (May 26, 2020a). En China, las aplicaciones de vigilancia del coronavirus llegaron para quedarse (In China, the surveillance apps for coronavirus are here to stay). *Clarín*, https://www.clarin.com/new-york-times-international-weekly/china-aplicaciones-vigilancia-coronavirus-llegaron-quedarse_0_yUOMdlusU.html.

Zhong, R. (May 26, 2020b). China's virus apps may outlast the outbreak, stirring privacy fears. *The New York Times*, https://www.nytimes.com/2020/05/26/technology/china-coronavirus-surveillance.html.

Chapter 15

The COVID-19 Pandemic and Transformation of Distance Education: Web 2.0 in Higher Education

Özlenen ÖZDİYAR[*,‡] **and Abdul Samet DEMİRKAYA**[†,§]

*Department of Educational Sciences,
Hacettepe University, Ankara, Turkey*

†*Department of Educational Sciences,
Burdur Mehmet Akif Ersoy University, Burdur, Turkey*

‡*ozlenen@hacettepe.edu.tr*
§*sdemirkaya@mehmetakif.edu.tr*

Abstract

This chapter introduces the challenges posed by the COVID-19 outbreak to educational systems. The pandemic exerted serious pressure on higher education systems, prompting the search for innovative solutions and triggering structural transformation. Online education had to replace face-to-face training and environments, with its opportunities and uncertainties. Web 2.0 tools promise to increase the effectiveness of online education with the opportunities it offers. The advantages offered by Web 2.0 tools should be taken into account and should be involved in the transformation process of higher education systems. Higher education institutions and their stakeholders should evaluate the experiences gained during the COVID-19 pandemic in detail, the opportunities and risks offered by technological transformation, and build the future of higher education aligned with the results. If the outputs of this process are evaluated effectively, accurate and operative inferences are made and innovative and sustainable solutions are developed. This process can carry educational systems to a brighter future.

1. The COVID-19 Pandemic

The COVID-19 (severe acute respiratory syndrome coronavirus 2, SARS-CoV-2) pandemic has severely affected human lives in all aspects. The lockdowns caused by the COVID-19 pandemic has affected almost every sector, including health, economy, and education, and required changes in social and cultural habits. The outbreak of the COVID-19 pandemic has caused drastic changes on the existing practices of education all over the world (Bryson *et al.*, 2020; Mishra *et al.*, 2020). From elementary to higher education institutions, the whole educational system faced with a crisis, and institutions needed to generate some strategic initiative to combat the situation (Dubey & Pandey, 2020; Mishra *et al.*, 2020).

Higher education institutions started contemplating how to deal with the challenges (Abdullah *et al.*, 2020). Many institutions delayed face-to-face education, were unable to conduct examinations, and were forced to move to online education in a very limited time span (Christian *et al.*, 2020; Dubey & Pandey, 2020; Toquero, 2020). They were not technologically competent to adapt to the urgent change and did not have an adequate infrastructure (Dubey & Pandey, 2020; Mishra *et al.*, 2020). Faculty competency in operating technology for the delivery of instruction was another uncertainty (Dubey & Pandey, 2020). Despite all the ambiguities, both faculty and students had to make the transition rapidly (Machynska & Dzikovska, 2020). The transition to online classrooms occurred and it altered usual teaching–learning processes and methods (Abdullah *et al.*, 2020). Transformation of educational processes required a paradigm shift in the students' thinking processes and mindsets (Dubey & Pandey, 2020). During this transition to online learning, students had to adjust to distance education environments, balance their technological competencies and higher workload, and also stay motivated and psychologically strong (Aristovnik *et al.*, 2020; Dubey & Pandey, 2020; Christian *et al.*, 2020; Machynska, & Dzikovska, 2020). In addition, the fact that some students live in rural and low socioeconomic communities and do not have access to internet facilities and technology was another obstacle (Dubey & Pandey, 2020; Yılmaz İnce *et al.*, 2020).

The COVID-19 pandemic has tested the sturdiness of educational systems and revealed their vulnerabilities. Meanwhile, it has also provided the educational systems with the opportunity to apply new technologies, redesign and improve by adopting them (Ali, 2020). This opportunity should be used prudently to address the identified deficiencies, and to rethink, redesign, and enhance educational systems with high quality and authentic digital extensions (Mishra *et al.*, 2020; Toquero, 2020). Higher education institutions especially should rebuild the curriculums based on distance learning experiences, responsive to the needs of technology-competent students and the changing and ambiguous times (Ali, 2020; Mishra *et al.*, 2020; Toquero, 2020).

2. Distance Education

As society was grappling with the COVID-19 pandemic and the challenges it brought, education had to continue as well (Christian *et al.*, 2020). Digital and online learning platforms quickly replaced educational institutions, and distance education became a new normal (Aristovnik *et al.*, 2020; Christian *et al.*, 2020; Dubey & Pandey, 2020). Most universities have started continuing their education with distance education, after determining the educational platforms to use (Machynska & Dzikovska, 2020; Yılmaz İnce *et al.*, 2020). Online learning settings that deliver learning activities and materials through centrally managed interfaces are called virtual learning environments (VLE) or learning management systems (LMS) (Brown, 2010). The online learning environments which give students the control of the environment and allow them to manage the technology, make decisions, and produce knowledge are named as personalized learning environments (PLE) (Rahimi *et al.*, 2014). PLEs provide students with choice, autonomy, control, and ownership over learning experiences, instead of possible restrictions stemming from pre-packaged materials, centralized structure, or instructor control (McLoughlin & Lee, 2010). Brown (2010) indicates that PLEs will become more popular than institutional VLEs and potentially replace VLEs because they address user needs better, and even claims that they might cause a paradigm shift in online education, change the nature of teaching and learning, and the portrayals of traditional institutions.

3. Web 2.0 Tools & Education

Web 2.0 tools, in other commonly used terms, "social software", "social web", or "user-created content", are user-driven, social, and collaborative web-based tools (Moore, 2007; Paily, 2013; Sigala, 2007). They are new generation internet applications, which provide ubiquitous access to information and allow individuals to interact with each other, work collaboratively work, generate new contents, and share information and artifacts as well (Kitsantas & Dabbagh, 2011; Oliver, 2010; Wheeler, 2009). The global diffusion of Web 2.0 caused a colossal effect on the way individuals search, reach, generate, consume, and share knowledge (Albion, 2008; Sigala, 2007). They offer extremely diverse open access content under dynamic and participative environments and provide with the opportunity to incorporate personalized and customizable systems, with the facility to form any kind of community of interest or practice (Albion, 2008; Shriram & Warner, 2010; Tyagi, 2012; Wheeler, 2009). They are also available to everyone who has access to web, mostly free and user-friendly (Tunks, 2012; Wheeler, 2009).

Web 2.0 tools are so dynamic and powerful that they even absorbed many of the older media, such as telephone, television, and printing press, into the internet (Wheeler, 2009). They are also changing the traditional teaching and learning processes, reshaping students' mindsets, impacting educational institutions, and they might even cause a paradigm shift on schooling (Brown, 2010; Tyagi, 2012). Both the flexibility of use without having any time or space dependence, and being user-friendly and free of cost, make them affordable for individuals and institutions (Çelik, 2021; Odom, 2010; Tunks, 2012). They offer new perspectives and opportunities to generate and process knowledge within educational settings, which were not available before (Rahimi et al., 2014). They present unlimited opportunities, by allowing learners to actively participate in learning experiences, interact, and collaborate with peers, design, generate and share knowledge, have ownership of their learning experiences, and personalize learning environments (Albion, 2008; An & Williams, 2010; Çelik, 2021; Den Exter et al., 2012: Kitsantas & Dabbagh, 2011; Oliver, 2010; Sigala, 2007; Tunks, 2012).

A broad number of Web 2.0 tools are available for students and teachers' instructional uses. Blogs, wikis, podcasts/vodcasts, avatars, social networking, content syndication, image and slide sharing, video sharing, audio/video conferencing, social bookmarking, mind mapping, communication, animation, and data mash up tools are among some of the widely recognized Web 2.0 tools (Boulos *et al.*, 2006; Costa, *et al.*, 2016; Eyyam *et al.*, 2011; Koehler *et al.*, 2017; Lee *et al.*, 2020; Oliver, 2010; Paily, 2013; Rahimi *et al.*, 2014; Shriram & Warner, 2010; Tunks, 2012). They offer abundant and extremely diverse resources in any discipline and numerous and unique pathways for online learning (Boulos *et al.*, 2006; Shriram & Warner, 2010; Tunks, 2012). They provide students with exploratory, expressive, reflective, constructive, engaging, and inspiring educational experiences, such as searching, mind mapping, remixing, blogging, and evaluating (Rahimi *et al.*, 2014; Sigala, 2007; Tyagi, 2012). The interactive and integrated nature of Web 2.0 tools enable students to actively participate in learning processes, to scaffold new ideas and knowledge, and to acquire authentic learning experiences, and these features of Web 2.0 tools make them compatible with constructivist approach (Çelik, 2021; Sigala, 2007).

Numerous Web 2.0 tools are available for students and institutions, and each offers unique features for specific uses, and most of them are free of cost (Boulos *et al.*, 2006; Oliver, 2010; Tunks, 2012). There are some that offer online spreadsheets for interactive use, ease research process, allow students to write and publish ideas, or help students develop conceptual understanding (Bull, 2008; Moore, 2007; Oliver, 2010). There are very diverse settings of Web 2.0 that can serve specific instructional purposes. Thus, deciding on instructional goals and selecting the most appropriate tools fitting the needs of students is an important instructional task, so teachers should have adequate knowledge and experiences about Web 2.0 tools (Albion, 2008; Costa *et al.*, 2016; Tunks, 2012; Tyagi, 2012).

3.1. *Blogs*

Blogs allow students compose their own texts or art and publish them online, (Bull, 2008; Oliver, 2010; Sigala, 2007). Blogs are content management tools, generally in the form of a personal web page, where individuals can publish writings about a theme or build online diaries, read and comment on others' content, and interact with other people (Ağır, 2014; Benson & Avery, 2009; Sigala, 2007; Wheeler, 2009). Blogs can help students improve their writing, literacy, critical thinking, teamwork skills, and can help teachers foster a learning community (Bull, 2008; Gitonga & Murungi, 2015; Sigala, 2007).

3.2. Wikis

Wikis are collaborative content management tools or digital repository of content where any registered user can create or edit content freely (Sigala, 2007; Wheeler, 2009). Its easy access from any computer and open content structure makes it user-friendly (Sigala, 2007). Any user can read, write, edit, and delete the content, so in educational settings, they can be used for online group discussions, collaborative group works and projects, and the generated content can be stored online (Ağır, 2014; Gitonga & Murungi, 2015; Sigala, 2007; Wheeler, 2009).

3.3. Social networking sites (SNS)

SNS are online communication tools and online communities that allow users to interact with each other in multiple ways, tag photos, etc., (Click & Petit, 2010). There are widely recognized and globally used SNS, such as Facebook and Twitter (Drexler *et al.*, 2008; Gitonga & Murungi, 2015; Stefancik & Stradiotová, 2020). SNS even changed the communication preferences and habits of children (Drexler *et al.*, 2008). Students can benefit from SNS to form class-based social groups to build a community or join existing groups based on their interests or majors (Gitonga & Murungi, 2015; Kitsantas & Dabbagh, 2011). Students can use SNS for chatting, content-sharing, and may benefit from social communities (Gitonga & Murungi, 2015).

3.4. Tagging/Bookmarking

Tagging is the process of categorizing or classifying the web content or resources by hyperlinking and assigning them key words called "tags" (Paily, 2013; Sigala, 2007). Bookmarking is saving bookmarks by tagging websites with key words to classify, store, and share links (Paily, 2013). Tagging and bookmarking make searching easier by using key words, support users by linking relevant knowledge, and storing useful information (Paily, 2013; Sigala, 2007). They create online communities through particular key words (Churchill *et al.*, 2009; Paily, 2013; Sigala, 2007). In educational settings, tagging and bookmarking can assist students to understand relational knowledge and see the contextual connections effectively, process information meaningfully, and learn constructively (Luo, 2010; Paily, 2013; Sigala, 2007).

3.5. *Presentations/Animations/Digital stories*

There are some Web 2.0 tools that allow users to add text and images, organize it as a presentation, and some of them enable users to animate the images and add sound or music as well (Rioseco, 2017). Prezi, Powtoon, Emaze, Buncee, Voki, and Scratch are among many of the diversified presentation and animation tools (Çelik, 2021; Gürsoy & Göksun, 2019). They provide eye-catching and engaging information and visuals, which make information easy to remember (Alameen, 2011; Rioseco, 2017) and allow students to present their work as well as their points of view and foster collaboration (Alameen, 2011). They also require hands on learning: prompting students to synthesize information and present it (Rioseco, 2017).

3.6. *Podcasts-vodcasts*

Podcasting or vodcasting is a digital audio or video distributing method, and they are delivered to the subscribers regularly over internet (Rajic, 2013; Whittaker, 2009). Podcasts/vodcasts have become a commonly used Web 2.0 tool in all levels of education, and they provide an alternative way of receiving information (Harris & Park, 2008; Stefancik & Stradiotová, 2020). There is an abundance of podcasts available in almost any subject area or for professional development (Solomon & Schrum, 2007). They help students to develop listening skills, process the content and information by listening, and spend their leisure time effectively (Stefancik & Stradiotová, 2020). They are easy to produce and edit and can easily be shared, so students can create podcasts for instructional purposes as well (Solomon & Schrum, 2007).

3.7. *Online collaborative writing tools*

In the class of Google Apps, Lino, Trello and others, Google Docs is the most recognized and widely used online collaborative writing tool, in other words, internet-based word processing tool which provides an online document to the user and the opportunity to share the document with others and work collaboratively on it (Koehler *et al.*, 2017; Odom, 2010; Parmaxi & Zaphiris, 2017). It enables synchronous or asynchronous collaboration, and this functionality allows students to work collaboratively from anywhere as long as they have internet access

(Odom, 2010). It offers the opportunity to all of the participants sharing the Google Docs to write on or edit the document and communicate with each other as well (Koehler *et al.*, 2017).

4. Web 2.0 Tools & Learners

Web 2.0 technologies offer numerous advantages including networking, interaction, collaboration, enrichment, and flexibility which are important aspects for educational settings (Costa *et al.*, 2016; Moore, 2007; Olea, 2019; Sigala, 2007; Tyagi, 2012). For instance, social networking tools have changed the communication habits of individuals, made document and idea sharing an easy task, and has provided easily accessible interactive and collaborative learning environments (Drexler *et al.*, 2008; Moore, 2007; Tunks, 2012; Tyagi, 2012). Intelligent search engines make researching and accessing knowledge a joyful job (Moore, 2007). Customized learning environments of Web 2.0 tools enable students to interact with people who have similar interests, to build learning communities, to provide them with constructivist learning experiences that improve higher-order thinking skills, and to stimulate them for inquiry and improving literacy (An & Williams, 2010; Çelik, 2021; Gitonga & Murungi, 2015; Moore, 2007; Sigala, 2007; Tyagi, 2012).

4.1. *Interaction*

In any online learning context, effective interaction is a key factor of success (Wan, 2010). Web 2.0 tools provide the instructors with numerous innovative ways to interact with students and allow them to interact with their peers (Click & Petit, 2010; Conole, 2010; Den Exter *et al.*, 2012; Tunks, 2012). The personalized learning environments and flexible usage options enable students to interact actively with each other (Azid *et al.*, 2020; Sigala, 2007). Web 2.0 tools provide more engaging learning experiences, entertaining and interactive learning environment to students, and increase their social presence (García-Morales, 2019; Olea, 2019). The selection of the proper Web 2.0 tool can improve the activity level of students, increase their motivation and enthusiasm, and transform the online learning environment into an engaging learning community (Sigala, 2007; Tunks, 2012).

4.2. *Collaboration*

Web 2.0 tools offer vigorous, unique, and innovative collaboration features (An & Williams, 2010; Boulos *et al.*, 2006). Collaboration and teamwork are among the main functions of Web 2.0 tools, aligned with flexible and interactive nature (Den Exter *et al.*, 2012; Paily, 2013; Tur & Urbina, 2016; Tyagi, 2012). In a collaborative learning environment, students share documents, work on it together, reflect on and evaluate each other's work. (Odom, 2010; Tur & Urbina, 2016). Interactive and collaborative nature of Web 2.0 tools also provide students with the control of the learning content, process information, and generate new ideas together with peers within an engaging learning community (Rahimi *et al.*, 2014; Sigala, 2007).

4.3. *Self-regulation*

Self-regulation is a concept defined as the ownership of an individual on his/her learning, and the self-regulation skills require behaviors such as setting goals, constructing strategies to realize these goals, and checking the outcomes, (Risemberg & Zimmerman, 1992; Zimmerman, 2008). The personalized learning environments and process-based learning experiences that Web 2.0 tools offer, require students to be active learners, to track their progress, and to display autonomous learning skills (Kitsantas & Dabbagh, 2011; McLoughlin & Lee, 2010). Time management skills of students are also important considering they all have varied levels of tool literacy (Lim & Newby, 2021). Educators using Web 2.0 should consider addressing the preferences and interests of students, providing choice, using materials proper for autonomous use, and promoting learning environments and experiences that can support self-regulation (McLoughlin & Lee, 2010).

4.4. *Educators*

Educators of the 21st century should have principles and skills such as entrepreneurship, creativity, dealing with ambiguity, and adapting to diverse contexts (McLoughlin & Lee, 2010; Tyagi, 2012). The evolving technology, and the complexities they bring, requires adaptation and active involvement of teachers (Brown, 2010; Parmaxi & Zaphiris, 2017).

Teachers should keep exploring new, dynamic, innovative, and authentic ways of providing high quality learning experiences (Wheeler, 2009). Web 2.0 tools offer quality and authenticity and are proper to use in varied forms and settings in numerous innovative ways (Boulos *et al.*, 2006; Conole, 2010; Oliver, 2010; Tunks, 2012; Wheeler, 2009). They are very dynamic and powerful applications, even forcing the traditional teaching and learning processes to change (Brown, 2010; Tyagi, 2012; Wheeler, 2009). Teachers' engagement with Web 2.0 tools enables them to explore the opportunities these technologies offer and to integrate these technologies with their ongoing teaching portfolios and enrich the educational implementations (Rahimi *et al.*, 2014). The majority of instructors still have limited knowledge about Web 2.0 tools, while such tools keep occupying students' lives (An & Williams, 2010). Providing in-service training to faculties and making them use Web 2.0 tools in educational settings can increase their knowledge and experience about Web 2.0 tools and confidence to implement them (Yuen *et al.*, 2011). The faculties and institutions that are currently using Web 2.0 tools should consider managing possible legal ramifications caused by openness and privacy of these settings (An & Williams, 2010; Oliver, 2010).

5. Conclusion

The outbreak of the COVID-19 pandemic has forced many institutions to delay face-to-face education and move to online education platforms rapidly (Christian *et al.*, 2020; Dubey & Pandey, 2020; Toquero, 2020). With such an unpredictable future, society is in need of resilient educational systems (Ali, 2020). Enriching resources and learning environments aligned with self-regulation needs of students and training the faculty are key to successful transformation of education (Kitsantas & Dabbagh, 2011). Web 2.0 tools have such a significant effect on students' and faculties' daily lives and educational practices, and considering the rapid development, Web 2.0 presence cannot be ignored (Brown, 2010; Odom, 2010). The rise of Web 2.0 tools and digital transformation should not be neglected due to the COVID-19 pandemic crisis (Mishra *et al.*, 2020). The 21st century educational landscape requires mashing the existing educational implications with the rising technologies and reformulating pedagogy (McLoughlin & Lee, 2010). Higher education stakeholders should overcome the challenge of integrating the effective Web 2.0 tools into the traditional educational settings by evaluating the data and outcomes of the practices (Kitsantas & Dabbagh, 2011). In order to cope with the complexity of the COVID-19 pandemic lockdown, and the online education dilemma, multimodal approaches should be developed (Mishra *et al.*, 2020). The COVID-19 pandemic triggered a transformative process in education, especially in higher education. However, this transformative process might lead education to a better pathway, considering how higher education institutions and the stakeholders focused on sustainable development (Sá & Serpa, 2020).

References

Abdullah, M., Husin, N. A., & Haider, A. (2020). Development of post-pandemic COVID19 higher education resilience framework in Malaysia. *Archives of Business Review*, *8*(5), 201–210, https://doi.org/10.14738/abr.85.8321.

Ağır, A. (2014). What are the usage conditions of Web 2.0 tools faculty of education students? *Turkish Online Journal of Distance Education*, *15*(3), 171–196, https://doi.org/10.17718/tojde.91465.

Alameen, G. (2011). Learner digital stories in a Web 2.0 Age. *TESOL Journal*, *2*(3), 355–369, https://doi.org/10.5054/tj.2011.259954.

Albion, P. R. (2008). Web 2.0 in teacher education: Two imperatives for action. *Computers in the Schools, 25*(3–4), 181–198, https://doi.org/10.1080/07380560802368173.

Ali, W. (2020). Online and remote learning in higher education institutes: A necessity in light of COVID-19 pandemic. *Higher Education Studies, 10*(3), 16–25, https://doi.org/10.5539/hes.v10n3p16.

An, Y.-J. & Williams, K. (2010). Teaching with Web 2.0 technologies: Benefits, barriers and lessons learned. *International Journal of Instructional Technology and Distance Learning, 7*(3), 41–48, http://www.itdl.org/Journal/Mar_10/article04.htm.

Aristovnik, A., Keržič, D., Ravšelj, D., Tomaževič, N., & Umek, L. (2020). Impacts of the COVID-19 pandemic on life of higher education students: A global perspective. *Sustainability, 12*(20), 8438, https://doi.org/10.3390/su12208438.

Azid, N., Hasan, R., Nazarudin, N. F. M., & Md-Ali, R. (2020). Embracing industrial revolution 4.0: The effect of using Web 2.0 tools on primary schools students' mathematics achievement (Fraction). *International Journal of Instruction, 13*(3), 711–728. https://doi.org/10.29333/iji.2020.13348a.

Benson, V. & Avery, B. (2009). Embedding web 2.0 strategies in learning and teaching. In M. Lytras, E. Damiani, & P. Ordóñez de Pablos (Eds.), Web 2.0, pp. 237–248. Boston, MA: Springer, https://doi.org/10.1007/978-0-387-85895-1_13.

Boulos, M. N. K., Maramba, I., & Wheeler, S. (2006). Wikis, blogs and podcasts: A new generation of Web-based tools for virtual collaborative clinical practice and education. *BMC Medical Education, 6*(1), 41, 1–8, https://doi. org/10.1186/1472-6920-6-41.

Brown, S. (2010). From VLEs to learning webs: The implications of Web 2.0 for learning and teaching. *Interactive Learning Environments, 18*(1), 1–10, https://doi.org/10.1080/10494820802158983.

Bryson, J. R., Andres, L., & Davies, A. (2020). COVID-19, virtual church services and a new temporary geography of home. *Tijdschrift voor Economische en Sociale Geografie (Journal of Economic and Human Geography), 111*(3), 360–372, https://doi.org/10.1111/tesg.12436.

Bull, G. (2008). Storytelling in the Web 2.0 era. *Learning & Leading with Technology, 35*(5), 10–11, https://www.researchgate.net/publication/2769 21955_Digital_Storytelling_in_a_Web_20_World.

Çelik, T. (2021). Web 2.0 tools usage competence scale development study. *Pamukkale Universitesi Egitim Fakultesi Dergisi (Pamukkale University Journal of Education), 51*, 449–475, https://doi.org/10.9779/pauefd.700181.

Christian, D. D., McCarty, D. L., & Brown, C. L. (2021). Experiential education during the COVID-19 pandemic: A reflective process. *Journal of Constructivist Psychology, 34*(3), 264–277, https://doi.org/10.1080/1072053 7.2020.1813666.

Churchill, D., Wong, W., Law, N., Salter, D., & Tai, B. (2009). Social bookmarking–repository–networking: Possibilities for support of teaching and learning in higher education. *Serials Review, 35*(3), 142–148, https://doi.org/10.1016/j. serrev.2009.04.006.

Click, A. & Petit, J. (2010). Social networking and Web 2.0 in information literacy. *International Information & Library Review, 42*(2), 137–142, https:// doi.org/10.1080/10572317.2010.10762855.

Conole, G. (2010). Facilitating new forms of discourse for learning and teaching: Harnessing the power of Web 2.0 practices. Open Learning: *The Journal of Open, Distance and e-Learning, 25*(2), 141–151, https://doi.org/10. 1080/02680511003787438.

Costa, C., Alvelos, H., & Teixeira, L. (2016). The use of Web 2.0 tools by students in learning and leisure contexts: A study in a Portuguese institution of higher education. *Technology, Pedagogy and Education, 25*(3), 377–394, https://doi.org/10.1080/1475939X.2015.1057611.

Den Exter, K., Rowe, S., Boyd, W., & Lloyd, D. (2012). Using Web 2.0 technologies for collaborative learning in distance education — Case studies from an Australian university. *Future Internet, 4*(1), 216–237, https://doi. org/10.3390/fi4010216.

Drexler, W., Baralt, A., & Dawson, K. (2008). The teach web 2.0 consortium: A tool to promote educational social networking and Web 2.0 use among educators. *Educational Media International, 45*(4), 271–283, https://doi.org/10.1080/09523980802571499.

Dubey, P. & Pandey, D. (2020). Distance learning in higher education during pandemic: Challenges and opportunities. *The International Journal of Indian Psychology, 8*(2), 43–46, https://doi.org/10.25215/0802.204.

Eyyam, R., Meneviş, I., & Doğruer, N. (2011). Perceptions of teacher candidates towards web 2.0 technologies. *Procedia — Social and Behavioral Sciences, 15*, 2663–2666, https://doi.org/10.1016/j.sbspro.2011.04.166.

García-Morales, V. J., Martín-Rojas, R., & Garde-Sánchez, R. (2019). How to encourage social entrepreneurship action? Using web 2.0 technologies in higher education institutions. *Journal of Business Ethics, 161*(2), 329–350, https://doi.org/10.1007/s10551-019-04216-6.

Gitonga, R. K. & Murungi, C. G. (2015). Web 2.0 Technology use by students in higher education: A case of Kenyan universities. In J. Keengwe & M. B. Maxfield, (Eds.), *Advancing Higher Education with Mobile Learning Technologies: Cases, Trends, and Inquiry-Based Methods*, pp. 278–287. IGI Global, http://doi:10.4018/978-1-4666-6284-1.ch015.

Gürsoy, G. & Göksun, D. O. (2019). The experiences of pre-service science teachers in educational content development using web 2.0 tools. *Contemporary Educational Technology, 10*(4), 338–357, https://doi.org/10.30935/cet.634168.

Harris, H. & Park, S. (2008). Educational usages of podcasting: Colloquium. *British Journal of Educational Technology, 39*(3), 548–551, https://doi.org/10.1111/j.1467-8535.2007.00788.x.

Kitsantas, A. & Dabbagh, N. (2011). The role of web 2.0 technologies in self-regulated learning. New *Directions for Teaching and Learning, 2011*(126), 99–106, https://doi.org/10.1002/tl.448.

Koehler, A. A., Newby, T. J., & Ertmer, P. A. (2017). Examining the role of web 2.0 tools in supporting problem solving during case-based instruction. *Journal of Research on Technology in Education, 49*(3–4), 182–197, https://doi.org/10.1080/15391523.2017.1338167.

Lee, G. L., Luo, T., Shah, S. S., & Muljana, P. (2020). Teachers' perceptions, proficiency, and integration of web 2.0 tools in literacy instruction in the united states of America. *Inted2020 Proceedings*, 2343–2343, https://doi.org/10.21125/inted.2020.0713.

Lim, J. & Newby, T. J. (2021). Preservice teachers' attitudes toward web 2.0 personal learning environments (PLEs): Considering the impact of self-regulation and digital literacy. *Education and Information Technologies, 26*, 3699–3720, https://doi.org/10.1007/s10639-021-10432-3.

Luo, L. (2010). Web 2.0 integration in information literacy instruction: An overview. *The Journal of Academic Librarianship, 36*(1), 32–40, https://doi. org/10.1016/j.acalib.2009.11.004.

Machynska, N. & Dzikovska, M. (2020). Challenges to manage the educational process in the HEI during the Pandemic. *Revista Romaneasca Pentru Educatie Multidimensionala, 12*(1Sup2), 92–99, https://doi.org/10.18662/ rrem/12.1sup2/251.

McLoughlin, C. & Lee, M. J. (2010). Personalised and self regulated learning in the web 2.0 era: International exemplars of innovative pedagogy using social software. *Australasian Journal of Educational Technology, 26*(1), 28–43, https://doi.org/10.14742/ajet.1100.

Mishra, L., Gupta, T., & Shree, A. (2020). Online teaching-learning in higher education during lockdown period of COVID-19 pandemic. *International Journal of Educational Research Open*, 1, 100012, https://doi.org/10.1016/j. ijedro.2020.100012.

Moore, M. (2007). Web 2.0: Does it really matter? *The American Journal of Distance Education, 21*, 177–183, https://doi.org/10.1080/08923 640701595183.

Odom, L. (2010). Mapping web 2.0 benefits to known best practices in distance education, http://contentdm.umgc.edu/digital/api/collection/p16240coll5/ id/55/download.

Olea, M. D. (2019). Application of web 2.0 tools in teaching 21st-century students in higher education in Calabarzon, Philippines. *IOER International Multidisciplinary Research Journal (IIMRJ), 1*(1), 1–8, https://www.ioer-imrj. com/wp-content/uploads/2019/03/WEB-2.0-TOOLS-DR.-OLEA-M.D.pdf.

Oliver, K. (2010). Integrating web 2.0 across the curriculum. *TechTrends, 54*(2), 50–60, https://doi.org/10.1007/s11528-010-0382-7.

Paily, M. U. (2013). Creating constructivist learning environment: Role of "Web 2.0" technology. *International Forum of Teaching and Studies, 9*(1), 39–50, http://etec512constructivismonline.weebly.com/uploads/2/3/7/5/23750641/ role_of_2.0_conference.pdf.

Parmaxi, A. & Zaphiris, P. (2017). Web 2.0 in computer-assisted language learning: A research synthesis and implications for instructional design and educational practice. *Interactive Learning Environments, 25*(6), 704–716, https://doi.org/10.1080/10494820.2016.1172243.

Rahimi, E., Van den Berg, J., & Veen, W. (2014). A pedagogy-driven framework for integrating web 2.0 tools into educational practices and building personal learning environments. *Journal of Literacy and Technology, 15*(2), 54–79, http://resolver.tudelft.nl/uuid:7fde0c8b-d301-4845-85e2-af236e37f8a3.

Rajic, S. (2013). Educational use of Podcast. 5. The Fourth International Conference on e-Learning (eLearning-2013), 26–27 September 2013,

Belgrade, Serbia, http://econference.metropolitan.ac.rs/files/pdf/2013/15-stajka-rajic-educational-use-of-podcast.pdf.

Rioseco, M., Paukner-Nogués, F., & Ramírez-Muñoz, B. (2017). Incorporating Powtoon as a learning activity into a course on technological innovations as didactic resources for pedagogy programs. *International Journal of Emerging Technologies in Learning, 22*(6), 120–131, https://doi.org/10.3991/ijet.v12i06.7025.

Risemberg, R. & Zimmerman, B. J. (1992). Self-regulated learning in gifted students. *Roeper Review, 15*(2), 98–101, https://doi.org/10.1080/02783199 209553476.

Sá, M. J. & Serpa, S. (2020). The COVID-19 pandemic as an opportunity to foster the sustainable development of teaching in higher education. *Sustainability, 12*(20), 8525, https://doi.org/10.3390/su12208525.

Shriram, R. & Warner, S. C. (2010). Connectivism and the impact of web 2.0 technologies on education. *Asian Journal of Distance Education, 8*(2), 4–17, http://library.oum.edu.my/oumlib/sites/default/files/file_attachments/odl-resources/4423/web-20.pdf.

Sigala, M. (2007). Integrating web 2.0 in e-learning environments: A socio-technical approach. *International Journal of Knowledge and Learning, 3*(6), 628–648, https://doi.org/10.1504/IJKL.2007.016837.

Solomon, G. & Schrum, L. (2007). *Web 2.0: New Tools, New Schools*. ISTE https://doi.org/10.5860/choice.45-5119.

Stefancik, R. & Stradiotová, E. (2020). Using web 2.0 tool podcast in teaching foreign languages. *Advanced Education*, 46–55, https://doi.org/10.20535/2410-8286.198209.

Toquero, C. M. (2020). Challenges and opportunities for higher education amid the COVID-19 pandemic: The Philippine context. *Pedagogical Research, 5*(4), 1–5, https://doi.org/10.29333/pr/7947.

Tunks, K. W. (2012). An introduction and guide to enhancing online instruction with web 2.0 tools. *Journal of Educators Online, 9*(2), n2, https://files.eric.ed.gov/fulltext/EJ985402.pdf.

Tur, G. & Urbina, S. (2016). Collaboration in ePortfolios with Web 2.0 tools in initial teacher training *Culture and Education, 28*(3), 601–632, https://doi.org/10.1080/11356405.2016.1203528.

Tyagi, S. (2012). Adoption of web 2.0 technology in higher education: A case study of universities in the National Capital Region, India. *International Journal of Education and Development using ICT, 8*(2), 28–43, https://files.eric.ed.gov/fulltext/EJ1084132.pdf.

Wan, L. (2010, May). Application of web 2.0 technologies in e-learning context. In 2010 International Conference on Networking and Digital Society, Vol. 1, pp. 437–440. *IEEE*, https://doi.org/10.1109/ICNDS.2010.5479229.

Wheeler, S. (2009). Learning space mashups: Combining web 2.0 tools to create collaborative and reflective learning spaces. *Future Internet, 1*(1), 3–13, https://doi.org/10.3390/fi1010003.

Whittaker, J. (2009). *Producing for Web 2.0 a Student Guide.* (Third Edition). Routledge: Taylor & Francis.

Yılmaz İnce, E., Kabul, A., & Diler, İ. (2020). Distance education in higher education in the COVID-19 pandemic process: A case of Isparta Applied Sciences University. *International Journal of Technology in Education and Science, 4*, 343–351, https://doi.org/10.46328/ijtes.v4i4.112

Yuen, S. C. Y., Yaoyuneyong, G., & Yuen, P. K. (2011). Perceptions, interest, and use: Teachers and Web 2.0 tools in education. *International Journal of Technology in Teaching & Learning, 7*(2), 109–123, https://sicet.org/main/wp-content/uploads/2016/11/ijttl-11-02-2_Yuen.pdf.

Zimmerman, B. J. (2008). Investigating self-regulation and motivation: Historical background, methodological developments, and future prospects. *American Educational Research Journal, 45*(1), 166–183, https://doi.org/10.3102/0002831207312909.

Index